PREFACE

This book is about a voyage, your voyage, down the west coast of France, calling in at any or all of the main harbours from Brest to Hendaye, near the Spanish border. For good measure it also includes a chapter outlining the canal route from Bordeaux to the Mediterranean.

It is intended both for the first-time visitor to these waters, and for those who have sailed here before, who may also find a few useful snippets of information. Conversely, you may have some gems for me which I would always be grateful to hear, better still read, and pass on to others.

The *Macmillan-Reeds Nautical Almanac* should be consulted for tides and certain background details which are not repeated here.

The book has two main aims:

a. To describe the lands off which you are coasting, together with the shoreside attractions (and demerits) of the harbours which you are about to visit. In this respect it is as much for browsing on a winter's evening, as for finding the nearest supermarket on the day.

b. To elaborate on navigational aspects which other guides may omit, gloss over or worse still simply take for granted. We are all at some time strangers to a new port and we hunger for clear, practical advice on the best approach to be taken and the pitfalls to be avoided.

To these ends the style is friendly and discursive, hence the title "Companion". If at times the words are colloquial, I make no apology – that is how we speak, not least when on holiday.

I know you will enjoy cruising one of the most attractive coastlines in Europe.

Neville Featherstone,
Trent, January 2001

The author is well aware that the three most useless things aboard a yacht are a retired Naval officer, a wheelbarrow and an umbrella

INTRODUCTION

Layout of the book Chapter 1 provides notes on various ways of getting to France's Atlantic coast which, with its offshore islands, has been described as France's finest and most interesting cruising ground — at least in part.

It may broadly be considered in the following three sections, covered by eight chapters each of which starts with introductory words about the region as a whole:

i.   Brest to the River Loire (Chapters 2 to 4). Once past the Raz de Sein and the Pointe de Penmarc'h, you can enjoy the gentler charm of South Brittany, the superlative waters of Quiberon Bay and the endless fun of the Golfe du Morbihan.

ii. River Loire to Ile d'Oléron (Chapters 5 and 6). The islands of Noirmoutier and Yeu and a series of harbours facilitate easy day hops down to the Pertuis Breton, Pertuis d'Antioche and the delights of La Rochelle, Rochefort and the islands of Ré and Oléron.

iii. Royan, gateway to the Gironde; or down the coast to Spain's border (Chapters 7 and 8). The Gironde is more than just part of the canal route to the Med; it is worth savouring like a bottle of good claret! So too are Arcachon and the four Basque harbours to the south.

Within these chapters all the main harbours, marinas and associated anchorages are covered, both ashore and afloat, in as much detail as possible. Only lack of space precludes coverage of some small, but popular islands, harbours and anchorages, eg Glénans, the Aven and Bélon rivers.

Chapter 9 gives a foretaste of negotiating the Canals to or from the Mediterranean Sea.

Acknowledgements The author and publisher gratefully acknowledge the material contributions of both the UK and French Hydrographic Offices.

I am most grateful to the following yachtsmen for their help:

Tony Boas and Nigel Ringrose for the arithmetic and local knowledge needed to get under Auray bridge with masthead and keel unscathed.

David Gilbey for updating and refining everything to do with Rochefort.

Hans & Mary Bye-Jorgensen for their words of wisdom on Royan, the Gironde, Bordeaux and its wines — and for fun, good claret and gourmet food whilst sailing and travelling in their company.

Nick & Jani Armstrong for their kind hospitality and detailed information about Arcachon.

John & Elizabeth Royle who passed on their most recent experiences in the Canals to the Med.

And most sincerely I thank my wife Ann who joins me when she can and selflessly cuts the grass when she cannot!

Photo credits Patrick Roach for the aerial photographs (excluding two by the author from a helium-filled balloon over Bordeaux); Hans & Mary Bye-Jorgensen, Nick Armstrong, John Royle, Detlef Jens and Chris Stevens; all other photographs by the author.

Nautical data has been corrected to Notices to Mariners Weekly Edition No 1, 4th January, 2001.

Conventions "Yachtsmen", need I say, embraces both ladies and gentlemen who sail and/or motor their yachts.

Times are local. All bearings and courses are related to True North. Magnetic variation in 2001 AD was about 5°W near Brest, about 4°W near St Nazaire and about 3°W off both La Rochelle and Biarritz; these values are decreasing at approx 7′ to 10′ per annum.

Distances are in nautical miles (M) or, if less than 1M, in cables (one tenth of a nautical mile or 185 metres).

In a few instances distances are stated in metres (m) and, when ashore, in kilometres.

Charted depths and drying <u>heights</u> are in metres respectively below and above Chart Datum.

Latitude and Longitude values are referenced to the European Datum 1950 (ED 50), since it is felt that the majority of yachtsmen will be using ED 50 charts for some time to come.

French Customs are active both at sea and in harbour. If boarded, business will be swiftly and pleasantly transacted if you remain polite and friendly throughout (no harm in offering a cup of coffee, although it is invariably declined). Above all it will create a favourable impression and expedite proceedings if your personal and yacht documents are presented in a folder, with clear plastic envelopes in which all are readily visible. Before the officers leave ensure that they give you a certificate "*Controle de la Navigation de Plaisance*", stating that they have cleared your vessel; this should save a repeat performance when next boarded.

TOURISM

Before leaving the UK find time to contact or visit the French National Tourist Office at 178 Piccadilly, London W1V 0AL. Tel 020 7629 2869; Fax 020 7493 6594; Info Tel 0891 244123. E-mail: info@mdlf.co.uk. Website: www.franceguide.com/.

Tourist Offices May I suggest that a close second to your first beer or plate of moules after arrival is a visit to the Tourist Office; details are listed under each harbour. Even quite small communities have one and they are a mine of useful information, including transport timetables and a *Plan de Ville*.

Talking of transport, if you haven't already got a folding bike or two aboard, do consider getting them. They add a new dimension to your runs ashore, especially if fitted with good shopping panniers or baskets. The French haven't yet cottoned on to them and think them rather droll.

Regional and Departmental Tourist Centres (CRT/CDT) also provide good literature and websites to help your winter planning.

RESTAURANTS

It is not easy to recommend restaurants since unfortunately neither time, wallet nor waistband permit one to eat in all of them. My list therefore includes those where I have enjoyed a good meal, plus many others where I could do no more than record the price of their set menus and my outside impressions. In some of the larger towns and cities I have grouped restaurants into areas where they proliferate so that you can browse at leisure before diving in.

Eating in France remains a huge pleasure and I recall only one occasion in the summer of '99 when the food was unsatisfactory. A pleasant welcome and good service can almost be taken for granted; do not feel disadvantaged if your French is less than fluent.

This is one of the better aspects of life in France: because you are a foreigner (and therefore of unsound mind), you will often be indulged where the French customer has to argue and cajole!

NAUTICAL MATTERS

"Sailing Tours" For those who appreciate a historical perspective I have quoted here and there from Part III of this five part work by Frank Cowper. From 1892 to 1895 he circumnavigated Great Britain, with a side trip down to St Nazaire. His writing is a rich blend of navigational facts laced with his own semi-libellous observations on the world around him; it makes fascinating reading. Original copies are hard to find, but a Reproduction edition was published in 1985 by Ashford Press Publishing, 1 Church Road, Shedfield, Hants.

Pilot books The *Channel Pilot* (NP 27, 4th edition 1999) includes coverage as far as the Pointe de Penmarc'h. The Admiralty *Bay of Biscay Pilot* (NP 22) covers the whole coast from Pointe de Penmarc'h to Cabo Ortegal on the NW tip of Spain. The current 7th edition (1998) is more yachtsman-friendly than of old, and contains some helpful aerial colour photographs.

Two Pilots, produced by the Royal Cruising Club Pilotage Foundation and published by Imray, also cover the French coast, specifically for yachtsmen:

North Biscay (6th edition, 2000) covers from the Chenal du Four to the Seudre River. Thereafter it contains only an abridged description of the Gironde and ports up to Bordeaux.

South Biscay includes a more complete description of the Gironde and ports up to Bordeaux.

Charts and maps Admiralty and SHOM charts are listed under each harbour; the largest scale chart is usually first. Unsurprisingly, French chart coverage is more comprehensive than British.

Michelin road maps (1 cm: 2 km scale) are very useful for your shore-side activities and a broad awareness of roads, railways, inland towns and cities. The whole coastline is covered by the following five maps:
- 58 Brittany peninsula, St Brieuc to Lorient, Chapters 1 to 3
- 63 Lorient to the River Loire, Chapter 4
- 67 River Loire to Bourgenay, Chapter 5
- 71 Bourgenay to Arcachon, including the Gironde, Chapters 6 to 8
- 78 Arcachon to the Spanish border, Chapter 7

The canals to the Med require four more which are truly a great asset (see chapter 9). Compare incidentally the 1999 French price of 19FF per map with £2·35 to £3·75 in the UK. *En passant* may I scotch the rumour that I navigate at sea on a Michelin road map, although I have used them up some rivers!

GPS Datum Both Admiralty and SHOM charts for this coast are currently referenced to ED 50 (European Datum 1950). This is the datum which you must select on your GPS receiver, so that GPS readouts can be plotted directly onto the chart. If unable to make this selection, for maximum accuracy manually apply the Datum shift, as printed on the chart, to the GPS readout (which is based on the WGS 84 datum) so that the corrected lat/long can be plotted onto the ED 50 chart.

Waypoints Usually only two waypoints are given for each harbour. In a few cases the lat/long of buoys or other marks may be given if deemed essential.

The first waypoint appears under the sub-headings of 'Approach' or 'Pilotage', and is an approach waypoint. This is a position in safe water, ie adequate depth and clear of nasties, from which you may either start an approach or can see your destination harbour. Thus it might be a few miles away, for example in a buoyed channel requiring further pilotage and/or buoy hopping, or as close as a few cables from the harbour entrance.

The second waypoint is the lat/long of the harbour entrance (or an appropriate, specified feature). This can serve as a final waypoint in your route plan – it should also help you find the place on a chart in the first instance. Three things are worth stressing:

a. Plot any waypoint before using it. Only by so doing can you possibly appreciate the full navigational situation and anticipate any potential problems. It may also help to eliminate finger trouble, ie inserting the wrong digits (forgive the pun); this of course applies to all waypoints.

b. The first waypoint is advisory only, but bear in mind that for 98% of the harbours it is based on personal experience and on a very careful study of charts and all available information. You are of course at liberty to discard it and substitute a waypoint of your own which may be influenced by prevailing conditions or other factors.

c. GPS is very good indeed with the lifting of Selective Availability, but despite the excellence of this equipment and any additional cross-checking which you might rightly employ, it is vital not to lose the Big Picture by over-reliance on the numbers.

By that I mean, keep your head "out of the office", be alert to everything around you, take nothing for granted and if you sense that all is not well – do something positive at once: eg stop the boat, turn back whence you came, plot a fix or three, re-assess the situation, pick up the threads and determine a safe course of action.

None of this is automatic or instinctive unless you have schooled yourself to act in this way.

Tidal stream atlases The Admiralty *English Channel* atlas (NP 250, referenced to Devonport and Dover) provides small scale coverage of the North Brittany coast down to 48°20′N (south end of the Chenal du Four, but has no tidal arrows therein).

The adjoining *France West Coast* atlas (NP 265, referenced to Brest and Dover) covers from 48°30′N (north end of the Chenal du Four) southward to 45°16′N (17M south of Pte de Grave). It provides only small-scale coverage of such key areas as the Chenal du Four, Raz de Sein and the mouth of the Gironde.

The same coastal area (west part of N Brittany to south of Pte de Grave) is covered by 3 French atlases, from north to south:

i. SHOM 560-UJA, covers the whole western end of the Brittany peninsula from Goulven (midway between Roscoff and L'Aberwrac'h) to Penmarc'h and has useful larger scale blow-ups of both the Chenal du Four and the Raz de Sein, all referenced to Brest.

ii. SHOM 558-UJA, covers south Brittany from Penmarc'h to Île de Noirmoutier with three large scale insets of Loctudy to Concarneau, including Île de Glénan; Île de Groix and Lorient; and Quiberon Bay and Belle-Île.

iii. SHOM 559-UJA, covers from Le Croisic to the mouth of the Gironde with three large scale insets of the mouth of the Loire; Bourgenay to Pte de la Coubre; and the mouth of the Gironde.

The French atlases are worth buying, especially if you plan to sail regularly in these waters or to indulge in intricate pilotage. There are no tidal stream atlases for the waters south of the Gironde.

Tidal Coefficients These are explained in the MRNA and listed under Brest for every day of the year. Suffice it to say here that they are used in France, in lieu of tidal Range, to quantify the size of a tide; a spring tide, for example, has a coefficient of about 100, an average tide 70 and neaps around 40. Hence the window of access to a tidally-restricted harbour is often quoted as a function of various values of coefficient. The strength of tidal streams may also be interpolated with reference to the coefficient. I commend them to you as quicker and easier than Range.

Lights These are always subject to change and are therefore omitted, unless their characteristics resolve a possible ambiguity or help to identify a buoy or beacon.

CROSS The French Coastguard has 4 centres (*CROSS = Centre Régionaux Opérationnels de Surveillance et de Sauvetage*) which equate to MRCCs. The Atlantic centres are:

- CROSS Corsen, covering the west coast only as far south as the Raz de Sein; CROSS Étel, Raz de Sein to the Spanish border.

Weather information Navtex provides a reliable service in English twice daily. The Corsen station (A) near Le Conquet routinely transmits weather messages at midnight and midday for sea areas West Brittany, North and South Biscay, Small Sole, Galicia and Romeo (see the MRNA for the boundaries of these areas, plus any changes in transmission times). It also transmits gale warnings on receipt and every 4 hours from midnight whilst they remain in force.

The CROSS stations shown above broadcast weather messages and gale warnings thrice daily in French (at about dictation speed) on VHF Ch 79 (Corsen and Soulac) and Ch 80 (Étel) through remote stations, at the times listed in the MRNA.

BBC Radio 4 shipping forecasts on 198 kHz LW at 0535, 1201, 1754 and 0048 UT/BST can be heard on a decent radio, (best reception at night), down to the Spanish border.

Forecasts and synoptic charts are provided daily at Capitaineries. Regional daily newspapers, eg *Ouest France*, contain similar information for up to a week ahead.

Le vent solaire A particular feature of this coast during the summer is the sea and land breeze cycle, known locally as *le vent solaire*. Typically after a quiet forenoon, a W'ly sea breeze sets in about midday, blowing onshore. It slowly veers to the NW, almost parallel to the coast, reaching Force 4 by late afternoon; it then veers further to the N, dying at dusk. Around midnight a land breeze may pipe up from the NE and freshen sufficiently to kick up rough seas – with resultant mayhem on the mooring buoys and in anchorages open to the NE. By morning the wind is calm.

Glossary Useful Breton and French words are listed in the MRNA. Extra French words include:

À couple = rafted up;

Biquille = bilge keel;

Béquilles = yacht legs;

Catway = finger pontoon;

Criée = fishmarket;

Défense = a fender;

Garde = a spring (back/fore).

HARBOURS AND MARINAS

Regattas/Rallies It can ruin the end of a long hard day's sail to find that your chosen marina is chock-a-block with racy types. The answer as you progress down the coast is to scan the mass of bumf pinned to each HM's notice-board for advance notice of forthcoming events elsewhere; newspapers and posters may also help. *Malheureusement* the French do not always divulge their future intentions, even if known.

VHF Channel 09 is the usual marina channel in France; there are inevitably a few exceptions.

Berthing Three types of berth are mentioned in this book:

a. Alongside/rafting. This implies a long pontoon with no fingers, on which you lie alongside the pontoon itself or raft up; the French are good at rafting ad infinitum. Thankfully they have not yet developed the xenophobic British habit of leaving a dinghy amidships on their outboard side or declaring an 0530 departure only to be still firmly turned in at 1100 ...

b. Finger berth (*catway*). Self evident, and the word *catway* is the key to requesting one.

c. Hammerhead. An alongside berth on the T-pontoon across the end of a long pontoon. They are fair game for a visitor; multihulls like them. Watch out for the tide in riverine marinas, eg Bénodet/Ste Marine, where hammerheads catch its full force.

The *accueil* (welcome) pontoon is a helpful feature but by no means universal. It gives you an obvious check-in berth where the paperwork may be sorted out before you shift to your assigned berth. La Rochelle's Les Minimes marina has an excellent example of the *genre*.

Mediterranean-style berthing is not in vogue along the Atlantic coast of France.

Fuel Many marinas have self-service diesel and petrol pumps which are automatically operated H24 by any appropriate French credit card. At present British cards are not electronically able to operate these pumps, although the RYA are investigating making their credit card acceptable.

Usually the solution is to advise the Capitainerie of the problem (it is well known); they will then switch on the pumps for your use and debit your credit card in the normal way.

If you are desperate for fuel outside office hours it may be possible to persuade a friendly French yachtsman to use his card on your behalf and then to reimburse him in cash.

Electrical plugs The blue three-pronged 'caravan' type socket is now widely used, especially in more modern marinas. However the classic two-pinned French lightweight socket still survives, often corroded and horrible – so bring both on separate cables, or buy an adaptor. If your kettle regularly trips the pontoon circuit-breaker, it may be because you have plugged into the only 5 amp socket, whereas all the others are 15 amp – get wise by reading the very small print. Also hone your skills at opening electrical control boxes to reset CBs.

Water connectors French marinas rarely provide a hose, so bring your own and ensure that it has a stout bronze screw-threaded connector attached. Plastic connectors, rubber faucets and jubilee clips will give you a soaking inside the first five minutes.

Nor do washbasins in the Sanitaire often have plugs, so get an array of different sizes from your good old-fashioned ironmongery (bare, creaking floorboards and brown-aproned assistants), if you can find one.

CATWAYS AND CLEATS

Any Guidebook to French harbours and marinas will have failed in its duty if it does not mention pontoons – finger pontoons to be precise – or as the French call them "*catways*". Catway is a vital word in the foreign yottie's vocabulary, because it may make the difference between lying undisturbed in your own berth or being rafted up ten deep with the equivalent of a French rugby scrum tramping across your foredeck, or through your cockpit, at all hours.

Catway is also appropriate because only a feline, preferably one with all its nine lives still intact, can safely manage to walk these wooden tightropes. Often little wider than a baulk of 4 x 2, these devices have all the resilient cunning of a trampoline.

If, for example, a single-hander leaps smartly over the side clutching a fistful of mooring warps, he is quite likely to be unceremoniously bounced back on board his *bateau*, or more probably into the water. If however your berthing party consists of several heavyweights they will all jump simultaneously onto the catway and the three nearest its outer end will ship water over the top of their wellies. It's all to do with buoyancy tanks, or lack of, and Archimedes' principle.

A side effect of the unstable nature of a catway is the severity of the shakes which it can induce. Who has not squatted on the end of a catway, trying to

secure a warp, to find himself quivering uncontrollably from the ankles upwards?

Assuming, however, that you have by now regained your balance or at least emerged from the water, there remains the problem of how to attach your fistful of warps to the catway (since despite all your troubles you will surely not have dropped them).

The French do not know what a cleat is – it does not appear in my Anglo-French *dictionnaire*. Ergo it does not exist, as was proven to me at one well-known marina where my catway, chosen by Hobson, was as naked of cleats as the trunk of a Californian redwood.

The French presumably invented the game of Croquet – why else would it be spelled so oddly? In that game one shoots Hoops, which may now be a dying breed. At any rate the French have acquired many millions of these hoops, sawn the legs off short and fitted the truncated version to their catways to serve as a cleat. A more fiendish device is hard to imagine!

You cannot belay to it with a figure of eight, whilst a round turn and two half hitches is anathema to a Hoop. In short it is quite impossible to secure your warp in a hurry – it all takes time, too much time – during which the bow will have blown off downwind trailing your headrope behind it. You will be incapacitated by a severe attack of the shakes and the French onlookers will be convulsed at the antics of another barking-mad Anglais.

So if you can't beat 'em, join 'em. Rig no fenders, eschew springs, merely pass a fistful of warps coiled like spaghetti to anybody who will accept it (normally the inboard end will not be attached to anything). Retire below to break out the Calva.

The visitors' pontoon at Morgat

ABBREVIATIONS AND SYMBOLS

The following abbreviations and symbols may be encountered in this book; many others will be found which are deemed to be self-explanatory:

AB	Alongside berth
aka	Also known as
⚒	Boatyard
⚓	Boathoist
Ⓛ	Chandlery
✝	Church
🛢	Diesel by cans
↯	Direction of buoyage
ECM	East Cardinal Mark
F	Fixed Light
Fl	Flashing light
🅕	Fuel berth
FV(s)	Fishing vessel(s)
⊖	Fish Harbour/Quay
H+, H–	Minutes after/before each hour
H24	Continuous
⚓	Holding tank pumpout
⊕	Hospital
⚓	Harbour Master
IDM	Isolated Danger Mark
ⓘ	Information Bureau
IPTS	International Port Traffic Signals
Iso	Isophase light
▣	Launderette
✦	Lifeboat
Ldg	Leading
L.Fl	Long-flashing light
M	Sea mile(s)
🛒	Stores/Supermarket
Météo	Météorologie/Weather
MHWN	Mean High Water Neaps
MHWS	Mean High Water Springs
MLWN	Mean Low Water Neaps
MLWS	Mean Low Water Springs
MRNA	Macmillan Reeds Nautical Almanac
NCM	North Cardinal Mark
Oc	Occulting light
PHM	Port-hand Mark
✉	Post Office
Q	Quick flashing light
✕	Restaurant
⇌	Railway station
SCM	South Cardinal Mark
SHM	Starboard-hand Mark
SHOM	French Hydrographic Dept
◣	Slip for launching, scrubbing
SNSM	Société Nationale de Sauvetage en Mer (Lifeboats)
SWM	Safe Water Mark
TSS	Traffic Separation Scheme
Ⓥ Ⓥ	Visitors berth/buoy
VQ	Very quick flashing light
WCM	West Cardinal Mark
WPT, ⊕	Waypoint
ZI/ZA	Industrial estate

DISTANCE TABLES

Approximate distances in nautical miles are by the most direct route, whilst avoiding dangers.

		1	2	3	4	5	6	7	8	9	10	11	12	13	14	15	16	17	18	19	20
1.	Le Conquet	1																			
2.	Camaret	13	2																		
3.	Morgat	22	16	3																	
4.	Douarnenez	29	21	11	4																
5.	Audierne	30	28	27	30	5															
6.	Loctudy	55	55	53	55	30	6														
7.	Bénodet	58	58	57	60	33	4	7													
8.	Port-la-Forêt	65	64	63	66	36	12	12	8												
9.	Concarneau	63	62	61	64	37	12	11	4	9											
10.	Lorient	84	86	85	88	61	38	36	33	32	10										
11.	Le Palais (Belle Ile)	95	99	98	101	74	54	52	48	47	26	11									
12.	Port Haliguen	100	105	104	107	80	59	57	55	53	32	11	12								
13.	La Trinité	108	110	109	112	85	64	62	60	58	37	16	8	13							
14.	Crouesty	108	110	109	112	85	64	62	60	58	37	16	9	8	14						
15.	Vannes	120	121	120	123	96	75	73	71	69	48	27	20	19	12	15					
16.	Arzal/Camoël	131	130	129	132	105	84	82	80	78	57	36	31	31	28	37	16				
17.	Le Croisic	124	125	124	127	100	79	77	75	73	48	27	26	26	22	33	18	17			
18.	La Baule/Pornichet	134	131	130	133	106	85	82	80	78	55	34	35	36	30	40	30	13	18		
19.	St Nazaire	145	138	137	140	113	95	91	90	87	66	41	42	45	40	50	39	24	12	19	
20.	Pornic	146	149	148	151	124	105	101	100	97	72	45	47	49	43	55	42	24	18	16	20

		1	2	3	4	5	6	7	8	9	10	11	12	13	14	15	16	17	18	19	20
1.	Le Conquet	1																			
2.	St Nazaire	145	2																		
3.	Pornic	146	16	3																	
4.	L'Herbaudière	144	16	10	4																
5.	Port Joinville	147	35	30	20	5															
6.	St Gilles-C-de-Vie	166	45	40	29	18	6														
7.	Sables d'Olonne	181	65	55	40	31	16	7													
8.	Bourgenay	190	74	64	49	40	25	9	8												
9.	St Martin (I de Ré)	208	92	75	67	55	44	27	20	9											
10.	La Rochelle	218	101	92	76	66	51	36	29	12	10										
11.	Rochefort	242	126	116	102	84	75	61	54	36	26	11									
12.	R La Seudre	242	125	116	100	89	71	58	52	33	24	30	12								
13.	Port St Denis	220	103	94	78	59	48	33	30	21	13	26	22	13							
14.	Port Bloc/Royan	234	122	115	107	97	85	71	60	56	52	68	27	42	14						
15.	Bordeaux	289	177	170	162	152	140	126	115	111	107	123	82	97	55	15					
16.	Cap Ferret	274	168	160	153	138	130	113	110	102	98	114	75	88	68	123	16				
17.	Capbreton	316	220	215	211	192	186	169	166	165	156	172	131	145	124	179	58	17			
18.	Anglet/Bayonne	328	232	223	223	200	195	181	178	177	168	184	143	157	132	187	70	12	18		
19.	Santander	300	243	237	229	212	210	204	204	206	202	218	184	192	180	235	133	106	103	19	
20.	Cabo Finisterre	382	404	399	390	377	395	393	394	406	407	423	399	397	401	456	376	370	373	274	20

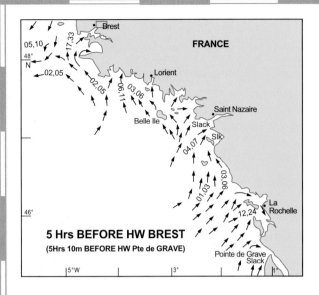

05,10
17,33
Brest

FRANCE

48°
N

02,05

02,05
06,11
03,06
Lorient

Belle Ile
Slack
Saint Nazaire

Slk

04,07

03,06

46°

01,03
12,24
La Rochelle

5 Hrs BEFORE HW BREST
(5Hrs 10m BEFORE HW Pte de GRAVE)

Pointe de Grave
Slack

5°W   3°   1°

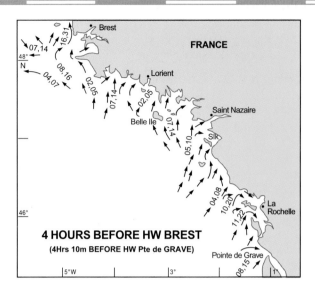

07,14
16,31
Brest

FRANCE

48°
N

08,16
04,07

02,05
07,14

02,05
Lorient

Belle Ile
Saint Nazaire

07,14
Slk

05,10

04,08
10,20
11,22

46°
La Rochelle

4 HOURS BEFORE HW BREST
(4Hrs 10m BEFORE HW Pte de GRAVE)

Pointe de Grave

08,15

5°W   3°   1°

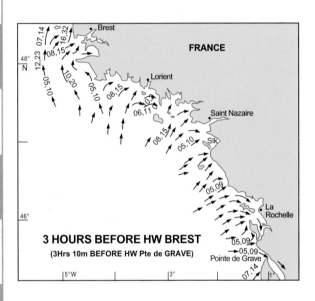

07,14
16,32
Brest

FRANCE

12,23
08,15

48°
N

05,10
10,20

05,10
08,15
Lorient

06,11
07,

08,15
Saint Nazaire

05,10
Slk

05,09

46°
La Rochelle

3 HOURS BEFORE HW BREST
(3Hrs 10m BEFORE HW Pte de GRAVE)

05,09
Pointe de Grave

07,14

5°W   3°   1°

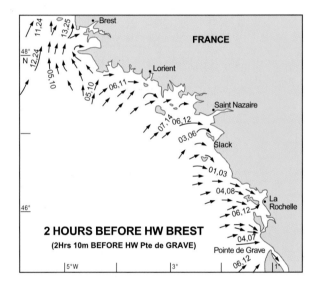

11,24
13,25
Brest

FRANCE

48°
N
12,24

05,10

05,10
06,11
Lorient

Saint Nazaire

07,14
06,12

03,06
Slack

01,03

04,08
La Rochelle

46°
06,12

2 HOURS BEFORE HW BREST
(2Hrs 10m BEFORE HW Pte de GRAVE)

04,07
Pointe de Grave

06,12

5°W   3°   1°

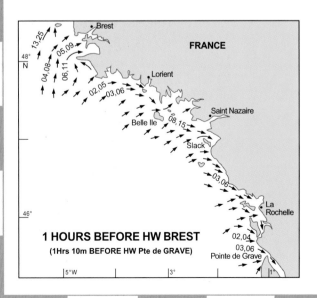

13,25
Brest

FRANCE

04,08
05,09

48°
N
06,11

02,05
03,06
Lorient

Belle Ile
08,15
Saint Nazaire

Slack

03,06

46°
La Rochelle

1 HOURS BEFORE HW BREST
(1Hrs 10m BEFORE HW Pte de GRAVE)

02,04
03,06
Pointe de Grave

5°W   3°   1°

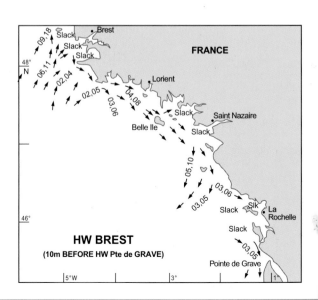

09,18
Slack
Brest

FRANCE

Slack
06,11
Slack

48°
N
02,04

02,05
04,08
Lorient

03,06

Belle Ile
Slack
Saint Nazaire

Slack

05,10

03,06
03,05
Slk
La Rochelle

46°
03,05
Slack

HW BREST
(10m BEFORE HW Pte de GRAVE)

03,05
Pointe de Grave

5°W   3°   1°

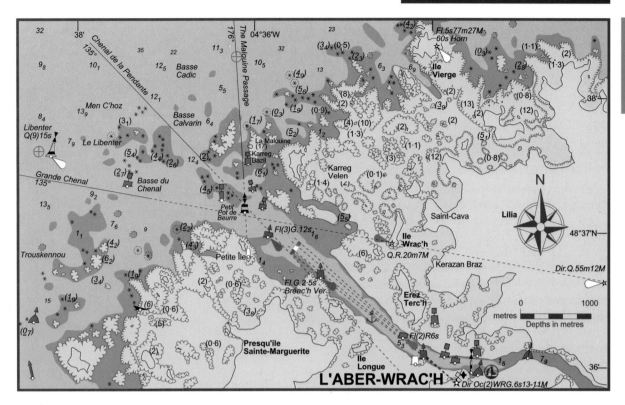

Facilities Capitainerie VHF Ch 09. Tel 02.98.04.91.62. Showers and bar in YC. Diesel approx HW±3 by the brow. A decent bar/restaurant, but nearest shops/bank are at Landéda 1½km SSW. Paluden: HM M. Gaby Appriaual, plus mongrel dog. Land at Rowing club slip on E bank for FW, showers; or at quay on W bank for FW and access to Lannilis (2km) for all facilities. A useful 5 days forecast for the western Channel can be had on 0806 691234, then press * 413 for clear, dictation French.

Paluden, looking NW

THE MALOUINE PASSAGE

The Malouine Passage is an interesting *divertissement*. It is a not too demanding short cut for yachts approaching/departing L'Aberwrac'h from/to the north or east. It saves a useful 3M against the Grand Chenal. From/to the west, it does not apply. The Passage is short (7 minutes) and sweet provided that it is tackled, as always, in the right conditions namely:

By day only (it is unlit) and in visibility of at least 2M. At neaps, to minimise any stream across the Passage. In only slight to moderate swell and a fair wind of no more than Force 4; there is no room to tack through the channel and stronger winds will raise a more difficult sea state. Timing is not too critical but above mid-flood (local HW–3 to HW) ensures generous depth of water and streams that are beginning to ease. Least depth at mid-tide neaps is likely to be more than 11m, whilst at LW Springs there will still be about 8m.

With experience more challenging conditions can be accepted.

Either BA chart 1432 or SHOM 7094 must be used. If your GPS was set to the OSGB 36 datum whilst crossing the Channel, ensure that you re-set your receiver to the ED 50 datum for use with these charts.

Navigational Marks Petit Pot de Beurre, a conspicuous ECM beacon tower, is the front leading mark on 176°/356°T. The slim white obelisk on Petite Île (3½ cables to the south) is the rear leading mark, also clearly visible although when exactly on transit it may be obscured by the height and girth of Petit Pot de Beurre – in which case you should "sidestep" a whisker to the east until the obelisk is just visible again. These two marks straddle the Grand Chenal to north and south respectively. The remaining marks, on the north side of the Grand Chenal are 2 PHM buoys and a PHM beacon tower (Karreg Bazil) close south of La Malouine rock itself. The direction of buoyage is of course from north to south.

First time The passage is more easily made northbound on the first occasion because:
i   The marks will already have been located and identified whilst using the Grand Chenal.
ii The three PHM marks provide a safe and clear funnel into the Passage proper, which is denied to you when approaching from the north.
iii La Malouine rock, 17m high, is more obvious from the south in close proximity to Petit Pot de Beurre. From the north it appears as one of many such rocks SW of Île Vierge lighthouse.

L'Aberwrac'h outer approaches, looking SW from Île Vierge with lighthouse in foreground

Chapter 1

Petit Pot de Beurre with the Île Vierge lighthouse bearing 050°

Directions north-bound Nearing Petit Pot de Beurre, identify the Petite Île obelisk. 1 cable east of Petit Pot du Beurre alter slowly starboard to the NNW, leaving the two PHM buoys about 15m to starboard. Glance over your port quarter to ensure that the leading marks are in transit 176° soon after passing the second PHM buoy and well before reaching the PHM beacon tower. Maintain the transit meticulously, adjusting for any stream across the channel.

The Passage now opens up ahead: off your starboard bow is the PHM beacon tower with La Malouine rock behind it. The west side of the Passage is fringed by drying rocks on which the sea usually breaks even in calm conditions, particularly at the northern end. Do not be intimidated! Depth of water is more than adequate; concentrate on maintaining the transit.

If eastbound, do not leave the transit until Île Vierge lighthouse bears 076° or more. This bearing clears a rock drying 1·7m, usually covered, off your starboard bow. A gradual turn to the NE for Lizen Ven Ouest WCM buoy will clear other outliers.

Directions south-bound Make good 48°38′·30N 4°36′·25W (267° Île Vierge lighthouse 1·5M). Positively identify both leading marks before leaving this position. If unable to do so, do not attempt the Malouine Passage; route via the Libenter buoy and Grand Chenal.

Once both marks are in your sights and in transit 176°, mirror the N-bound procedure.

L'ABERWRAC'H TO THE NORTHERN END OF THE CHENAL DU FOUR

The shortest (about 10M) practicable route from Libenter buoy is via Basse Paupian WCM buoy (48°35′·38N 04°46′·16W) to the Waypoint 'LF' (48°31′·50N 4°49′·00W), 5 cables west of Le Four lighthouse.

The leg from Libenter to Basse Paupian passes safely about 3 cables to seaward of the outliers of Roches de Portsall (of *Amoco Cadiz* notoriety). If you feel the need for more searoom, take the slightly longer route via Grande Basse de Portsall WCM buoy (48°36′·78N 04°46′·05W), instead of Basse Paupian; thence to LF.

Note that these two WCM buoys are just under 1·5M apart and can be confused. Basse Paupian is however a small, unlit spar buoy; Grande Basse de Portsall is a much larger, lattice-structure light buoy with solar panels, radar reflector and whistle.

Inshore route A shorter route from Libenter to Le Four, shown on BA 1432 and SHOM 7150, runs inshore of Roches de Portsall. However this route needs at least 5M visibility in order to see and identify the none-too-obvious transit marks.

If you have a couple of spare days, potter from L'Aberwrac'h to Portsall and Argenton, with perhaps a night-stop in L'Aberildut. You might thereby gain a dose of that invaluable, oft-quoted, but elusive commodity - local knowledge!

View NE from the Grand Chenal, Île Vierge lighthouse bearing 055°

THE CHENAL DU FOUR

Looking ESE toward Le Conquet. Note S-going stream at Grande Vinotière

For some yachtsmen, even those who are happy with the rocks and tides of North Brittany, the Chenal du Four poses something of a barrier (largely psychological) to progress round into South Brittany. These notes aim to simplify and alleviate such problems as do exist.

The deepwater route There are six lighthouses on the mainland (Trézien, Pointe de Corsen, Pointe de Kermorvan, Lochrist and the twin towers on Pointe St Mathieu) which provide transits by day and night or directional beams (sectors) for both the CdF and the Chenal de la Helle, as charted. They define the deeper water and are therefore used mainly by larger vessels, (over 1600 grt). The yachtsman may find it time-consuming and difficult to locate, identify and align on these daymarks and lights with absolute certainty, whilst at the same time looking for buoys and beacons which are more immediately to hand. In any case he is not greatly constrained by depth of water (unless close inshore); he may therefore elect to take a more direct "buoy-hopping" route.

A direct route of only three legs is shown below from N to S. It can be used by day or night in either direction (reciprocal track °T in brackets), and has been found to be safe, expeditious and above all simple in any weather. Plot the positions on BA 3345 and study the leg notes.

Leg 1 Waypoint 'LF' (48°31´·50N 4°49´·00W) 188°(008°)/5M to Valbelle PHM light buoy (48°26´·49N 04°49´·96W);

Leg 2 Valbelle 167°(347°)/4·6M to Grande Vinotière PHM light tower (48°22´·00N 04°48´·48W. This position is 1 cable west of the tower);

Leg 3 Grande Vinotière 156°(336°)/2·85M to Vieux Moines PHM light tower (48°19´·40N 04°46´·70W. This position is also 1 cable west of the tower); thence to Camaret or Brest.

If continuing south to the Raz de Sein, substitute La Fourmi buoy for Vieux Moines, thus:

Leg 3A Grande Vinotière 172°(352°)/2·7M to La Fourmi unlit SHM buoy (48°19´·31N 04°47´·88W); thence to Raz de Sein.

NOTES ON EACH LEG

Leg 1 From Waypoint 'LF' the direct, rhumb line track to Valbelle clears Les Liniou reefs and Plateau des Fourches by at least 0·5M to the west; these drying and above water rocks (highest 9m) will normally be clearly seen.

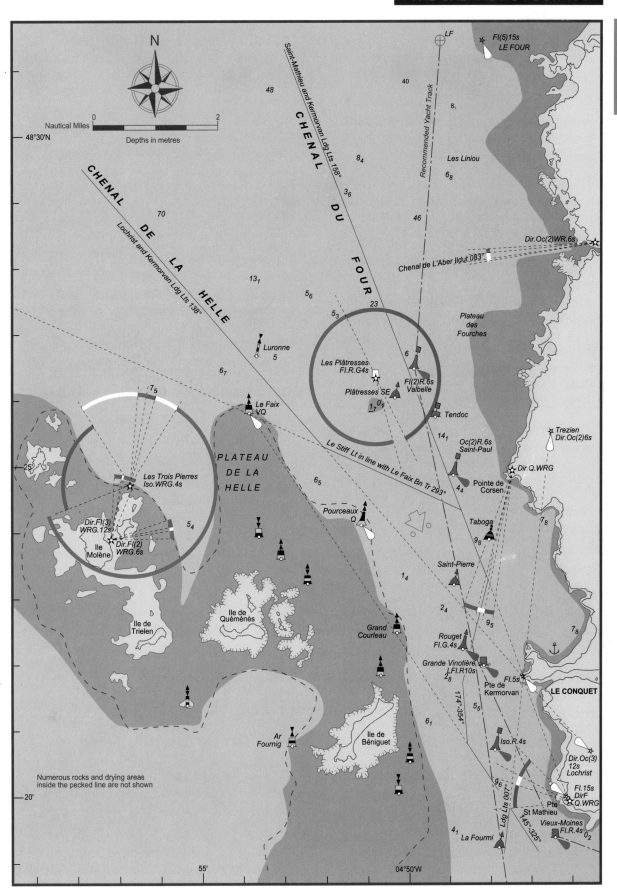

It is obviously important not to deviate to the east of the rhumb line track. GPS is an invaluable aid in this respect, backed up by radar and/or visual bearings on Le Four light and Valbelle buoy.

In the vicinity of Valbelle expect to meet rough water or at least a sharp chop as depths shoal from 40 metres in the north to 6 metres or less around the adjacent Les Plâtresses rocks.

Les Plâtresses beacon light tower, brilliantly white and looking from afar like a three-master under full sail, will be seen 0·6M west of Valbelle, together with an unlit SHM buoy. 2M further west is Le Faix NCM light tower .

Leg 2 As you pass them, carefully tick off those buoys which lie within a few cables either side of track, namely from north to south:

Tendoc, a small unlit PHM buoy; St Paul lit PHM buoy; Taboga unlit isolated danger buoy; St Pierre unlit SHM buoy; and the large Rouget SHM light buoy; 3 cables ESE of which is Grande Vinotière, a 16m high unmistakable red masonry tower.

Depths to north and south of Grande Vinotière are around 6 - 10 metres and navigable water between Pointe de Kermorvan and Ile de Béniguet has narrowed to less than 2 miles. This is likely to be the roughest area in the whole of CdF. Expect therefore to be bounced around by short, steep seas with overfalls, but these are easily seen and of brief duration as the tide sweeps you through at groundspeeds of about 9 - 10 knots.

Leg 3 Spare a quick glance at Le Conquet and its navigational marks, as you hurtle past. It is mainly a fishing port but could be a useful bolt hole in the event of gear failure. Anse des Blancs Sablons, just north of Le Conquet, is about the only anchorage where you can get out of the tide and shelter from S and W winds, tucked well in to the lee of Presqu'île de Kermorvan.

The only two buoys visible on this leg, whether going to Vieux Moines or to La Fourmi, are:

Les Renards unlit IDM buoy, marking a 1·2m patch; and Tournant et Lochrist PHM light buoy, almost on the track to La Fourmi.

Finally, marking the southern end of the CdF, are Vieux Moines, another massive red beacon tower with light, and the rather small, unlit La Fourmi SHM buoy.

There is room to cut between Vieux Moines and Pointe St Mathieu, if you must, but take account of the evil fang-like rock, 1·5m high and 100m NNE of Vieux Moines; the rocky reefs close W and NW of Pointe de St Mathieu; and to the SE the more insidious dangers of Les Rospects (off chartlet) for which a clearing bearing is essential.

TIDAL TACTICS

Tidal streams are the dominant factor in navigating the CdF and will determine all your timing. On chart 3345 tidal diamond 'H', just south of Grande Vinotière, shows rates of 5·2 knots springs and 2·6 knots neaps. There are 9 more diamonds on this chart. Avoid bucking a foul stream; even at neaps it is not a race-winning tactic.

Two adjoining Admiralty tidal stream atlases, "The English Channel" (NP 250; referenced to Dover and Devonport) and "France West coast" (NP 265; referenced to Brest and Dover), are needed. The former extends down to 48°20´N (abeam Pointe de St Mathieu), but has no tidal arrows within the CdF itself.

The latter covers from well south up to 48°30´N (1M south of Le Four light house). The scale of each atlas differs and is in any case fairly small. Thus much cross-referring between atlases, page turning, interpolation and conversions between Brest and Dover tide times, are required to obtain the Big Tidal Picture for both the CdF and its approaches.

In contrast the equivalent French atlas, SHOM 560-UJA, covers the whole western end of the Brittany peninsula from Goulven (midway between Roscoff and L'Aberwrac'h) to Penmarc'h

Coastguard station   Main light

Pointe St Mathieu, looking north

and has useful larger scale blow-ups of both the Chenal du Four and the Raz de Sein, all referenced to Brest – well worth buying.

Timing southbound Slack water off Le Four is at about HW Brest and the south-going stream starts to make at HW Brest +1 and runs until HWB +5. It is slack off Le Conquet by HWB +6. Thus the stream is fair in the CdF for about $5\frac{1}{2}$ hours, but passage through the 12·5M long CdF usually only takes just under 2 hours for a yacht with 5 knots boat speed.

Applying these tidal ingredients, two examples illustrate the planning equation:

i   A yacht bound for either Camaret or Brest would leave L'Aberwrac'h at HW Brest +$2\frac{1}{4}$ (HW Dover –5) against the last of the east-going stream, to arrive abeam Le Four (13·5M) at about HW Brest +$4\frac{3}{4}$ and off Vieux Moines at about slack water (HWB +6). The 8·5M to Camaret would be against the last of the ebb, but the young flood would assist over the 15 miles to Brest's Moulin Blanc marina.

ii   The same yacht, if bound through the Raz de Sein for Audierne, would need to utilise the first of the fair stream through the CdF and to stay on this tidal conveyor belt so as to arrive at the Raz at about HWB +6, spot on the critical slack water. The distance is some 30M (12·5M in the CdF and about 17M onwards to the Raz).

Thus the yacht would leave L'Aberwrac'h at HWB –3 against a foul tide, to be abeam Le Four at HWB (slack water); off La Fourmi buoy at HWB +2 and entering the Raz at HWB +5 as the stream goes slack.

The last 10M to Audierne would be against a weak foul stream. Although Audierne itself is tidally constrained, a buoy can be picked up off Ste Evette at any state of the tide. Await the tide up-river to Audierne or stay overnight on the buoy; Ste Evette is well sheltered.

Timing northbound Similar tactics apply, but of course in the opposite sense.

For example, a yacht bound for L'Aberwrac'h would leave Brest at HWB +5 or Camaret at the next HWB –$6\frac{1}{2}$ in order to be at Vieux Moines by HWB –5 where the north-going stream is already running strongly. From abeam Le Four at HWB –3, the yacht will carry the east-going stream for the next $6\frac{1}{2}$ hours, comfortably making L'Aberwrac'h (14M) or Roscoff (39M) on that tide and, with a fair wind, possibly Trébeurden (52M).

If proceeding from Audierne to L'Aberwrac'h, leave Audierne at about HWB +4 so as to be in the

Raz de Sein at HWB +$5\frac{1}{2}$ (slack water). The north-going stream should have you off La Fourmi at about HWB –4, abeam Le Four at HWB –2 and entering L'Aberwrac'h soon after HWB, having efficiently covered about 55M in 9 hours.

General notes Concentrate on steering a steady course. Pick up the next mark ahead as soon as possible. The navigator should talk the helmsman on to it, never distracting him with extraneous features and only occasionally with the Test match score. If beating, keep careful track of progress and dangers to either side of track, bearing in mind the higher than usual groundspeeds.

Safety If poor visibility is forecast it may be sensible to wait another day. If visibility shortens unexpectedly and you do not have radar, consider requesting navigational assistance or information on other vessels from *Cross Corsen* on VHF Ch 16; they will usually oblige in English.

From the outset be prepared for patches of rough water, ie washboards in, crew hooked on in the cockpit, lifejackets on, engine either idling or at instant readiness, headsail partly rolled to improve visibility ahead, main with a precautionary slab in. Conditions can change rapidly; better safe than horribly unprepared.

On the other hand you may enjoy an exhilaratingly fast passage in relatively calm water. Either way the CdF is always an interesting two hours. If you keep ahead of the game, it will stimulate rather than intimidate.

Les Vieux Moines PHM beacon

BREST TO POINTE DE PENMARC'H

CONTENTS

THE SEA AND THE LAND

There is no sudden change from North to South Brittany, other than the fact that you are at last steering roughly 180° from the moment you passed abeam of Le Four light house. (That heading incidentally will do nicely for the Raz de Sein). The slate roofs and white gable ends are still there along the cliff tops and amongst the Abers. The lunar landscape of coastal rocks will not fade until you are well south of Pointe de Penmarc'h.

But there has been a sea change, and not just in name. The English Channel with its short steep seas is astern. Ahead is the Atlantic Ocean with a three thousand mile fetch from the New World to the Old. Swell has altered the appearance and feel of these waters, not always present but never far from your mind.

Brittany is a vast region which extends westward from Mont St Michel in the north to Nantes and the Loire in the south. The département of Finistère is one of five such administrative packages within Brittany. From a north-south line drawn between Locquirec on the north coast, and Le Pouldu on the south, Finistère stretches west to

Chapter 2

the end of the old world. Along its coasts are the harbours and fishing villages which have drawn British yachtsmen like a magnet for so many years. Every name recalls a visit, an incident, pilotage well executed, perhaps a great meal or a meeting of minds with a friendly local inhabitant.

Before you hurry south try to make time to visit some of the places for which no space could be found in this book. The islands of Ushant (Ouessant) and Molène lie challengingly to the west of the Chenal du Four. Further south call in at Île de Sein before or after you pass through the Raz. Respect the rocks which guard the fishing ports of St Guénolé, Le Guilvinec and Lesconil along the bleak and never-ending promontory east from Penmarc'h.

Venture inland when it would be foolish or unpleasant to put to sea. East of Brest is the huge Armoric Regional Park which sprawls from Camaret towards Morlaix and Guingamp. Innumerable attractive byways and hidden valleys are there to be explored on foot or bicycle. The high desolate moorlands and rocky outcrops of the Monts d'Arrée punctuate much of the Park. From the highest point (380m) you can see the Channel coast and the Rade de Brest on a clear day. Further south the Black Mountains rise east of Chateaulin and Quimper.

Or of course you can sail inland to explore the rivers Aulne and Élorn in complete shelter.

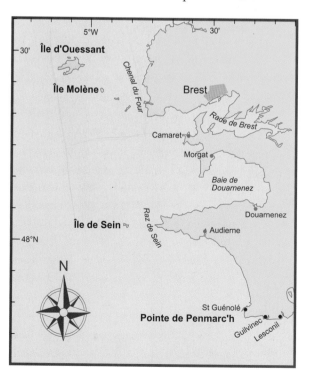

BREST

Brest has a lot going for it, even if it lacks the charm of older French cities. It is one of France's largest cities, a thriving commercial port and major naval base (shades of Plymouth/Devonport). It has good road, rail, air and ferry connections for the UK. The Rade de Brest is a well sheltered mini-cruising ground into which the Rivers Élorn and Aulne flow; both are worth exploring, particularly if you are delayed by bad weather offshore.

HISTORICAL

When the city was occupied in 1940, impregnable submarine pens were built for the U-boat fleet which in the Battle of the Atlantic sank a huge tonnage of Allied merchant shipping, threatening to cut off vital supplies flowing from America to Europe. By 1944 four years of Allied bombing had reduced the city, but not the submarine pens, to rubble.

It was rebuilt along severely geometric lines and some new buildings appear starkly functional. Green parks and tree-lined avenues do exist, but less so than in other cities. The naval base and commercial docks lie cheek by jowl. Near the latter,

on the water front at Blaveau (bus-stop) the atmosphere is rather more villagey with bars and restaurants. This area is overlooked by the American war memorial in pink stone, rebuilt after WW2. The marina is further east, a mile before the conspicuous double bridges across the Élorn.

TOURISM

A major attraction in the marina is Océanopolis, a vast and unusually striking design for all things oceanographic; a must for school parties and underwater buffs, perhaps a slightly less riveting visit for normal mortals! Two new buildings dealing with Tropical and Polar waters opened in 2000. Entrance is 50FF for adults, 30FF for 4-17 year olds and opening hours are 0930 to 1900 in season (1800 M-F, out of season; weekends as in season); Tel 02.98.34.40.40.

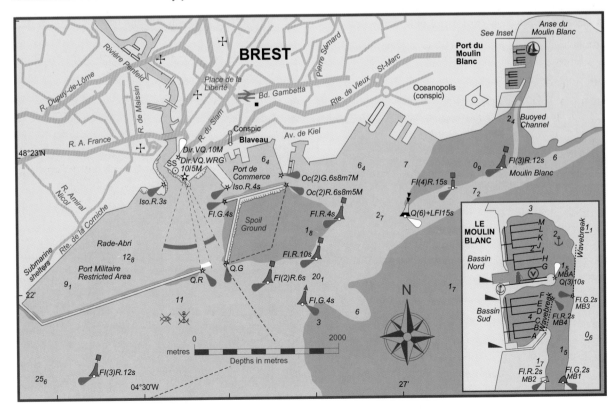

Looking west through the Goulet de Brest

Labels on image: Pte des Espagnols, Pte de Cornouaille, Pte du Portzic, Naval Base

Buses Station 02.98.44.46.73; Bibus 02.98.80.30.30 is the city/suburban network. The No 7 bus leaves the marina from either the north, end or behind Océanopolis, to the city centre. Destination: Place de la Liberté. The service is at least twice per hour (much less frequent at weekends) and takes 15 mins. Tickets, 6FF return, are bought on the bus. The Tourist Office is on the south corner of Place de la Liberté, about 100m from the bus stop.

Taxis (via Capitainerie) Allo Taxi 02.98.42.11.11; Les Taxis Brestois 02.98.80.43.43.

What to see/do Brest itself could not be rated highly as a tourist attraction.

There is a Maritime Museum in a small part of the 15th century Chateau, but it is a poor cousin to the Paris original. Entry 29FF, daily except Tues 0915-1200 & 1400-1800; follow a rather oddly signed route, taking care not to end up in the Dungeon! There are fine views across the Rade and through the Goulet.

To the west, Tour Tanguy by the Pont de Recouvrance (a colossal lifting span bridge across the Penfeld River), depicts scenes from Brest's past until 1939; open daily 1000-1200 & 1400-1900 in season, free.

A tour of the Naval base (Arsenal) and a French warship is possible only for French citizens; nor can you visit the former German U-boat pens, but see Lorient, St Nazaire and Bordeaux for this slightly dubious pleasure.

From the commercial docks there are boat trips to Ushant, Île de Molène and around the Rade.

Tourist Office Place de la Liberté, BP 24, 29266 Brest Cedex. Tel 02.98.44.24.96. Fax 02.98.44.53.73. e-mail: Office.de.Tourisme.Brest@wanadoo.fr

Hours in season (15/6-15/9): Mon-Sat 0930-1230 & 1400-1830; Sun 1000-1200 & 1400-1600.

Out of season Mon-Sat 1000-1230 & 1400-1800; Sun closed.

Car hire Avis 02.98.44.63.02, 230 bis, rue de Siam; Budget 02.98.41.70.60; Europcar 02.98.44.66.88, 43 rue Voltaire; Hertz 02.98.80.11.51.

Bike hire Torch VTT, 20 rue Yves Collet, Brest; 02.98.46.06.07.

ACCESS TO UK

For yachtsmen Brest's two great strengths are:
a. The marina is a safe haven in which to leave a boat; and
b. It has good access to the UK.

Océanopolis

Trains Gare SNCF 08.36.35.35.35. Paris (Montparnasse) is about 4¼ hours by TGV; thence on to London by Eurostar.

Flights Brest Guipavas Airport 02.98.32.01.00, is only 10 minutes by taxi from the marina. Air France 08.02.80.28.02, 55 mins to Paris; Finistair 02.98.84.64.87; Britair 02.98.32.01.10, fly direct to Gatwick.

Ferries Brittany Ferries, Roscoff - Plymouth. Roscoff 02.98.29.28.00 65km can be reached by bus or train/bus via Morlaix in under an hour, less by car. Also St Malo 02.99.40.64.41 - Portsmouth.

EATING ASHORE

In the marina central area after a shower, have a drink in *Le Tour du Monde*, a conspicuous and convivial bar above the showers, before eating at the nearby *Bar à Huitres*, open 1200-2359.

Otherwise, you have two choices at the north end of the marina: *Le Balaou*, a useful combination of grocer's shop (épicerie) and restaurant, which serves breakfast and modest 56FF and 62FF lunch/dinner menus, plus à la carte. Tel 02.98.41.79.87. There is also a Tabac/Bar a few metres up the road if you just want a drink.

Or you can eat close by in far greater style (and expense) at *Ma Petite Folie*, a converted crayfish boat, firmly aground on the sands (which make a safe and attractive playground for kids – there are also attractive lawns and shady trees at the north end for a family picnic). At *Ma Petite Folie*, run by Brigitte and François Fer, choose superb seafood from a set menu at 110FF or a far more elaborate à la carte menu. After a long day's sail from Roscoff I enjoyed a memorable meal here. All credit cards, including Amex. Tel 02.98.42.44.42. Closed Sun and 2 weeks in mid-August!

Restaurants in Brest The following are grouped roughly in popular eating areas. At Blaveau (near the docks, overlooked by the American Monument) on Quai de la Douane, try:
- La Maison de l'Océan, at No 2; 02.98.80.44.84.
- A l'Abri des Flots, at No 8; 02.98.44.07.31. Closed late Sep-mid Oct.
- Aux Patrouilleurs, at No 26; 02.98.44.10.25.

Rue de Siam (SW of Place de la Liberté):
- Bella Notte, at No 6; 02.98.44.44.21. Restaurant/pizzeria.
- La Jonquière, at No 12; 02.98.46.05.52. Traditional.
- Océania, at No 82; 02.98.80.66.66. Seafood. Closed first 3 weeks in August.

Rue Fautras, (3 blocks NW of and parallel to rue de Siam):
- Le Vieux Gréement, at No 2; 02.98.43.20.48. Seafood. Shut Sun & Mon.
- Le Roi Gradlon, at No 19; 02.98.80.17.28. Crêpes. Shut Sun and Mon am.
- Le Vatel, at No 23; 02.98.44.51.02. Gastronomic; menus 89-299FF. Shut Sun pm & Mon.

Rue Jean Jaurès (NE of Place de la Liberté):
- MacDonalds, at No 50; 02.98.43.03.27. Yes, MacDonalds ...! beyond the Town Hall.
- La Taverne St-Martin, at No 92; 02.98.80.48.17. Brasserie/restaurant; steak specialities.
- L'Auberge de la Crêpe, at No 142; 02.98.46.47.30. Corner of rue de la Turenne.
- La Boucherie, at No 164; 02.98.43.64.68. Grills. 52-200FF.

Rue Yves Collet (SE of Place de la Liberté, NW of Gare SNCF):
- La Ruffé, 1 rue Yves Collet; 02.98.46.07.70. Seafood 75-170FF. Closed pm Sun. Bon appetit.

SHOPPING
Supermarkets Nearest is In Brest at St Marc

Banks All

Brest was rebuilt along severely geometric lines

Conspic tower

Roche Mengam

Goulet de Brest and Roche Mengam isolated danger mark, looking NNW

NAVIGATIONAL MATTERS

Charts AC 3427 covers from Pte de St Mathieu and Pte de Toulinguet up to Brest commercial docks, but just excludes Moulin Blanc marina. It does however include Camaret at large scale. AC 3429 includes Moulin Blanc marina, the Rade de Brest, the first 3 miles of the River Élorn and the River Aulne as far as Pont Térénez; neither river is charted beyond these points. Equivalent SHOM charts are 7401 and 7400. AC 3428 (SHOM 7399) and SHOM 7397/7398 are not essential for yachts.

Pilotage The waypoint 48°18′·30N 04°44′·00W is on the 068° leading line used by large vessels and French warships, some of which are moving quite fast; a good lookout astern is essential. The twin light houses at Pte du Petit Minou (front leading mark) and Pte du Portzic light house (rear leading mark) are both obvious. The steep rocky sides of the Goulet (narrows or straits) de Brest paint a good radar picture.

It may be better, especially in poor visibility, for a yacht to avoid the leading line altogether, ie from the Chenal du Four stay north of Le Coq, Charles Martell and Basse Beuzec PHM buoys, keeping close inshore between Pte du Petit Minou and Pte du Portzic. This approach will also cheat the worst of any foul tide.

From the south, by day, you may decide to route through the Chenal du Toulinguet (perfectly straightforward) and along the south side of the Goulet. By night the lit route via Basse du Lis SCM light buoy, La Parquette light beacon and Swansea Vale IDM light buoy is slightly longer, but safer.

Once past Pointe des Espagnols, the Rade de Brest opens out and there is room for all. If making for Moulin Blanc, it is probably easier to stay just north of the line of PHM channel buoys, but watch for warships entering/leaving the naval harbour.

Océanopolis is not always conspicuous, because its white roof cannot be seen at or near LW and might in any case be mistaken for one of the many oil/gas tanks in the adjacent industrial area.

Tides and tidal streams Brest is a Standard Port. Try to work a fair tide in the Goulet where the stream reaches 3·9kn at Sp, 2·2kn at Nps (see notes for the Chenal du Four); there is often quite a chop on the water near Roche Mengam.

Hazards In the Goulet the Plateau des Fillettes is a rocky bank in mid-stream which might pose a problem but only in poor visibility. Its west end is marked by a WCM lt buoy and the east end by Mengam IDM bcn tr. The south side of the bank is marked by two PHM lt buoys. Yachts are free to pass either side of it, but must not impede large

Front:
Pointe du Petit-Minou

Rear:
Pointe du Portzic

068° leading marks

vessels which are navigating a narrow channel (Rule 9) and are directed by Brest Port Control to route north or south of Mengam.

Access The marina is accessible at all tides, but be aware that outside the buoyed channel depths shoal rapidly. At or near LW, stand on for about a cable beyond the Moulin Blanc PHM buoy before turning onto approx 005° for the marina. Inside the marina the 'MBA' ECM light beacon on a concrete wave-break marks the turn-in point for the **Ⓥ** pontoon.

VHF Monitor Brest Port Control Ch 08 for traffic movements. The marina is on Ch 09.

MOULIN BLANC MARINA

This large (1325 berths) marina has virtually every facility and engineers to fix most problems. The office staff are friendly and mostly bi-lingual. Information handouts are comprehensive.

Capitainerie (at the head of the **Ⓥ** pontoon) is open 0800-2000 in season, 0900-1230 & 1330 to 1800 out of season. VHF Ch 09. Tel 02.98.02.20.02; Fax 02.98.41.67.91. Director Marc Lambert. Weather forecasts are posted at 0830 daily.

Where to berth Alongside the **Ⓥ** pontoon (first to port beyond the ECM beacon), rafted up in season; no finger pontoons. There is often a colossal French multihull berthed here and numerous small fry, so that space can be tight. Request a vacant berth elsewhere if you plan to stay a while.

Tariff Daily rates, all seasons, for selected LOAs on pontoon:
8m = 86FF; 9m = 102FF; 10m = 107FF;
11m = 117FF; 12m = 125FF; 13m = 131FF.

Fuel The fuel berth is at the inner end of the **Ⓥ** pontoon. Diesel and petrol are available 0900-1130 and 1400-1700, or 24 hours by French credit card. If, as is likely, your credit/bank card will not work the dispensing machine, first speak to the Capitainerie who will activate the pumps and debit your card in longhand.

Showers 10FF per jeton for a good shower, below the Tour du Monde bar, opposite G pontoon. The launderette is in the shower block.

NAUTICAL NEEDS

Chandlery There are 5 chandleries, some in rue Alain Colas, behind the marina:
Comptoirs Maritimes, 02.98.02.30.04, SHOM chart agent; Navi Ouest, 02.98.42.03.57; Occase Mer, 02.98.42.03.01; UShip, 02.98.02.49.02, SHOM chart agent; Servie Mer, 02.98.46.38.86;

Sailmakers Yucca Voiles, 02.98.80.14.00; Voiles Ocean, 02.98.80.28.32; Incidences, 02.98.44.79.80;

Engines Jet-Marine, 02.98.41.80.25 (Volvo, Suzuki, Yanmar); Mecamar, 02.98.43.14.22 (Bukh, Nanni, Sabb, Yanmar); Navi Ouest, 02.98.42.03.57 (Evinrude); St Marc Plaisance, 02.98.44.51.40 (Honda, Mariner).

Moulin Blanc marina looking west across Brest to the open sea

RADE DE BREST

When the weather is set foul and you have exhausted the limited delights of Brest and the Moulin Blanc, head across the great roadstead of Brest for either the River Élorn or the Aulne. The latter is particularly well sheltered from all that the wind gods can hurl at you;

most of it goes literally over your head. It is easily navigated, there are a number of safe anchorages and both Port Launay and Chateaulin are very pleasant places.

Charts AC 3429 and SHOM 7400 (both 1:22,500). Neither of these cover the Rivers Élorn and Aulne beyond their first few miles. Thereafter, in all seriousness, the IGN (National Geographic Institute) TOP 25 series at 1:25,000 are excellent, with depth contours but no actual depths. Sheet 0516 (W) covers the Élorn to Landernau; 0517 (W) and 0518 (E) cover the Aulne to Chateaulin, the limit of navigation for masted boats. Michelin road map No 58 would be better than nothing.

GEOGRAPHY

On the west side of the Rade Presqu'Île de Quélern, with Pointe des Espagnols at its NE tip,

is an impressive peninsula which provides excellent shelter from the prevailing winds; see Camaret for good walks or bicycle rides. On its east side anchor off Roscanvel and up to six cables north or south; beyond these limits the ground becomes shallow, foul or rocky.

To the east a deepwater channel leads up to Île des Morts and Île Tréberon on which landing is prohibited. Further east the military installations on Île Longue are surrounded by extensive no anchoring/no fishing areas and an inner Prohibited area. (These military installations made it impossible to obtain aerial photographs of Camaret and Morgat). A ferry runs thrice daily from Brest, 25 mins, (Azénor; Tel 02.98.41.46.23) to Le Fret at the base of Île Longue, with useful bus connections to Camaret, Crozon and Morgat.

The southern shore of the Rade is pleasantly

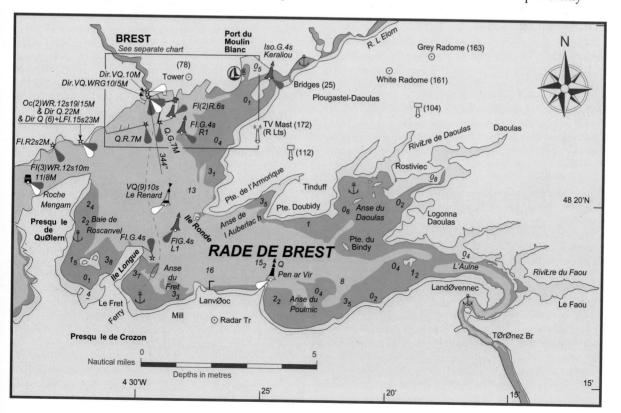

wooded, but another Prohibited area lies at the west end of Anse du Poulmic, which is generally shallow until the entrance to the River Aulne.

Backtracking to the vicinity of Pte des Espagnols, the main fairway ESE to the Aulne is entered between Basse du Renard WCM buoy and Île Ronde off Pte de l'Armorique. If coming from the marina, route to Île Ronde only via R1 SHM buoy, thus avoiding the shoal ground and obstructions that lie on a direct track from Moulin Blanc buoy.

Eastwards from Île Ronde the fairway starts to narrow at No 4 PHM buoy (4°22′W). To the north are attractive anchorages and local moorings in the Anse de L'Auberlac'h and the much wider, shallower Baie de Daoulas; both these inlets are open to the SW, but are well sheltered in an anti-cyclonic easterly. The buoyed fairway is at its narrowest at Traverse de l'Hôpital, opposite the drying river of that name. The buoyed, drying Faou river flows in from the east past Île d'Arun.

RIVER AULNE

From here the Aulne describes a large reversed S curve, passing the Abbaye de Saint Guénolé at Landévennec and the moored naval hulks by Port Styvel, where buoyage ceases. The river passes between steeply wooded banks and below the Pont de Térénez (27m clearance) – only to fall off the edge of AC 3429!

About 7 miles further on it runs tangential to the N165 autoroute for a short stretch; after another 4 miles the lock at Guily-Glaz (Tel 02.98.86.03.21) is reached, during its opening hours of HW-2 to +1½, if your timing is right. Beyond it the canalised

Port Launay quayside berths

river carries 3 metres. After 7 mile the generous quays of Port Launay lie to port on a long, gentle bend to starboard. This is a peaceful spot to berth and perhaps dine at Hotel Au Bon Accueil (Tel 02.98.86.15.77).

The attractive town of Chateaulin is 1·5 miles upstream with a mooring pontoon to starboard near the modern tourist office; supermarket nearby. Restaurants: Le Lotus; La Belle Epoque (Tel 02.98.86.31.21), 26 Quai Charles de Gaulle, closed Mon.

RIVER ÉLORN

Leave Moulin Blanc at about HW Brest –2. Landernau is approx 6½M from the two road bridges (25m clearance). The river is buoyed, but at ever longer intervals and above St Jean PHM beacon the best water (3m at HW neaps) is not easy to find; the author grounded in a bilge-keeler whilst 50m inside the buoyed channel.

The lifting bridge 0·5M short of Landernau must be pre-booked (Tel 02.98.85.16.16; mobile 06.11.03.31.20). In the town on the north bank yachts dry against the quay on hard, flat ground just before the new road bridge.

This attractive market town has several 17th century buildings and most facilities.

Tourist Office on Pont de Rohan (02.98.85.13.09).

Market days Mon, Fri & Sat.

Restaurants
- Le Clos du Pontic (02.98.21.50.91);
- Château de Brézal (02.98.85.12.19);
- L'Amandier (02.98.85.10.89);
- Le Printanier (02.98.21.49.50).

Twin bridges over River Elorn, from Moulin Blanc marina

Bare bones

CAMARET

This little fishing and yachting harbour is tucked in almost at the end of the Crozon peninsula, well placed between the Chenal du Four and the Raz de Sein.
It also lies just west of the Rade de Brest and within easy
striking distance of the Baie de Douarnenez.

Fishing vessels berth in the SE corner of the harbour. There are marinas near the entrance and at the NW end of the harbour. Camaret has successfully combined fishing with yachting; the ambience is a happy one with friendly people. No wonder it is popular either as a base or for yachts on passage.

Camaret wears its heart on its sleeve. Features include the stout bulk of Le Tour Vauban with the Rocamadour chapel close by and the sad rib-like bones of beached *chalutiers* slowly rotting in the sun. The waterfront by day is a colourful kaleidoscope of hotels, restaurants, bars; at night it is brightly illuminated and thronging with people. If a festival is in progress your ears may be assaulted/soothed (depending on taste) by mega-decibels of music and song into the small hours.

TOURISM

Tourist Office 15 Quai Kleber, BP 16, 29570 Camaret. Tel 02.98.27.93.60; Fax 02.98.27.87.22. Hours in season: Mon-Sat 0915-1900; Sun 1000-1230 & 1530-1830.

What to see/do The rugged coastal scenery near Camaret lends itself to cycling and walking. Go west to Pointe du Toulinguet and study the Chenal du Toulinguet if planning to sail south. Near here are the megalithic alignments of Lagatjar, 143 menhirs, dating back to 2500BC. Continue down to Pointe de Pen-Hir, passing the huge granite Cross of Lorraine memorial to the Bretons of the Free French forces. Here you can get a close-up of Les Tas de Pois, plus a panorama stretching from Pointe St Mathieu to the Raz and Île de Sein.

Plage de Corréjou. Masts at La Pointe Marina in the background

Bike hire Vauban Sport 2000, 3 rue du Loch; 02.98.27.86.82.

ACCESS TO UK

See under Brest and Rade de Brest, noting that regular ferries ply between Brest and Le Fret which can be reached from Camaret by bus (13 minutes via Crozon).

EATING ASHORE

Restaurants The following are in sequence southwards from the NW end of the harbour:

- Hotel Thalassa. Menus at 100 and 158FF.
- Hotel-Restaurant du Styvel; 02.98.27.92.74. Yveline et Georges Téphany. Seafood, 72-185FF.
- Hôtel de France (Logie); 02.98.27.93.06. Menus at 78, 100, 148 and 190FF.
- La Licorne. Menus at 68, 94, 118, 158 and 225FF.
- There are several crêperies, pizzerias etc; also 2 Irish-type pubs serving Guinness and Murphy's.

Or head north up the Presqu'Île de Quelern to Pointe des Espagnols for views across the Goulet and Rade de Brest, returning via the village of Roscanvel.

Beaches Excellent, the nearest is Plage du Corréjou; hop over the harbour's north wall (Digue du Sillon). Otherwise a bike ride to Anse du Pouldu, Anse de Pen-Hat (windsurfing, dangerous bathing) and Plage de Veryarc'h, respectively ENE, WSW and SSW of the harbour.

Also tennis and a mini golf course at rue du Stade.

Music On Monday evenings in July and August there are varied musical concerts and recitals; see Tourist Office for details.

Buses to Crozon (10 mins; for Morgat), Quimper (1h 30m) and Brest (1h 40m).

Taxi 02.98.27.84.84.

Car hire See Tourist Office

SHOPPING

Supermarkets Huit à Huit on the waterfront. For the much bigger Super-U, continue south, turn right up rue du Loch (between the Post Office and Tourist Office).

Markets Third Tuesday of the month, daily in July/August, in Place St Thomas.

Banks BNP and Credit Agricole on waterfront.

Tour Vauban   *SHM beacon*   *Rocamadour chapel*

La Louve west cardinal and Les Tas de Pois

NAVIGATIONAL MATTERS

Charts AC 3427 (1:22,500 with 1:10,000 of Camaret) and 798 (1:60,000). SHOM charts are 7401 (1:22,500) and 7148 (1:50,000).

Approaches From the NW quadrant the approach to the waypoint 48°17´·50N 4°36´·00W is direct and simple, except perhaps in gale force easterlies – despite being partially protected by the massif of Presqu'ile de Quélern. At night stay in the white sector of the N mole light.

From the south the outer approach is past Les Tas de Pois and through Chenal du Toulinguet. Even in a southerly Force 6 this is perfectly manageable by day and eyeball navigation between the 8m high Le Pohen rock and La Louve WCM beacon is certainly easier than the charted 156·5° leading line astern of you.

From the west, or by night from the south, it is more practicable to take a longer route via Basse du Lis SCM light buoy, La Parquette light beacon (black and white spiral bands) and north of the unlit Trépied SHM buoy.

Daymarks On rounding Pointe du Grand Gouin you will see, grouped closely together, a bright green SHM beacon at the west end of the North mole; Tour Vauban, a bulky fort of stone and mellow brick; and Rocamadour chapel (minus its spire which was shot off by the British in the 17th century – you would be forgiven for not noticing this).

Pilotage From the waypoint, about 2 cables N of the rugged Pointe du Grand Gouin, set course 137°/8 cables for the east end of the harbour's North mole (48°16´·90N 04°35´·10W) which is rather less obvious than the bright green SHM beacon referred to above.

From Brest skirt round Presqu'ile de Quélern and steer south to the harbour entrance.

Within the harbour, if making for Plaisance Styvel, keep clear of mooring trots in the middle and a 0·5m shoal patch off the end of the slipway on the N side.

Tides HW and LW Camaret are 10 and 13 minutes respectively before HW and LW Brest. MHWS is 6·6m, MLWS 1·0m; MHWN is 5·1m, MLWN 2·5m.

Tidal streams There is a back eddy in the Anse du Camaret, clockwise during the flood; and counter-clockwise during the ebb. Rates are not strong.

Access At all tides and in all weathers.

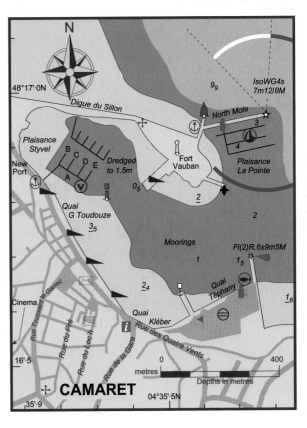

Styvel marina: Juno on 'E' pontoon;
'A' pontoon in the foreground is vacant

MARINAS

There are two marinas, sharing one harbour-master, but otherwise with separate facilities:

Plaisance de la Pointe The original marina, immediately to starboard of the entrance on rounding the North mole. Least depth is about 3m. No finger pontoons; it has its own office and showers below Tour Vauban, but is a fair walk to the town. 12 ⚓s are close S/SE. Good shelter except in easterlies.

Plaisance du Styvel At the NW end of the harbour, comprises two separate pontoon blocks: the northerly block is only for locals.

The southerly block has ❷ finger pontoons on the east side of 'E' pontoon (the first you reach); visitors also berth alongside/raft up on the SW side of 'A' pontoon which lies NW/SE. The HM may insist on this allocation of berths and, even if other berths at Styvel are vacant, may re-direct you to La Pointe. Least depths are about 1·5m. An unlit PHM perch close SE of 'E' pontoon warns of shoal water. Excellent access to Capitainerie, showers etc and the town. Good shelter.

Anchorage Anchoring in the harbour is forbidden, but there is an anchorage east of the entrance and fairway, clear of fish farms and mussel rafts.

Capitainerie Open 0900-1230 & 1400 to 1900 Mon-Sat, but Wed 0900-1230 & 1700-1900; Sun 0900-1230 & 1600-1900. Tel (La Pointe) 02.98.27.95.99, (Styvel) 02.98.27.89.31; Fax 02.98.27.96.45. VHF Ch 09. HM Noël Tretout. Weather forecasts are posted 0900 daily.

Showers 0800-2100. 9FF per jeton; machine gives change. The launderette is in adjacent block.

Tariff Daily rates 1 Jun-30 Sept, for selected LOAs on pontoon at either marina:
8m = 85.50FF; 9m = 98FF; 10m = 113.50FF; 11m = 128FF; 12m = 143.50FF; 13m = 158FF.

Fuel The diesel (only) berth is at La Pointe at the foot of the gangway leading to the pontoons. Available via Mecamar (Tel 02.98.27.95.29): Tue-Fri 0900-1200 & 1600-1800; Sat 0900-1200 & 1700-1800; Sun & Mon 1100-1200 & 1700-1800.

NAUTICAL NEEDS

Chandlery & repairs

- Comptoirs Maritimes, 02.98.27.91.03, Quai Téphany (by fishing harbour). SHOM chart agent.
- Maison de la Presse in Place St Thomas (first right after Huit à Huit supermarket) keeps a small stock of SHOM charts/publications, and English newspapers.
- Chantier Nautique de l'Iroise, 02.98.27.82.74, Quai Téphany. Boatyard, 25 ton crane.
- Charpentiers Marine Camaretois (near Tour Vauban). Shipwright.
- Mecamar, Le Sillon, (Tel 02.98.27.95.29). Engineering repairs (Sabb, Bukh, Nanni, Tohatsu, Yanmar). Runs the diesel pump at Plaisance la Pointe.

Styvel marina. Red perch warns of shoal

MORGAT

Morgat is off the beaten track, a delightful sleepy hollow, a place for lazy days. Yet it has rallies, regattas, an active dinghy school, enthusiastic divers and a modest fishing presence. It is protected from the prevailing winds by the mass of the 4M long promontory which culminates in the Cap de la Chèvre (nanny goat), a 90m high headland. Morgat is exposed only to winds from N to SE. The harbour nestles below pine-covered slopes; its mile-wide bay to the N boasts blue waters and a magnificent golden curve of sandy beach.

To be specific: Morgat is the port, Tréflez is the village and Crozon 3km away is the commune. The village, about 10 mins walk from the marina, is pleasantly attractive without being charming; it is purely a seaside resort devoted to beach and hotels, the latter having some style. At the end of the 19th century Monsieur Peugeot (a bicycle-maker, later car-maker) launched an estate agency here; most of the hotels and villas date from that time.

Nowadays Morgat is frenetic in July and August, the rest of the year it recuperates. Crozon, by the way, has been rather unkindly described as "a one-way traffic system to distribute tourists among the various resorts (of the Crozon peninsula)" – but that need not concern you too much.

TOURISM

Tourist Office At Crozon, reached by bike or bus (times indeterminate). Open all year, at Bd Pralognan la Vannoise, 29160 Crozon. Tel 02.98.26.17.18. Fax 02.98.27.24.89. In season the Syndicat d'Initiative at bd de la Plage, Morgat, Tel 02.98.27.29.49, fulfils the same role.

Things to do A bike ride to Cap de la Chèvre and back via Pte de Dinan is a bracing 11km. On foot perhaps a shorter walk along the clifftops to the south of the lighthouse would suffice.

Vedette trips to Les Grandes Grottes are a local attraction; or go by dinghy if the weather is OK. These caves are at either end of Anse de St Hernot, the first bay south of Morgat lighthouse. The largest is 80m long and 15m high. Les petites grottes are on the Pte des Grottes at the NE end of Morgat beach and can be reached on foot at LW.

Buses from Camaret to either Brest or Quimper stop at Crozon, but not Morgat. A local bus was glimpsed leaving Morgat possibly for Crozon, but no bus-stops or timetables were to be seen.

Taxi 02.98.27.11.85.

Car hire via Syndicat d'Initiative, bd de la Plage (in season); Tel 02.98.27.29.49.

Bike hire Cycles Failler, 34 rue de Poulpatré, Crozon; Tel 02.98.27.06.35.

EATING ASHORE

Restaurants The following are a selection in sequence from the marina to the north end of the village:

ACCORDING TO LOCAL LEGEND ...

There is a Basse d'Ys, 2·5M WSW of Cap de la Chèvre and according to local legend Ys was once the capital city of Cornouaille, ruled by King Gradlon in the 6th century. Ys was protected from the sea by a dike, opened by locks to which the King alone had the keys. However his naughty daughter, having been seduced by the Devil, stole the keys and let the sea in. The city was drowned forever beneath the waves, but the memory lives on. Ys is said to lie in the Baie de Douarnenez or Baie des Trépassés (Raz de Sein) or off Audierne and, no doubt, a few other places.

Entry buoy NE of the wavebreaks, looking SW

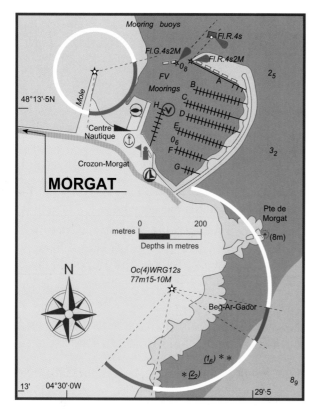

MORGAT

48°13'·5N

Mooring buoys

Fl.R.4s

Fl.G.4s2M

Fl.R.4s2M

0·8

FV Moorings

2·5

Mole

Centre Nautique

Crozon-Morgat

B A
C
H V
D
E
0·6
F
G

3·2

0
metres
200

Depths in metres

N

Oc(4)WRG12s
77m15-10M

Beg-Ar-Gador

Pte de Morgat

(8m)

(1·6) **

* (2·2)

13'   04°30'·0W   29'·5   8·9

- Les Échoppes, 24 Quai du Kador; characterful cottage/roses on wall etc, menus from 100FF. Tel 02.98.26.12.63. Closed in winter.
- Irish beer next door at Le Kerguelen bar.
- Hotel-Restaurant de la Ville d'Ys, impressive place up the hill behind Les Échoppes, good views to seaward; menus 85-240FF. François Moulin. Tel 02.98.27.06.49. Closed in winter.
- La Grange de Toul Boss, crêperie on the main square; menus from 79FF. Pleasant garden for eating alfresco. Tel 02.98.27.17.95.
- Les Flots, main square next to Proxi mini-supermarket; good for snacks.
- Le Julia, 43 rue de Treflez; follow the beach northward to Le Galion (conspic monkey puzzle tree), turn left for about 400m, quite a walk but worthwhile. Menus from 82-260FF. Tel 02.98.27.05.89. Closed Nov-Feb.

SHOPPING

Supermarkets Proxi is a mini-supermarket/grocery in Morgat's square. U-Marché at 7 rue Alsace, Crozon, Tel 02.98.27.06.08.

Market days Morgat, grand sale every Wed morning in summer. Crozon market on 2nd and 4th Weds of the month in Place de l'église.

Banks Only in Crozon.

NAVIGATIONAL MATTERS

Charts AC 798, 1:60,000 with 1:15,000 inset. Or SHOM 6676 (1:15,000) and 6099 (1: 45,800).

Approaches The entrance to the Baie de Douarnenez is 3M wide, adequate for any camel. But if you round Cap de la Chèvre inshore of Basse Vieille IDM buoy a more needle-like finesse is needed, precisely because it looks so deceptively easy. Take note, particularly in bad weather, of the reef stretching almost a mile SW from the headland; La Lentille, a rock drying 1m, under the nose of the CG station; and Basse Plate reef, drying 5·6m, off the SE corner. But Basse Laye 0·4m is the most dangerous rock, bearing 150°/7 cables from the CG station.

To clear these nasties fix yourself by traditional means, by radar or by GPS (nothing north of 48°09'·40N will do nicely). At night it might be wise to shape a course outside Basse Vieille.

Once clear, set course for the waypoint at 48°13'·70N 04°29'·00W from which the harbour entrance should be clearly visible. Morgat is hidden by wooded cliffs until you are north of the clifftop light house, Oc (4) WRG 12s.

Pilotage From Cap de la Chèvre the east side of the promontory is sheer delight, a succession of sandy bays amongst the cliffs and wooded slopes – choose your picnic stop! If beating be aware of the rocky plateau about 2M ESE of Morgat: Les Verrès and La Pierre Profonde are 9m and 4·1m high respectively, whilst Le Taureau, the nearest rock to Morgat, dries 1·8m.

In January 2000 the French authorities designated 24 anchor berths for the use of large vessels. These berths lie up to 1·5M east of the Cap de la Chèvre promontory, from north of 48°10'·70N (Anse de St Nicholas) to the coast north of Morgat.

Keep at least 2 cables off the shore and harbour breakwater as you make for the waypoint. From

To the visitors pontoon in front of a yellow crane

there track 264°/4 cables to the PHM entry buoy 48°13'·66N 04°29'·58W; this is at the entrance to the short channel, dredged 1·5m, which leads SW between concrete wavebreaks into the marina.

Tides HW Morgat is 8 mins before HW Brest; LWs are 10 mins nps or 20 sp before LW Brest. MHWS is 6·5m, MLWS 1·0m; MHWN is 5·0m, MLWN 2·4m.

Tidal streams may reach 1 knot off Cap de la Chèvre, but in the Baie rarely exceed ½ knot.

Access At all tides and in all weathers.

MARINA

On the east side of the marina are 6 pontoons for locals, lettered B-G from the north. Pontoon A is actually part of the wavebreak, but there are 8 finger pontoons at its inboard end (16 boats). Its outer end is made up of 5 concrete wavebreak barges with no boats berthed on them.

Visitors berth on 'H' pontoon (north/south) by the yellow crane. It has short, narrow fingers (max LOA 12m); unhappily most berths are occupied by local workboats and small craft. Check with HM for a vacant berth on pontoons B-E.

Anchorage on sand in the centre of Anse de Morgat clear of local moorings, but not in strong E winds or with SW swell. Anchoring prohibited within the port due to fishing boat moorings.

Capitainerie is open 0800-2000 daily in season; winter 0800-1200 & 1400-1800. VHF Ch 09. Tel 02.98.27.01.97; Fax 02.98.27.19.76. HM Pierre Carn. Weather forecasts are posted daily.

Showers 10FF and Launderette (open 0800-1800) are adjacent.

Tariff Daily rates for selected LOAs Jul/Aug; 2nd figure is Apr-Jun & Sep; Oct-Mar is half the 2nd figure:
8m = 71/53.5FF; 9m = 80/59.5FF; 10m = 89/67FF; 11m = 98/74FF; 12m = 109/82FF.

Fuel The diesel (only) berth is at the root of the **Ⓥ** pontoon, west side. Open Jul/Aug 0800-1200 & 1400-1900 (1730 Sep-Jun).

Yacht Club Centre Nautique de Crozon-Morgat (CNCM), Tel 02.98.27.01.98.

NAUTICAL NEEDS

Chandlery There is a chandlery midway between port and village, but for a greater choice go to Camaret (10 mins by bus) or to Douarnenez (145°/10M by rhumb line) for repairs. The garage on the left as you leave Morgat (up the hill) for Crozon is helpful for mechanical problems.

The harbour nestles below pine-covered slopes

DOUARNENEZ

Douarnenez is well worth a detour, both on its own merits and to savour the other-worldliness of the Baie de Douarnenez, on the edge of the ancient kingdom of Cornouaille. Yet it is not so very remote, 24M from Pointe St Mathieu with Camaret and Morgat as intermediate ports of call;

and 18M east of the Raz de Sein. The Pouldavid river flows out through the harbour which partly dries below the tidal sill at Port Rhu. Douarnenez lies on the east bank and Tréboul on the west. The latter houses the marina with pleasant tree-shaded pavements on its N side.

Douarnenez is rather larger, but has few yacht facilities. Instead there is a substantial and active fishing basin (yachts prohibited) NNE of the town. South of this is Port de Rosmeur which has charm and quayside cafés/bars, but mostly dries and has no room for yachts.

Port Rhu boat museum, looking up-stream

TOURISM

Tourist Offices The Tréboul office, Quai de l'Yser (near Capitainerie) only opens Jul/Aug. The main tourist office is in Douarnenez, 2 rue du Dr Mével and sports a red British telephone box outside! Tel 02.98.92.13.35; Fax 02.98.92.70.47. Hours: Jul/Aug, Mon-Sat 0900-1900; Sun 1000-1300 & 1600-1900. Out of season: Mon-Sat 0900-1200 & 1400-1800.

What to see The major attraction is undoubtedly the Boat Museum on the east bank at Port Rhu, open daily 1000-1900, mid-Jun-end Sep; out of season 1000-1230 & 1400-1800, except Mon, 30FF

entry. Tel 02.98.92.65.20; Fax 02.98.92.05.41. In the basin are about 20 boats of all types and sizes. In the museum more than 100 boats from all over Europe are on display, some of them recalling the heyday of Douarnenez as a sardine port and one of the largest canneries. Traditional boatbuilding and sailmaking are exemplified by actual craftsmen working in the boatyard and sailmaker's loft. An interesting, if exhausting, visit. Look down on Port Rhu from the metal road bridge (clearance 16·5m) which crosses upstream; otherwise use the pedestrian bridge over the barrage, sill and gate to reach Douarnenez.

Climb up to Place Gabriel Péri at the centre of Douarnenez, enjoy the old-fashioned atmosphere, before dropping down to Port de Rosmeur, always interesting and very evocative of the past. Complete the circuit by walking past the Fish Basin and the Rade du Guet where there are good views down-river to Île Tristan. Return to the marina by the pedestrian bridge.

Rail The line to Quimper is disused. Quimper is on Brest-Vannes line.

Bus 50 mins from Tréboul marina to Quimper.

Taxi 02.98.74.14.14; 02.98.92.35.90; 02.98.92.13.13.

Beaches There are two good beaches close NNW and NW of marina, Plage St Jean and Plage des Sables Blancs, marked on chart 798.

Unfortunately it is out of order

Tréboul marina, looking west

ACCESS TO UK

See under Brest.

SHOPPING

Supermarkets
- There is a mini-supermarket, Score (Tel 02.98.74.00.67) on the north side of the marina.
- LeClerc Hypermarket (Tel 02.98.74.00.67) is about 600 metres SW of the marina off Route de Toubalan.

Tréboul is compact, friendly and has virtually everything you could want for normal needs, but for more upmarket shopping go to Douarnenez (about 15 mins walk).

Market days Tréboul market is at the far end of quai de l'Yser, every morning except Sunday.

Banks Two banks on the quai de l'Yser at Tréboul. Many more in Douarnenez.

EATING ASHORE

Restaurants in Tréboul
- La Capitainerie is next door to the Capitainerie (would you believe) and closest to the Ⓥ pontoons, if you need a quickish bite.
- You can eat very pleasantly at Un P'tit Grain, 02.98.74.14.19, a small restaurant/pizzeria at No 1 rue Jeanne d'Arc, near the conspic Boulangerie Le Guellec on NW corner of marina.

In Douarnenez
- Le Doyen at the Hotel de France, 4 rue Jean Jaurès, 02.98.92.00.02; some gentle gourmandising, from menus 95-195FF, closed Sun pm and Mons except Jul/Aug.
- Le Tristan, 25 rue de Rosmeur, 02.98.92.20.17 (M. Daden), overlooks Port de Rosmeur; *un bon table, pour un repas qui sort de l'ordinaire.* Menus 99-210FF, closed Wed & mid-Nov to mid-Jan.

NAVIGATIONAL MATTERS

Charts AC 798, 1:60,000 with 1:15,000 inset. SHOM charts are 6677 (1:15,000) and 6099 (1:45,800).

Entrance to Port Rhu   Passe du Guet   Tréboul marina   Île Tristan

Chapter 2

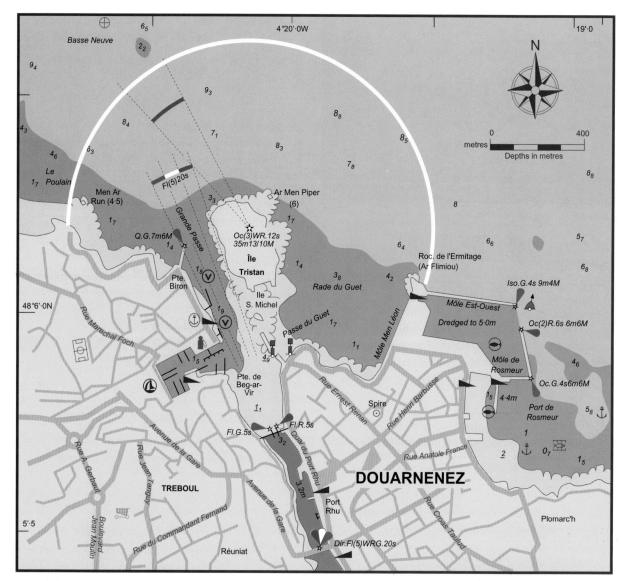

Approaches Straightforward. From the west (Raz de Sein) the coast is clean. From WNW, see Morgat for notes on rounding Cap de la Chèvre. The SE corner of the Baie de Douarnenez is free of dangers and studded by a series of wide sandy beaches, ideal as day anchorages.

Pilotage A waypoint of 48°06′·70N 04°20′·68W is in the white sector of the Fl (5) WRG 20s directional light which covers the Grande Passe; and in the red sector of Île Tristan light, Oc (3) WR 12s, which covers Basse Veur (4·7m) and Basse Neuve (1·8m).

By day this waypoint is almost on the 146° transit of the two church spires marked as "Belfry" on AC 798. These church spires and Île Tristan light house are very conspicuous, even looking into the mid-morning sun. Île Tristan is a chunky, cliffy, tree-covered island.

Basse Veur should not be a problem and Basse Neuve, even at LW springs, may only concern deep-draught yachts. The 146° leading line clears it close to the SW.

Tides HW Douarnenez is 10 mins nps or 15 mins sp before HW Brest; LWs are 8 mins nps or 18 mins sp before LW Brest. MHWS is 6·4m, MLWS 0·9m; MHWN is 4·9m, MLWN 2·3m.

Passe du Guet and Île Tristan, looking N at high water

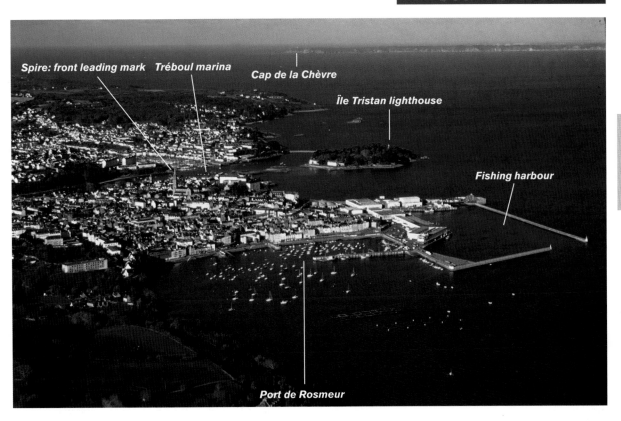

Spire: front leading mark Tréboul marina Cap de la Chèvre

Île Tristan lighthouse

Fishing harbour

Port de Rosmeur

Tidal streams are slight in the Baie de Douarnenez.

Access At all tides and in all weathers to the ♥ pontoons off Tréboul marina.

MARINA

Where to berth Within Tréboul marina there is no visitors' pontoon and quite simply no room; it is chock-a-block with local boats even in early June. The two ♥ pontoons on the west bank of the Grande Passe are quite exposed to NW'lies.

Berth/raft against either side of the northerly pontoon. The southerly pontoon has finger berths which may prove uncomfortable. There are 7 white ♥s close by.

Port Rhu is entered over a sill drying 1·1m. A 10m wide gate is normally left open, but if not it opens approx HW±1, but HW±2 in Jul/Aug if the Coefficient is >70. A lifting pedestrian bridge is usually down, but lifts when vessels are cleared to enter/exit. Rhu's Bureau du Port is aboard the adjacent moored tug *Courageux*, VHF Ch 09.

Île Tristan
lighthouse

Church spires
in transit 146°

Grande
Passe

Pte Biron
mole head

Outer transits and Grand Passe

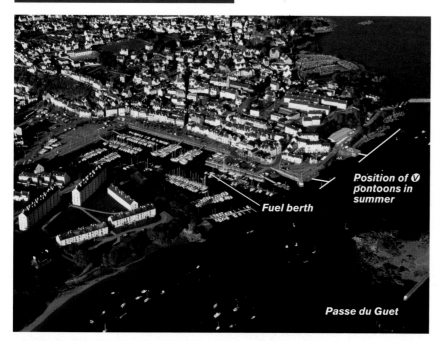

Fuel berth

Position of **V** pontoons in summer

Passe du Guet

122FF; 12m = 135FF; >13m = 7FF per metre.

Daily rates for selected LOAs on pontoons in Port Rhu (advisable to pre-check availability): 8m = 77FF; 9m = 85FF; 10m = 92FF; 11m = 98FF; 12m = 108FF; >13m = 6FF per metre.

Fuel The fuel berth (diesel & petrol) is on the north side of Tréboul marina, behind the pontoon for small fishing boats; available H24 by credit card or office hours for other payments.

Pontoons and moorings are available in at least 3m. If you want to berth here you will first have to prove your boat's antiquity or curiosity value, rather than your own!

Anchorages There is little or no room to anchor in the Grande Passe. The Rade de Guet, SE of Île Tristan, offers anchorage in about 2-4 metres, but is exposed to winds from N to E. From here the Passe de Guet leads SW into the Pouldavid river through a gap marked by 2 PHM beacons and drying 2 to 3·5m; best water is on the S side. Before using it, survey this Passe at LW. A useful anchorage, protected from south and west, but open to the north, is about 2 cables east of Port du Rosmeur mole, clear of local yacht moorings in 3-5m.

Tréboul Capitainerie (between the two **V** pontoons) is open Jul/Aug 0700-1200 & 1330 to 2100 Mon-Fri; Sat/Sun 0800-1200 & 1400-1800. Sep-Jun 0800-1200 & 1330 to 2100 Mon-Fri; Sat 0800-1200; Sun shut. VHF Ch 09. Tel 02.98.74.02.56; Fax 02.98.74.05.08. HM Robert Lappart. Weather forecasts are posted daily at the Capitainerie, below which are showers (jeton) available in office hours. For launderette try Le Lavoir, Les Halles, Douarnenez, 02.98.92.84.47, open daily 0700-2100.

Rhu Capitainerie VHF Ch 09. Tel 02.98.92.00.67; Fax 02.98.92.47.87.

Tariff Daily rates for selected LOAs on visitors' pontoons off Tréboul marina:
8m = 96FF; 9m = 106FF; 10m = 115FF; 11m =

NAUTICAL NEEDS

Chandlery & repairs at Tréboul

- Comptoir Maritime, Quai de l'Yser. Tel 02.98.92.14.00. Chandlery. SHOM chart agent.
- Cooperative Maritime, Quai de l'Yser. Tel 02.98.74.33.68. Chandlery. SHOM chart agent.
- Iroise Nautic. Tel 02.98.74.29.38. Chandlery, Electronics, Engineering (Yamaha).
- Chantiers Baloin, Pouldavid industrial zone. Tel 02.98.92.10.40. Boats/engines. (Honda, OMC, Johnson, Yanmar, Nanni).
- Ets Le Guellec. Tel 02.98.74.33.10. (Volvo, Perkins, Suzuki).
- Scop Navale de Cornouaille, BP 27. Tel 02.98.74.33.03. Shipwright, wood and GRP.

At Douarnenez

- Ets Poënot, Fishing basin. Tel 02.98.92.02.98. Electrics/Electronics.

Visitors' pontoons, looking NNW

RAZ DE SEIN

Pte du Van

Baie des Trépassés

CG station

La Vieille

Pte du Raz

La Plate WCM beacon

The second of the potential barriers to progress toward South Brittany is the
Raz de Sein. Raz incidentally is pronounced 'Rarh' by the French.
The problem with the Raz is simply that it is in the way
and has to be tackled rather than circumnavigated,

unless of course you wish to deviate about 15
miles to seaward and go round the western end of
the Chaussée de Sein.

But the Raz is a classic example of a problem
which taken at the right moment almost ceases to
be a problem. "What was all the fuss about?"
people ask when they emerge unscathed at the
other side. I recall my two crewmembers who
slept right through it, feet first, whilst I tackled it
single-handed at night – it was not a problem,
purely because the timing was right.

Having said that, do take all the seamanlike
precautions as outlined in the Chenal du Four

notes. Take note of the various dire warnings
which you will read both here and elsewhere. The
Raz is not a pushover and should be treated with
the utmost respect!

GEOGRAPHY

The geography of the Raz is shown on BA charts
798 (1:60,000 scale with northern approaches) and
2351 (1:75,000 scale with southern approaches).
The equivalent French charts, both at 1:50,000
scale, show more detail; they are SHOM 7148 from
the north and 7147 from the south.

The main features which roughly delineate the

La Vieille   CG station   La Plate

Raz area are (clockwise from the NW):

Tévennec light house (from afar vaguely resembling a ship with high superstructure and funnel); Basse Jaune, unlit isolated danger buoy to the NE; Baie des Trépassés (the deceased) to the ENE; to the east, Pointe du Raz with a conspicuous signal station on the mainland and La Vieille light house and La Plate WCM light beacon off the end of the Pointe; to the SW, Le Chat SCM light beacon; and to the west the outliers of Île de Sein and Chaussée de Sein, marked by several lights and light buoys.

There is no specific "epicentre" of the Raz, but for plotting/planning purposes a waypoint 'D' at 48°02′·42N 04°45′·80W, 2 cables west of La Plate, is safe by day in any normal seastate and can easily be related to La Plate by the Mark One Eyeball.

By night a waypoint 'N' at 48°02′·90N 04°46′·40W (6 cables NW of waypoint 'D') is in more open water and in a cocked hat formed by the white sectors of Tévennec, La Vieille and Le Chat lights, where position can readily be checked by bearings.

These are the waypoints towards which you should shape your course, taking care to correct any minor deviations from track before they become major.

DANGERS

Avoid a close encounter with the following: The rocky outliers around Tévennec and the rocks off the northern tip (Pointe du Van) of the Baie des Trépassés; the shallows (7·4m) of Masklou Greiz and Kornog Bras (3·6m), respectively about a mile south and south-west of La Plate. Your course should pass east of these whether you are bound to/from Audierne or to/from Penmarc'h. Do not even contemplate the Passe du Trouz Yar, inshore between the mainland and La Vieille; mistakes in timing, misidentification of rocks or gear/engine failure could be terminal.

TIDAL STREAM DATA

The Admiralty tidal stream atlas "France West coast" (NP 265) shows tidal streams at quite small scale. On BA 798, but not 2351, there are two tidal diamonds in the vicinity of the Raz.

The equivalent French tidal stream atlas, SHOM 560-UJA, covers the end of the Brittany peninsula from Goulven (midway between Roscoff and L'Aberwrac'h) to Penmarc'h and includes useful, larger scale blow-ups of both the Raz and the Chenal du Four – recommended.

TIMING

Slack water, lasting about 30 minutes, occurs abeam La Plate at about HW Brest –1, at the end of the north-going flood; and at about HW Brest +0525, at the end of the south-going ebb.

So, aim to be abeam La Plate at slack water, plus or minus 15 minutes.

The only possible exception to this diktat is when wind and tide are known to be in unison – but this cannot always be guaranteed as the wind can shift considerably around the Pointe du Raz and the tidal streams can be fickle.

Arriving early or late, even by as little as an hour before or after slack water, may make for a surprisingly rough ride. Maximum spring rates in the middle and south parts of the Raz are quoted by the Admiralty *Bay of Biscay Pilot* as 6 knots north-going and 5·25 knots south-going.

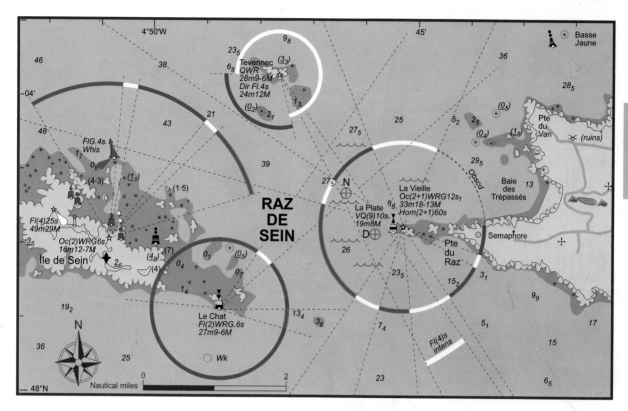

RAZ
DE
SEIN

A large mass of water is after all being squeezed through a misshapen channel less than 2 miles wide, over an uneven rocky seabed with depths of around 25 metres as opposed to 45 metres further north. The result will always be some turbulence, but to an acceptable degree at slack water before the new stream has had time to get established.

In addition there will also be the classic conditions when it might be unwise to transit the Raz, depending on your boat, your crew and your own experience as skipper. These could include, for example, winds of Force 6 or above; any wind-against-tide situation, especially at times other than slack water, when steep, breaking seas can be expected; and in fog or visibility below one mile if not radar-equipped.

PILOTAGE

All the features referred to are easily seen, identified and can be used for checking position. No special skills are required, simply an early awareness of deviations from track, an appreciation of the dangers off track and the need for accurate timing.

From the north everything unfolds in the fulness of time as you draw near. If you are seriously early, rather than anchor in the Baie des Trépassés

(not good for morale?), consider waiting to the east of Basse Jaune isolated danger buoy in an east-west racetrack pattern. The buoy will enable you to refine your timing at the Raz.

From the Baie de Douarnenez Basse Jaune is again a key feature. On leaving it, make for Tévennec until you are clear of the rocks west of Pointe du Van and able to turn south.

From the south Audierne/Ste Evette remains your bolt hole, especially if you are battling a fresh west to north west wind. Keep this refuge up your sleeve until your timing comes good and you are finally committed to the Raz. Stay tucked in to the east side of the Raz, ie skirting round La Plate two cables off; this makes visual assessments of progress much easier, is more fun and generally is the shortest possible track.

Clearing to the southeast If making for Audierne, you can hug the cliffs on your port side as closely as your instinct for self-preservation dictates. If bound for Penmarc'h there is nothing in the way. Do not be too surprised if what was a modest south-westerly wind whilst north of the Raz backs southerly and freshens once south of the Raz, only just allowing you to lay your course. It may veer again as you get further south.

Marina

Fishmarket and
second chevrons 045°

Note the shallow water

First chevrons 359°

AUDIERNE

Audierne and nearby Ste Evette between them really have everything for everybody, although on an unassuming scale. Strategically important for the Raz de Sein and Chenal du Four, the all-tide anchorage/moorings at Ste Evette are well known to British yachtsmen hurrying north or south. But pause a day or two and go up to the little marina in the heart of Audierne; the pilotage is simple enough and the ambience is relaxed and welcoming. Even Brits, having made it south of the Raz, unbend a little and a multi-national gathering for a sundowner and the exchange of war-stories is the norm rather than the exception.

Where were you when Princess Diana died in 1997? I had just berthed in Audierne when a French crew broke the news to me "This is a sad day for Britain ...." – we shared a glass or two and sailed in company the next day.

TOURISM

Tourist Office 8 rue Victor Hugo, 29770 Audierne. Tel 02.98.70.12.20; Fax 02.98.75.01.11.

Hours in season: Mon-Sat 0930-1200 & 1400-1800; closed Sun.

The Tourist Office, located in an ancient hospice on the SW side of the main square (Place de la Liberté) is above average in terms of assistance and quantity/quality of information available.

Behind it are some very old alleyways and houses which are revealed in three good walk leaflets.

Buses to Douarnenez and Quimper.

Taxi 02.98.70.27.69; 02.98.70.06.06; 02.98.70.02.96.

Car and Bike hire Ford garage, rue Lamartine, 200m before Casino supermarket, qv.

Beaches There are very good, dazzlingly white sandy beaches between Audierne breakwater

(Fl(3) WG 12s) and Ste Evette, open only to the SE; about 5-10 mins bike ride from Audierne marina.

EATING ASHORE

Restaurants A stone's throw from the marina, around the Place de la Liberté or in rue Jean Jaurès are:
* Le Cornouaille, 02.98.70.09.13. Seafood specialities.
* Hotel-Restaurant Le Goyen; 02.98.70.08.88. Place Simon, along rue Jean Jaurès. Upmarket and impressive 3 star. Seafood, 149-210FF.
* La Goélette, 6 quai Pelletan; 02.98.70.29.06. *La marmite de fruits de mer.*

On the way to Ste Evette are:
* Le Grand Large, Bar-Brasserie; 02.98.70.08.22. Seafood and informal snacks at 79 and 85FF. 1, rue du Möle. Marvellous views to seaward; beach access.
* Hotel-Restaurant Au Roi Gradlon; 02.98.70.04.51. 3, ave Manu Brusq; a little further along the coast road, right on Ste Evette beach. Seafood, 85-180FF.

SHOPPING

Supermarkets The "Casino" is quite a long walk, best on a bike. Just before the river bridge turn left into rue Lamartine; it is approx 500m on the right. Hours: Mon-Fri 0900-1215 & 1430-1915; Sat 0900-1915; Sun 0900-1200.

Market days Wednesday mornings - fruit and vegetables; Sat mornings - megamarket.

First chevrons 359°

Banks Most of the usual in or near Place de la Liberté.

NAVIGATIONAL MATTERS

Charts AC 3640, inc 1:24,000 inset, and 2351 (1:75,000). SHOM charts 7147 and 7148, both 1:50,000.

Approaches La Gamelle, a drying shoal on which the sea always breaks, dominates the outer central part of the bay and is marked on its SW side by a WCM light buoy and by an unlit SCM buoy to the SE. The entry channels to the west and east of La Gamelle are defined by directional and leading lights.

Note that La Gamelle extends about 5 cables north of the two cardinal buoys. Therefore, from the SE, stand on well past the SCM buoy before turning west for Ste Evette.

From the west do not cut the corner past Pte de Lervily light house due to drying offliers.

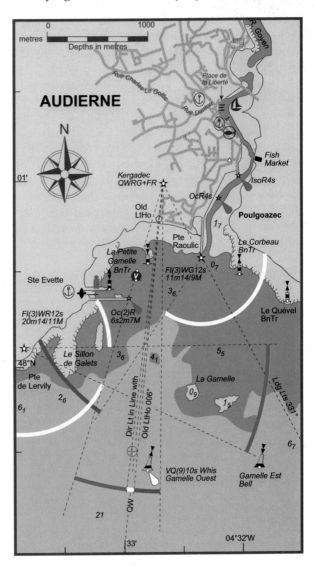

Front chevrons on lamp post   Rear chevrons on fish market

Second chevrons 045°

Pilotage Anse de Ste Evette is easy to enter even at night, once the long east/west breakwater, Oc (2) R 6s, has been identified. Watch out for many small buoys.

Audierne: From the light house, *Fl(3)WG12s*, keep 20-25 metres off and parallel with the long breakwater, aligning 359° on a pair of red/white chevrons on the roadside ahead. Follow the bend round to starboard the same distance off.

Looking NE, aim to leave close to port the Oc R 4s light and the Iso R 4s light on an estacade, whilst aligning 045° on the second set of red/white chevrons which are on the black and white fish market building on the east bank. When about 15 metres from the front chevron alter 90° to port onto 315°, making for the long line of fishing boats berthed on the quays to port.

Keep very close (2-3 metres) to these vessels, as drying banks lurk close to starboard. Similarly, whilst manoeuvering for a berth, keep close to the three pontoons which form the marina. Night arrival/departure is not recommended.

When leaving Audierne the reverse procedure applies, but note that on the stretch from the fish market another set of red/white chevrons on the roadside should be aligned on 225°. Binoculars may be needed to find the various chevrons for the first time; thereafter they are clear enough.

Tides HW and LW Audierne are approx 30 minutes before HW and LW Brest. MHWS is 5·2m, MLWS 0·8m; MHWN is 4·1m, MLWN 2·0m.

Tidal streams Slight in the bay. There are 3 tidal diamonds on chart 3640.

Access
Ste Evette: anchorage/moorings: all tides and in all weathers.

Audierne marina: HW−2 to +1 for 2m draft, but HW±3 is possible subject to reduced clearances, careful tidal calculations and exact adherence to leading lines. At neaps the predicted height of tide at HW±3 is 3 metres. The River Goyen is dredged approx 1m, so Audierne is accessible by dinghy even if a visit by yacht is not feasible.

In strong onshore winds seas break on drying sandbanks close east of the entrance.

HARBOUR AND MARINA
Audierne Bureau du Port in Place de la République facing pontoons, is open 0800-1200 daily. Tel 02.98.75.04.93. HM Guy Tapon. Weather forecasts are posted daily.

Showers, across the square at the side of Les Halles (covered market), are good and include one for handicapped persons. Open 0900-2200 daily Jun-Sep; 0900-1200 & 1400-1700 Oct-May. 10FF per jeton gives 6 mins of hot water; but only cold water in washbasins, mirrors removed. The heads were smelly. No launderette, but try La Laverie du Port, 2 Place de la République.

Ste Evette Tel 02.98.70.00.28. HM Jean-Pierre Conan. There are showers, WCs, launderette, restaurant and bar. Vedette trips to Île de Sein; dep 1000, back 1600; 115FF return.

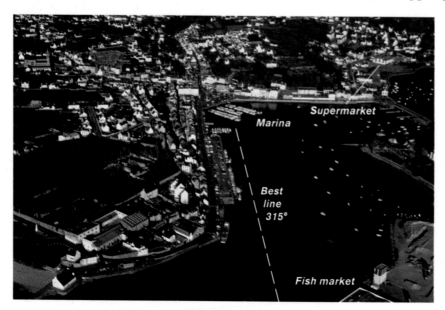

Supermarket

Marina

Best line 315°

Fish market

Audierne and Ste Evette looking SSW

Where to berth/moor

Ste Evette: There are numerous white ⚓s, some rather close together. Or anchor east of the buoys and clear of other traffic, especially *vedettes*; swell may intrude.

Audierne: berth in 1·5-2 metres on the first or second of 3 pontoons with finger berths or on the hammerheads, or on pontoons close NE. Unmarked drying sandbanks are close east of the pontoons. See pilotage notes.

Tariff

Audierne: daily rates for selected LOAs on pontoon at marina:
8m = 81FF; 9m = 92FF; 10m = 101FF; 11m = 104FF; 12m = 106FF.

Drying sandbanks close east of the pontoons

Third chevron outbound 225°

Ste Evette: mooring buoy 55-65FF for 8-10 metres.

Fuel At Ste Evette diesel (only) is available from a pump at the head of the jetty/slipway with an ECM beacon off its end. Neither diesel nor petrol are available alongside at Audierne.

NAUTICAL NEEDS

Chandlery & repairs

- There is a very good chandlery, Comptoir Maritime (Tel 02.98.70.05.37) down the Quai Jean Jaurès; it is also a SHOM chart agent.
- Ornoc'h Marine is across the river bridge and turn left along the river bank. There is not too much in the way of boatyards and yacht repairers.

LOCTUDY TO THE RIVER ÉTEL

CONTENTS

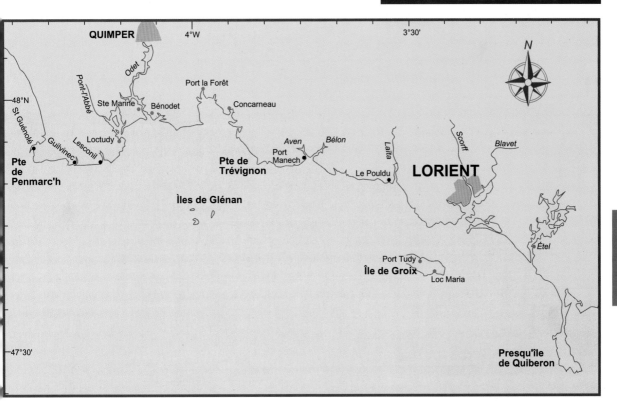

Chapter 3

THE SEA AND THE LAND

At last we can say that we have arrived in South Brittany! The rocks are still around us, not quite literally, but the coastline is lower, the beaches are a white strand backed by the dark green of the wooded land. The amazing jumble of reefs, crags and inlets which characterises the shores of North Brittany has mostly faded away, yet the next 50 miles are still very much Brittany, albeit gentler and – dare I say it – warmer.

From Lesconil to Pointe de Trévignon (SE of Concarneau) there are fine and interesting waters to be cruised. Loctudy, Bénodet, Port-la-Forêt and Concarneau are our bed-fellows, never more than a few hours apart. The Rivers of Pont l'Abbe and Odet beckon us a few miles inland. Offshore lie the Îles de Glénan, far enough away to feel remote, but still in sight of the mainland and a mere couple of hours dash to safety should the weather turn bad.

Further east between Concarneau and Lorient low cliffs predominate, punctuated by a string of inlets and tiny harbours which recall instantly the south coast of Cornwall, here mimicked as the Côte de Cornouaille. Port Manech and the Aven and Belon rivers (the former famed for Gauguin, the latter for its oysters – and where better to eat them than at Chez Jacky, a few metres from your mooring) are both pure delight

and a base for two or three days quiet exploration. Brigneau, Merrien, Doëlan and Le Pouldu on the drying Quimperlé (aka Laïta) river are all quintessential Breton harbours which smack of Polperro, Gorran Haven, St Mawes and Coverack in no particular order – but none of these Breton harbours are as easy of access and therefore rarely visited.

Next is Lorient, once a great seaport now faded from the trading days of the C17/18, but a useful port of refuge for coasting yachts. Close offshore Île de Groix is both a rocky bulwark to protect Lorient and an escape for its citizens, which is why Port Tudy is best avoided at a high season weekend – simply no room at the inn.

Finally as the eye follows the curve of land southeastward towards the Quiberon peninsula, pause at the Etel river. If conditions are right and you have done your homework, go for it. You will be neither over-crowded nor disappointed.

If you have time for the hinterland, visit Quimper for its charm and history. Cycle to the fishing ports west of Loctudy as you are unlikely to visit them by sea. Or follow the attractive valleys of the Scorff and Blavet rivers N and NE of Lorient. The rest is the Argoat (a wooded region or inland area) peaceful, bucolic, dotted with small farms – find a local bus and enjoy a day's walk.

LOCTUDY

Château Loubrière bearing 274°

Perhaps Loctudy's greatest charm is the Pont l'Abbé river which flows between the woods of Île Garo and the typically Breton houses of Île Tudy (a peninsula), giving attractive views from the marina, both upriver and to seaward.
The marina, to which new buildings and extra pontoons have been added in recent years, is about 1 km from the village. Walk via the Fishing Basin where in the early evening ultra-fresh fish straight off the boats can be bought from retail shops. The village itself is as unremarkable as many a working port; it straggles from the waterside up rue du Port and then westward past the interesting 12th century church towards a hinterland of modern developments. All is redeemed, however, by the Manoir de Kerazan, a little further to the NW.

TOURISM

Tourist Office Place des Anciens Combattants, 29750 Loctudy (near the church).
Tel 02.98.87.53.78. Hours in season: Mon-Sat 0900-1200 & 1400-1700; closed Sun.
The peaceful Pont l'Abbé river can be navigated on the tide by yachts (or by dinghy), drying out alongside on mud at Pont l'Abbé, 3 miles. Or go on foot or bicycle, up the west bank, back on the east bank and ferry from Île Tudy to Loctudy. Pont l'Abbé is capital of the pays Bigouden which is noted for traditional costumes and head-dress. It is a pleasant town with castle and huge church. A Festival of embroidery is held in the second week in July.

The Manoir de Kerazan, 2·5km NW on the D2 road to Pont l'Abbé, is well worth a visit. It is a 16th century manor house of considerable style and elegance, set in wooded parkland with estate farms. In the 19th century it was restored by the Astors and bequeathed to the French equivalent of the National Trust. Today it recalls an almost feudal Breton lifestyle and houses many works of art in exquisite rooms. Part of the building is a museum, open daily 1030-1900 from mid-Jun to end Aug; entry 32FF. Tel 02.98.87.40.40.

At Penmarc'h the disused light house contains an interesting Centre of Maritime Discovery, Tel 02.98.58.72.87. Open 1100-1900, Jul/Aug; entry 20FF. Temporary exhibitions, terrific ambience and sobering views to seaward of the rocks which you have circumnavigated.

Buses to Quimper for railway station, Tel 08.36.35.35.35, and airport, Tel 02.98.94.30.30.

Taxi 02.98.87.55.35 (mobile 06.07.53.68.72); 02.98.87.36.29; mobile 06.07.27.43.37.

Car hire Budget, 8 rue de Concarneau, 29000 Quimper. Tel 02.98.52.04.87.

Bike hire La Pedale Bigoudene, 13 rue du Général de Gaulle. Tel 02.98.87.42.00.

Beaches Nearest is Plage de Langoz, immediately south of Pte de Langoz. Plage de Kervilzic is the next bay south.

EATING ASHORE

Restaurants Loctudy is not exactly a gourmet's paradise, but in addition to the usual array of crêperies, pizzerias etc, here are a few possibilities:
- Le Gwenn Ha Du, 24 rue du Port Tel 02.98.87.95.20. Brasserie: seafood, grills.
- Maison Gouzien, 1 rue de Kerpaul. Tel 02.98.87.40.19. Restaurant open for lunch only.

- Le Relais de Lodonnec, 3 rue des Tulipes, Plage de Lodonnec. Tel 02.98.87.55.34. This is about 180°/1·5M from the marina, going south on rue de Kerpaul. Take your hand-held GPS and home in on 47°48´·75N 04°10´·50W. The Relais is in an old fisherman's cottage, just off the beach, with suitable decor and good seafood. Menus 100-200FF. Worth the walk or bike ride.

SHOPPING

Supermarkets
- Champion, Route de Pont-L'Abbé. Open in season, Mon-Sat 0900-1930; Sun 0900-1230. Tel 02.98.87.94.94. Because it is about 1·3km NW of the marina it delivers free.
- Supermarket Le Lay, 70 rue St Guiziou. Tel 02.98.87.42.52. Smaller but nearer.

Market days Tues mornings, Place de la Mairie. Fishmarket (criée) Tel 02.98.87.40.11. 0630 & 1700 Mon-Fri.

Banks Two in rue St Guiziou; one in rue du Port.

NAVIGATIONAL MATTERS

Charts AC 3641 (1:20,000), 2351 and 2352 (both 1:75,000). SHOM charts: 6649 (1:15,000), 6679 (1:20,000) and 7146 (1:50,000). ECM Navicarte 543 covers the area, including the Pont l'Abbé river.

Approaches From the west, skirt the interminable low spit of land between Pointe de Penmarc'h and

Loctudy looking WNW

Marina

Île Tudy

Les Perdrix tower

Pte de Langoz

Karek-Soaz

Labels on photo: Menhir tower — Eckmühl Lt Ho — Disused Lt Ho — Coastguard station

Pointe de Penmarc'h

Loctudy itself. Observe the gaunt tower of Menhir and behind the serried ranks of Eckmühl octagonal light-house, its disused namesake and the signal tower beyond. In bad weather this is a scene of sombre awfulness and you will be glad to have it all astern. Even the names (never mind the appearance) of offlying rocks strike a chill note: Lost Moan, Rat, Guisty, Les Putains (the Whores). In heavy onshore weather it will be less rough to keep 1-2M seaward of the buoys rather than buoy-hopping along a dangerous lee shore. See also notes on Swell.

In good weather: *Pas de problème!* Look out for fishing vessels from/to St Guénolé, Guilvinec and Lesconil; these harbours should only be used by yachts in emergency.

From the east and south the Anse de Bénodet is generally shallow, but adequately marked.

Pilotage The approach waypoint is at 47°50′·26N 04°09′·00W, 200m south of Men Audierne unlit SHM bn. From the WPT make good 272°/9 cables toward the eastern side of the marina, passing the PHM buoy and two SHM buoys, all lit. Les Perdrix, an unlit, conspicuous black and white chequered tower, dominates the approach channel. Near LW it should be left no closer than 100m to starboard to clear rocky ledges and the drying spit SE of the SHM bn (Fl(4)G.15s).

Château Durumain is easy to see amongst the trees and gives general orientation. Château Loubrière is hard to see through the forest of

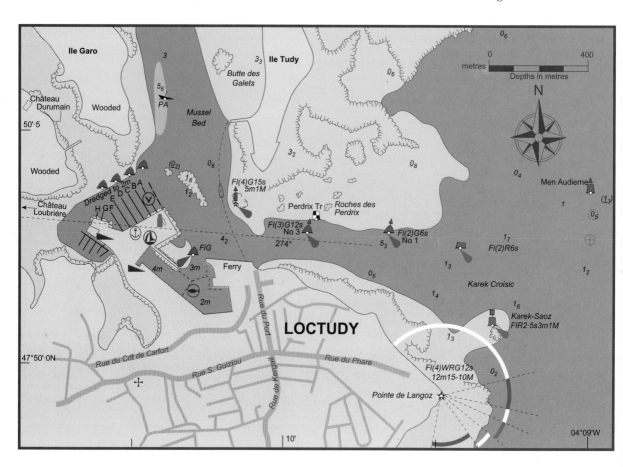

masts which provide as good guidance as any.

Tides HW Loctudy is 13 mins nps or 33 mins sp before HW Brest; LWs are 25 mins nps or 35 mins sp before LW Brest. MHWS is 5·0m, MLWS 0·8m; MHWN is 3·9m, MLWN 1·9m.

Tidal streams Slight in the bay, but very strong in the Pont l'Abbé river and near approaches.

Access In all weathers and at most tides. Keep north of the PHM buoy to avoid Karek Croisic, a dangerous 0·9m shoal. From the S keep at least 100m off Karek-Saoz bn tower (Fl.R.2·5s)

It is compulsory to enter/leave under power. Engineless boats must not navigate the approach channel between 1630 and 1830 when the fishing fleet returns; all yachts would do well to avoid this busy period when fishing vessels are rushing to meet commercial deadlines.

Men Audierne   SHM beacon   Les Perdrix

Les Perdrix and starboard-hand beacon looking east at LW

MARINA

Bureau du Port at the head of 'E' pontoon, is open 0730-2100 daily Jul/Aug; Mar-Jun & Sept, 0830-1200 & 1330-1800 Mon-Sat, Sun 0900-1200; Oct-Feb 0830-1200 & 1330-1800 Mon-Sat. Tel 02.98.87.51.36; Fax 02.98.87.96.77. VHF Ch 09. HM Didier Furic.

Weather forecasts are posted daily. Showers, by jeton during office hours, and launderette are in the Capitainerie building.

Where to berth/moor/⚓ Pontoon 'A' is for visitors <12m LOA in berths A16-A54, ie on the SW side of the pontoon; in practice visitors tend to berth on both sides or even on 'B' pontoon. If >12m LOA, berth on the inside of the concrete wavebreaks. There are 68 white mooring buoys NE of the marina. Space for anchoring is limited. Caution: very strong tidal streams.

Tariff Daily rates in Jul/Aug for selected LOAs on pontoons (mooring buoys in brackets): 8m = 109 (86)FF; 9m = 123 (97)FF; 10m = 144 (113)FF; 11m = 160 (125)FF; 12m = 182 (142)FF; >14m, 20 (15)FF per extra metre.

Daily rates on pontoons in Apr/May/Jun & Sep are approx 75% of those shown above; for buoys the figure is approx 53%.

Fuel Diesel and petrol during office hours. Fuel berth by concrete wavebreaks.

NAUTICAL NEEDS

Chandlery & repairs

- Cooperative Maritime, at marina, 29750 Loctudy. Tel 02.98.66.50.70. SHOM chart agent.
- Locamarine, at marina, 29750 Loctudy. Tel 02.98.87.95.95. (Yanmar, Tohatsu).
- Chantier Nautique Pichavant, at marina, 29750 Loctudy. Tel 02.98.87.01.41. (Boatyard, repairs mechanical and electrical, crane).
- Voilerie Pichavant. Tel 02.98.87.23.29. Sail repairs.

Château Durumain   SHM beacon Fl(4)G 15s   Île Garo

Château Durumain and starboard-hand beacon

Chapter 3

BÉNODET AND SAINTE MARINE

Bénodet, or, to be more precise, the Odet river flanked by Bénodet on the east bank and Sainte Marine on the west, is delightful – as many thousands of yachtsmen will attest! Bénodet is a fair-sized seaside resort with good beaches and all the tourists that go with such places.

Ste Marine is smaller, quieter and therefore more appealing to some.

The approaches and entrance are straightforward. Inside are marinas at Sainte Marine and Penfoul (Bénodet) and there are many moorings either side of the fairway. Above the Pont de Cornouaille is where the late Eric Tabarly used to moor his famous yacht *Pen-Duick*. The river winds past fine châteaux and through beautiful wooded scenery for about 6 miles, before opening out into a shallow bay which is navigable almost as far as Quimper. Some of the anchorages are completely secluded, away from the *vedettes* and out of the tide.

Bénodet approach

Quimper is a fascinating city whose potteries (*faïence*), massive cathedral and old quarter are particularly worth visiting.

TOURISM

Bénodet Tourist Office 29 Ave de la Mer, BP 10, 29950 Bénodet, (near the water tower). Tel 02.98.57.00.14; Fax 02.98.57.23.00. Hours in season: Mon-Sat 0900-1900; Sun 1000-1230 & 1400-1900. A small tourist office, Tel 02.98.56.48.41, near the SW end of Pont de Cornouaille opens 0900-1200 & 1400-1700, only in season. There is no Tourist Office in Ste Marine.

Bus to Quimper (35m).

Rail station 08.36.35.35.35 (Paris 4½hrs).

Airport 02.98.94.30.30.

Taxi 02.98.57.00.44; 02.98.57.07.27.

Car hire Europcar, 14 ave de la Libération, Quimper (near railway station). Tel 02.98.90.00.68.

Bike hire Cycletty, 5 ave de la Mer, Bénodet. Tel 02.98.57.12.49.

Beaches Bénodet: Anse du Trez, east of the front ldg lt; Plage de la Pte St Gilles, east of Pte du Bénodet. Ste Marine: Plage du Treven, west of Pte de Combrit.

EATING ASHORE

Restaurants
Bénodet:
- Hotel-Restaurant Les Bains de Mer, 11 rue de Kerguélen. Tel 02.98.57.03.41.
- Hotel Le Cornouaille, 62 ave de la Plage. Tel 02.98.57.03.78.
- La Ferme du Letty, 5 route du Letty. Tel 02.98.57.01.27. M J-M Guilbault. ESE from Bénodet to 47°52´·1N 04°05´·08W by GPS. Gastronomique. 160-540FF, Amex. Closed: Wed & pm Thurs.
- Several large resort hotels have restaurants. There are also crêperies, brasseries, pizzerias

Ste Marine (Vieux Port):
- Hotel Ste Marine. 99-195FF.
- Café du Port. Tel 02.98.56.44.36. 77-250FF.
- L'Agape, Tel 02.98.56.32.70. 170-290FF. Closed Tues pm & Wed, except in Jul/Aug.

SHOPPING

Supermarkets At Ste Marine, 200m south of the showers on the roadway, "Ravalec Gourmet" is a highly recommended mini-supermarket-cum-delicatessen, open 0800-1245 & 1430-1900, closed Mon pm. Tel 02.98.51.94.00. Also at 11 rue de Cornouaille, Bénodet. Tel 02.98.57.01.02. The launderette at Ste Marine has closed down.

At Bénodet
- Champion, Penfoul roundabout (the junction of D34/D44). Tel 02.98.57.27.20.
- A launderette (laverie) is at No 2 (bottom of) rue de Kerguélen; open daily.

Market day Monday 0730-1330 in Place du Méneyer, Bénodet.

Banks Crédit Mutuel de Bretagne, 68 ave de la Plage, Bénodet; plus various cash dispensers.

NAVIGATIONAL MATTERS

Charts AC 3641 (1:20,000), 2351 and 2352 (both 1:75,000). Equivalent SHOM charts: 6649 (1:15,000), 6679 (1:20,000) which covers the Odet river up to Quimper and 7148 (1:50,000).

Sainte Marine, a riverside walk

Château et bateau at Ste Marine

Approaches From the west the shortest route, by day or night, is via Karek Greis ECM, Basse Boulanger SCM and Basse Bilien ECM, all light buoys; thence towards the approach waypoint (47°51′·00N 04°06′·10W) in order to establish on the 346° leading line.

Note: The 005° alignment of Pte de Combrit light and La Pyramide (Bénodet) light house must be used with caution, if at all, because it leads <u>not</u> into the river but onto Pte de Combrit itself.

From the east or southeast, pass La Voleuse SCM light buoy on course for the waypoint, leaving all rocky dangers and Le Taro unlit WCM beacon to starboard; thence enter on the 346° transit.

Pilotage The river entrance is marked by two PHM buoys and a beacon tower, all unlit; and by two unlit SHM beacon towers. All is obvious by day and the 346° leading marks are easily seen. At night, before reaching the first channel marks, it is important to be firmly on this transit. When 250m short of Pte du Coq alter onto 315° into the river

where the fairway can usually be navigated by background lights – but not beyond Pont de Cornouaille.

Outside the river proper, SE of the Pte du Coq, yachts can anchor in the Anse du Trez in 3-4m. Anchoring in the fairway between Pte du Coq and the bridge is prohibited. Speed limit 3 knots.

Tides At neaps HW Bénodet is the same as HW Brest; at springs it is 20 mins before HW Brest. LWs are 13 mins neaps, or 23 mins springs, before LW Brest. MHWS is 5·2m, MLWS 0·9m; MHWN is 4·1m, MLWN 2·1m. See Almanac for differences at Port du Corniguel, 8M upstream.

Tidal streams In the Anse de Bénodet streams are rotatory clockwise and fairly weak. Be aware that in the river the spring stream reaches 3 knots at mid-flood/ebb; see below re berthing.

Access At all tides and in all weathers, but it is best to arrive/depart around slack water to avoid the very strong stream (above) which can make manoeuvering in the marinas interesting or even stressful depending on your handling skills and engine power. It is essential to berth head to tide. At Ste Marine the hammerheads are most exposed to the stream. At Penfoul marina the outside of the long concrete outer wavebreak is similarly exposed; better protection is on the inside. Slack water in the fairway occurs at about HW Brest –5h35m and –0h20m. If the river is in spate the ebb runs longer and harder. The wind also has a considerable effect.

The 346° leading marks are easily seen

Labels on image: *Anse de Penfoul* *Capitainerie* *Fuel* *Wavebreak (visitors)*

Bénodet marina

MARINAS

Ste Marine Bureau du Port Cale du Bac, Ste Marine, 29120 Combrit. Tel 02.98.56.38.72. Fax 02.98.51.95.17. VHF Ch 09. HM Jean Plouzennec. Hours 0800-2000 in season; out of season 0800-1200 & 1400 to 1730. Weather forecasts are posted daily. In Jul/Aug a small Accueil annex operates at the north end of A pontoon.

Showers 0830-1700, up the hillside path from the gangway by B pontoon.

Visitors berth alongside/raft on the long A pontoon at the S end (no fingers); if full, berth on F pontoon (furthest north) or on a hammerhead and enquire further. Watch the tide.

It is a pleasant walk via the pontoons to the Bureau du Port which is in Le Vieux Port. This is a delightful and much-photographed spot: boats dry out below shady trees; an old chapel and several restaurants/bars cluster at the water's edge. The views up/down river and across to Bénodet provide endless interest as coasters, sand-

dredgers, vedettes, ferries and yachts variously interpret the Rules of the Road. Rule 9 rules, OK!

In Jul/Aug, 0900-2100, a pedestrian (& bike) ferry crosses to Bénodet from a slip by the Bureau du Port. In other months call the marina Ch 09 for their dory at specified times. Alternatively "On your bike!" The view downstream from the Pont de Cornouaille is worth the effort.

Penfoul Bureau du Port 29950 Bénodet. Tel 02.98.57.05.78. Fax 02.98.57.00.21. VHF Ch 09. HM Georges James. Hours 0800-2000 in season; out of season, Mon-Sat 0800-1200 & 1400 to 1800; Sun & Hols 0800-1200. Weather forecasts are posted daily.

Showers Behind the Bureau du Port (jetons); also launderette.

Visitors berth on the outside (west) of Pontoon D (fingers), the north side of Pontoon E, and inside (east) of the long concrete wavebreak, where larger yachts should berth on the outside. Caution: all outside berths and the north side of

Sainte Marine, le Vieux Port

the buoyed channel decrease with patches of 0·5m. Similar depths obtain over the last 1·5M from Port de Corniguel to the road bridge (5·8m clearance) near Château de Poulguinan, just short of Quimper.

Above Pont de Cornouaille anchorages off the (W) or (E) banks are at: Anse de Combrit (W), Porz Keraign (E), Anse de Kérautret (W), Porz Meilou (E), Anse de St-Cadou* (E) off which the Anse de Toulven forks to the NE; off Les Trois Tourtres (W) and in 1 metre below Quimper.

*This anchorage is a secluded creek where kingfishers, other birds and wildlife may be seen. In most of the riverside anchorages the *vedettes* can be a nuisance (wash and loud commentaries).

Pontoon E are affected by the tidal stream, especially the ebb. See notes under Access. A riverside footpath leads to Bénodet.

Tariffs

Ste Marine: Daily rates Jul/Aug, for selected LOAs on pontoons (mooring buoys in brackets): 8m = 116 (74)FF; 9m = 134 (87)FF; 10m = 152 (96)FF; 11m = 172 (110)FF; 12m = 193 (123)FF; 13m = 208 (131)FF. Daily rates on pontoons and buoys in Apr/May/ Jun & Sep are approx 75% of those shown above.

Penfoul: Daily rates Jul/Aug, for selected LOAs on pontoons* (mooring buoys in brackets): 8m = 131 (86)FF; 9m = 145 (100)FF; 10m = 159 (111)FF; 11m = 180 (130)FF; 12m = 200 (150)FF; 13m = 218 (163)FF. Daily rates on pontoons and buoys in Apr/May/ Jun & Sep are approx 80% of those shown above.

*These pontoons are E, F, G & H in the Nouveau Port (more southerly, aka Kergait); B, C & D at Penfoul are slightly cheaper.

Fuel The Penfoul fuel berth is at the foot of the gangway leading to pontoon E (there is no fuel at Ste Marine). Available in season 0800-1830; out of season 0830-1200 & 1400-1730, Mon-Sat; Sun & Hols 0900-1200.

Up the Odet River SHOM chart 6679 is desirable. Keep to the middle of the river which carries at least 2m as far as Château Lanroz (47°57′N); most depths are from 4 to 8 metres. Between Pte de Kersabiec (47°55′·60N) and Pte du Canon the river does a sharp S-bend, marked by SHM perches. In the drying Baie de Kérogan depths in

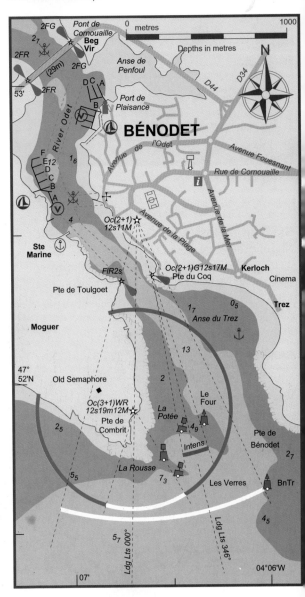

Sainte Marine, 'A' pontoon is in the foreground

Chapter 3

NAUTICAL NEEDS

Chandlery & repairs

Ste Marine:
- Chantier Naval Structures, Kerbenoën ZI. Tel 02.98.51.94.73. Boatyard.
- Coop Maritime, 1 quai Jacques-de-Thezac. Tel 02.98.56.31.74. Chandlery. SHOM chart agent.

Bénodet:
- LVA, at marina. Tel 02.98.57.15.82. Boat and engine repairs.

- Accasting 29, 45 route de Quimper. Tel 02.98.57.20.83. Boatyard.
- Accastillage de l'Odet, at marina. Tel 02.98.57.26.11. Chandlery, SHOM chart agent.
- Coop Maritime, 50bis Ave de la Plage. Tel 02.98.66.20.67. Chandlery.
- Le Bihan Voiles, 68 ave de l'Odet. Tel 02.98.57.18.03. Sailmaker.

Ste Marine marina

PORT LA FORÊT

Once upon a time at the head of the Baie de la Forêt there was a secluded, drying creek where oysters were cultivated. Cherry and cider apple orchards encircled the little village. Then came a 1000 berth marina – but surprisingly the quiet ambience of this pleasant spot has survived;

little has changed. Oysters, cherries and cider are still celebrated; the local palate and economy may even have been stimulated. Motor cars choke the D44 road in summer.

TOURISM

Tourist Office 2 rue du Vieux Port, BP 2, 29940 La Forêt-Fouesnant, (next to the church).
Tel 02.98.56.94.09; Fax 02.98.51.42.07. Hours in season: daily 0900-1200 & 1400-1700; out of season 0900-1215 & 1430-1900.

Bus to Quimper (30m). Rail station 08.36.35.35.35 (Paris 4½hrs); Airport 02.98.94.30.30.

Taxi 02.98.56.84.88//06.03.50.27.68.

Car hire Le Douce, C'Hastel industrial park. Tel 02.98.56.05.40.

Bike hire ask at Capitainerie or tourist office.

Beaches The beach immediately south of the marina on the east side of the entry channel is the nearest. To the southeast of the marina is the extensive main beach, Plage de Kerléven. Other beaches are to the west of Cap Coz and south towards Beg Meil.

EATING ASHORE
Restaurants
- Hotel du Port, 4 corniche de la Cale (on the walk into village). Tel 02.98.56.97.33. 75-210FF.

La Forêt-Fouesnant

Marina

Oyster beds

Cap Coz

Les Ormeaux

Waiting buoys

- Hotel Beauséjour, place de la Baie (roundabout at the head of the creek). Tel 02.98.56.97.18. Traditional fare and surroundings. 75-168FF.
- Jardin de la Baie, on the roundabout. 65-170FF.
- La Mouclade, on the roundabout. Tel 02.98.56.90.57. *Moules à gogo ici.* 65-120FF.
- Manoir du Stang, rue du Menez Plenn (15km north from the roundabout). Tel 02.98.56.97.37. Dine in baronial splendour, Jul/Aug only.
- Hotel-Restaurant de l'Espérance, place de l'Église (just above the church). Tel 02.98.56.96.58. Garden and lots of greenery. Seafood. 95-235FF. Logie. Closed pm Wed.
- Hotel aux Cerisiers, 3 rue des Cerisiers, higher up the hill on the right. Tel 02.98.56.97.24.

There are cafés and crêperies etc at the marina.

SHOPPING

Supermarkets Alimentation mini-supermarket, at marina, 0800-2000. In the village a well-stocked mini-supermarket is just below the church.

Market day Sunday morning in the village.

Banks Two banks up the hill in village. Cash dispenser near Capitainerie.

NAVIGATIONAL MATTERS

Charts AC 3641 (1:20,000) and 2352 (1:75,000). SHOM 6650 (1:15,600)and 7146 (1:50,000).

Approaches From the SW make good 060° from Rostolou ECM buoy to Beg Meil ECM buoy at the entrance to Baie de la Forêt, passing between Île aux Moutons and La Voleuse SCM buoy; the latter will have to be rounded if approaching from Loctudy or Bénodet. The coastline here is generally low, with sandy beaches and a wooded skyline. The signal station and red/white lattice tower on Beg Meil are conspicuous. The white buildings of Concarneau loom beyond.

From the East the approach is less cluttered unless you elect to pass north of Île Verte and Men Du IDM beacon. In any event you will have to round Pointe de Trévignon (looking a little like a submarine from afar) and the tall WCM beacon

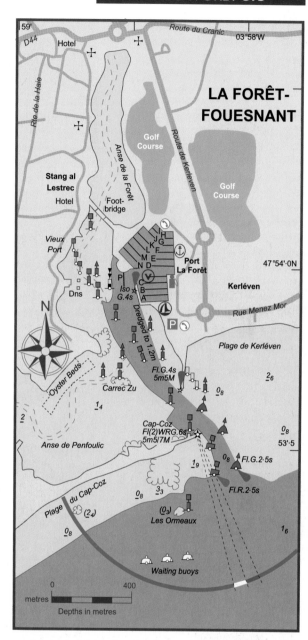

Beg Meil ECM buoy; Concarneau beyond

tower off Les Soldats; thence set course 330° direct to Port la Forêt, keeping a wary eye open for rocks and fishing vessels off Concarneau.

Pilotage From the waypoint 47°52'·70N 03°57'·80W the harbour entrance bears 343° / 0·9M. The white sector of the new directional light, Fl (2) WRG 6s, at Cap Coz covers this approach. There are no unambiguous marks to pinpoint the marina until the usual forest of masts is seen. The east side of the bay is shallow, especially SW of Concarneau and abeam the waypoint where Le Scoré rock is marked by a slender SCM perch (unlit and hard to see by day). Basse Rouge 0·8m is close WNW of the waypoint. The entrance channel is marked by a lit PHM and SHM buoy, then by two unlit SHM buoys and one PHM buoy, all small; thereafter by perches.

Tides HW Port la Forêt is 10 mins neaps, or 30 mins springs, before HW Brest. LWs are 20 mins neaps, or 30 mins springs, before LW Brest. MHWS is 5·0m, MLWS 0·8m; MHWN is 3·9m, MLWN 1·9m.

Tidal streams Slight within the bay.

Access A 0·9m shoal patch about 300 metres SSE of Cap Coz makes entry unwise LW±1½, except for shoal draft vessels. Three white waiting buoys are south of Les Ormeaux PHM perch in about 2·5m. The channel inwards from the light buoys was dredged 1·8 metres in March 1999.

Anchorages Along the west side of Baie de la Forêt there are attractive day anchorages off Pain du Sucre, Kerveltrec and the jetty, Fl R 2s, at Kervastard, all well sheltered from westerlies.

Port-la-Forêt marina

Le Vieux Port

A secluded drying creek at the head of the bay

MARINA

Capitainerie Port de Plaisance, 29940 La Forêt-Fouesnant. Tel 02.98.56.98.45, Fax 02.98.56.81.31. VHF Ch 09. HM Jean-Claude Lannurien. Hours 0800-2000 Jul/Aug; Mar-Jun & Sep 0830-1200 & 1330 to 1800; Oct-Feb 0900-1200 & 1330-1730. Weather forecasts are posted daily. The staff are very helpful indeed.

Showers H24, by A and E pontoons; jeton 11FF.

Tariff Daily rates Jun/Jul/Aug for selected LOAs on pontoons (half price 1 Sep to 31 May): 8m = 99FF; 9m = 124FF; 10m = 154FF; 11m = 154FF; 13m = 186FF; >14m = 38FF per extra m.

Fuel The fuel berth is at the inner end, N side of the Ⓥ pontoon (between 'C' and 'D'). Diesel and petrol are available 0800-1200 & 1330-1900 in season.

Launderette (Lavomatique) at the marina. Tel 02.98.56.96.72. Open 24 hours, self-service. An international meeting place!

NAUTICAL NEEDS

Chandlery & repairs

- Atelier Motonautique, at the marina. Tel 02.98.56.90.66. Roland Louedec. Chandlery, boat and engine repairs (Volvo, Nanni, Mercury).
- CDK Technologie, at marina. Tel 02.98.51.41.00. Boatyard and shipwrights.
- PLF Marine, at marina. Tel 02.98.56.96.04. Gérard Constant. Chandlery. Repairs.
- Concarneau Electronique Service, at marina. Tel 02.98.51.42.27.
- Le Bihan Voiles, at marina. Tel 02.98.51.40.40. Sailmaker.

CONCARNEAU

Concarneau somehow blends the rough-tough, working atmosphere of a major fishing port with the ancient charm and massive granite ramparts of the Ville Close. Overlaid on this hard exterior is an all-engulfing veneer of tourism, of which the marina is but one small part.

Yachts occupy the outer harbour, fishing boats the inner, separated by the Ville Close on a small rocky islet. The centre of the town is close at hand, a mélange of old and new, mostly the latter. Come and see for yourself – ideally not in July or August!

TOURISM

Tourist Office Quai d'Aiguillon, 29185 Concarneau. Tel 02.98.97.01.44; Fax 02.98.50.88.81. May/Jun, Mon-Sat 0900-1200 & 1400-1830, Sun 0930-1230; Jul/Aug 0900-2000; Sep-Apr, Mon-Sat 0900-1200 & 1400-1830.

Bus to Rosporden (20 mins) for nearest railway station with trains to Rennes, Quimper, Nantes. Bus to Quimper (30m). Rail station 08.36.35.35.35 (info, Paris 4½hrs); Airport 02.98.94.30.30. Local buses to Pont-Aven (25 mins), Port Manech (40 mins) and Quimperlé (55 mins).

Taxi rank near Tourist Office. Or call 02.98.97.24.18; 02.98.97.13.82.

Car hire Tel 02.98.50.79.00; 02.98.97.36.06.

Bike hire Ets Gloanec, 65 ave Le Lay (near Stoc supermarket). Tel 02.98.97.09.77.

Beaches Walk/cycle from the Bureau du Port along the sea front to the west, then north, passing: Plage Rodel, Plage des Dames, Plage de Cornouaille and Plage des Sables Blancs. SE of the harbour, Plage de Cabellou in Anse de Kersos is close enough for a dinghy trip on a calm day.

Festivals etc Two dates for your diary: 14 July, Bastille Day, is celebrated every year by a fleet of old sailing vessels gathering in the bay. In mid to late August, the Fêtes des Filets Bleues (Blue Nets festival) takes place; folk dancing, processions etc. It was originally (1905) a charity event in aid of

---

WHAT TO SEE/DO

La Ville Close is of course the star attraction, rightly so. It has been described at such length by others that only the following are highlighted here: Walk the ramparts, almost a complete circuit with good views across the fishing basin and to seaward. Stroll the length of the main drag (rue Vauban and rue Saint-Guénolé), taking in as you go: the Musée de la Pêche (who fishes what, where and how), including a visit to *Hémérica*, a paid-off trawler; and Carré des Larrons (open air theatre) at the far end for music, song and dance. Pause for refreshments!

The Fishing Port walk round on your own or get a conducted tour with one of two enterprising

fishermen – Michel Pencoat (*Authentique*, Tel 02.98.50.55.10) or Simon (*A l'assaut des remparts*

La Ville Close: clock tower

02.98.50.56.55) – who take you round trawlers, canning factory and fish auction. See the Tourist Office for details.

Marinarium (or aquarium, on which the French are hooked!) at Place de la Croix, close to the Capitainerie, is part of the Laboratoire Maritime. Blend in with the inmates on a rainy day.

Château de Keriolet a break from *nautisme*, at Beuzec-Conq (home of the rear leading light) is a 15th century manor house, face-lifted in the 19th century and later owned by a Russian prince, who assassinated the monk Rasputin. Irresistible at 25FF, open 1030-1830 Jul/Aug.

Rear mark
Beuzec spire

Front mark
La Croix light

Marina

Approaching to port of 028° leading line

fishermen who had lost their jobs with the demise of sardine fishing.

EATING ASHORE

Broadly, you either dive into La Ville Close, along with half the French nation (the other half is in Le Palais, Belle Île), where you will find several acceptable eating places – whether you can find a table is another matter. Or you scout around by the Quai Carnot, ie adjacent to La Criée (fish market), where some good little places will feed you today's catch. Restaurants have also been found elsewhere in Concarneau. Recce the possibilities below and pre-book if in high season.

Restaurants In La Ville Close:
- Le Saint-Guénolé, 1 rue Saint-Guénolé. Tel 02.98.60.55.00. Menus 68-135FF.

- L'Assiette de Pecheur, 12 rue Saint-Guénolé (near Le Galion). Tel 02.98.70.75.84. Seafood!
- Le Galion, 15 rue Saint-Guénolé (at the far end). Tel 02.98.97.30.16. Dark, intimate and discreet gourmandising. Menus 119-299FF. Rooms available. Closed Sun pm and Mon, except Jul/Aug.

In/around Quai Carnot (NW side of Fishing harbour):
- Aux Vieux Gréements, 4 Quai Carnot. Tel 02.98.60.75.56. From 59FF.
- L'Escale, 19 Quai Carnot. Tel 02.98.97.03.31. Popular. Open 0400-2300 (yes, that's correct!)
- Le Chalut, 20 Quai Carnot. Tel 02.98.97.02.12. Menus 50-150FF.
- Le Pouce (*manger sur le pouce* = to have a quick snack), 29 Quai Carnot. Tel 02.98.97.01.71. Menus 78-160FF. *Plateau de Fruits de mer* for two is 280FF.

Capitainerie   Marina   La Ville Close   La Médée

- Les Océanides, 3 rue du Lin. Tel 02.98.97.08.61. Menus 76-150FF. Large recommended hotel.

Elsewhere in town:
- Le Buccin, 1 rue Duguay-Trouin (across from Bureau du Port). Tel 02.98.50.54.22.
- À l'Ancre, 22 rue Dumont d'Urville (near the town hall). Tel 02.98.97.02.68. Menus 65-170FF.
- Chez Armande, 15bis ave Dr. Nicholas (across from marina). Tel 02.98.97.00.76. 98-190FF.

SHOPPING

Supermarket Stoc, 17 Quai Carnot. Tel 02.98.97.50.40. Mon-Sat 0845-1930; Sun 0900-1200.

Market days Fish market Mon-Fri 0600 at Quai d'Aiguillon. Fish/seafood/vegetable/fruit market every morning in Les Halles, rue Jean-Jaurès. Open air market in front of Ville Close, Mon-Fri 0800-1300.

Banks All you might need Mon-Sat, plus cash dispensers.

Access to UK See under Brest. Ferries from Roscoff, St Malo and Cherbourg.

NAVIGATIONAL MATTERS

Charts AC 3641 (1:20,000) and 2352 (1:75,000). SHOM charts are 6650 (1:15,600) and 7146 (1:50,000).

Tides HW Concarneau is 10 mins neaps, or 30 mins springs, before HW Brest. LWs are 20 mins neaps, or 30 mins springs, before LW Brest. MHWS is 5·0m, MLWS 0·8m; MHWN is 3·9m, MLWN 1·9m. Tidal streams are slight.

Access At all tides and in most weather, but in a fresh to strong S-SW wind it is probably best to lower all sail not later than La Médée tower, whilst there is adequate searoom. Or, if it is blowing really hard, Port-la-Forêt will usually be a safer bet providing there is adequate depth in the entrance, since it is better protected than Concarneau; as witness the wholesale destruction of the latter's marina in the storm of 1987.

Approaches From the SW track 062° from Rostolou ECM buoy to the approach **waypoint** 47°50´·75N 03°56´·18W, passing between Île aux Moutons and La Voleuse SCM buoy; the latter must be rounded if approaching from Loctudy or Bénodet. The coastline is generally low, with sandy beaches and a wooded skyline. The signal station and red/white lattice tower on Beg Meil are

Le Cochon beacon; Anse de Kersos behind

Les Soldats WCM beacon; Concarneau in the background

Lanriec leading light – located in green window above 'LANRIEC'

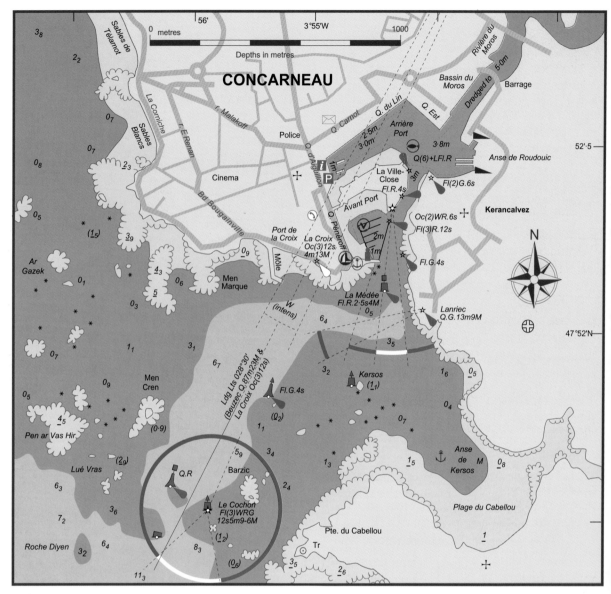

conspicuous. The long, low, white apartment buildings of Concarneau loom beyond.

From the E/SE the approach is less cluttered, unless you elect to pass north of Île Verte and Men Du IDM beacon. In any event you will have to round Pointe de Trévignon (looking a little like a submarine from afar) and the tall WCM beacon tower off Les Soldats; thence set course 330° to the waypoint, watching out for fishing vessels to/from Concarneau.

Pilotage At the waypoint turn onto the 028½° leading line to pass Le Cochon SHM beacon tower, conspic 0·9M ahead. By day the leading marks are hard to see: the front is a small white tower which does not stand out against other buildings (at night its light is amongst shore lights); the rear mark is a church spire, 3M

distant, just visible over the wooded skyline. When in the QG sector from Lanriec N, turn onto 070°; then onto 000° in the white sector of the ☆, Oc (2) WR 6s, to enter the harbour. The marina is entered at the north end of the wavebreak. Note: Close SW of La Médée tower, Fl R 2·5s, there is a 0·5m patch which could stop you dead if you should cut the corner near LW springs.

Anchorages There is no space to anchor within the harbour. Anse de Kersos to the south and the next bay round, Baie de Pouldohan, are both sheltered from easterlies but have many moorings and are really only suitable as day anchorages. See also anchorages shown under Port-la-Forêt. Port de la Croix, close west of the front leading light, is only a small drying harbour with mole.

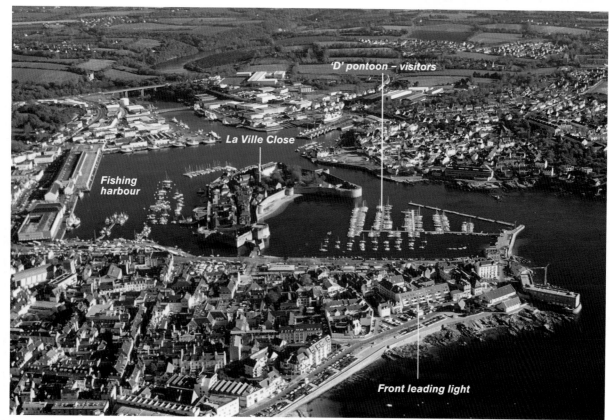

Concarneau marina and fishing harbour, looking ENE

MARINA

Bureau du Port Môle Pénéroff, 29900 Concarneau. Tel 02.98.97.57.96, Fax 02.98.97.15.15. VHF Ch 09. HM Didier Picard. Hours in season 0700-2100; out of season 0900-1200 & 1400-1800. Weather forecasts are posted daily.

Visitors berth on N side of 'D' pontoon (the second from the north), better protection the further in you go; or on the inside of the wavebreak. Yachts have no place in the Arrière Port.

Showers next to Bureau du Port; 0800-1130 & 1400-1930.

Tariff Daily rates Jul/Aug for selected LOAs on pontoons; second figure is for other summer months:
8m = 98/88FF; 9m = 118/98FF; 10m = 134/108FF; 11m = 149/118FF; 12m = 160/129FF; 12m-14m = 175/139FF; 14m-16m = 191/149FF.

Fuel Berth at the south end of the wavebreak is safer near HW due to 1m depth. Diesel and petrol are available Jul/Aug 0700-2030 daily; 0800-1130 & 1400-1930 out of season; pay via Bureau du Port. Or refuel H24 if you have an acceptable (French) bank card.

Launderette Place de l'Hôtel de Ville (near Mairie). Tel 02.98.50.86.74. Open daily 0700-2000.

NAUTICAL NEEDS

Chandlery & repairs If heavy repairs are needed, substantial engineering facilities are on the east side of the fishing basin, to which a pedestrian ferry runs from the NE corner of Ville Close.

* Accastillage de Moulin-Mer, route de Trégunc. 02.98.97.46.79. Chandlery, hull & engine repairs.
* Ets Barzic, 26 Quai Carnot. Tel 02.98.97.01.57. Chandlery and SHOM chart agent.
* Coop Maritime, rue des Chalutiers (north end of fishing basin). Tel 02.98.97.55.76. Chandlery. SHOM chart agent.
* Concarneau Electronique Service, 10 Quai Est. Tel 02.98.50.51.09.
* St Gué Électronique, 15 Quai Est. Tel 02.98.97.50.86.
* Sail Loft Le Rose, 19 ave Dr Pierre-Nicolas (by marina). Tel 02.98.97.04.28. SHOM chart agent.

Approaching the harbour entrance from the SSW

LORIENT

Lorient is one of those ports at which one is pleased to arrive and pleased to leave – rather like having one's mother-in-law to stay. After being almost wiped out in WW2, it was re-built, but sadly is not known to have won any prizes for architectural excellence. The city and suburbs sprawl around a huge natural harbour which embraces separate commercial, naval (de-activated), fishing and yachting ports. The harbour is criss-crossed by ferries and vedettes, especially to/from Île de Groix, which breaks the full force of the prevailing south westerlies.

WEST SIDE

Kernével and Lorient marinas (also misleadingly referred to as Port du Commerce) are run by the same company (SEM) and charge identical fees.

MARINAS AND ASSOCIATED SHORESIDE FACILITIES

The five marinas are far apart around Lorient harbour; the two largest are on the west side and the other three on the east. For convenience's sake they are shown below, together with their shore facilities, as separate geographic entities under the west and east sides of the harbour. Engineering support is also widely dispersed, such that for technical problems or repairs you might be better served at Port-la-Forêt, Concarneau, La Trinité or Crouesty.

Kernével is close to the harbour entrance but remote from shops/restaurants and is rather exposed to strong westerlies. Lorient marina is well sheltered in the city centre, but has relatively few vacant berths and at peak times or regattas may turn visitors away. The inner, wet basin would be a good place to leave a boat.

Tariffs. Kernével and Lorient

Daily rates Jun/Jul/Aug for selected LOAs on pontoons (2nd figures are for Sep-May): 7m-8·5m = 100/50F; <10m = 130/65F; <11·5m = 150/75F; <14m = 190/95F; <16m = 230/115F.

Kernével

Capitainerie 56260 Larmor-Plage. Tel 02.97.65.48.25, Fax 02.97.33.63.56. VHF Ch 9. HM Bruno Dagorne. Hours in season 0800-1230 & 1330-2000; out of season 0830-1230 & 1400-1800. Weather forecasts are posted daily. Enter at the north end between two yellow buoys. At the south end of marina berth only on east side of ❷ pontoon (fingers), or on the wavebreak.

Capitainerie *Fuel pontoon*

Kernével marina, south end, looking NW

Lorient

Capitainerie quai de Rohan, 56100 Lorient. Tel 02.97.21.10.14, Fax 02.97.21.10.15. VHF Ch 9. HM Bruno Dagorne. In season 0800-1230 & 1330-2000; out of season 0830-1230 & 1400-1800. Weather forecasts are posted daily. Caution: Beware of vedettes and Île de Groix ferry. Visitors' pontoon is first to port just before pyramidal-roofed Capitainerie. See HM for a berth in the wet basin; access approx HW±1.

Showers 12FF, in small building on N side of road bridge by wet basin.

Launderette (laverie), Cours de la Bôve.

Taxi Tel 02.97.21.29.29.

Bus to Quimper, Brest, Vannes, Nantes.

Rail station Tel 02.97.85.41.64; info 08.36.35.35.35 (Paris 4½hrs, Brest-Nantes);

Airport Lorient/Lann-Bihoue Tel 02.97.87.21.50. Flights to Paris, Lyon, Belle Île.

Car hire Rentacar, 4 place de la Libération, Lorient. Tel 02.97.35.12.12.

Access to UK See under Brest. Ferries from Roscoff, St Malo and Cherbourg.

Fuel See Kernével.

Nautical Needs
- Cap Océans, 14 rue F. Toullec, Lorient. Tel 02.97.37.34.78. Engineering.
- Comptoir de la Mer, 87 av de la Perriere. Tel 02.97.87.08.63. Chandlery. SHOM chart agent.
- L'Alcandre, Maison de la Mer, quai de Rohan. Tel 02.97.64.20.41. SHOM chart agent.
- Metalunox, ZI de Kerandre, Hennebont. Tel 02.97.85.01.73. Stainless steel work.

Showers/launderette in Capitainerie building; jeton 12FF. After 2000LT get jeton from bar in Villa Margaret and use night showers.

Fuel Diesel and petrol (the only source in Lorient) from the fuel berth at the south end of the marina; approach from the south, ie leaving the ☆ Fl Y 2·5s to starboard. Self-service H24 if you have an acceptable (French) bank card; otherwise call Ch 09 in office hours and pay at the Capitainerie.

Nautical needs
- Chantier Kernével Nautic, bd Roger Le Port, Larmor-Plage. Tel 02.97.65.55.72.
- Shipchandler, marina. Chandlery and SHOM chart agent.
- Allard Voiles Services, ZA de Kerhoas, Larmor-Plage. Tel 02.97.83.72.07. Sailmaker.
- Waterbuses to Lorient and Port-Louis, afternoons Jul/Aug. Few amenities at Kernével; bus to Larmor-Plage.

Tourist Office Larmor-Plage: Ave Gen de Gaulle. Tel 02.97.33.70.02. Hours 0930-1830, Jul/Aug. Bike hire: Larmor Cycles, 2 bld de Toulhars. Tel 02.97.33.79.50. Good beaches at Plage de Toulhars and Plage de Port-Maria. Market on Sun am. Spar minimarket, 3 rue des 4 Frères Le Roy. Tel 02.97.65.49.94; hours 0800-2000, Jul/Aug. Banks.

Lorient marina: inner wet basin, looking ESE

Lorient marina: capitainerie

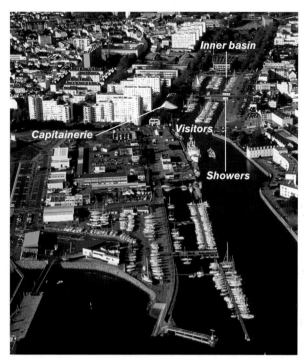
Lorient marina, looking west

Market days Big fish market Wed and Sat mornings.

Supermarkets Shopi, 28 rue Auguste Nayel, Lorient. Tel 02.97.64.40.60. Mon-Sat 0845-1300 & 1430-1945. Free delivery to your boat when you buy more than 400FF worth.

Tourist Office (next to Capitainerie), Tel 02.97.21.07.84, Fax 02.97.21.99.44; open Mon-Sat 0900-1230 & 1330-1800. The Inter-Celtic Festival, 10 days from 1st Friday in August, is big business if you are a Celt; music, song, dance etc in or near Place Jules-Ferry. Other than that, there are few cultural or historical "must-visit" attractions in Lorient.

Restaurants
- Le Poisson d'Or, 1 rue Maître Esvelin. Tel 02.97.21.57.06. Pamper yourself in this rather elegant restaurant, 2 mins walk WNW from the marina along quai de Rohan. 120-280FF.

- Le Pic, 2 bd du Maréchal Franchet d'Esperey. Tel 02.97.21.18.29. Traditional fare, 100-200FF.
- Victor-Hugo, 36 rue Carnot. Tel 02.97.64.26.54. SSW from the wet basin bridge. 95-225FF.

EAST SIDE

Port-Louis, of French East India Company fame, is today a quiet and charming backwater east of the harbour entrance; the walled town has character. The marina is municipally run and suffers from a lack of funding (the mayor is said not to like yachts – a pity, it shows!).

Sainte Catherine and Pen Mané marinas are a little further up-harbour and about 6 cables apart. They are run by the same company (Sagemor), charge identical fees and access the same shops at Locmiquélic nearly a mile away. Shelter is good in all three marinas. A new marina at Locmalo was due to start building in 2000.

Tariff. Port-Louis
Daily rates Jun-Sep for selected LOAs on pontoons (Oct-May rate is 50% of Jun-Sep): 7·5m-8m = 84F; <9m = 92FF; <10m = 100FF; <11m = 108FF; <12m = 120FF; <13m = 132FF; <14m = 150FF; >14m = 176FF.

Tariff. Sainte Catherine and Pen Mané
Daily rates 1 Jun-31 Aug for selected LOAs on pontoons (2nd figure is for Apr, May & Sep): 7m-8·5m = 75/40FF; <10m = 100/50FF; <11·5m = 120/60FF; <14m = 145/75FF.

Note: the Jun-Aug rates apply for each of the first 5 days; thereafter the daily rate doubles.

Port-Louis

Bureau du Port quai de la Pointe, 56290 Port-Louis. Tel 02.97.82.59.55. Mobile 06.08.64.49.52. VHF Ch 9. HM Roberto Gabellec. Hours M, T, Th, F 0830-1200 & 1330-1730; Wed, Sat 0815-1200. Approach via No 1 and D1 SHM buoys. Unlit SHM perch marks the end of slipway; small yellow buoys mark the edge of dredged basin. Enter with care, especially at night. Caution: works are in progress to enlarge berthing facilities for fishing vessels; the former

Approach to Port-Louis marina

visitors pontoon has been wiped out! Berth on a vacant finger berth and see HM. When the office is shut, a list of vacant finger berths is posted on the door (what a brilliantly simple idea); ditto weather forecasts.

Fuel See Kernével. Water bus to Lorient every afternoon via Kernével.

Supermarket Intermarché, 65 ave de Kerbel. Tel 02.97.82.46.65.

Market days Sat morning; and, in Jul/Aug only, Tues evenings 1830-2200 – a big event.

Tourist Office 47 Grande Rue, 56290 Port-Louis. Tel 02.97.82.52.93; Fax 02.97.82.43.66. Jul/Aug, M-F 0930-1230 & 1430-1830 (Tues 2000); Sat 0930-1300 & 1430-1630; Sun 1000-1230.

Bike hire Cycles Réchaussat, 9 rue du Mézat. Tel 02.97.82.13.86.

Taxi 02.97.82.19.81.

La Citadelle Museum of the East India company and a maritime museum, Apr-Sep 1000-1830. Tel 02.97.12.10.37.

Beaches nearest is SE of La Citadelle.

Restaurants

* Hotel du Commerce, Place du Marché. Tel 02.97.82.46.05. Looks staid and a bit of a time-warp, but excellent cuisine. 89-195FF.
* La Belle Vue, 1 rue de la Pointe (across from Bureau du Port). Tel 02.97.82.46.03. 85-225FF. As the name suggests, good views up-harbour.
* Au St Pierre, 6 Grand Rue. Tel 02.97.82.57.71. Seafood.

Ste Catherine

Capitainerie quai Rallier du Batty, 56570 Locmiquélic. Tel 02.97.33.59.51; Fax 02.97.33.89.25. VHF Ch 9. HM Catherine Gautier. Hours in season M, T, Th, F 0845-1200 & 1330-1800; Wed, Sat 0845-1200; Sun/Hols 0900-1230. Weather forecasts are posted daily. Entry H24 is simple; berth in 2-3m on 'A' pontoon, first to starboard.

Showers/Launderette next to Capitainerie.

Fuel At Kernével. Frequent Transrade ferries to

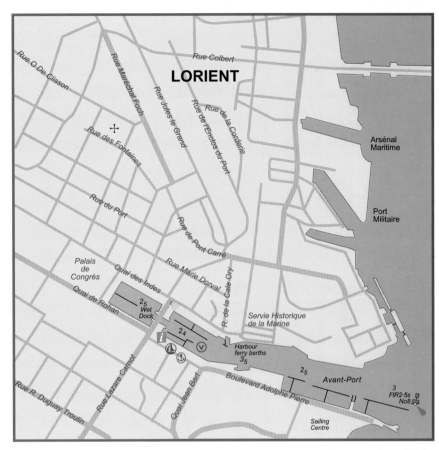

Lorient marina. All normal shopping in Locmiquélic; nearest supermarket is at Port-Louis. Some minor eating places & bars by the marina.

Taxi 02.97.33.41.48.

Nautical needs

* Demi-clé, 25 rue du Port, Locmiquélic. Tel 02.97.33.53.87. Chandlery.
* Chantier Nautique de la Combe, ZI Pen Mané. Tel 02.97.33.89.80. Boatyard.

Pen Mané

Capitainerie A small office and showers are at the head of the gangway; if closed, contact or cycle to

Pen Mané marina. Lorient in the background

Harbour entrance: La Citadelle and grain silos

Labels on image: Le Cochon beacon · Grain silos · Île St Michel · La Jument PHM beacon · La Citadelle · IPTS

Ste Catherine marina (above) which is in any case the preferred option for visitors. Entry H24 is simple, leaving Rohu No 1 GRG buoy, Fl (2+1) G 10s, to starboard; berth in a vacant finger on the outer wavebreak. Fuel, shopping, ferries as for Ste Catherine.

NAVIGATIONAL MATTERS

Charts AC 304 (1:10,000 with a 1:12,500 inset of the Blavet river) and 2352 (1:75,000). SHOM 7140 (1:10,000), 7139 (1:20,000) and 7031 (1:50,000).

Approaches There are two approaches, the West and the South Passes, which meet close north of Les Trois Pierres, black-and-white banded beacon tower. Both are well marked/lit and present no difficulty, although the South Pass has some shallow patches.

The waypoints are: West Pass 47°40′·80N 03°24′·92W, 057°/5M to the front leading light, Q; and South Pass 47°40′·50N 03°22′·40W, 008½°/ 2·1M to abeam La Citadelle.

Check that the International Port Traffic Signals on La Citadelle do not prohibit your entry or departure, as appropriate, whilst certain categories of large or constrained vessels are transiting. Rule 9 applies and the onus is on yachts to keep clear.

Daymarks The most conspicuous daymarks for general orientation are: La Citadelle; the WW2 submarine pens; the grain silos, white with blue stripe, on the quayside opposite Pen-Mané; and a large water tower west of Kernével which is useful when approaching from the southeast.

Pilotage The main channel through the narrows (only about 130 metres wide) is well marked by buoys, beacons and leading lights. Here, if conflicting traffic requires and there is enough water, yachts can use an unlit alternative channel, dredged 1·0 m, which passes west of La Jument PHM red tower and its reef. When entering, leave to starboard a preferred-channel-to-starboard RGR buoy south of La Jument, and further north the preferred-channel-to-starboard RGR Le Cochon beacon. Careful prior study of AC 304 or

the rather clearer SHOM 7140 is needed to 'fathom' the details of this secondary channel.

After passing La Citadelle, keep straight ahead for Kernével or turn starboard for Port-Louis.

Up-harbour the main channel leads west of Île Saint-Michel to Lorient marina, Pen Mané marina and the entrance to the Blavet river. East of that island a buoyed, but unlit secondary channel gives access to Sainte Catherine marina and also to Pen Mané marina.

Tides HW Lorient at neaps is 3 mins after, and at springs 20 mins before, HW Brest. LWs are 10 mins neaps, or 20 mins springs, before LW Brest. MHWS is 5·1m, MLWS 0·8m; MHWN is 4·0m, MLWN 2·0m.

Tidal streams at springs reach 1kn in the approaches, 2·5 knots in the narrows and 1·8 knots within the harbour.

Access At all tides and in all winds by day and night. A port of refuge.

Anchorages There is an anchorage close NE of La Citadelle, clear of moorings and the fairway to Port-Louis. Within the harbour, anchorage may be found outside the fairways, eg off Sainte Catherine marina. Note that the former submarine base, north of Kernével marina, and the de-activated naval base north and east of Lorient marina is a prohibited area (no hardship), and the deactivated, and the de-activated naval base north and east of Lorient Marina is restricted.

The Blavet river which flows into Lorient harbour abeam Pen Mané marina, grows increasingly attractive the further up-river you go. Anchor or moor up/downstream of the first bridge (22m clearance), or higher up-stream just out of the fairway. The channel winds and narrows upriver where there are 0·3m patches, so at LWS expect a least depth of 1·0m. At Hennebont, the limit of masted progress, there are some mooring buoys and a small pontoon where keels sink into soft mud. It is a pleasant ramparted town with the usual facilities and a market on Thurs mornings.

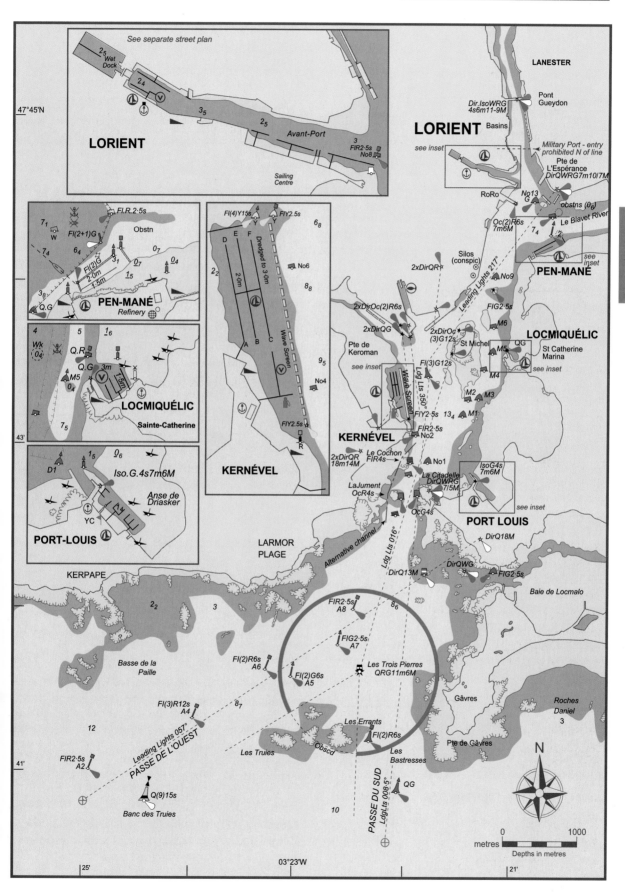

47°45'N

See separate street plan

Wet Dock
2·5
2·4

LORIENT

LANESTER

Pont Gueydon
Dir.IsoWRG 4s6m11-9M

LORIENT Basins
see inset

3·5
2·5
Avant-Port
3
Fl.R2·5s No8

Sailing Centre

Military Port - entry prohibited N of line
Pte de L'Espérance DirQWRG7m10/7M

RoRo

No13 G

obstns (0₆)
Le Blavet River
see inset

PEN-MANÉ

Oc(2)R6s 7m6M
7·4 2

Chapter 3

Fl.R.2·5s
7·1
W
Fl(2+1)G
7·4
6·4
Obstn
0·7
0·4
Fl(2)G 2.0m 1.5m
3·1
1·5
0·7
3·8
Q.G
PEN-MANÉ
Refinery

Fl(4)Y15s
Y Y
Fl.Y2.5s
6·8
D E F
Dredged to 3·0m
2·2
2·0m
No6
8·8
A B C
Wave Screen
9·5
No4
Fl.Y2.5s
R
KERNÉVEL

2xDirQR

Silos (conspic)
No9

Leading Lights 217°
Fl.G2·5s
2xDirOc(2)R6s
2xDirQG
2xDirOc (3)G12s
St Michel
M6
M5
LOCMIQUÉLIC
QG
St Catherine Marina
see inset

4
Wk 0·4
5
Q.R
Q.G
M5
0·4
1·6
3m
1·5m
LOCMIQUÉLIC
Sainte-Catherine
7·5

Pte de Keroman
see inset

Lgd Lts 350°
Wave Screen
Fl(3)G12s
Fl.Y2.5s
13·4
KERNÉVEL
Fl.R2·5s
No2

M4
M2
M3
M1

D1
1·5
0·6
Iso.G.4s7m6M
Anse de Driasker
A4
YC
PORT-LOUIS

2xDirQR 18m14M
Le Cochon Fl.R4s
No1
La Citadelle DirQWRG 7/5M

IsoG4s 7m6M
see inset
PORT LOUIS

LaJument OcR4s
OcG4s
DirQWG
DirQ18M

KERPAPE

LARMOR PLAGE

Alternative channel

Ldg Lts 016°

DirQ13M

Fl.G2·5s

Baie de Locmalo

Fl.R2·5s A8
8·6

Fl.G2·5s A7

Fl(2)R6s A6

Fl(2)G6s A5

Les Trois Pierres QRG11m6M

Gâvres

Roches Daniel
3

Basse de la Paille

2·2
3

Fl(3)R12s A4
8·7

Les Errants

Fl(2)R6s

Pte de Gâvres

N

12

Fl.R2·5s A2

Leading Lights 057°
PASSE DE L'OUEST

Les Truies
Obscd

Les Bastresses

PASSE DU SUD
LdgLts 008·5°

QG

Q(9)15s
Banc des Truies

10

0   1000
metres
Depths in metres

25'

03°23'W

21'

41'

43'

PORT TUDY

Port Tudy (Île de Groix)

As you head southeast, Groix is the first of eight offshore islands that you may visit, excluding the Glénan archipelago. It is a flat-topped chunk of granite, roughly 40 metres high, 4M long by about 1½M wide – virtually the same size as Alderney, but greener and more wooded.

Port Tudy is the harbour and half a mile up the hill is Le Bourg ('The Town'), the island's capital (again not unlike the walk from Braye harbour to St Anne). The only other village of any size is Loc Maria, a mile SE of Port Tudy. This is well worth a visit either for a picnic or to recce the harbour from land before venturing to enter in your *bateau* (see navigational notes). The south coast is generally rugged and exposed, especially at its western end.

TOURISM

Tourist Office Mairie, 56590 Île de Groix. Tel 02.97.86.53.08 (all year); 02.97.86.54.96 season.

Bus The Route 1 bus leaves Le Bourg (in front of the church) at 0915 and 1115 on Tues and Fri, to cover the western half of the island. Route 2 bus, Wed & Sat same times, does the eastern half.

Taxi Call 02.97.86.80.65; 02.97.86.81.62.

Bike and car hire On the quays:
- Coconut's Hire, Tel 02.97.86.81.57.
- Cycles Martin, from 30FF/day. Hrs 0900-1200 & 1400-1900. Tel 02.97.86.84.17.
- Joël Tristan, from 56FF per day. Tel 02.97.86.80.03.

Ferry to Lorient (45 mins): 110FF return foot passenger Jun-Sep; 5-8 daily sailings from Groix.

Beaches At the east tip of the island, just below Pointe de la Croix light house, is the Plage des Grands Sables a massive white sandbank projecting out from the land. It is just over a mile

WHAT TO SEE/DO

Groix is ideal for walking or cycling. The coastal footpath hugs the clifftops and is 25km long; possibly best done over two days. The cycle route goes inland at times to avoid the more difficult clifftop sections; it can be done in 4 to $4\frac{1}{2}$ hours, but a full day allows for stops along the way.

At the west end of Groix, between the light house and the Signal station, is a Nature Reserve, not surprisingly home to many different seabirds et al. Preferably before visiting it, look round the Maison de la Réserve in Le Bourg to get a feel for whatever else you might see. Entry is free; Jun & Sep, Mon-Sat 1030-1200. Jul/Aug, Mon-Sat 0930-1230 & 1730-1900, Sun 0930-1230.

Meanwhile back in Port Tudy, if you yearn for *le patrimoine et l'art de vivre* without too much effort, call in at the Ecomuseum, a former canning factory overlooking the harbour, which traces the history of the island from earliest times, its inhabitants and their toil in the fields and at sea.

Entry: 24FF; 1 Jun-30 Sep, 0930-1230 & 1500-1900.

from Port Tudy, not commercialised and has plenty of space even at high water. Close south of this beach is the Plage des Sables Rouges, so coloured by minerals in the granite; here you may even find garnet, a deep red transparent gem (worth taking a bucket and spade). There are other sandy inlets and coves around the island – just a question of finding your secret spot!

EATING ASHORE

Restaurants At Port Tudy:
- Le Ty Mad, Tel 02.97.86.80.19. Seafood, what else?
- Les Courreaux, Tel 02.97.86.82.66. Arguably the best on the island; please report!
- Also Café du Port, Café de l'Escale, Café de la Jetée: all good for a drink and a snack.

At Le Bourg:
- La Marine, rue Gén de Gaulle. Tel 02.97.86.80.05. Seafood on the terrace.
- L'Esméralda, near the cinema. Tel 02.97.86.50.57. Elegant townhouse surroundings.

SHOPPING

Supermarkets Both are a fair walk uphill westward out of Le Bourg: Ecomarché, route du Pen Men; Tel 02.97.86.88.19. Comod, route de Port-Lay; Tel 02.97.86.80.07.

Banks Credit Agricole, 6 place du Leurhé, Le Bourg (behind town hall).

NAVIGATIONAL MATTERS

Charts AC 2352 (1:75,000) and SHOM 7031 (1:50,000) permit coastal, rather than inshore, navigation. SHOM 7139 (1:20,000) covers the island and adjacent mainland with a larger scale inset of Port Tudy.

Approaches From the west the approaches are clear, except for: a one mile wide no-anchoring zone halfway between the west tip of the island and Port Tudy (protects submarine cables); three large unlit yellow naval mooring buoys 5-7 cables WNW of Port Tudy; and floating mussel lines off Port Lay, 3 cables W of Port Tudy.

From Lorient most vessels, including some fairly rapid vedettes, will track from Banc des Truies WCM light buoy direct to the harbour entrance, passing the waypoint (47°39´·14N 03°26´·28W) and leaving Speerbrecker unlit ECM buoy 100 metres to starboard. Don't get run down by this stream of marine commuters from/to Lorient, especially numerous at weekends and public holidays.

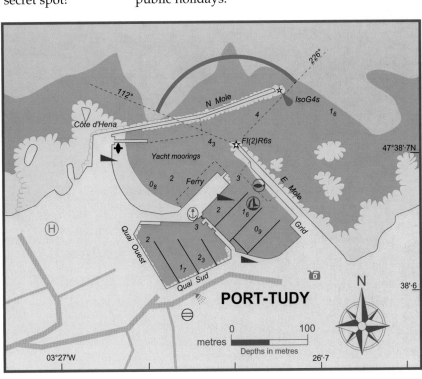

Ferry berth   Avant Port moorings

Entrance to the Avant Port

From SE or E it is best to keep outside Les Chats SCM light buoy and Edouard de Cougy ECM buoy (marking a wreck). Closer in you must keep north of Basse Mélite NCM buoy guarding the eponymous shoal. West of this buoy, do not cut the corner too fine as there are offlying reefs.

Daymarks Pen Men 28 metre high, square white light house with black top, Fl (4) 25s, at the west end (with nearby white Signal station) and the water tower in the centre of the island are the two most conspicuous features. At the SE end of the island Pointe des Chats light house is on a low spit of land and on Pointe de la Croix the small light house is partly hidden by trees.

Pilotage The water tower in transit 216° with the church spire at Le Bourg leads directly to Port Tudy.

Tides HW Port Tudy (which is a French Standard Port) at neaps is the same as, and at springs 25 mins before, HW Brest. LWs are 15 mins neaps, or 25 mins springs, before LW Brest. MHWS is 5·1m, MLWS 0·9m; MHWN is 4·0m, MLWN 2·0m.

Tidal streams do not exceed 0.5 knots on the north side of the island. SHOM Tidal stream atlas (558-UJA) covering Penmarc'h to Noirmoutier contains a large scale inset of Île de Groix.

Access At all tides and all weathers, but in strong north to northeast winds a heavy swell enters the outer harbour. The inner wet basin is accessible via a 7m wide gate HW±2 between 0630 and 2200LT; possibly for a shorter period at small coefficients, and not at all if there is much swell.

Anchorages Anchoring is prohibited in the harbour due to lack of space. There are however up to 18 (at the last count) yacht moorings in the outer harbour, some dull red conical-shaped, others dayglow orange spherical.

Showers

First pontoon   Gate into wet basin

Inner harbour pontoons and entrance to wet basin

MARINA

Capitainerie Port Tudy, 56590 Île de Groix. Tel 02.97.86.54.62. HM Michel Prevel. VHF Ch 09. In season daily 0630-2100; out of season 0800-1200 & 1400-1800. Weather forecasts are posted daily. Visitors have three options:

i. a finger berth on the first or second pontoons in the tidal east basin;

depths 1·5 to 2·5m.

ii. a finger berth in the wet basin (access HW±2, as detailed above); depths 2 to 3m.

iii. a buoy in the Avant Port.

Visitors tend to go for the first option because it is simplest and because the window into the wet basin is relatively short; in any case this basin is now rather taken up by local boats.

Buoys in the Avant Port are not a favourite occupation of mine. They are often used by sailing school boats and inevitably suffer some wash and noise from the ferries; they are also subject to the mayhem which erupts if/when the *vent solaire* blows in the small hours. The buoys are now laid for fore-and-aft mooring, ie no longer the bows-in petal pattern to a single buoy.

In July & August the whole harbour becomes chock-a-block and visitors can expect to be turned away, but Lorient is not too far. Prior booking and/or arrival around noon are the better solutions.

Showers On the quay next to the wet basin; open 0830-1100 & 1700-1900. These limited times guarantee maximum queuing and unfortunately the use of boat heads! In the block a formidable Madame sits at the receipt of customs – do not cross swords with her. 13FF for a shower and jetons cannot be bought in advance; fresh water is a precious commodity on the island.

Tariff Daily rates all year for selected LOAs on pontoons:
- East basin: 7-9m = 112FF; 9-12m = 154FF; 12-15m = 196FF; >15m = 224FF.
- Wet basin: 11FF per metre LOA. Avant Port: buoy 50FF.

Fuel Diesel and petrol pumps at the Renault garage in the SE corner of the harbour, but cans only, as hoses do not reach a yacht alongside the drying quay. Tel 02.97.86.59.19. Open 0800-1200 & 1330-1900.

Launderette Loca Loisirs, on the quayside (next door to Tristan the Bike). 0800-2200. Tel 02.97.86.80.03.

NAUTICAL NEEDS

Chandlery & repairs Atelier Naval Ar C'hanot (south quay), Tel 02.97.86.81.86. Boatyard. Coop Marine (south quay), Tel 02.97.86.80.03. Chandlery. SHOM chart agent.

LOCMARIA

This is a peaceful anchorage, sheltered in winds from the west, through north to east. But it is completely exposed to southerly winds, swell and sea. Consult the MRNA for brief directions which are amplified in the Pilot with a sketch and photograph.

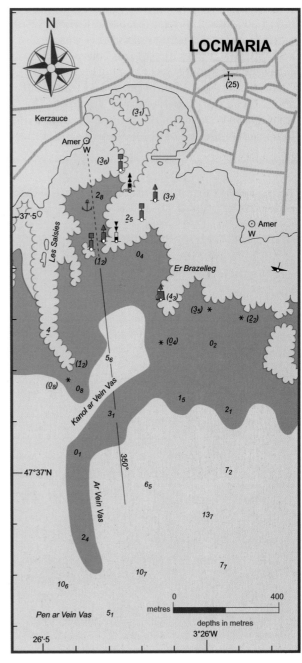

Chapter 3

RIVER ÉTEL

I must admit it: I have always fought shy of visiting this place, imagining labyrinthine pilotage, maelstroms and tidal streams akin to the jetstreams which blow aloft.
I was shamed into it by a two-female Brit crew (aka Scylla and Charybdis) who told me they went in, liked it, stayed a night

and left without turning a hair. So I did likewise; *pas de problème*.

The toughest part was seeking the help of the only Lady Pilot in France (Madame Josiane Pene) – due to my excruciating French. She was economical with her directions *"Vous pouvez entrer"*. After that it's up to you.

There is a palpable air of peace and tranquillity about Étel. People are friendly and relaxed. The light has an almost luminous quality, perhaps due to its being reflected off the extensive sand dunes either side of the entrance.

TOURISM

Tourist Office Place des Thoniers, BP 29, 56410 Étel; at south end of La Criée (fishmarket). Tel 02.97.55.23.80; Fax 02.97.55.58.26. Closed out of season, when you should call at the Mairie.

What to see/do Mostly relax and do little except sit on the beach, eat, drink etc! It's that sort of place. Take advice from the HM on a dinghy trip up-river, under the Lorois bridge into La Mer (or Ría) d'Étel, a sizeable inland sea dotted with islets; uncharted and with strong tides. Or go by bike and cross the 50 metre causeway to the little island of St Cado. Here there is a Romanesque chapel, a Calvary and fishermen's cottages; best seen near high water.

A pedestrian ferry (bikes free) runs from near the Lifeboat shed to La Magouër. Daily 0900-1300 & 1500-1900, but Tues 0900-1400 & 1600-1900.

Étel harbour, middle reach

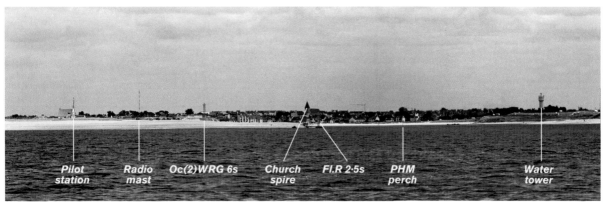

Pilot station | Radio mast | Oc(2)WRG 6s | Church spire | Fl.R 2·5s | PHM perch | Water tower

Approaching the waypoint from well west of the 020° leading line

15FF return. This would enable you to visit the Pilot station and have a chat with Madame Pene about the infamous bar.

Another interesting visit is to the CROSS Étel(Coastguard station) at the north end of the town by the red and white radio mast. Best to make the initial arrangement through the HM.

If you are in Etel in August you will be engulfed in the Fête du Thon (Tuna festival).

Bus (Routes 1 and 27/27A) from Rue du Souvenir (north of Place de la République) to Lorient, Auray, Vannes, Carnac and Vannes. Railway station at Auray 02.97.42.50.50.

Taxi Call 02.97.55.45.40; 02.97.55.31.18; 02.97.55.30.84.

Car and Bike hire Ask at Tourist Office.

Beaches On your way in you will have seen most of the beaches, both outside the entrance and within the river. You are spoiled for choice, but do be wary of the tidal streams.

EATING ASHORE

Restaurants
- La Chaloupe, 12 Cours des Quais (abeam S end of marina). Tel 02.97.55.32.13. Seafood menus 80-115FF.
- Le Lamparo, 42 rue de Libération. Tel 02.97.55.42.96. Inexpensive moules/frites & seafood.
- Le Trianon (Logie), just beyond the church. Tel 02.97.55.32.41. Menus 90-190FF.
- Le Bar Breton, 2 rue du 8 Mai (opposite Coop Maritime). Tel 02.97.55.45.40. Pleasant bar, restaurant/pizzeria including takeaway.

A little bit of history: Here you can drink beer at the very table on which the Germans signed the surrender of the Lorient pocket on 7 May 1945. A plaque and photograph record the event.

SHOPPING

Supermarket Shopi, NE corner of La Piscine. Open 0830-1215 & 1500-1900, except pm Wed and Sunday.

Fishmarket daily 0830-1230. Retail sales at La Criée, Place des Thoniers. Fresh tuna at 33FF/Kg.

Market day Tuesday.

Banks Rue du Général Leclerc and Place de la République, plus cash dispensers.

NAVIGATIONAL MATTERS

Charts SHOM 7138 (1:10,000) is essential. AC 2352 (1:75,000) and SHOM 7032 (1:50,000) are both too small scale to be of real assistance.

Approaches From the west (Lorient or Île de Groix) keep to seaward of Roheu SCM beacon (two-tone grey rather than yellow/black); from the south leave Les Pierres Noires IDM beacon to starboard. Make for the waypoint, 47°38´·10N 03°12´·96W, in about 6 metres depth.

Access The position and depths over the bar can change almost daily. The current SHOM chart shows 0·6m depth, but exceptionally the bar has been known to dry by up to 5m. In onshore winds, especially against the ebb, the sea breaks right across the entrance making it impassable. For a first visit, choose neaps, calm

PHM perch abeam the Pilot station

Chapter 3

Oc(2)WRG 6s   Fl.R 2·5s   Lifeboat house   Radio mast   PHM perch   Church spire

Closing the 020° leading line from west to east

weather and good visibility; a night approach is not advised.

The best time to cross the bar is between HW Port-Tudy –2 and –1, although the flood will still be running at 1-1·5 knots. Others suggest at HW Port-Tudy –3 and +2, both times when the stream is almost slack (truly) and depths should be adequate.

Navigational marks There are 3 conspicuous landmarks in the town of Étel, from west to east: a red/white radio mast, 76 metres high; the church spire, 44m, and a water tower, 51m. The latter two marks are too far offset to the east to be

Lifeboat   Fl(2)G 6s   Radio   Fl.G 2·5s
house   mast

Starboard-hand marks and radio mast almost aligned

Turn starboard   Fl(2)R 6s   Fish market and
into marina   Tourist office

PHM buoy and marina

properly aligned with the axis of the river, so that bearings on them pass near to or across the drying spit which extends south from Le Bout du Havre.

However a bearing of 020°T on the radio mast leads through the entrance and aligns closely with the four navigational marks which can be seen inside. The waypoint is on this line, approx three cables outside the bar and 7 cables from the PHM perch. The best advice is to track initially straight up the middle. The banks either side are quite steep-to.

Pilotage Call Semaphore d'Étel on VHF Ch13; Madame Josiane may do no more than clear you to enter, assuming that you are on a satisfactory course and that there is adequate depth of water over the bar. If however your course is incorrect, expect to be directed accordingly (*"Tournez à gauche/droite"*). The red signal arrow (see MRNA for signals) mounted on a black-and-white mast is now only used for non-radio vessels by prior arrangement, Tel 02.97.55.35.59.

On your port hand the two red light beacons and the Pilot's white-gabled building are all clearly visible, but need not directly concern you. Concentrate on leaving the sole unlit PHM perch close to port, then alter to about 010° to leave the SHM light buoy some 50m to starboard. Thence a course of 032° will take you between the SHM light beacon and the final PHM light buoy. Thereafter relax as the river broadens; steer 000° towards the marina.

Be very wary of following local boats. They may deviate east of the various marks into a shoal water anchorage/mooring off the drying Banc du Stang.

Tides HW Étel at neaps is 20 mins after, or at springs 10 mins before, HW Brest. LW is 10 mins neaps, or 30 mins springs, after LW Brest. MHWS is 5·1m; MLWS 1·5m; MHWN is 4·0m, MLWN

2·1m. Heights of LW may vary depending on the state of the bar.

Tidal streams are slight a mile or two offshore. In the narrows, abeam the unhappily named Pointe de Secours, and up to the marina, the spring ebb reaches 5 knots, 4 knots on the flood. Just beyond the marina, tidal diamond 'B' shows a maximum of 1·5 knots.

Slack waters here occur at about HW −4 and HW +2. Thus at LW the ebb is still running at 1·2kn springs, 0·6kn neaps and at HW the flood is still making at 1·2kn springs, 0·8kn neaps.

Anchorages Anchoring is prohibited outside the entrance from shore to shore, within 5 cables of the Oc (2) WRG light. It is also prohibited in the river from the PHM light buoy to just beyond the marina, due to a submarine cable and shellfish beds (not shown on the chart). Which leaves only the upper reaches as far as the Lorois bridge for possible anchoring, clear of oyster beds.

MARINA

Capitainerie Cours des quais, 56410 Étel. Tel 02.97.55.46.62. HM Bernard Philippe. VHF Ch 13. Hours in season: Mon-Sat 0800-1200 & 1400-1800; Sun 1000-1200. Weather forecasts are posted daily.

Visitors berth on 'E' pontoon, the fourth from the north, or on hammerheads in about 3m at LW; max LOA is 15m. Caution: in June 1999 some seaweed was found in the fresh water supply on pontoon 'H'.

Showers Free, modern showers/toilets behind the Capitainerie.

Tariff Daily rates 1 May to 30 Sep for selected LOAs on pontoons:
7-8m = 78FF; <9m = 84FF; <10m = 92FF; <11m = 102FF; <12m = 114FF; <13m = 120FF.

Fuel No fuel in the marina, although duty-free diesel might be available from the fish quay.

Launderette "Pressing" (dry cleaner and launderette), rue de la Libération (close to the church). Open Tues-Sat 0830-1200 & 1430-1900; closed Sun & Mon.

NAUTICAL NEEDS

Chandlery & repairs
- Coop Marine, Cours des quais. Tel 02.97.55.30.76. Chandlery. SHOM chart agent.
- Chantier Naval du Magouër (west bank), Tel 02.97.36.76.59. Boatyard.

There is also a boatyard about 300m north of the marina in Impasse de la Corderie.

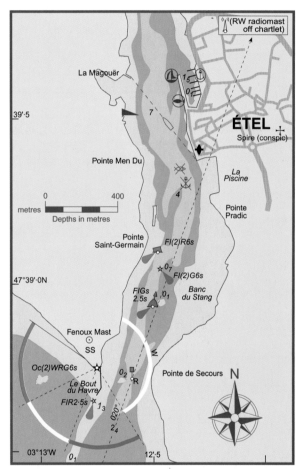

Outward bound

Chapter 3

BELLE ÎLE, QUIBERON BAY, AND THE GOLFE DU MORBIHAN

CONTENTS

THE SEA AND THE LAND

To many these waters are their goal for a summer cruise. It is a heady cocktail: the great bight of Quiberon Bay, protected by the peninsula to the west and Belle Île to the southwest, embraces an inner string of rocky reefs and islets. The Chaussées de la Teignouse, du Béniguet and de l'Île aux Chevaux make for fascinating pilotage and rock-hopping with irresistible anchorages off Île Houat and Île Hoëdic. Between La Trinité and Crouesty the Golfe du Morbihan is at once a cruising delight and a safe haven from gales.

Presqu'île de Rhuys is briefly touched upon under Crouesty (4.5).

To the south east the Vilaine River is entered by the lock at Arzal/Camoel and is navigable up to Redon without having to lower the mast. La Roche Bernard is particularly attractive.

Students of naval history will relish the Battle of Quiberon Bay 1759, fought in a rising gale amongst the reefs of these then largely uncharted waters.

But step ashore here for your first serious encounter with megaliths, menhirs, dolmens, cromlechs and the like. A few definitions may be

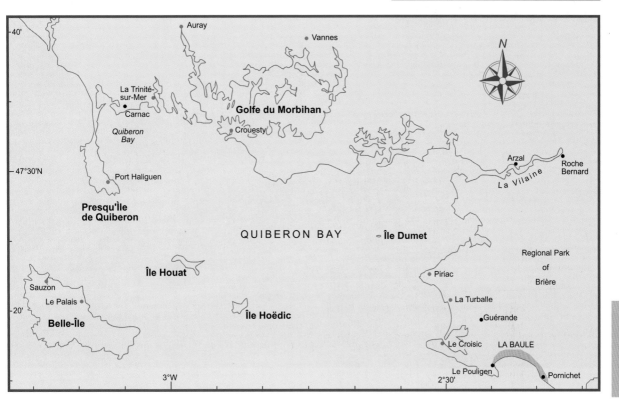

Chapter 4

in order: megalith means 'large stone' and is a generic term, just as shellfish refers to a whole range of oysters, mussels, crabs, lobsters, *langoustines* and others infinitely more appetising than megaliths. A menhir is a single standing stone; if laid out in lines these are referred to as alignments. If arranged in a semi-circle this is known as a cromlech. Where a flattish stone is laid horizontally across two menhirs these are dolmens and probably form part of a burial chamber. Some of these are covered by mounds of earth (tumuli). Near Carnac there are about 3000 menhirs, dated between 2000 and 5000 BC, long before the Pyramids and Stonehenge came into being. Here endeth the lesson.

The Carnac site is easily accessible from Port Haliguen, La Trinité, Auray or Vannes. There are other megaliths at Lagatjar near Camaret, at Locmariaquer near the mouth of the Morbihan and on Presqu'Île de Rhuys, to name but a few.

Frank Cowper wrote about them over a century ago in 1894, a mere blip in the vast timescale which they span. He was exasperated that no definitive explanation had ever been advanced as to how and why the stones came to be there. But even today theories abound of which none can be proven. His final advice is:

'To my mind the best way to see these weird processions of gaunt rocks is to climb up to Mont St Michel, on which there is a lowly chapel, and, sitting at the foot of a rude granite cross, look out over the West as the sun goes down.'

Mont St Michel should not of course be confused with the one of that name near St Malo. This one is a tumulus just outside Carnac and is visible as soon as you cycle west out of La Trinité. Nowadays there is an Archeoscope at Carnac which, in case you wondered, is a place where you can watch an audio-visual presentation explaining that the origins and purpose of the stones are not known. For this you will be charged 45FF. Try a visit to Carnac and formulate your own theory – it could be a winner.

Moving to the eastern end of Quiberon Bay we can enter the Regional Park of Brière which is equally accessible from Piriac, La Turballe and Le Croisic. This is largely marshland where local craft industries used to flourish in a now vanishing lifestyle. Peat-cutting, fishing for eels, gathering rushes still are amongst those activities.

Visit nearby Île de Fédrun to see the old thatched cottages; also La Hutte Brièronne, a restaurant serving eels and other local delicacies.

To the SW is the Presqu'Île Guérandaise, an area centred around the tiny, charming mediaeval town of Guérande. Here you can stroll around the outside of the C15 ramparts and gaze out across the salt-pans which stretch from La Turballe south east to La Baule. Local history is on view at the small museum in St Michael's Gate.

Drying inner harbour   Fuel   Citadel   Yacht moorings

Le Palais, looking NW

LE PALAIS, BELLE ÎLE

Another day, another offshore island ... If you want to know what it's like inside a sardine tin, come to Le Palais any weekend in August, or possibly any other summer month. OK, if you still insist, get there early, bring plenty of fenders and a king-sized sense of humour.

The problem revolves around where you are going to park your boat, because, *mon ami*, half the French nation is vying for the same few square metres as you. (You will recall that the other half has already occupied Concarneau). More anon ...

Assuming your boat is now secured, you'll be glad you persevered because this is a charming island where you can relax after the hurly-burly of its capital, Le Palais. It's plenty big enough – 9½ miles long, 5 miles wide (maximum) and about 50 metres high – to escape the hordes and take a break from the nautical routine. Walk, cycle, ride a horse, drive a mini-Moke or hop on a bus – there's no problem getting mobile.

Belle Île also boasts real countryside, farmed in the middle, where gorse permits, and slashed by small, wooded valleys (*abers*) which run down to hidden creeks and beaches. Sauzon (qv) is one of the largest of these and a most attractive former fishing port on the northern tip. A far smaller version of an *aber* is the nearby Port du Vieux Chateau, or Stêr-Vraz, off which the narrow cleft and anchorage of Ster Wenn opens.

Other such inlets are, on the west coast: Port du Borderon, Port de Donnant, Port Coton (see Les Aiguilles) and Port Goulphar; on the south coast: Port Kerel ⚓, Port Herlin ⚓, Port Blanc, Port de Pouldon and Port Loscan; and on the east end: Port Maria ⚓ and Port An Dro ⚓ (to name quite a few). Those marked ⚓ are the more feasible anchorages on a really calm settled day. Try one by land for a picnic and if you like what you see, return by boat.

Apart from Le Palais and Sauzon (qv), the only other communities of any size are Bangor near the centre of the island and Locmaria at the SE end.

switched and if/when the bridge-operator forgets to switch them – the first hint of chaos ...

Once inside, berth as directed by a very efficient bald, English-speaking Ace in baseball cap and fast dory. The south quay is more convenient for the town. The north quay is partly occupied by supply coasters, so grit from building materials gets everywhere. Eventually yachts will be rafted from quay to quay such that you scarcely need to walk on water. The chaos is unbelievable and order is only restored if/when everybody keeps a sense of humour! Good spectator sport.

Marina (Bassin de la Saline). In contrast this is a haven of semi-rural peace. Speak nicely to the baseball Ace who will do his best for you, if any residents' finger berths come vacant. It's further out of town, but worthwhile if you plan to stay a few days. Electricity and water are laid on.

Showers next to Capitainerie: 0815-1230 & 1415-2030. 13FF for 6 mins. There are also showers at Les Glacis, a municipal campsite north of the wet basin – convenient for the sardines therein. At the west end of the basin turn right up the hill.

Tariff Daily rates for LOA bands, in sequence: avant port buoy/wet basin berth/marina finger berth:
7-8·5m = 36/51/67FF;
<10m = 51/67/82FF;
<11·5m = 67/82/93FF;
<13m = 82/93/134FF;
<15m = 93/134/164FF.

Fuel Diesel, petrol and water tap alongside the inner end of Quai Bonnelle. Tel 02.97.31.84.68. Daily 0800-1200 & 1500-1800. Caution: check depths near LW.

Launderette Laverie de l'Ocean, rue J le Brix (behind south quay of wet basin, opposite the Petit Casino mini-supermarket). Open 0830-1900.

NAUTICAL NEEDS

Belle Île would not be a good place for serious repairs to hull, engine, rigging or sails. La Trinité and Crouesty both have far better facilities.

Chandlery & repairs

- Cooperative Maritime, ave Carnot. Tel 02.97.31.82.48. Chandlery.
- Le Filet Bleu, 3 rue Jules Simon. Tel 02.97.31.34.82. Chandlery.
- Ilo Marine, La Saline, BP 55, Le Palais. Tel 02.97.31.82.05. Repairs, engines.

Marina La Saline

Lifting bridge

Wet basin

Coaster berth

Entry gate and bridge

SAUZON, BELLE ÎLE

Sauzon is delightful! The name, by the way, is said to derive from Port Saxon, or English Port. Despite many visitors in season it manages to remain relaxed and peaceful. The pace of life is gentle, perhaps because almost everything comes to a halt for a few hours when the harbour and creek have dried out. Only the occasional Brit beavers away scrubbing his/her bottom over the lunch hour, whilst the rest of the world are enjoying good food and a glass or three of wine. The drying creek, over 5 cables long, is a paradise too for the kids who can safely paddle around in the remaining pools and rivulets, covering themselves and the family boat in seaweed, mud and sand!

The surrounding countryside and coastal scenery lend themselves to walking, or biking if you prefer – particularly around the lower, but no less breezy, northwestern tip of the island. A stay of several days would surprise nobody, even if you originally picked up a buoy "just to have a quick look" before rushing on to the next port of call. There is a loose analogy with Guernsey: Sauzon is to Le Palais what Beaucette is to St Peter Port's Victoria marina – The Calm and the Storm!

TOURISM

Tourist Office (Point I), Quai Guerveur, Sauzon. Tel/Fax 02.97.31.69.49. Easter - 30 September, 0800-1230 & 1600-2030.

What to see/do Please read the entry for Le Palais, but essentially in a place like Sauzon you make your own entertainment. The setting is almost perfect – the rest is up to you.

Transport public and hired: See also Le Palais.

Bus A bus (marketed as *Le Pass'Ports*) runs from Sauzon (13FF single) to Le Palais, about 6 times daily.

Bike hire Cyclotour, ferry pontoon and Pen Prad. Tel 02.97.31.65.25. Bikes & motor scooters.

Horse Charter La Ferme du Poney bleu, Anterre, Sauzon. Tel 02.97.31.64.32.

Ferries Vedettes run Sauzon-Quiberon (July to mid-Sep, 30 mins, 3 times a day).

Beaches The closest beaches to Sauzon are at: The sandy isthmus to Pte des Poulains and the beach at the head of Ster Vras. See also Le Palais.

EATING ASHORE

Restaurants Almost all the eating places line the Quai Guerveur on the west side of the harbour. There is always something interesting on the water (or mud) at which to gaze – unless you are looking into your beloved's limpid pools – and some places have stunning views to seaward.
- Hôtel du Phare is one such, where from the Terrace restaurant, shaded by bright yellow parasols, you can look across the rim of your glass to the

Anchorage east of the harbour entrance

Pte des Poulains
light house

Drying inner
harbour

Avant port
visitors' moorings

Le Gareau
beacon

Pen Prad
small local boats

Sauzon, looking NW

Quiberon peninsula or peer into the inner light-house. The food is good, too! Menus 90-200FF. Book on 02.97.31.60.36 or get there very early.
- L'Abri-côtier. Tel 02.97.31.60.50. Seafood specialities and Café-Bar.
- Café de la Cale. Tel 02.97.31.65.74. More seafood in a pleasant, sheltered corner. Next door to:
- Le Comptoir. Tel 02.97.31.62.81. Specialising in mussels; 85FF menu.
- Roz Avel, good fish restaurant in rue de l'Eglise (behind the church). Tel 02.97.31.61.48.
- Le Contre Quai, rue St Nicolas. *Une très bonne table*. Tel 02.97.31.60.60. Moving out of Sauzon:
- Le Cardinal is an upmarket *** hotel overlooking the outer moorings. Tel 02.97.31.61.60.

SHOPPING

Market day Thursday morning.

Banks Crédit Agricole, Quai Guerveur, Sauzon.

NAVIGATIONAL MATTERS

Charts AC 2353 (1:75,000) shows very little detail. SHOM 7142 has a 1:7,500 inset of Sauzon.

Approaches and pilotage Sauzon is 1·6M ESE of Pointe des Poulains lighthouse on the NW tip of the island. There are no unmarked hazards in the offing. Off Pointe du Cardinal the key feature is Le Gareau, an unlit green masonry beacon. 250 m ENE of it is the

waypoint (47°22´·88N 03°12´·73W) in about 12 metres of water.

Tides Use time and height differences for Le Palais, 4M to the ESE.

Tidal streams reach a knot or so off the NW end of the island, but are slight in the approach.

Access is at all tides and in all weathers to the anchorage, outer moorings and avant port where yachts can remain afloat in 1·5m. Shelter is good except in strong winds from N to E, including the *vent solaire*, when swell enters the Avant Port. The inner harbour dries about 1·6m to 2m in the first 250m where most of the moorings lie. Access is about HW±1½, depending on draught, under-keel clearance, springs/neaps and how far south you plan to go.

QG   Fl.R 4s

Inner harbour, looking NE. Visitors' moorings are within the pecked line

Chapter 4

Avant port, looking south past moorings into the inner harbour. The vedette Gourinis *is in the foreground*

HARBOUR

Bureau du Port Quai Guerveur, 56360 Belle Île. Tel/Fax 02.97.31.63.40. HM M. Kerignard. VHF Ch 09. Hours in season, daily 0900-1230 & 1700-2000; closed Sun. Weather forecasts are posted daily. Launderette. Showers: 0800-1230 & 1600-2030; 12FF.

Fuel None.

The harbour is in three parts:

a. An outer area where there are moorings and an anchorage.

b. The avant port, 47°22′·53N 03°12′·93W enclosed by a west and an east mole, each with a squat light tower, Fl G 4s and Fl R 4s, respectively. Here yachts can stay afloat on Øs.

c. A drying inner harbour enclosed by moles, full of moorings and extending 5 cables inland. The entrance is 20m wide, marked by a taller light tower, QG, on the short west mole.

From the waypoint the ☆ Fl G 4s and ☆ QG are in transit 205°, with 3½ cables to run. You can see through the avant port into the inner harbour and creek beyond, with the village to starboard.

Visitors have four options for anchoring or mooring – from seaward:

a. Anchorage. Outside, east of the harbour entrance, anchor in 4-6m.

b. Outer moorings. 22 white buoys, of which Nos 1-15 are Øs, lie outside the harbour on the west side; those numbered 16-22 are rented by locals. Anchoring prohibited.

c. Avant port moorings. Inside the avant port on the west side in 1·5m there are 9 white Øs on which yachts moor fore-and-aft, usually rafted up; no multihulls. Caution: close inshore of these Øs is a drying ledge, marked at its southern end by a yellow SPM perch.

Note: The vedette "Gourinis" berths about 3 times daily, July to mid-September, on a pontoon inside the west mole; keep clear.

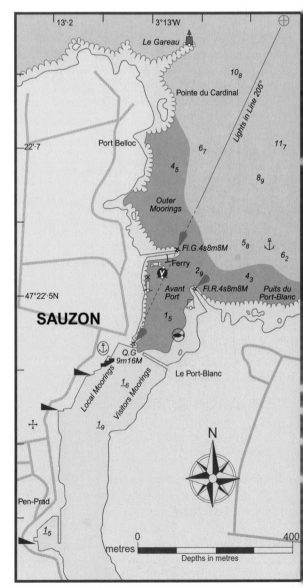

Only fishing boats and locals moor on the east side. Anchoring prohibited.

d. Inner harbour, drying moorings (the bottom is mainly level mud; firm enough for legs). Rule of thumb: Visitors occupy the east side on red buoys; locals are on the west side on green buoys. Thus on the east side there are 41 red ⚓s for fore-and-aft mooring. On the west side there are 60 green fore-and-aft mooring buoys and 46 quayside berths for locals only. Exception to every rule: also on the east side, nearest to the entrance, there are 12 green fore-and-aft mooring buoys for locals. In the S part of the creek, between the last line of moorings and Pen-Prad Basin, up to 80 boats can dry out at anchor.

Tariff Daily rates for LOA bands, ⚓s: 7-8·5m = 50FF; 8·5-10m = 60FF; 10-11·5m =

Le Gareau SHM bn

Outer moorings, west side, looking north

70FF; 11·5-13m = 80FF; >13 and multihulls = 90FF.
At anchor in drying area only: <8·5m = 20FF; 8·5m-11·5m = 30FF; >11·5m and multihulls = 40FF.

NAUTICAL NEEDS

Sauzon has no facilities for boat repairs; see also Le Palais. La Trinité and Crouesty both have far better facilities than Belle Île.

AND FINALLY ... A WORD OR TWO ABOUT STER WENN

This narrow cleft in the rocks has become over-popularised and a visit by boat may not appeal. A 3km bike ride from Sauzon is always a good starter, so that you can make up your own mind. For ordinary mortals it is definitely a fair weather anchorage, whatever you may read about riding out north-westerly gales within its narrow rocky confines.

The sailing directions and SHOM chart 7142 are more than adequate, but the following is a quick summary. Arrange yourself a spell of settled weather with minimal swell.

From Sauzon get round Pointe des Poulains, **outside** the north and west cardinal buoys. From the latter a track of 136° (OK, call it southeast) will get you to Stêr Vras, the main inlet, a mile and a half ahead. When close, you may notice the golf course to port and bird sanctuary to starboard, with a large hotel further south. Enter Stêr Vras, shunning the offliers on its northern side. As you come abeam the 5th hole (truly) to the north, Ster Wenn opens up to starboard and in you go! Anchor where space and other boats permit, taking a stern line ashore; there are some rings in the rocky sides.

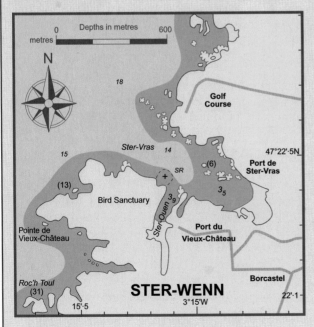

STER-WENN

PORT HALIGUEN

Launderette

Capitainerie annex

Visitors' pontoon

Vieux Port

Main Capitainerie

Fuel

Port Haliguen, looking west

Port Haliguen, or Hooligan as some illiterate Brits call it, is a straightforward place – noticeably so if you've just fought your way out of innermost Le Palais.
From within Quiberon Bay make for the harbour entrance;
no pilotage worthy of the name need trouble you,

unless you are rounding the Quiberon peninsula. Inside the harbour entrance turn 90° starboard and berth on either side of the **V** pontoon on your starboard bow.

Unsurprisingly Haliguen is a long-standing favourite with many Brits due to its sheltered position at the west end of Quiberon Bay, easy access, pleasant surroundings and good beaches. Get the bikes out asap, because you need them just to pedal round to the Capitainerie, even more so to reach the little village and the fleshpots of Quiberon beyond.

TOURISM

Tourist Office There is no Tourist Office in Haliguen, although the main Capitainerie keeps a

few tourist brochures. In Quiberon the Tourist Office is at 14 rue Verdun. Tel 02.97.50.07.84. Open in season Mon-Sat 0900-1230 & 1330-1930; Sun/Hols 0900-1230 & 1500-1900.

What to see/do Visit (free) one of the famous canning plants where sardines, tuna, anchovy, fish soups and mackerel, inter alia, find their way into tins. One such is La Belle Iloise, Zone Artisanale Plein Ouest; NW of the station, off rue d'Armorique de Kerné, close to the cemetery! Guided tours, Mon-Sat 0900-1130 & 1400-1800.

The rugged west coast of the peninsula, about 8km from the south to the narrowest point, is ideal for cycling or walking (bus back?). Small coves, jagged cliffs and open spaces abound.

Quiberon is on the edge of Mégalithic country; see the first page of this chapter for details.

Bus Presqu'ile Transport runs about 6 buses per day, Jul/Aug, from Port Maria to the N end of the peninsula (6FF).

Railway A special train, Le Tire-bouchon (corkscrew), links Quiberon station 02.97.50.07.07, near the church, to Auray, Jul-Sep; thence TGV takes 35hrs to Paris. *Pour éviter les bouchons* = to avoid the bottle-necks/traffic-jams!

Taxis Tel 02.97.50.41.41; 02.97.50.15.52; 02.97.50.24.30; 02.97.50.19.09.

Bike hire
- Le Long des Quais, Port Haliguen. Tel 02.97.30.45.70.
- Cyclomar, place Hoche, Quiberon. Tel 02.97.50.26.00. Bikes, scooters, mopeds.
- Cycles Loisirs, 3 rue Victor Golvan, Quiberon. Tel 02.97.50.10.69.

Car hire Tel 02.97.50.21.92 in season.

Ferries 7 daily trips from Quiberon (Port Maria) to Le Palais, Belle Île (45 mins). Vedettes run Quiberon-Sauzon (July to mid-Sep, 30 mins, 3 times a day). Also trips to Houat and Hoëdic.

Airport (airstrip really, just south of the marina). Flying club Tel 02.97.50.11.05. Have a French flying lesson or just take a *promenade aérienne*.

Beaches The nearest are Plage de Kermorvan and Plage de Castéro, immediately north of the marina; there are more further up the east side of the peninsula. The west side of the peninsula is rocky with low cliffs except at the north end where there are more beaches. South of the marina, choose from Plages du Porigo, du Fort Neuf, de l'Aérodrome and du Congeul. There is a huge, crowded beach, La Grande Plage, at Port Maria (Quiberon).

EATING ASHORE

Restaurants
- Crêperie-Restaurant du Vieux Port, 44 rue Surcouf, Haliguen. Tel 02.97.50.01.56. Jean-Marc and team. Ivy clad house tucked away behind the Vieux Port. Open 1200-1500 and 1900-2200. Eat in the flower garden or by a log fire. Ever popular with French and Brits alike.
- Le Relax. From the ❤ pontoon walk the coastal path north for 5 cables. (The blue neon sign is conspic at night). 1200-1400 and 1900-2200. Menus 78-190FF. Tel 02.97.50.12.84. Sea views.
- La Pêcherie (below Hotel Port Haliguen, in main square). Menus 98-220FF.

In Quiberon/Port Maria
- L'Ancienne Forge, 20 rue de Verdun. Tel 02.97.50.18.64. Just above the Tourist Office and set back from the road. Peaceful charm. Seafood menus 82-168FF.

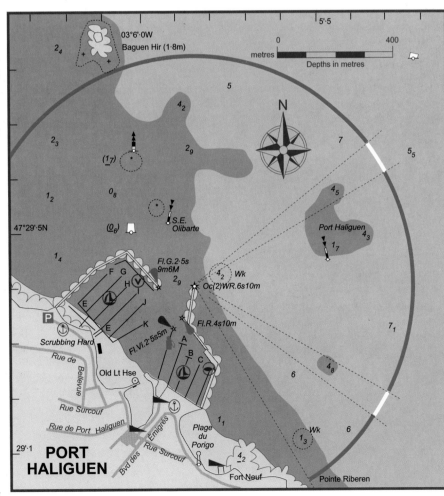

La Teignouse lighthouse, looking NW

- La Criée, 11 quai de l'Océan. Tel 02.97.30.53.09. Eat the morning's catch from 89FF.
- Le Jules Verne, 1 bld de Hoëdic, NW corner of Port Maria harbour. Tel 02.97.30.55.55. Yellow sun awning. Seafood and lobster specialities. Menus 90-345FF. Closed Wed lunch.

SHOPPING

Essential foods are available from a small *épicerie/alimentation* near the root of 'G' pontoon. A wider choice is on offer at a similar shop on the SE corner of Le Vieux Port. Close by, the Café du Midi sells bread and some English newspapers in season. For more serious shopping walk or cycle up the hill on rue de Port Haliguen, towards Quiberon. After 600 metres the Casino Supermarket is on your left. Tel 02.97.50.07.67. Open 0830-2000 Mon-Sat; 0900-1230 Sun.

In Quiberon's rue Verdun (the main street) Spar and Comod supermarkets are respectively uphill and downhill of the Tourist Office. Intermarché is just north of the railway station; open 0830-2000 in summer.

Markets Haliguen, main square, Wed mornings in Jul/Aug. Quiberon, Saturday mornings.

Banks In Quiberon.

NAVIGATIONAL MATTERS

Charts AC 2353 (1:75,000) covers Haliguen and the whole of Quiberon Bay. Haliguen is also on the very edge of AC 2352. SHOM 7141 (1:20,000)

Mildly disconcerting when your waypoint (NE Teignouse buoy) is removed for a bottom scrub

Château Turpault at south end of Quiberon peninsula, looking west

covers Haliguen and La Trinité, with details of the Chaussée and Passage de la Teignouse and Passage du Béniguet. SHOM 7032 (1:50,000) covers from Lorient to La Trinité, including Île de Groix and Belle Île.

Approaches and Pilotage If approaching from within Quiberon Bay, there are no uncharted hazards except a large, unlit, rusty white mooring buoy (shown NE of the harbour entrance on the chartlet); this could hurt you. By day go straight to the harbour entrance 47°29′·40N 03°06′·00W. At night go to the waypoint 47°29′·80N 03°05′·00W, so as to approach on 240°, in the white sector of the ☆ Oc (2) WR 6s.

From the SE, ie between La Teignouse light house and Quiberon Sud SCM light buoy, it is more direct to approach on 303° in the other white sector (299°-307°) of the same light.

If rounding Quiberon peninsula from the NW, or arriving from Belle Île or from south of Houat and Hoëdic, the simplest route by day or night is via the Passage de la Teignouse which is wide, well buoyed and lit.

From the NW, by day only, there are at least three short cuts through Chaussée de la Teignouse which the more experienced navigator may work out for him/herself. These are briefly:

a. Le Pouilloux SCM buoy–Les Trois Pierres NCM beacon–SCM and ECM perches rounding Roc'h er Vy–ECM perch off En Toul Bihan– harbour entrance. This is the shortest route, saving 3M+ against Passage de la Teignouse. It requires

SHOM 7141, good visibility, moderate sea state and precise pilotage at close quarters with rocks. Take care; if unhappy, do not persist.

b. Le Pouilloux SCM buoy–Basse Cariou WCM buoy–then east, towards NE Teignouse SHM light buoy, but turning short onto NNE to track through Passage de la Teignouse.

c. Le Pouilloux SCM buoy–Goué Vaz Nord NCM buoy–then northeast to pick up Passage de la Teignouse; this is a minor variation on route (b).

Landmarks The Quiberon peninsula, when first sighted (especially from the NW), looks like clumps of trees growing out of the water – they are rocks! At the SW tip, on Beg el Lan, Château Turpault is conspicuous, gaunt and lonely. La Teignouse light house is also distinctive, a squat white tower perched on a rocky base and topped by a slimmer white tower with red lantern. Quiberon's large and conspicuous church is in transit 246° with Port Haliguen's entrance.

Tides HW Port Haliguen at neaps is 15 mins after, and at springs 20 mins before, HW Brest. LWs are 10 mins neaps, or 15 mins springs, before LW Brest.

MHWS is 5·2m, MLWS 0·7m; MHWN is 4·1m, MLWN 2·0m.

Tidal streams reach 3 knots in the Passage de la Teignouse and 2 knots in Quiberon Bay. SHOM Tidal stream atlas (558-UJA: Penmarc'h to Noirmoutier) has a large scale inset of Quiberon Bay.

Access At all tides and all weathers.

Anchorage No anchoring in harbour. Some of the beaches up the east side of the peninsula are suitable for anchoring to swim or picnic. Oyster beds start to proliferate at the northern end.

HARBOUR AND MARINA

Capitainerie BP 15, 56170 Quiberon. Tel 02.97.50.20.56; Fax 02.97.50.50.50. VHF Ch 09. HM P Dubois. The main office is on the east side of Le Vieux Port; an annex in the west basin deals with routine yachting matters. If planning to enter the wet basin at Le Palais, gate opening times are posted here. Hours in season, Mon-Sat 0830-1230 & 1330-2000; Sun 0900-1200 & 1400-1900. Weather forecasts are posted daily. Haliguen marina is run by Sagemor who also run La Trinité, Crouesty and some smaller marinas in the Golfe du Morbihan.

Showers next to Capitainerie: 0800-1230 & 1630-2130. 12FF.

The harbour is in 3 sections:
a. East basin (pontoons A-D), aka Port Haliguen I; mostly local boats. Fuel at end of central jetty (see below). Workshops, boatyards and engineering facilities in this area.
b. Le Vieux Port dries and is used by small fishing boats.
c. West basin (pontoons E-K, plus V for ❷), aka Port Haliguen II; some marine retailers.

Tariff Daily rates for LOA bands, first figure is Apr, May, Sep; second Jun-Aug:
7-8·5m = 60/100FF; <10m = 80/130FF; <11·5m = 90/150FF; <14m = 110/190FF.

Fuel At outer end of the jetty with ☆ Fl Vi 2·5s. H24 by French bank card, or call VHF Ch 09 for foreign cards/cash 0900-1145 & 1400-1700.

Launderette Laverie on west side of Vieux Port; open 0800-2100.

NAUTICAL NEEDS

Chandlery & repairs
- ATOL Chantier Naval, Port Haliguen II. Tel 02.97.30.45.45.
- Loc'Haliguen Marine, Port Haliguen II. Tel 02.97.30.40.81. Perkins, Lombardini and outboards.
- Kergroix, Port Haliguen II. Tel 02.97.50.07.16. Chandlery.
- Kergroix Boatyard at the St Pierre-Quiberon industrial area. Tel 02.97.30.92.70.
- Cooperative Maritime, 2-4 bld de Hoëdic, Port-Maria. Tel 02.97.50.07.75. Chandlery.
- Librairie de Port-Maria, 1 quai de l'Océan. Tel 02.97.50.01.43. SHOM chart agent.

PORT MARIA
Except in emergency keep away from this harbour. It is shallow and hectic with ferries/vedettes.

Large unlit mooring buoy; marina in background, looking SW

The drying Vieux Port

Market-place

Launderette

Fl.R 4s

Oc(2)WR 6s

Fl.G 2·5s

Entrance to Vieux Port with statue of a fisherman looking seaward – or at the other statue?

La Trinité, looking ENE with the Golfe du Morbihan in the top right

Kerisper Bridge

Visitors' pontoon

Capitainerie and fish market

Fuel

LA TRINITÉ

La Trinité has been described as the Atlantic Mecca for the racing fraternity, a description which might well be contested by La Rochelle. It matters not because only a faintly racy air prevails and cruising yachtsmen need not be off put. The bonus is a large range of engineering support facilities (see below). Sailing in all its forms has long since overtaken fishing as the prime water activity at La Trinité, but do keep clear of the extensive oyster beds both in the river/harbour and outside in the NW corner of Quiberon Bay.

TOURISM

Tourist Office is behind the Capitainerie, next to La Criée (fishmarket) all housed under one pyramid-style slate roof, so beloved by the French. Môle Loïc Caradec, BP 46, 56470 La Trinité. Tel 02.97.55.72.21; Fax 02.97.55.78.07. e-mail: tourisme@ot-trinite-sur-mer.fr Internet: www.ot-trinite-sur-mer.fr Hours in season Mon-Sat 0900-1900; Sun/Hols 1000-1300 & 1400-1900.

What to see/do La Trinité is close to the heart of Mégalithic country – see the opening pages of this chapter for details – and the Carnac alignments are an easy bike ride away. The town itself is crowded with tourists and is a little short on charm and character. It is a base rather than a must-visit place.

If the Cabin Boy/Powder Monkeys feel like a little Swallows and Amazons exploration, a dinghy trip beyond Kerisper bridge up the River Crac'h is fun. The upper reaches mostly dry so go up on the flood, return on the ebb having enjoyed a picnic or banyan. On the wall by the inner end of the ❷ pontoon is an air clearance gauge calibrated for Kerisper bridge (11m).

Buses run from La Trinité to Auray and Vannes or south to Quiberon; bus stop is at the marina.

Railway A special train, Le Tire-bouchon (corkscrew), links Quiberon station 02.97.50.07.07, near the church, to Auray, Jul-Sep; thence TGV takes $3\frac{1}{2}$hrs to Paris. *Pour éviter les bouchons* = to avoid the bottle-necks/traffic-jams!

Taxis Tel 02.97.55.72.87; 02.97.55.73.18.

Bike hire

- ABC Location, 42 cours des Quais.
  Tel 02.97.30.10.80. Bikes and canoes.
- Bruno Gouzerh, 20 cours des Quais.
  Tel 02.97.55.73.15. Bikes and scooters.
- AA Triniloc, 35 cours des Quais.
  Tel 02.97.30.10.00. Scooters.

Car hire At Auray, or ask at Tourist Office.

Beaches South of the harbour on the west bank are Plages du Port, de la Vanneresse, de Port Biren and at Pointe de Kerbihan. Round this point, towards Carnac are Plages de Kervillen, Men Du and Beaumer. Carnac has the well-populated Grande Plage stretching along the front.

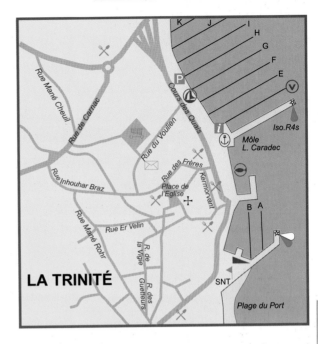

LA TRINITÉ

EATING ASHORE

Restaurants roughly from south to north:
- L'Arrosoir, rue du Men Dû (at south end of the quays next to the Mairie). Tel 02.97.30.13.58. No set menus. Good views from the terrace across the harbour.
- L'Azimut, 1 rue du Men Dû. Tel 02.97.55.71.88. Menus 98-188FF. Pour les gourmands.
- L'Ecailler, 41 cours des Quais, opposite K pontoon. Tel 02.97.55.83.73. Menus 128-245FF. Amex. Small and civilised.
- L'Ostréa, cours des Quais, opposite K pontoon. Tel 02.97.55.73.23. Menus 82-168FF. Good view down harbour from 1st floor terrace restaurant.

- Le Commerce Hotel-restaurant, 4 route de Carnac (behind L'Ostréa). Tel 02.97.55.72.36. Menus 99-160FF. More traditional establishment.
- Le Petit Lougre pizzeria, 8 route de Carnac (next to Le Commerce). Tel 02.97.55.71.63. Menus 49-95FF. Cheap and cheerful.
- Le Surcouf, at the W end of Kerisper bridge. Tel 02.97.55.73.59. Really good food at extremely reasonable prices. Crowded with locals, so essential to book in season; or eat moules at the bar.

SHOPPING

A Comod Supermarket is a short way up rue du Voulien, the turning opposite the end of 'F' pontoon. Tel 02.97.55.75.15. Open Mon-Sat 0800-2000; Sun 0800-1300 & 1700-2000. There is another and better supermarket at the south end of the town near the Mairie.

Markets Tues and Fri mornings in Place du Marché, next to Comod. Daily fishmarket on the quay and in La Criée, behind the Capitainerie.

Banks The usual, in and around Place du Marché, rue du Voulien and cours des Quais.

Front leading mark, Q WRG

Front leading mark 347° blends well with background

Rear leading mark 347° is also hard to see by day

NAVIGATIONAL MATTERS

Charts AC 2353 (1:75,000) covers La Trinité and the whole of Quiberon Bay. La Trinité is also on the western edge of AC 2358 (1:25,000). SHOM 7032 (1:50,000) covers from Lorient to La Trinité, including Île de Groix and Belle Île. SHOM 7141 (1:20,000) covers La Trinité and Port Haliguen, with details of the Chaussée and Passage de la Teignouse and Passage du Béniguet.

Approaches If approaching from within Quiberon Bay, there are no uncharted hazards. If rounding Quiberon peninsula from the NW, or arriving from Belle Île or from south of Houat and Hoedic, the simplest route by day or night is via the Passage de la Teignouse which is wide, well buoyed and lit.

By day only, there are at least three short cuts through Chaussée de la Teignouse which the more experienced navigator may work out for himself. For an outline see Port Haliguen.

Pilotage By day and night make good the waypoint 47°33´·38N 03°00´·30W which is

3 cables SE of Petit Trého PHM light buoy. It is also within the white sectors of both the front leading light, Q WRG, on Pte de Kernevest, and of the N Oc WRG 4s at the head of the river.

By day in average visibility you can safely navigate the River Crac'h by buoy-hopping the first 4 unlit PHM buoys and then following the lit lateral buoys which mark the inner bend.

At night the approach is in two stages using long and short range navigational lights:

a. At longer range track inbound 347° on the leading lights, Q WRG and Q. Be aware of unlit marks and dangers to either side. Leave this leading line well before Mousker rock.

b. When about 5 cables from the waypoint, jink some 30° to port to intercept the white sector (346°-348°) of the ☆ Oc WRG 4s, which only becomes visible against shore lights at lesser ranges than the leading lights. Thereafter track 347° up-river within the white sector.

At the river bend alter onto 297° tracking within the white sector (293·5°-300·5°) of a second Dir ☆, Oc (2) WR 6s, towards the entrance to the harbour proper.

Between Nos 5 and 12 light buoys, by day / night, alter starboard 340° for the jetty head, ☆ Iso R 4s, and ❶ pontoon.

Daymarks The shoreline consists of white, sandy bays backed by extensive pine woods. There are no obvious landmarks and both leading marks are hard to pick out. However before reaching the

Nearing the conspicuous Estacade and marina beyond

waypoint, the usual forest of masts will be seen up-river where the distinctive Kerisper bridge at the head of the marina will confirm your suspicions that you are indeed approaching the right harbour; it was built in 1901 and apes the steel skeleton of the Eiffel Tower.

Directional light, 347°, at head of river

Tides HW La Trinité at neaps is 20 mins after, and at springs 20 mins before, HW Brest. LWs are 5 mins neaps, or 15 mins springs, before LW Brest.

 MHWS is 5·4m, MLWS 0·8m; MHWN is 4·3m, MLWN 2·1m.

Tidal streams reach 3 knots in the Passage de la Teignouse and 2 knots in Quiberon Bay. SHOM Tidal stream atlas (558-UJA: Penmarc'h to Noirmoutier) has a large scale inset of Quiberon Bay.

Access At all tides and all weathers.

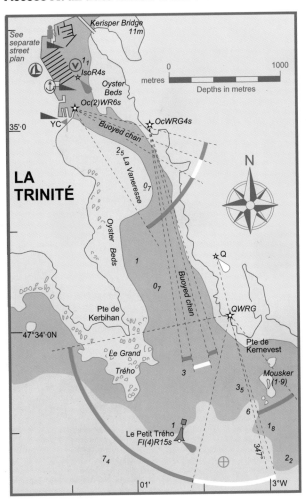

Shelter is very good. La Vaneresse, a large drying mudflat off the west shore immediately down-river of the harbour, affords considerable shelter before half-tide against southerly winds, but when covered quite a lot of movement can be felt on the Ⓥ pontoon.

Anchorage No anchoring in harbour. Formula 1 racing multihulls of semi-futuristic design are usually moored just south of the Môle Loïc Caradec.

HARBOUR AND MARINA

Capitainerie, at the head of the Ⓥ pontoon. Tel 02.97.55.71.49; Fax 02.97.55.86.89. VHF Ch 09. HM J-J Prevot. Hours in season, daily 0800-1300 & 1400-2000. Weather forecasts are posted daily. La Trinité marina is run by Sagemor who also run Port Haliguen, Crouesty and some smaller marinas in the Golfe du Morbihan. The harbour is in 4 sections, from south to north:

a. South Basin (pontoons A & B); mostly sailing school boats.

b. Fishing Basin: mostly small fishing boats.

c. Central Basin: The Môle Loïc Caradec, ☆ Iso R 4s, is theoretically C pontoon but is actually a substantial estacade, through which the tide runs (care needed). Pontoon D, next one to the north, is for Ⓥ; E-K are for berth holders.

d. North Basin: Pontoons L-Q. Workshops, boatyards and engineering facilities are nearby. The rest of the harbour is full of moorings, leaving little or no space for anchoring.

Showers in Capitainerie: same hours; 12FF. A good public loo in the same building is H24.

Tariff Daily rates for LOA bands, first figure is Apr, May, Sep; second Jun-Aug:

7-8·5m = 60/100FF; 8·5-10m = 80/130FF; 10-11·5m = 90/150FF; 11·5-14m = 110/190FF.

Fuel By the boat-hoist, between ends of K and L pontoons. H24 by French bank card, or 1000-1300 & 1600-1930 for foreign cards/cash.

Launderette cours des Quais, opposite K pontoon: Open Mon/Tues 0800-1300 & 1500-2000; Wed-Sun 0800-1330 & 1500-2030.

NAUTICAL NEEDS

Chandlery & repairs There are 3 main areas where these retailers/services are located:
a. La Trinité. (Along the quayside; up and behind the Place du Marché).
- U-Ship, cours des Quais. Tel 02.97.55.72.07. Chandlery.
- Marine-Ship, 5 cours des Quais. Tel 02.97.55.79.74. Chandlery.
- Quai Ouest, 36/7 cours des Quais. Tel 02.97.55.80.80. Chandlery. SHOM chart agent.
- Sedan, 42 cours des Quais. Tel 02.97.55.78.06. Electrical and Electronic equipment.
- Rioux-Nautique, 30 rue du Voullien. Tel 02.97.55.72.43. Volvo, Evinrude, Zodiac.

- Le Cuillier, 6 rue Inouarh Braz. Tel 02.97.55.82.01. Chandlery, marine supplies, SHOM Agent.
- Delta Voiles, 2 rue de Carnac. Tel 02.97.55.80.77. Sailmaker.

b. ZA (Zone Artisanale) de Kermarquer, 1·5km NW of Kerisper bridge.
- Sitel, ZA de Kermarquer. Tel 02.97.55.88.39. Electrical and Electronic equipment.
- Technique Gréement, ZA de Kermarquer. Tel 02.97.55.83.02. Rigging, spars. Lewmar, Harken.
- Technique Voile, ZA de Kermarquer. Tel 02.97.55.77.26. Sailmaker.

b. ZA de Kerran, across Kerisper bridge towards St Philibert.
- Top Loisirs, ZA de Kerran. Tel 02.97.55.09.65. Boatyard. Mechanical engineering.
- Kervilor, Anse de Mané Braz, St Philibert. Tel 02.97.55.00.26. Boatyard. Yanmar. Perkins.
- Kyrran-Services, ZA de Kerran. Tel 02.97.55.13.94. Engines, all makes.
- Technologie Marine, ZA de Kerran. Tel 02.97.55.14.98. Shipwright (GRP and wood), boatyard.

Masts and the Kerisper Bridge are the most conspicuous features

CROUESTY

Quiberon Bay lies to seaward and the Golfe du Morbihan is just inland, around the Pointe de Port Navalo, with Crouesty almost at the end of the crab-like claw which is Presqu'île de Rhuys. Sounds like a quote from a tourist brochure, but actually it is geographic fact. Coupled to this handy situation, Crouesty marina and associated "village" are amongst the most successful of such combinations in France. The place is alive and humming, with even a couple of night-clubs.

TOURISM

Tourist Office is at the NE end of Darse 4 in the Maison du Port, BP 47, 56640 Arzon. www.crouesty.com, e-mail: crouesty@crouesty.com. Tel 02.97.53.69.69; Fax 02.97.53.76.10. Hours in season Mon-Sat 0900-1200 & 1400-1900; Sun/Hols 1000-1300.

What to see/do This is a good place for a little light walking. You might like to devise your own circuit to include the Chapelle du Croisty at the SW corner of the marina, where a Pardon de la Mer is held on 15 August every year; the Tumulus at Petit Mont (from Jun-Sep there are 5/6 visits per day, 3 person minimum, 20FF adult; or make your own arrangements) and also enjoy the fabulous views. Carry on round the coast to Port Navalo light house and the attractive fishing harbour and bay. For the smaller kids there is a one hour ride round Arzon in Le Petit Train with commentary; their French may be better than yours? There is an 18 hole golf-course at Kerners, just NE of Arzon.

Further afield you can bicycle round the southern shores of the Golfe du Morbihan, particularly for bird watching in the nature reserves. You are bound to bump into some of the lesser known megaliths along the way and climb the Butte de César (politely translated as Caesar's Hillock) from which JC watched his fleet defeat one of the revolting local tribes in the 1st century BC.

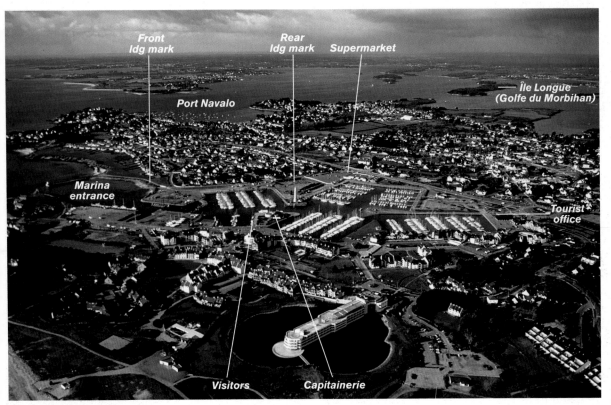

Crouesty marina, looking NW

Start of the approach channel, coming from the north

Go further east along the Presqu'Ile de Rhuys to the C13 Château du Suscinio, built on marshes at the sea's edge. Once a proud favourite of the Dukes of Brittany it is now ruined, but none the less impressive.

Bus Coach service (CTM Vannes) runs from Port Navalo, via Crouesty/Arzon, to Vannes, 30km.

Railway Nearest station is at Vannes, qv.

Taxis Tel 02.97.53.81.95; 02.97.53.94.06.

Ferry A vedette "Lez V" runs in Jul/Aug, 0930-1830, from Port Navalo across to Locmariaquer.

Bike hire
- Abbis Location, 9-11 quai des Voiliers, at marina. Tel 02.97.53.64.64. 600 bikes!
- Cycles de L'Océan, 50 rue Centrale, Arzon. Tel 02.97.53.74.19. M-S 1000-2000. From 60FF/day.

Car hire Ask at Tourist Office.

Beaches Plage du Fogeo, due south of the marina, is the nearest and longest; others lie further away to the SE. To the west there are two sandy coves on the way to Port Navalo.

EATING ASHORE

Restaurants The following eating places are along the marina quayside (quai des Voiliers):
- La Marina, Tel 02.97.53.98.92. Menus 88-198FF. Seafood, grills, bar, pizzeria.
- La Transat, Tel 02.97.53.86.76. Menus 60-125FF. Seafood, glacier, bar, brasserie.
- Le P'tit Crabe, Tel 02.97.53.89.56. Menus 99-169FF. Seafood, covered terrace.

- L'Huitrière, Tel 02.97.53.91.95. No prizes for guessing the menu!
- Le Yacht, above Capitainerie. Tel 02.97.53.96.08. Menus 65-90FF. Simple fare, good ambience.

Away from the marina, try:
- Le Grand Largue at Port-Navalo, by the ferry. Tel 02.97.53.71.58. First class seafood in elegant surroundings with fantastic views. Prices to match.
- Auberge de Kerstéphanie, route de Roaliguen, Sarzeau. Tel 02.97.41.72.41. Seafood and log fire.

SHOPPING

Supermarkets
- Intermarché is close north of Darse 2 on the outskirts of Arzon village. Tel 02.97.53.71.12; or
- fax your orders on 02.97.53.74.22. Super U, Tel 02.97.53.83.84, is at the Kerjouanno roundabout, approx. 0·5M ESE of the Tourist Office on D780 to Vannes.

Markets Mon morning Jul/Aug in Crouesty. Tues morning year round in Arzon. Fri morning Easter to Sept. in Port Navalo.

Banks Crédit Agricole in Arzon. Cashpoints on the marina quayside.

NAVIGATIONAL MATTERS

Charts Crouesty is covered by AC 2358 (1:25,000) and by AC 2353 (1:75,000) which also covers the whole of Quiberon Bay. SHOM 6992 (1:10,000) covers the entrance to the Golfe du Morbihan. SHOM 7034 (1:25,000) covers all the Golfe du

No 6 PHM buoy

Shoal ground just off the channel

board with a vertical white stripe (and ☆ Q) which near LW may be partially obscured by the tops of the breakwaters. Note: The same waypoint also applies when approaching the Golfe du Morbihan on the 001° leading line.

The approach channel, dredged to 1·8m, is marked by 4 PHM buoys, 1 PHM perch and 3 SHM buoys, all unlit; it narrows to about 80m at the entrance.

Morbihan. SHOM 7033 (1:50,000) covers from Quiberon to Le Pouliguen, including the south half of Golfe du Morbihan.

Approaches There are no uncharted hazards in the approaches which are straightforward. From the north, if sluicing out of the Golfe du Morbihan on the ebb, expect to ride briefly through tide-rips and overfalls in the vicinity of Basse du Taleg (2·3m), 700m S of Port Navalo light house.

From the SW or from La Trinité keep south of Méaban islet and the offlying rocks.

Pilotage By day and night make good the waypoint (47°32′·04N 02°55′·21W), which is on the 058° leading line and 800m from the first channel buoys. The rear leading mark is easily seen by day. The front leading mark is a red ☐

Daymarks The grey concrete light tower (Q, rear ldg mark) dominates the marina and is easily seen from the SW, but from further S or from the NW it is obscured by higher ground. You may see a small chapel close SE of the breakwater ☆ Fl G 4s, if not too busy avoiding other craft. The Capitainerie's slate-roofed pyramidal building is easily seen, as well it might be.

Tides HW Crouesty at neaps is 30 mins after, and at springs 5 mins before, HW Brest. LWs are 5 mins neaps, or 10 mins springs, before LW Brest.

MHWS is 4·9m, MLWS 0·7m; MHWN is 3·9m, MLWN 1·8m.

Tidal streams reach 4 knots off Port Navalo and set NNW/SSE at 1·1 knots across the approach

Entrance to the marina near low water

Oc(2)R 6s

Fl.G 4s

*Front Rear
058° leading marks, both Q*

Chapter 4

channel to Crouesty. SHOM Tidal stream atlas (558-UJA: Penmarc'h to Noirmoutier) refers.

Access At all tides and all weathers. Near LW do not stray outside the buoyed approach channel (why ever would you?!) because there are drying rocky ledges on both sides.

Shelter is good, except when strong SW to NW winds blow into the marina causing quite a lot of movement on the ❺ pontoons.

Anchorage No space for anchoring in the marina nor outside due to rocky patches.

MARINA

Capitainerie conspicuous on S side beyond ❺ berths. Tel 02.97.53.73.33; Fax 02.97.53.90.22. VHF Ch 09. HM Michel Mergault. Hours in season, daily 0800-2100. Weather forecasts are posted daily. Crouesty marina is run by Sagemor who also run Port Haliguen, La Trinité and some smaller marinas in the Golfe du Morbihan.

Major expansion work has continued throughout 2000 and should be completed for the 2001 season, when there will be 380 extra berths. The work comprises from seaward:
a. To port, just beyond the front leading light, a new basin, Darse Nord, pontoons Q-T;
b. To starboard, opposite Darse Nord, another new basin, Darse Sud, pontoons U-Z;
c. To starboard, just before the Capitainerie, an enlarged Visitors' basin, pontoons V1 and V2;
d. To port, the fuel pontoon has been moved to immediately below the lighthouse; and

e. To port, the pontoons in Darse 2 and 3 have been relaid as I-M, accessed from their W end. The other basins are unchanged, ie on the N side: Darse 1 (pontoons N-P) in front of the light ho; on the S side, Darse 5 (pontoons A-C); and Darse 4 (pontoons D-H) mostly sailing school boats.

Visitors should berth in the visitors' basin (120 berths, but soon gets crowded) or in a vacant berth as arranged with the Capitainerie. There are no longer visitors' pontoons along the south side of the fairway. There is no space for anchoring in or outside the marina.

Tariff Daily rates for LOA bands, first figure is Apr, May, Sep; second Jun-Aug:
7-8·5m = 60/100FF; 8·5-10m = 80/130FF; 10-11·5m = 90/150FF; 11·5-14m = 110/190FF.

Showers are in the Capitainerie and elsewhere: 0800-2130, except Fri 0800-2030; 12FF.

Fuel pontoon is immediately south of the light-house. H24 by French bank card, or office hours if paying by non-French cards/cash.

Launderette at Intermarché supermarket north of Darse 2; Tel 02.97.53.71.12.

NAUTICAL NEEDS

Chandlery & repairs The retailers below are located along the quayside (Le quai des Voiliers):
• Nautiloc, BP 7. Tel 02.97.53.76.57. Chandlery. SHOM chart agent.
• Electronique du Golfe, facing the boat hoist. Tel 02.97.53.75.32. Electrics, heating, refrigeration.
ZA (Zone Artisanale) du Redo, beyond the roundabout at the NE end of the marina, is

Capitainerie

where the following engineering facilities can be found:

- AMC, BP19. Tel 02.97.53.71.30. Boatyard, engine repairs. Volvo, Yanmar, Perkins, Mariner.
- Yachts & Racing. Tel 02.97.53.62.53. Boatyard, electronic repairs.
- Massif Marine. Tel 02.97.53.61.94. Boat and engine repairs. Volvo, Mercury, Zodiac.

- Ets Michel Le Gal, BP 23. Tel 02.97.53.89.40. Engines and hydraulic repairs.
- Chantier naval du Redo, BP 26. Tel 02.97.53.78.70. Wood specialist, GRP, engines, outboards.
- Technique Gréement. Tel 02.97.53.95.02. Rigging, spars.
- North Sails. Tel 02.97.53.78.58. Sailmaker, repairs.

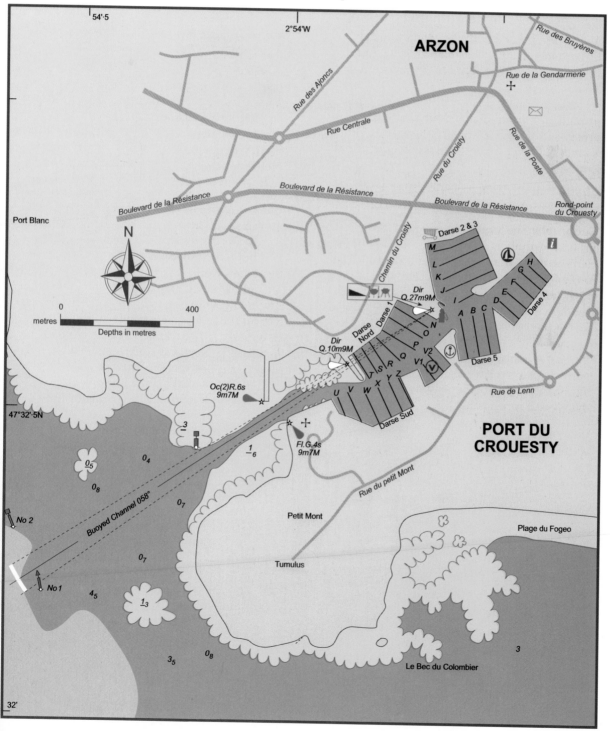

Chapter 4

GOLFE DU MORBIHAN

OK, let's be pedantic for two moments: Golfe du Morbihan is the proper name for this large and delightful inland sea – it *is* a sea, as the tides will constantly remind you! Most people, including this Companion, refer to it simply as the Morbihan (or 'little sea', depending on etymology).

Not to be confused with the Morbihan, the Département whose coastline stretches from Le Pouldu (8M WNW of Lorient) to just south of the Vilaine River.

Semantics apart, this is truly a superb cruising ground and the following thumbnail sketch briefly sets the scene; see also the entries for Vannes (4.7) and Auray (4.8), the two principal towns.

Charts With BA 2358 or SHOM 7034 (both 1:25,000) spread out on the table, read on ...

Geography The Morbihan, roughly 10M wide by 5M north/south, is at least twice the size of Poole Harbour and – dare I say it – far more fun! The Auray River flows in at the western end and the much smaller Noyalo River at the eastern end. The shoreline is to say the least intricate, fretted like the pieces of a gigantic jigsaw puzzle. Throw in a myriad islands, admit the Atlantic Ocean twice a day, stir well with equal amounts of mud and rock and you have a recipe which will stimulate or relax you depending largely on where you happen to be.

Frank Cowper neatly summarises the comparison with Poole Harbour:

'The Morbihan is a sort of rocky Poole Harbour. Instead of mud, however, there is granite mostly. Both can bring the unwary amateur to a full stop, the difference being that the amateur leaves his impression on the mud, while the granite leaves its impression on the amateur, generally too of a rather more permanent character.'

Tidal streams are well documented in the MRNA and on charts. The newcomer to the Morbihan is nevertheless often surprised not only by their speed but more especially by the narrow, jet-like core of the stream, adjacent to relatively still water. For example a boat may drift out of the back waters between Île Longue and Gavrinis, barely making headway; but a few metres out into the fairway, she will be making 7 or 8 knots over the ground.

Yet these powerful streams seem benign, not bent on your destruction. They divide and sweep past a rocky islet, taking the line of least resistance. Back eddies are a useful attribute –

Entrance to the Morbihan, looking NNE

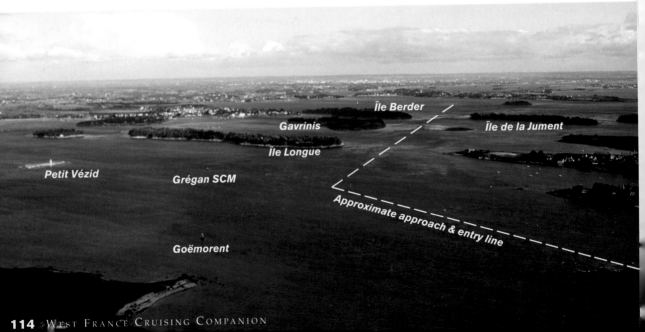

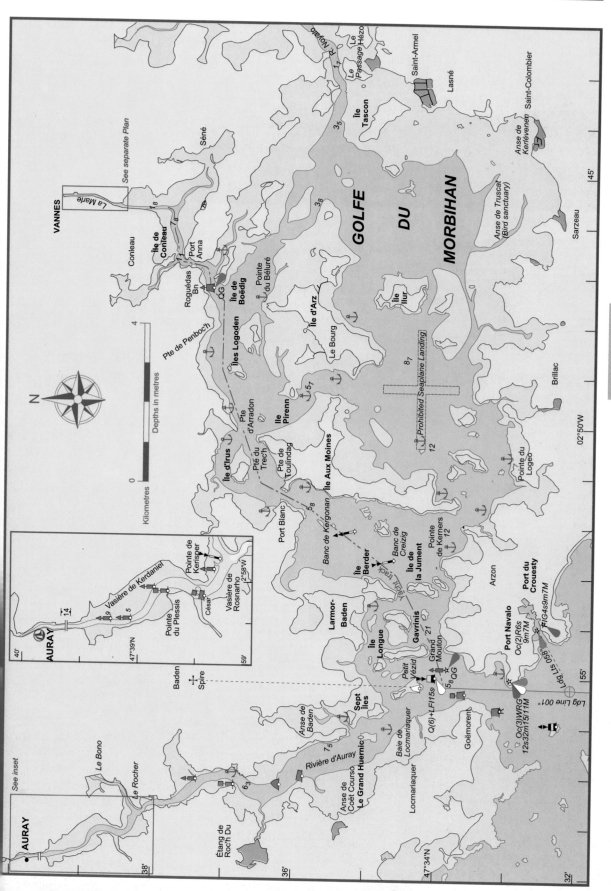

Chapter 4

001° leading marks

Grand Vézid house — Baden church spire, rear mark — Petit Vézid obelisk, front mark

Port Navalo lighthouse

Petit Vézid obelisk Front ldg mark 001° — House on Grand Vézid — GRÉGAN

Grégan SCM beacon, looking NNW

ROGUÉDAS

Roguédas SHM beacon

watch a local boatman row his steady way close round an islet in such an eddy, whilst a boat's length further out your craft is being pushed in the opposite direction.

Approach For a first-time visitor, start at the waypoint 47°32′·04N 02°55′·21W, about a mile south of the entrance proper. This gives you a chance to identify the 001° leading marks: Front is on Petit Vézid islet, a white obelisk which is easily confused with yacht sails; the rear is Baden church spire, 5M north of the waypoint and therefore hard to see in poor visiblity. Once established on the line you are fully prepared for a roller-coaster ride on the flood tide, with Port Navalo light house moving rapidly down your starboard side.

If going to Vannes, pass Navalo no later than local HW –30 mins so as to reach Vannes at about local HW. In any event do not attempt entry against the ebb, unless you know the back-eddies.

Entrance This two-way "plug-hole" is only 700 metres across, through which a mass of water is inexorably accelerated. Expect a few tide-rips and overfalls over the irregular bottom, but above all concentrate on maintaining the leading line, or a little west of it. Unless bound up the Auray River (4.8), bias your track slightly toward Goëmorent PHM beacon tower, then shape a course south of Grégan SCM beacon so as to be well clear of a SHM beacon, QG, marking the rocks of Grand and Petit Mouton, towards which the bulk of the flood stream sets strongly ($6\frac{1}{2}$ knots).

Once past, relax a little and, as you surge away to the NE, check that Île Longue, Gavrinis and Île Berder to port, and to starboard Erlannig and Île de la Jument, are all correctly identified.

The main fairway Many yachts will follow the main fairway as shown on the chartlet, north-eastwards past the Banc de Creizig (small S and N cardinal buoys), leaving to starboard Île aux Moines, the longest island. Nip through the narrows off Pointe de Toulindag, keeping a safe distance from the many vedettes which rush to offload their passengers, sometimes with scant regard for yachts.

More narrows and a tidal gate off Pointe

Petit Vézid front ldg mark   Île Longue   Gavrinis   Île Berder   Île de la Jument

Port Navalo

Port Navalo lighthouse

Port Navalo and Morbihan entrance, looking north

d'Arradon where the fairway bends NE past extensive moorings to the north. It then broadens out and turns eastward past Îles Logoden and Pointe de Penboc'h. Stand on almost to Boëdic WCM buoy before turning NE for Roguédas SHM beacon tower. At this stage, please read the entry for Vannes (4.7) if that is your destination.

The wider scene Whilst piloting yourself north-eastwards in the Morbihan, take note of where three channels lead off into the less frequented parts of this inland sea. When sated by the activity of Vannes, return to these and explore:
a. Eastsoutheast from Boëdic WCM buoy towards Le Passage at the remote eastern end;
b. Southward between Île aux Moines and Île d'Arz thence east; and
c. South around Îles aux Moines, thence NE and east towards Île Ilur.

Whichever route or circuit you take, the waters around the two principal islands are ideal for a row ashore and unspoiled walking and picnics. Peaceful anchorages can be found out of the tide and sheltered from the wind of the day. Most of the bays and inlets along the southern shore of the Golfe are almost full of moorings, but you may still find room to anchor clear of these.

Further east large areas are shallow and unmarked, but navigable with care and sufficient rise of tide. Many islets and rocky outcrops are marked as bird sanctuaries and should be respected. There is a strong away-from-it-all feeling ...

Old working boat among the islands.
This is truly a superb cruising ground

Vannes

Vannes is quite a lively city and the Place Gambetta at the head of the marina is possibly as far as you will get on your first run ashore. It epitomises café life and the serious business of watching the world go by – across the rim of a sparkling glass, no doubt.

When/if you stir yourself, either go NE to walk round the ramparts and the semi-formal flower gardens below, noting of course the much-photographed ancient lavoirs. Or leave by the Port St Vincent, behind you, and meander through the old streets and half-timbered mediaeval buildings. Either way, you will inevitably end up near the Cathédrale St Pierre, towering above the maze of narrow streets and surrounded by charming squares, Place Henri-IV being amongst the best. Pavement artists, buskers, minstrels – they're all here. Pause for refreshment and to recce the evening's eating place, probably in the tiny rue des Halles.

Well that's it for Day One; see below for other touristy distractions ...

The ancient and much photographed wash houses

Gardens and Château de l'Hermine

TOURISM

Tourist Office bears NW a good stone's throw from the Bureau du Port; it is in a half-timbered building, 1 rue Thiers, 56000 Vannes. Tel 02.97.47.24.34; Fax 02.97.47.29.49. Hours: Sep-Jun, Mon-Sat 0900-1200 & 1400-1800, shut Sun; Jul/Aug, Mon-Sat 0900-1900, Sun/Hols 1000-1300 & 1500-1900.

What to see/do Watch a jousting tournament on water (inner marina) usually around 8 August. 20 local teams participate, attempting to knock the other guy off his perch into the water; predictable fun if you have the body mass of a Japanese wrestler.

The annual open-air Jazz Festival is one of Vannes' biggest claims to fame. It is held in the Théâtre de Verdure, first week in August, and more or less takes over the city for 3 or 4 nights.

La Cohue, itself a historic building in front of the cathedral, now houses the Musée de Vannes should you feel in need of some local history, or it's pouring with rain (open Jun-Sep 1000-1800; Oct-May 1000-1200 & 1400-1800). Close by, on the corner of rue des Halles and rue Noe, is the Archaeological Museum – back to Megaliths again, but you can see them all rather more realistically at Carnac. The Tourist Office will fill you in with other cultural delights, but basically stroll around the city and savour its ancient charm.

Or leap on your bike for a pleasant 5 km spin down to Île de Conleau, the place you always sail past without stopping. Stop for a picnic or local lunch and take a look at the anchoring prospects. For a longer spin (10km) in the opposite direction, cross the swing bridge and head SSE on D199 to Séné, not easy to reach by water and atmospheric home, as they say, of the traditional *sinagots* (two-masted, undecked fishing boats in use up to WW2). If energetic, continue to Montsarrac which looks across the River Noyalo to the anchorage off Le Passage.

Bus Nos 23 & 24 buses run from Vannes, via Auray, La Trinité and Carnac, to Quiberon.

Railway The station (Info Tel 08.36.35.35.35) is at the north end of Ave Victor Hugo, a brisk 25 mins walk from the marina, a definite taxi ride if crew-changing. Paris in 3 hours by TGV. Other mainline stops are Bordeaux and Toulouse. Local trains run from Quimper to Redon, via Vannes.

Airport A small airfield is about 12 km north. The nearest commercial airport is at Lorient, qv.

Taxi Tel 02.97.47.40.62; 02.97.54.34.34.

Bike hire Cycles Le Mellec, place de la Madeleine. Tel 02.97.63.00.24.

Car hire

- Avis, place de la Gare. Tel 02.97.47.54.54.
- ADA, 45 bd Ed. Herriot. Tel 02.97.42.59.10.
- ECO , 9 ave de la Marne. Tel 02.97.46.09.08.

Vedettes will take you round the Morbihan with stops at Île aux Moines and Île d'Arz, but this is not to be contemplated unless your own boat is seriously out of commission for a few days!

EATING ASHORE

Restaurants The nearest eating places are roughly behind the Bureau du Port. These include:

- La Saladiere, 36 rue du Port. Tel 02.97.42.52.10. Menus 65-120FF.
- Le Vieux Port, 26 rue du Port. Tel 02.97.47.93.93. Seafood menus at 75 & 82FF.

Pink house and concealed turning

Chapter 4

- L'Atlantique, 16 Place Gambetta, opposite Tourist Office. Tel 02.97.47.05.49. Menus 64-208FF.
- La Table des Gourmets, 6 rueAlexandre Le Pontois. Tel 02.97.47.52.44. Slightly garish red and timber facade, NE out of Place Gambetta. All cards inc Amex.

In Rue des Halles, at the heart of the old Quarter's narrow streets, by the Cathedral:
- La Jonquière, No 9. Tel 02.97.54.08.34. Part of a chain, pleasant and functional. 69-124FF.
- Breizh Café, No 13. Tel 02.97.54.37.41. Cosy, kids, traditional. Menus around 89FF.
- Le Pavé des Halles, No 17. Pre-book 02.97.47.15.96. Small and elegant. Menus 109-215FF.
- L'Epée, 2 rue J Le Brix, near to Monoprix. Tel 02.97.47.10.11. 1st floor, stained glass windows! Traditional and slightly formal. Menus 69-178FF. Closed Wed pm and Sun.

Or for something different, walk from your boat down to the swing bridge for:
- Bayous, route de Conleau. Tel 02.97.63.04.52. Trendy Franco-American jazzy bar-restaurant. A must during the Jazz festival. Menus 59-129FF. Closed Sun and Mon pm.

Waiting pontoon

Swing bridge

Waiting pontoon

Although the swing bridge is operated efficiently and punctually, boats should be prepared for some delays at peak periods. Once through the bridge, you are obliged to motor at the speed of the slowest boat in the convoy, the cut being far too narrow for safe overtaking.

SHOPPING

Supermarkets Both are on the north side of the old city: Monoprix, Place J le Brix. Open 0830-2000. Stoc, rue du Méné, downhill from Monoprix.

Market day Wed and Sat mornings, a bustling friendly market in Place du Poids Public.

Banks All banks. There is a convenient cash dispenser on the north wall of the Bureau du Port.

NAVIGATIONAL MATTERS

Charts Vannes and the whole Golfe du Morbihan are covered by AC 2358 and by the equivalent SHOM 7034, both at 1:25,000.

Pilots North Biscay Pilot (RCC/Imray). Admiralty Bay of Biscay Pilot (NP 22).

Approach and Pilotage See under Golfe du Morbihan for navigation as far as the Roguédas beacon tower. From here avoid cutting the corner northwards into the narrow passage past the pink house (being painted more white than pink in August '99) and Port Anna. At Île de Conleau there is an attractive but very crowded anchorage

Inner basin

Entry gate

Visitors on D & G pontoons

Fuel and boatyard

Near the entry gate the marina dory will usually meet you to ask for LOA and beam; the latter may be the limiting factor in finding a berth for you. If it all gets too difficult, you will simply be told to berth on D or G pontoons.

from the HM at the address below.

At Vannes tidal heights are: MHWS is 3·3m, MLWS 0·5m; MHWN is 2·7m, MLWN 1·0m.

Tidal streams upstream of Roguédas reach 1·1 knots at extreme springs in the narrows, but thereafter are slight.

Access to the marina is by day only, when the 10m wide lock gate is open, ie local HW ±2½. Note: HW −2½ at Vannes just happens to be HW at Port Tudy (Île de Groix). The latter is a French Standard Port, so if you pick up a free set of Port Tudy tide tables, you could save yourself a few calculations. The lock gate shows Ⓡ & Ⓖ lights when shut; when open, usually obvious, there are no lights.

During the 5 hour open period the swing bridge opens on the hour and half-hour, mid-Jun to mid-Sep and at weekends throughout the year. Out of season opening is only on the hour. During the first and final half hours (of the overall 5 hour block), the bridge may open on request Ch 09. During school terms the 1200 opening is at 1150 and the 1700 opening is at either 1650 or 1710.

The bridge operator is in the control tower at the west end of the bridge; he sometimes addresses the assembled fleet by loudspeaker. He can also be contacted by an intercom on the upstream and downstream waiting pontoons.

Outbound boats have priority, but traffic is controlled by R/G/Y lights on the bridge's main pier, as follows: 2 Ⓡ = no passage; 2 Oc Ⓡ = get ready; 2 Ⓖ = Go; 2 Oc Ⓖ = only transit if committed; 1 Ⓨ = unmasted boats may transit.

Anchorage The nearest anchorage is in the vicinity of Île de Conleau, as shown on AC 2358.

MARINA

Bureau du Port is on the west side of the inner basin; Port de Plaisance, La Rabine, 56000 Vannes.

in the creek. Follow the channel east to buoys 5 and 6 where there is a 0·7m patch and the channel turns sharply north, shallowing to 0·9m in places. There will probably be insufficient water for many boats until after HW −3.

Tides HW Vannes at neaps is 2 hrs 20 mins, and at springs 2 hrs, after HW Brest. LWs are 1 hr 25 mins neaps, and 2 hrs springs, after LW Brest. Times of HW become progressively later as one sails NE'wards into the Morbihan; thus HW Vannes occurs 2 hours after HW Port Navalo. Obviously it pays to make use of this moving tidal conveyor belt. Note: Order a free timetable of lock gate opening hours (*Horaire d'ouverture du Bassin*),

Waiting pontoon and bridge, boats leaving

Tel 02.97.54.16.08; Fax 02.97.54.00.47. VHF Ch 09. HM M. J-Y Le Norcy. Open Jul/Aug: Mon-Sat 0800-2100, Sun 0800-1900; Sep-Jun Mon-Fri 0900-1200 & 1330-1800, Sat 0900-1200 & 1400-1800, Sun 0830-1200. Weather forecasts are posted daily. Shelter is excellent.

Tariff Daily rates for selected LOA, in season: 7m = 71FF; 8m = 81FF; 9m = 96FF; 10m = 110FF; 11m = 124FF; 12m = 142FF; 13m = 156FF; 14m = 169FF.

Visitors are often directed willy-nilly by the marina dory to pontoons D and G, beyond the last finger pontoons. Here boats raft up as best they can; in season this is fairly chaotic and less than ideal. It is better to pre-book a vacant finger berth, even 24 hours beforehand (English is spoken in the Bureau du Port), and then to arrive early to stand the best chance of actually getting a slot.

Particularly in season, quarts into pint pots (or metric equivalents) simply will not go!

There are long-standing plans to move the Bureau du Port and all the finger berths, plus pontoon, from the west to the east bank. The inner basin, 99% locals, would not change. Whether Visitors' berthing will improve remains to be seen.

Showers are inside the Bureau du Port, at the back; 10FF. Similar hours to Bureau du Port.

Depth gauge   *Upstream waiting pontoon*   *Traffic lights, not yet illuminated*

Bridge opening and traffic lights

Vannes is a good place for crew-changing: Rail services are very good and the N165 motorway links Brest to Nantes, via Vannes. The N166 is a more rural route to Dinan and St Malo.

Launderette in the Bureau du Port, pay by jetons.

Fuel is available by hose from a boatyard downstream of the swing bridge, adjacent to No 12 PHM buoy; Tel 02.97.63.20.17, open Mon-Sat 0830-1200 & 1330-1800. Also from a boatyard between the swing bridge and the lock, on the east side of the narrow canal (sloping sides and too narrow for most boats to turn); Tel 02.97.47.32.09, open Mon-Sat 0900-1200 & 1400-1800.

NAUTICAL NEEDS

Chandlery & repairs
- Voilerie Daniel (UShip), 37 rue Ferdinand le Dressay. East side of the inner basin facing Bureau du Port. Tel 02.97.47.14.41. Sailmaker, chandlery, gas. SHOM agent.
- Voilerie Le Port, 11 rue St Vincent. Tel 02.97.42.54.01. Chandlery, SHOM chart agent.
- Le Pennec, rue du Commerce. Tel 02.97.47.32.09. Boat yard and fuel (see under Fuel, above).
- Chantier Navale Caudard, Parc du Golfe. Tel 02.97.63.20.17. Boat yard and fuel, by No 12 buoy.

Lockgate open into marina

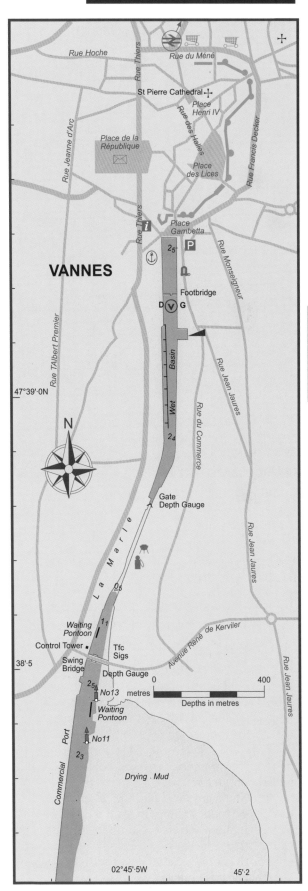

Vieux Pont

Visitors' moorings

Capitainerie

AURAY

Of all the places in the Golfe du Morbihan, you should not omit a trip upriver into Auray even if it means the loss of your VHF aerial, or worse – more anon!
It is a fun place, as a few thousand tourists every day of the week will confirm.
If you can mentally pretend that the tourists do not exist,

then it is not hard to visualise the scene as it was four hundred or more years ago. Much of the old port of St Goustan still exists: The ancient stone bridge, the cobbled quays, steeply wooded banks, ramparts and narrow alleyways threaded between overhanging timbered houses ... come and see for yourself.

Auray itself is quite a large, pleasant town reached by a steep climb up from the bridge. It is a mixture of old and new, dominated by the huge church of St Gildas. Good transport by road and rail and of course a useful base for the Morbihan, less frenetic than Vannes.

TOURISM

Tourist Office is at 20 rue du Lait, near the church. Tel 02.97.24.09.75; Fax 02.97.50.80.75. Hours: Jan-Jun & Sep-Dec, Mon-Sat 0900-1200 & 1400-1800, shut Sun; Jul/Aug, Mon-Sat 0900-1900; Sun/Hols 0900-1200.

Bus Nos 23 & 24 buses run from Quiberon, via Carnac, La Trinité and Auray, to Vannes.

Railway The station (Tel 02.97.24.44.66) is up Ave Gén de Gaulle, over a mile NW of the town centre, a definite taxi ride if crew-changing. Paris is 3h 30m by TGV. The local train (Le Tire Bouchon; see under Port Haliguen) also runs from Auray to Quiberon in Jul-Sep.

Taxi Tel 02.97.56.37.25.

Car hire
- Avis, place de la Gare. Tel 02.97.29.00.29.
- Europcar, 38 rue Jean Jaurès. Tel 02.97.24.23.33.

EATING ASHORE

Restaurants The nearest eating places are along the quayside at St Goustan. All are crowded with tourists in season, but should provide a satisfactory meal. Here are just a few:
- La Licorne,15 place St Sauveur. Tel 02.97.24.06.46. Seafood.
- Le Relais Franklin. Tel 02.97.24.82.54. Seafood.
- L'Eglantine, 17 place St Sauveur. Tel 02.97.56.46.55. Seafood. Menus 75-179FF

Up in the town try:
- La Chaumière, 1 rue Abbé Philippe Le Gall. Tel 02.97.50.77.75. (Ballon crossroad, opposite Stoc supermarket). Seafood. Closed Wed, except in season.
- Le Bretagne, Hotel-bar-restaurant, 1 place aux Roues. Tel 02.97.24.09.96.
- La Chebaudière, 6 place du Loch. 72-180FF. Closed Wed and in Jul/Aug.
- La Closerie de Kerdrain, 20 rue Louis-Billet. Tel 02.97.56.61.27. Gastronomy in the garden of this 16th century manor house. Closed Mon.
- Auberge La Plaine, rue du Lait, near the church. Tel 02.97.24.09.40. Menus 80-195FF.

Half-timbered houses

SHOPPING

Supermarkets Monoprix, 11 ave du Marechal Foch, NW of church. Tel 02.97.24.05.26. Stoc, ave du Gén de Gaulle, further NW of church. Tel 02.97.24.03.96.

Market day Mon mornings, one of the major and most colourful open-air markets in Brittany.

Banks Crédit Agricole.

Launderette Laverie du Centre, 1 place Gabriel Deshayes is up by Auray church, quite a haul. Tel 02.97.56.50.97. Open daily 0800-2200.

NAVIGATIONAL MATTERS

Charts Auray and the whole Golfe du Morbihan are covered by AC 2358 and by the equivalent SHOM 7034, both at 1:25,000.

Tides HW Auray at neaps is 55 mins after, and at springs the same as, HW Brest. LWs are 5 mins neaps, or 20 mins springs, after LW Brest.

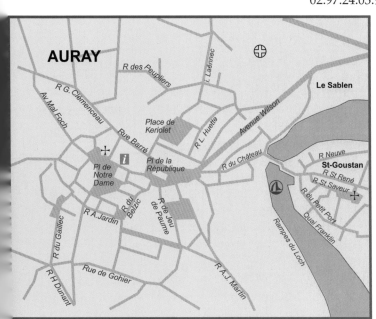

At Auray MHWS is 4·9m, MLWS 0·8m; MHWN is 4·0m, MLWN 1·8m.

Notes

i   Port Navalo is a French Standard Port. Pick up a freebie set of Navalo tide tables, with secondary port differences, (all calculated by SHOM) and you will probably find the results more accurate than the Admiralty figures.

ii   The tidal curve for Auray is not identical to the classic tidal curve for Brest. At Auray there is a longish stand at HW followed by an abrupt ebb. This reinforces the advice that it is not wise to leave (or approach) on the ebb.

iii Strong winds have a considerable effect on water levels. In 1999 by far the highest tide of the year occurred when the coefficient was only average.

Tidal streams reach 4 knots at extreme springs in the narrows between Sept Iles and Le Grand Huernic. Here the stream reverses about 30 minutes after HW and LW Port Navalo. Above Le Bono streams are less than 5 knots.

Tidal aspects down-river from the bridge should also be considered:

a. If coming from outside the Morbihan, do not arrive too early or you will be plugging a foul ebb off Port Navalo;

b. A premature arrival may also put you on the putty off Pointe de Kerisper (1·3M S of Auray bridge) where the least charted depth of 0·2m is found; and

c. Just N of this, César PHM buoy marks a patch drying 1·0m (remains of a Roman bridge) 100m to the NNE. So if you turn onto north leaving the buoy close to port, there is every chance of hitting the Pons Romanus. You must therefore keep as far to starboard of the buoy as possible until at least 200m beyond it when normal navigation can be resumed.

d. Consider the converse effects when deciding your departure time. It is not usually sensible to leave on the ebb for the obvious reasons should you run aground.

Access In all weathers, but consider depth limitations and Auray bridge, as discussed below. Between Le Bono and Auray the least charted depth is 0·2m, but near mid-flood there should be adequate water under you. The best time to start up-river depends both on your masthead height and its ability to pass unscathed below Auray bridge, and also on your draught.

Shelter is excellent on the ⚓s at St Goustan.

Bridge span

Anchorage There are anchorages, some drying, in the river as shown on AC 2358; also tucked in out of the tide at Sept Iles and off Le Rocher. Also some ⚓s downstream of the bridge.

Pilotage From abeam Locmariaquer the 6M passage up the Auray River is straightforward.

There is plenty of water up to Le Bono inlet (47°38'·2N) and any drying banks or narrows are buoyed or perched.

AURAY BRIDGE

It is better to scratch your head over tidal calculations than to scratch (or worse) your VHF aerial on the underside of the concrete road bridge; or alternatively your keel(s) on the river bed. Some might even manage to do both simultaneously (!) which highlights the nature of the problem. The following fairly detailed notes may assist:

Dimensions Essentially the vertical distance between the river bed and the underside of the

looking upriver through the bridge

ridge at centre span is 19·3 metres. That is a physical and incontrovertible fact; it has nothing to do with the state of the tide, recent drought/rains or any other ephemeral happening. It is the sum of 0·4m charted depth (see AC 2358), 4·9m height of MHWS and 14m the height of the bridge above MHWS. The Maître de Port, M. Raymond Coasmat, endorses these figures.

So, if your keel-to-masthead dimension (K-M) exceeds 19·3m you don't have a problem – you simply will not get past Auray bridge, but there may be a vacant ⚓ downriver.

If your K-M is less than 19·3m, draw a sketch (it always helps) and work out the tidal window through which you will, almost literally, squeeze. But first decide on the safety margins, above masthead and below keel, acceptable to you: let's say 0·5m above and below, an extra 1m to add. Then, for your boat – using your water and air draughts (including VHF aerial etc) plus these safety margins – do your sums and sketches for HW and LW, at neaps, springs or in between, as applicable to your visit. These will enable you to work out the times either side of HW when both keel and mast are safe – and when not! *Caution*: If water levels are higher than normal as a result of heavy rains, masthead clearance will be correspondingly reduced.

Examples Here are three, at very different states of the tide, for a 9·7m (32ft) LOA fin keeler, with 2·1m water draught and 15·2m air draught (fairly high-masted); the 0·5m safety margins are already included. Both Range and Coefficient have been included to indicate the size of the tide. The following windows emerge for a safe passage under the bridge:

a. Springs (Range 4·6m/Coeff 105): HW $-3\frac{3}{4}$ to HW $-2\frac{1}{2}$; and HW $+2\frac{1}{2}$ to HW $+3\frac{3}{4}$. This is a $1\frac{1}{4}$ hour window around mid-flood (also mid-ebb) when both keel and mast will clear the river bed and the bridge. However during the 5 hours at the top of this big spring tide (ie HW $\pm2\frac{1}{2}$), the mast will not clear the bridge.

b. Neaps/Springs (Range 3·2m/Coeff 70): HW $-4\frac{1}{2}$ to HW $-2\frac{1}{4}$, and HW $+2\frac{1}{4}$ to $+4\frac{1}{2}$. On an average tide, midway between neaps and springs, the window expands to $2\frac{1}{4}$ hours but the tallish mast will still not clear the bridge for $4\frac{1}{2}$ hours around HW.

c. Neaps (Range 1·2m/Coeff 29) no restriction at all because LW works out at 2·5m, and HW at 3·7m which enables the mast and its safety margin to be preserved – just. Hold your breath!

From the above you might say "Go through at HW–3 (or +3)", but it's better to work it out. Have faith in your calculations. Accept that a "low"

Moorings and bridge looking downriver

bridge will always look perilously close aloft. Set your depth-sounder alarm to sound at the 0·5m below-keel clearance. Enjoy Auray!

Tide gauge Below the bridge on a post there is a tidal gauge (see photograph) which indicates simultaneously on two scales, one for depth of water and the other for air clearance. If you don't like what you see on either scale, you can still back off. The present gauge is however partly obscured between two trots of moored boats both of which should be left to starboard on arrival. In early 2000 a new electronic indicator had been due for installation up on the bridge span. Funding for it has been diverted unexpectedly to replace mooring chains on the ⚓s. It is hoped that the new indicator may be installed in 2001.

HARBOUR (ST GOUSTAN)

Bureau du Port is on the east quay, south of the last eating place, at 4 place du Rolland, 56400 Auray. Tel 02.97.56.29.08; Fax 02.97.24.16.56. VHF Ch 09. HM M. Raymond Goasmat, a genial part-time gentleman who is also contactable on mobile ☎ 06.08.42.18.62. Hours from Apr to mid-Oct: Mon-Fri 0800-1200 & 1330-1730; and on the flood tide, year round. Weather forecasts are posted daily, mid-Apr to mid-Sep.

Visitors moor fore-and-aft on two trots of white buoys in 1·4m to 2·3m on the west side of the harbour, well beyond the bridge. A small red or white pick-up buoy is secured to a line joining each pair of mooring buoys. Fenders are essential as rafting one-on-one is the norm. Messing about in boats remains a favourite source of endless

amusement and bonhomie. You may be able to lie alongside the drying east quay for an hour or two around High Water; ask HM. 2500 boats visit Auray each year of which 1300 are British.

Tariff Daily rates, year round, on buoys: 7-8m = 58FF; <9m = 64FF; <10m = 69FF; <11m = 75FF; <12m = 80FF; <13m = 86FF; <14m = 91FF; >14m = 102FF.

Showers are behind the Capitainerie, open 0930-1730 only, due to vandalism: jetons 11FF.

Fuel is not available by hose. Cans from the nearest garage are the only possibility.

NAUTICAL NEEDS

Chandlery & repairs Auray is not too well served for yacht repairs or even for nautical supplies. If you have technical problems, the nearest and best equipped centre is Crouesty.
- Le Comptoir de la Mer, ZI de Kerbois. Tel 02.97.24.04.97. Chandlery. SHOM chart agent. (Kerbois is 2km WSW of the town centre, just inside the southern ring road, RN165).
- Accastillage Diffusion, ZA de Kerfontaine, Pluneret. Tel 02.97.24.18.89. Chandlery. SHOM chart agent. (Pluneret is 2km ESE of the town centre).

Down river at the drying Port du Parun, east bank at 47°36´·80N, are:
- Chantier Lobrichon, a traditional boatyard. Tel 02.97.57.15.22.
- Le Borgne boatyard, hull and engineering repairs. Tel 02.97.57.00.15.

Visitors' moorings, west quay and old bridge at St Goustan

THE VILAINE RIVER

The seaward portion of the Vilaine River, ie downstream of the lock at Arzal, is the subject of this little briefing. It assumes that you are locking-in, to meander up-river to such delightful spots as La Roche Bernard, Foleux and Redon, with your mast still vertical.

You may then be bound north via the canal to Dinan and St Malo – or of course you may have come thence. *N'importe.*

NAVIGATIONAL MATTERS

Charts AC 2353 (1:75,000) covers La Vilaine up to the lock at Arzal, as well as Quiberon Bay; SHOM 7033 (1:50,000) is the equivalent. SHOM 2381 (1:14,400) gives full details at large scale.

Approaches There are two options:

1. If coming from the west, keep NW of Île Dumet and approach via the Passe de la Grande Accroche (loosely and ominously translated as 'Pass of the Great Crunch'). By day/night make good the waypoint, 47°29´·00N 02°33´·90W, which is in transit 052° with Penlan light house and Les Prierès abbey tower, the rear mark. It is also 5 cables abeam Les Mâts SCM spar buoy and on the edge of the 8° white sector (052°-060°) of Penlan light, 3·3M away.

When 1M from Penlan light and with Basse de Kervoyal SCM light beacon bearing 270°, turn starboard 090° towards Nos 1 & 2 lateral light buoys at the river entrance proper.

Note: At night the 2° white sector (269°-271°) of Kervoyal covers this 090°-270° track section.

2. From the S, keep SE of Île Dumet and approach via the Passe de la Varlingue. La Varlingue is the name for an awkwardly placed pair of rocks, one awash at CD, the other drying 0·3m; more anon. See also Piriac for a description of the outer dangers.

By day/night make good the waypoint, 47°28´·30N 02°31´·95W, which is in transit 025½° with Penlan lighthouse and Billiers church tower, the rear mark. It is also on the edge of Penlan's adjoining Green (to port) and Red (to starboard) sectors. La Varlingue will be left close to starboard. When 7 cables from Penlan light and with Basse de Kervoyal SCM

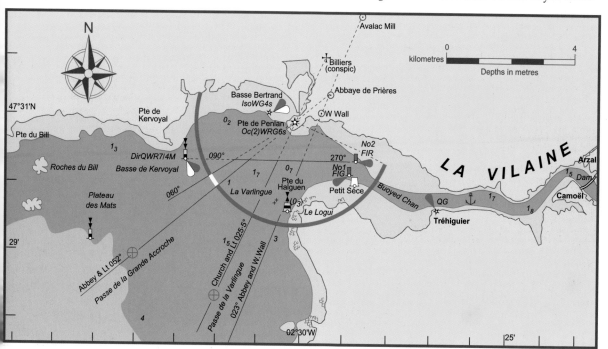

The Vilaine barrier, sluices and lock, looking west downriver

light beacon bearing 270°, continue as in option (1).

Note: An alternative transit 023°, as shown on AC 2353, passes between La Varlingue rocks and the shore. The marks are a whited wall and Les Prierès abbey tower (rear), neither of which are at all easy to see, nor are they lit.

Option (1) has about 1m more water than (2). Option (2) is slightly more sheltered from strong westerlies by the intervening shoal (1·3m) bank of La Grande Accroche. La Varlingue rocks need not be a problem with sufficient rise of tide.

Daymarks Penlan lighthouse is an 18m high tower, white with red bands. It is the only sure-fire mark serving both approaches since other charted marks are mostly obscured by trees.

Pilotage The 090°-270° section between Basse de Kervoyal SCM light beacon and Nos 1 & 2 lateral light buoys is part of a broad bar with a least charted depth of 0·9m, but as little as 0·5m (due to silting) may be found, together with rough water in strong onshore winds.

Once inside the buoyed/beaconed river channel least depths of about 2m are likely at first, except near the edges of the fairway. Depths reduce markedly as the barrage is neared. Due to encroaching mudbanks some buoys may be further outboard than they should be; keep a central course and approach in the top half of the tide. The lock is at 47°30'·10N 02°22'·90W.

The lock is in any case unusable for a period either side of LW due to lack of water. There are waiting buoys downstream of the lock and space to anchor.

Tides At Tréhiguier (nearly half-way to the lock) HW at neaps is 35 mins after, and at springs 20 mins before HW Brest. LW Tréhiguier at neaps is 5 mins, and at springs 10 mins before LW Brest. MHWS is 5·5m, MLWS 0·7m; MHWN is 4·4m, MLWN 2·1m.

Tidal streams north of Île Dumet set NE/SW, do not exceed 1 knot at springs. Off Tréhiguier rates are said to reach 3 knots at springs in both directions but this rate is probably exaggerated. The Barrage at Arzal has distorted the tidal streams in the estuary, and no details are available. When sluicing is in progress at the Barrage the flow of water can change rapidly especially if the River Vilaine is in spate.

Arzal lock operation The lock is large (85m x 13m wide x 2m deep over the sill), but despite its size is often crowded in season. A road bridge operates in unison with the lock.

The lock opens on the hour (subject to tides) from 0700 to 2200 in July and August. Call the lock on VHF Ch 18. Times vary with the tides from day to day, so you should check beforehand with the Capitainerie at Camoël on tel 02.97.45.01.15 for recorded information, or call the marina, not the lock, on VHF Ch 09; or obtain prior information from other marinas around Quiberon Bay and in the Golfe du Morbihan, bearing in mind that Camoël/Arzal, La Roche Bernard, Port Haliguen, La Trinité, Port Blanc, Île-aux-Moines, Arradon and Crouesty marinas are all run by the same company, Sagemor.

The lock control tower is a conspicuous red building. On the lock walls there are vertical chains around which you can rig and tend your warps. The lock may be quite turbulent; rig all fenders.

Shelter within the river and in both marinas is very good.

Anchorage No anchoring in the marinas; anchor in the river clear of the fairway.

MARINAS

There are two marinas immediately upstream of the Barrage: Arzal on the NW bank and Camoël on the S bank. Arzal is the larger with all the

facilities of a major marina and a visitors' pontoon M/N. Camoël is quieter and more secluded, but can only be reached by circumnavigating the Prohibited Area (marked by yellow buoys) upstream of the Barrage sluices.

Capitaineries are located at both marinas, but share the same numbers: Tel 02.99.90.05.86; Fax 02.99.90.08.08. VHF Ch 09. HM Marc de Ghellink. Postal address: Le Vieux Château, Port de Camoël, 56130 Camoël. Web site: www.baie-de-quiberon.com

Hours in season, daily 0830-1230 & 1430-2130. Weather forecasts are posted daily. Showers at both marinas.

Tariff Daily rates for LOA bands, first figure is Sep-Jun; second Jul/Aug:
7-8.5m = 35/60FF; <10m = 45/75FF; <11.5m = 50/90FF; <14m = 60/105FF.

Fuel diesel and petrol, is immediately upstream of the lock on the Arzal side; open 0830-1230 and 1430-2100.

NAUTICAL NEEDS

Chandlery & repairs
* Chantier Nautique du Barrage, 56190 Arzal. Tel 02.97.45.03.50. Chandlery, hull repairs.
* Chantier Naval de la Vilaine, 56190 Arzal. Tel 02.97.45.04.97. Boatyard, chandler, sail repairs.

Shops Arzal and Camoël are 5km apart, equidistant from the Barrage, but with limited facilities. La Roche Bernard is about 10km by road from either village and has good facilities.

Taxis 02.97.45.02.83.

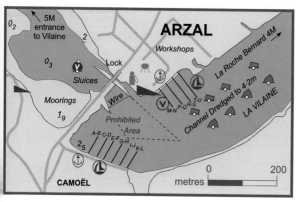

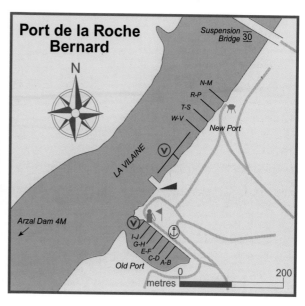

PIRIAC

This self-effacing little harbour is pure delight, one of my favourites along the whole of France's Atlantic coast! If you get no further south than Quiberon Bay, make every effort to include it in your cruise. You have moved out of Brittany and the Morbihan département and into the Loire Atlantique. The peat bogs of La Grande Brière are 20km east, 13km to the south east is the mediaeval walled town of Guérande and further south east the sophistication of La Baule.

Here in Piriac the ambience is unsophisticated, tranquil and pleasing. Flowers fill the narrow cobbled streets and squares, ivy covers the walls of half-timbered, 17th century houses. Gaze seawards over the drying reefs which you so carefully avoided. Watch the mussel dredgers selling their catch direct to eager buyers at the slipway. Linger over a drink outside the Hôtel du Port, HQ of the Royal Canot Club, as the world passes by along Quai Verdun.

See also the introduction to this chapter.

TOURISM

Tourist Office is 7 rue des Cap-Horniers, 44420 Piriac. Tel 02.40.23.51.42; Fax 02.40.23.51.19. Hours in season Mon-Sat 0900-1200 & 1400-1900; Sun/Hols 1000-1300.

Bus Line 80 runs to St Nazaire (1 hour), via La Turballe (10 mins) and Guérande (30 mins).

Railway Nearest station is at Le Pouliguen (18km).

Piriac, looking east. The pecked line denotes a retaining wall

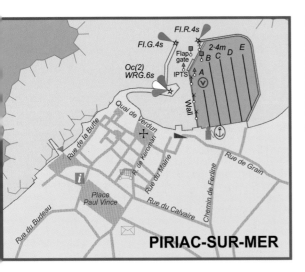

PIRIAC-SUR-MER

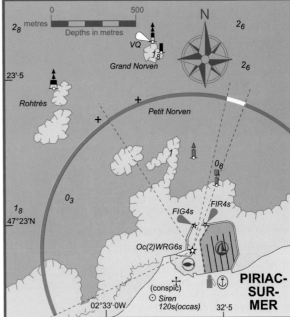

PIRIAC-SUR-MER

Taxi Tel 02.40.23.59.52.

Bike and Car hire SARL Garage Patalane, 6 rue du Calvaire. Tel 02.40.23.50.62.

Beaches Plage St Michel is the nearest, on the SW side of the town. To the south are Plages du Castelli and du Petit Lanroué.

EATING ASHORE

Restaurants

- Poivre et Sel, 1 rue Neuve. Tel 02.40.23.56.03. Menus 84-140FF. Seafood.
- Bodega Bay, rue de la Plage. Tel 02.40.23.62.24. Plateful of tapas for 75/89FF. Seafood 149FF.
- L'Île Dumet (within Hôtel de la Poste), 26 rue de la Plage. Tel 02.40.23.62.24. Menus 90/120FF.

SHOPPING

Supermarkets Comod, 22 rue de Kerouman (behind the church). Tel 02.40.23.56.92. Small, but stocks most essentials. Nearest proper supermarket is at La Turballe (6km).

Markets In season Mon, Wed and Sat mornings. Out of season Tues morning.

Banks None; nearest at La Turballe.

NAVIGATIONAL MATTERS

Charts AC 2353 (1:75,000) covers Piriac and all of Quiberon Bay. SHOM 7033 (1:50,000) is the French equivalent.

Approaches From the NW skirt round low-lying Île Dumet. Its south side is steep-to, but shoals extend north and east. From the W or SW be aware of the well marked Plateau du Four.

A rocky plateau extends 1½M west and 1M north from Piriac. From Les Bayonelles WCM buoy, Q (9) 15s, a track to Grand Norven NCM beacon, VQ, passing inside the 0·6m and 0·3m patches and clear of Les Rohtrès unlit NCM beacon tower, will avoid the drying offliers. There is no safe inner short cut to the south of either of these North Cardinal marks.

Chapter 4

Grand Norvern NCM beacon

Disused beacon

Île Dumet

Grand Norvern NCM beacon, VQ; Île Dumet on the horizon, looking WNW

Marina: flapgate up, retaining wall clearly visible

Daymarks On Pointe du Castelli a white Signal station, supported by a prow-like base. Piriac's church tower with bell-shaped belfry and the stumpy white light beacon tower are roughly aligned with the approach channel (197°).

Pilotage By day/night make good the waypoint (47°23′·88N 02°32′·26W), in the white sector of Piriac's directional light, Oc (2) WRG 6s; from it the harbour entrance bears 197°/9 cables. Once east of Grand Norvern it may be acceptable to cut the corner inside the waypoint.

Marina wall Inside the harbour entrance the marina lies to port, water being retained by a wall marked by 4 yellow SPM perches; do not attempt to cross this wall at any state of the tide. Near the north end of the wall the marina is entered over a flapgate, located between two very obvious PHM and SHM perches.

Flapgate operation
starting from the position shown in the above photo: The flapgate is up, retaining 2·4m water in the marina. When, on the rising tide, the water level outside equals that inside the marina the flapgate drops giving an immediate

1·5m of water above it. The adjacent depth gauge shows 15 (or 1·5m), its bottom mark. Binoculars help in reading the gauge clearly, especially at night.

As the concrete support base covers, the gauge shows 29 (2·9m), its top mark, meaning at least 2·9m over the lowered flapgate. The depth gauge too now covers, which is why you cannot see it if/when you arrive near HW! On the ebb the sequence reverses.

The IPTS on the south side of the flapgate indicate:

| ®®® (vert) | = Flapgate up; no entry/exit. |
| © © © (vert) | = Flapgate down, at least 1·5m water over it. Proceed, if adequate depth on gauge. |

Marina entrance: viewed from within marina; flapgate down, wall covered, depth gauge unreadable!

ides Interpolating tidal differences for Le Croisic, le Höedic and Penerf, HW Piriac at neaps is 15 mins fter, and at springs 32 nins before HW Brest. LW Piriac at neaps is 17 mins, nd at springs 21 mins efore LW Brest. MHWS is ·3m, MLWS 0·7m; MHWN is 4·2m, MLWN ·0m.

idal streams between Piriac and Île Dumet set NE/SW, reaching 2-3 knots t springs to quote the Admiralty Pilot, although hese rates are "thought to e overstated". The UK and French Tidal stream atlases both appear to suggest that these rates ould be halved.

Buying mussels on the slipway

Access At about HW ±3, depending on draught, to clear both the flapgate and the ledges drying approx 1·6m outside the harbour. In strong northerlies, particularly at night, care is needed.

Shelter is good, except when strong NW to N winds blow into the marina.

Anchorage No anchoring in the marina; outside anchor NE of the entrance in about 3m on sand.

MARINA

Capitainerie is on the 1st floor of a tall grey building south of the marina; 1 rue du Fort Baron, 44420 Piriac. Tel 02.40.23.52.32; Fax 02.40.15.51.78. VHF Ch 09. HM Louis Bolzec. Hours in season, daily 0900-1200 & 1400-1700. Weather forecasts are posted daily. Showers are inside. Marina is run by St Nazaire's Chamber of Commerce, as is Le Pouliguen marina.

Tariff Daily rates for LOA bands in Jul-Aug: 7-8·5m = 91-101FF; 8·5-10m = 106-119FF; 10-11·5m = 127-142FF; 11·5-12·5m = 151-162FF.

Fuel installation, diesel and petrol, is at the head of A pontoon; closes at 1130 and 1900.

Launderette at corner of Chemin de Ferline and rue du Calvaire (due south from the marina).

Chandlery & repairs
• Atout Vent, 2 venelle du Sourd, BP3. Tel 02.40.15.51.48. Chandlery, hull repairs, rigging.
• Cargot, 1 quai de Verdun. Tel 02.40.23.50.86. Boatyard, chandler, engine repairs.

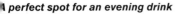

A perfect spot for an evening drink

Chapter 4

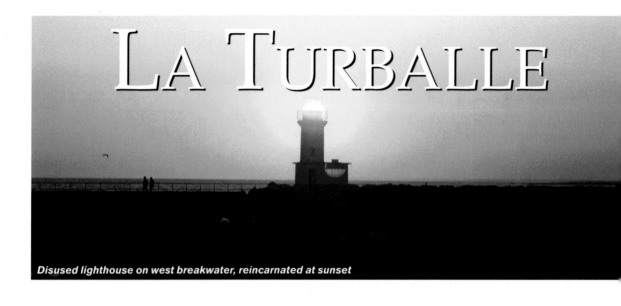

LA TURBALLE

Disused lighthouse on west breakwater, reincarnated at sunset

Fishing boats in this bustling port are outnumbered only by the seagulls which noisily follow their every move, screeching for scraps of sardines. Yachts co-exist quite happily, along with several thousand holiday-makers in what is fast becoming a popular seaside resort.

The town, as you might expect, is an uneven blend of traditional fishery and modern resort architecture, but it's friendly. Both residents and visitors seem to enjoy themselves.

La Turballe can be entered at all tides, which gives it the edge over neighbouring harbours. Piriac is delightful, but a half-tide marina. Le Croisic is similar, and the little marina dries 1·7m. Round the corner, Le Pouliguen is rather fun; the drying approaches offer some challenge, because the channel is not over-endowed with good marks. Pornichet marina, at the east end of the bay, is the archetypal nautical parking lot, useful if that's what you need, access H24! See also the introduction to this chapter.

TOURISM

Tourist Office place Charles de Gaulle, BP 40, 44420 La Turballe. Tel & Fax 02.40.23.32.01. Open 7/7 days in Jul/Aug. Out of season Mon-Sat 1000-1300 & 1430-1830; closed Wed & Sun.

Bus Line 80 runs via Guérande (15 mins) to St Nazaire (50 mins), and to Piriac (10 mins).

Railway Nearest station is at Le Pouliguen (13km), qv.

Taxi Rio Robert, Tel 02.40.62.02.67.

Bike hire Cycles Herigault, 52 rue du Maréchal de Lattre de Tassigny. Tel 02.40.23.30.59.

Car hire Ask at Tourist Office.

Beaches The sandy Plage des Bretons extends 2N south in a great sweep from the harbour towards Le Croisic. The smaller Plage de la Bastille is NW of the harbour.

Pontoon 'B' looking north
Visitors' area cleared for visiting rally

W breakwater
Fl(4)WR 12s

Rear: F Vi
006.5° leading line

Front: F Vi

SHM bn
Fl.G 4s

Fish market
roof

Entering harbour. After the SHM beacon turn starboard to the marina

EATING ASHORE

Restaurants

- Les Sarments, rue du Croisic (behind quai St Jacques). Menus 92-132FF. Grills on a wood fire.
- La Chaumière, 6 quai St Jacques. Tel 02.40.23.32.11.
- Le Terminus, 18 quai St Paul. Tel 02.40.23.30.29. Menus 95-210FF.

Shopping

Supermarkets Comod is 400m NE of marina, at junction of Rue du Maréchal de Lattre de Tassigny and Rue de la Poste. Intermarché is 800m N of marina, at La Marjolaine roundabout.

Markets Fishmarket daily (next to the fish basin). A covered market is behind the Espace Galahy.

Banks Crédit Lyonnais and others.

NAVIGATIONAL MATTERS

Charts AC 2353 (1:75,000) covers La Turballe and the whole of Quiberon Bay. SHOM 7033 (1:50,000) is the French equivalent. SHOM 6826 (1:17,000)

covers La Turballe and Le Croisic.

Approaches From the SW be aware of the well marked/lit Plateau du Four and the shoals off Pointe du Croisic, marked by Basse Castouillet WCM lt buoy. From the WNW there are offliers between Les Bayonelles WCM buoy, Q (9) 15s, and the harbour. The rest of the bay is clear.

Pilotage By day and night make good the waypoint 47°20´·45N 02°31´·50W, 5 cables WSW of the harbour. Maintain the 070° leading line (church tower on with Trescalan water tower) to a position about 250m south of the harbour. Here the entrance 47°20´·78N 02°30´·80W, hitherto invisible against an apparently seamless line of bouldered breakwater, suddenly opens up – go for it! Inside the harbour turn sharply starboard for the marina, watching out for large fishing vessels.

At night approach in the white sector of the west jetty ☆ Fl (4) WR 12s, until picking up the intensified 006·5° leading lights, both F Vi, into harbour.

Daymarks On Pointe du Castelli a white signal station, on a prow-like base. To the south, Le Croisic church tower and the rather similar one at Batz-sur-mer are conspicuous; as is the large white roofed fish market in the centre of La Turballe harbour. A disused white light tower on the west jetty is more obvious than the lattice light tower, Fl (4) WR 12s, on the end of this jetty.

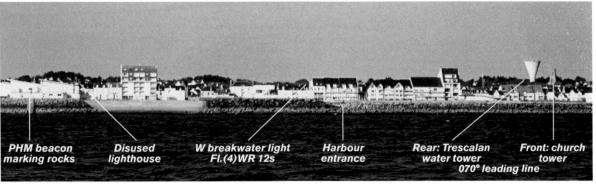

PHM beacon
marking rocks

Disused
lighthouse

W breakwater light
Fl.(4)WR 12s

Harbour
entrance

Rear: Trescalan
water tower

Front: church
tower

070° leading line

Approaching from the west

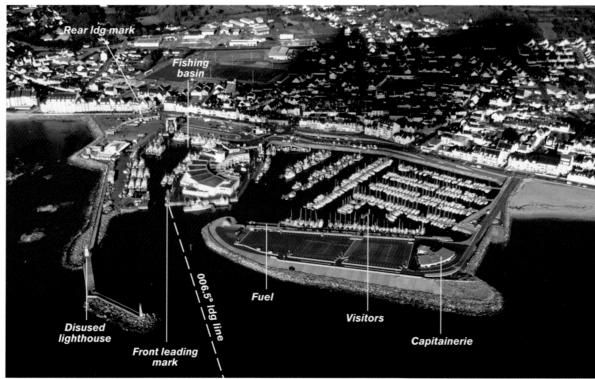

La Turballe, looking north

Tides Use tidal differences for Le Croisic, where HW at neaps is 15 mins after, and at springs 40 mins before HW Brest. LW Le Croisic at neaps is 15 mins, and at springs 20 mins before LW Brest. MHWS is 5·4m, MLWS 0·7m; MHWN is 4·3m, MLWN 2·0m.

Tidal streams in the bay (Rade de Croisic) are rotary clockwise at 1 knot, a constant spring rate.

Access is at all tides and is straightforward once the harbour entrance has revealed itself, but at MLWS there may be only 2·2m depth in the marina entrance. Be wary of swell in westerlies.

Entrances to the Fishing Basin and marina

Hazards Rocky ledges 80m west of the harbour are marked by a large unlit red beacon tower.

Shelter is very good, but in strong SSW winds a heavy swell may work into the harbour.

Anchorage A fair weather anchorage is about 2-3 cables SSE of the entrance in approx 3m on sand; no anchoring in the marina.

MARINA

Capitainerie is a modern building south of the marina on Môle le Tourlandroux, 44420 La Turballe. Tel 02.40.23.41.65; Fax 02.40.23.47.64. VHF Ch 09. HM G Pasquier. Hours in season, Mon-Sat 0800-1200 & 1700-2000; closed Wed. Weather forecasts are posted daily.

Showers 10FF and **Launderette** are inside.

Visitors berth near the end of B pontoon around 3 sides of a rectangle, with a detached pontoon in the middle; no finger berths, but much rafting. In high season berths are quickly filled and visitors may have to be turned away, especially if a regatta or rally is in progress.

In which case the nearest options are Le Croisic if you can dry out or Piriac, both half-tide harbours; or Pornichet if you want a cast-iron certainty at all tides.

Tariff Daily rates for LOA bands in Apr-Oct, (Rate) is Nov-Mar:
6-7m = 63(32)FF; <8m = 74(39FF); <9m = 85(44)FF; <10m = 96(49)FF; <11m = 115(58)FF; <12m = 133(68)FF; <13m = 157(78)FF.

Fuel berth is at the head of A pontoon, on finger pontoon for yachts; fendered berth is for fishing vessels. Available H24 only if you have a French-type credit card, otherwise pay at Capitainerie.

NAUTICAL NEEDS

Chandlery & repairs
- Voilerie Biscay. Tel 02.40.23.49.21. Sailmaker.
- Inter Coop Marine, 2 quai St Jacques. Tel 02.40.62.80.05. Chandlery, SHOM chart agent.
- Cargot Piriac Diffusion, 1 quai de Verdun. Tel 02.40.23.50.86. Chandlery, engine repairs.
- Atlantic Meca Plaisance, ZA La Marjolaine. Tel 02.40.62.86.86. Engine repairs.

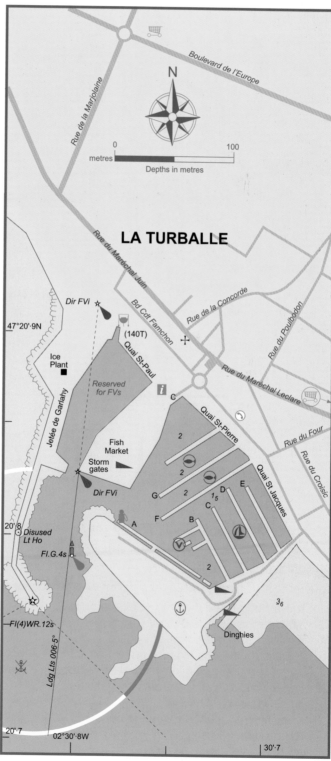

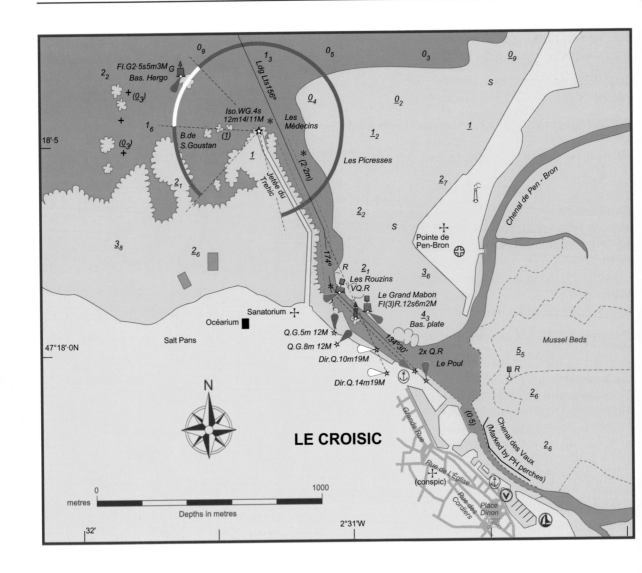

LE CROISIC

Brilliant light, big skyscapes and far horizons are the backdrop to Le Croisic.
Vast expanses of mussel beds, salt marshes and salt pans stretch inland
almost to La Turballe, Guérande in the NE and Le Pouliguen
to the East. There is an away-from-it-all feeling about

Le Croisic, heightened if anything by seeing the TGV roll in from Paris not many yards from the marina.

The waterfront is divided into several basins (*Chambres*) by the intervening arms of terra firma (*Jonchères* or islets), but Grande Jonchère is now little more than a carpark and fairground, whilst Petite Jonchère is an overgrown and derelict islet – in sad contrast to the several well-preserved 17th century buildings along the quays.

Yet these detailed shortcomings do not greatly detract from the charm of Le Croisic. It is an attractive and enjoyable town, well worth the effort of parking your *bateau* - literally, as the marina and quay dry.

TOURISM

Tourist Office rue des Poilus, 44490 Le Croisic (between the marina and the railway station). Tel 02.40.23.00.70. Open 7/7 days in Jul/Aug.

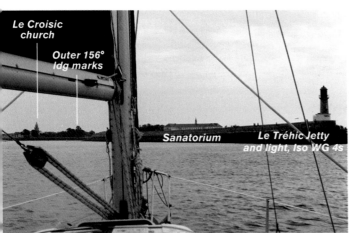

Le Croisic church

Outer 156° ldg marks

Sanatorium   Le Tréhic Jetty and light, Iso WG 4s

Approaching the seaward end of Jetée du Tréhic, near low water

What to see/do Cycle round the peninsula, pausing to admire the view from Pointe du Croisic. Visit the Océarium (sic), just beyond the Jetée du Tréhic. Once again the French fascination with the underwater world and its inhabitants surfaces, if that is the right word? But this is an above average exhibition. There is even a tunnel running through the aquarium. Great for the kids; I actually managed to stifle my usual cynical yawn! Open 1000-1900 Jun-Aug; Sep-May 1000-1200 & 1400-1800.

Watch the daily fish auctions in La Criée; nothing to do with the previous attraction!

See also the introduction to this chapter.

Beaches The sandy Plage de St Goustan is on the NW side of Jetée du Tréhic. The smaller Plage de Port-Lin is 1km SW of the marina; walk/cycle via station and bld du Général Leclerc.

Bus Line 81 runs via Le Pouliguen (20 mins) and La Baule (35 mins) to St Nazaire (70 mins).

Railway Station is 300m SE of the marina. Paris is 3h 15m by TGV, via St Nazaire and Nantes.

Taxi Tel 02.40.23.26.49; 02.40.23.06.17.

Bike and Car hire Ask at the Tourist Office.

EATING ASHORE

Restaurants
• Le Lénigo, 11 quai Lénigo, opposite the fish market. Tel 02.40.23.00.31. Menus 89-170FF.
• L'Estacade, 4 quai Lénigo. Tel 02.40.23.03.77. Menus 88-238FF. Timbered facade.
• La Marina, 12 rue de la Marine (near to the marina). Tel 02.40.15.79.70.
• Bretagne, 11 quai Petite Chambre. Tel 02.40.23.00.51. Seafood 100-265FF.

SHOPPING

Supermarkets Corsaire (a bit basic) in Place Dinan is very close to the marina. Intermarché, rue Kerdavid is about 1km west of the marina, near the root of Jetée du Tréhic. Tel 02.40.62.92.49.

Markets In Place Dinan, close to the marina, and sprawling through the small back streets towards the church.

Banks Enough to refill your coffers.

NAVIGATIONAL MATTERS

Charts AC 2353 covers Quiberon Bay at 1:75,000 with an inset of Le Croisic at 1:20,000. SHOM 7033 at 1:50,000 is the French equivalent. SHOM 6826 covers Le Croisic at 1:17,000. AC 2986 (1:50,000) just includes Le Croisic and its southern approaches.

Approaches From the W and SW be aware of the well marked/lit Plateau du Four and the shoals off Pointe du Croisic, marked by Basse Castouillet WCM lt buoy. Near HW it is feasible to cross these shoals, avoiding patches of 0·6m, 0·7m and the rocks drying 0·3m just west of Basse Hergo SHM beacon/tower which must be left well to starboard. From the NNW there are offliers between Les Bayonelles WCM buoy, Q (9) 15s, and La Turballe. The rest of the bay is clear.

Chapter 4

Le Grand Mabon PHM tower Fl(3)R12s

Church tower

156° ldg marks

Estacade

174° leading marks

Pilotage By day and night make good the waypoint 47°19′·00N 02°31′·55W, which is on the 156° leading line, 4½ cables from the head of Jetée du Tréhic. Three sets of leading lines must be followed precisely:

a. The outer 156° daymarks are red □s on white pylons, just visible through a gap in the trees with the large, domed church tower almost in transit beyond. Both lights are Dir Q, intensified.

b. The middle set 174° are even more coy, appearing at the last moment from behind pine trees. Both are yellow □s with a green vertical stripe, QG. They lead through the channel bend.

c. On passing Les Rouzins PHM light buoy, VQ R, the inner set leads 134·5°. The marks are red/ white chequered □s: the front on the quay and the rear atop the black-roofed Fish market (Criée); both QR.

Here *Le Poul* opens out to port, whilst the channel continues SE, marked by port-hand perches. Ignore the various inlets (*Chambres*) to starboard. Stand on for 4 cables to a conspicuous white walled/roofed boatyard shed with travel hoist; in front of this, turn 90° starboard into the marina.

Daymarks Le Croisic church tower is virtually on the 156° leading line and is seen well before the leading marks; not to be confused (as if you would) with the rather similar tower at Batz-sur-Mer, 1·7M SE. The massive stone Jetée du Tréhic dominates the entry channel and its 12 metre high light tower is easily seen. The sanatorium and Pen-Bron hospital are visible either side of the root of Jetée du Tréhic, but you will be too busy with leading marks to really notice them!

Tides HW Le Croisic at neaps is 15 mins after, and at springs 40 mins before HW Brest. LW Le Croisic at neaps is 15 mins, and at springs 20 mins before LW Brest. MHWS is 5·4m, MLWS 0·7m; MHWN is 4·3m, MLWN 2·0m. Tide gauges at the head of Jetée du Tréhic and by the fish quay indicate the height of tide above chart datum.

Le Croisic approach and marina, looking north

Tidal streams in the bay (Rade de Croisic) are rotary clockwise at 1 knot, a constant spring rate. In the channel between Grand Mabon and the fish market the spring stream reaches 4 knots at mid-flood and mid-ebb; it is said to be even stronger further to the NW.

134.5° Fishmarket
ldg marks

Inner leading marks 134.5°

Access at HW±2 neaps, ±1 springs. No access LW ±1½. Best time to enter is HW slack, about 30 minutes before local HW. As far as the fish market the channel is dredged 2·2m, thereafter it narrows and shoals steadily to about 0·5m. The marina dries approx 1·7m. I once crept in at LW with a coefficient of 68 and 1·6m draught; unsurprisingly I had to turn back just before the Criée. Leading mark photos were taken at LW.

Hazards The white sector of Tréhic light covers a safe arc across the Rade de Croisic, but closer in it embraces the rocks near Hergo SHM beacon tower; so establish on the 156° leading line not later than the waypoint. Drying sandbanks east of the channel are marked by Les Rouzins PHM light buoy and Grand Mabon lit PHM beacon tower.

Shelter is very good.

Anchorage in The Pool is prohibited due to many moorings. Anchoring on sand and gravel near the waypoint to await the tide would be feasible, but beware the strong tidal streams.

MARINA

Capitainerie is a small modern building to starboard of the marina entrance, 44490 Le Croisic. Tel 02.40.23.10.95; Fax 02.40.15.75.92. VHF Ch 09. HM Jacques Lecallo. Hours in season, daily 0800-2000; out of season 0800-1200 & 1330-1715, closed Sun. Weather forecasts are posted daily. Showers are inside.

Visitors berth on the inboard side of the Capitainerie, bows in to ❶ pontoon, sternrope to buoy. Max LOA 13m, space for up to 10 boats; ideal for bilge keels, lifting keels or on legs. Fin keelers can dry out on hard, clean, level ground against the quay outboard of the Capitainerie.

Tariff Daily rates for LOA bands year round: 7-8·5m = 51-55FF; 8·5-10m = 57-63FF; 10-11·5m = 66-74FF; 11·5-13m = 78-82FF.

Fuel *Il n'y a pas*, except by cans from a garage.

NAUTICAL NEEDS

Chandlery & repairs
- Inter Coop Marine, 1 rue du Mail de Broc. Tel 02.40.15.71.01. Chandlery.
- Gérard Lemerle, ave Aristide Briand (opposite the station). Tel 02.40.62.92.12. Chandlery.

The following are in the Zone Artisanale (east of the railway station):
- Marine Atlantique, rue du Pré-du-Pas. Tel 02.40.23.09.00. Boatyard.
- Chantiers Navals de la Presqu'ile. Tel 02.40.23.14.33. Boatyard.
- Méca Navale. Tel 02.40.23.04.10. Mechanical engineering.
- MGEM. Tel 02.40.62.92.89. Electrical and electronic repairs.

Outside the Capitainerie quay:
drying berth for fin keelers against the wall

Inside the Capitainerie quay. Bows-in berthing

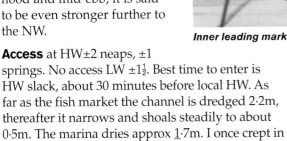

RIVER LOIRE TO BOURGENAY

CONTENTS

THE CHÂTEAUX AND WINES OF THE LOIRE

If you get held up along this stretch of coast (either for repairs or bad weather), then rejoice because this could be a golden opportunity to visit the great Châteaux of the Loire. To do so hire a car and make for Saumur, some 50km upstream from Angers. Saumur is about 160km from anywhere on the coast between Pornic and Bourgenay.

At Saumur, armed with Michelin map 64, you can start a delightful pilgrimage up-river as far as time permits. Certainly you might hope to cover the 120 km past Chinon and Tours to Blois. In this stretch you could "do" in best tourist mode a few of the better known châteaux, ie Saumur, ruined Chinon, Azay-le-Rideau, Villandry with its superb gardens, Chenonceaux, Amboise, Chaumont, Blois and Chambord.

Some of these incomparable architectural masterpieces originated as fortresses in feudal times. In the 14th and 15th centuries they gradually evolved into fine castles in which the Kings and Dukes of France gathered and court life blossomed. The artistic effect of the Renaissance is seen in the more elaborately decorated 16th century châteaux of Azay-le-Rideau and Chenonceaux; if time permits visits to only two châteaux these would be the prime candidates. Do not in any case make the mistake of trying to visit too many châteaux or your enjoyment will be blunted.

There is still of course the important matter of Loire wines to be addressed. You might combine a château visit in the morning with a little wine-tasting around noon, followed by a picnic lunch

*Port de la Meule,
Île d'Yeu*

somewhere along the grassy banks of this majestic river ... after that it's up to you. The Loire provides the summer drinking wines of France - ideal for visiting yachtsmen.

Mention Loire wine and the average Brit is programmed to say Muscadet – which is a grape variety and can be a fine wine. There is a vast difference between that labelled Muscadet and the far better Muscadet-sur-lie which has been allowed to ferment on the lees (*lie*), thereby acquiring extra flavour and a certain 'zip'. The best wine is Muscadet de Sèvre-et-Maine from the area east of Nantes and between the Sèvre and Maine rivers.

Further up-river a wide variety of wines are produced: Rosé d'Anjou is perhaps best avoided, but there are some good Anjou whites made from the Chenin Blanc grape. Saumur produces some dry sparkling wines which lack the flavour of Champagne. Then, in the area around the confluence of the Loire and the Cher, excellent red wines made from the Cabernet Franc grape are produced around Saumur and Chinon. In the Touraine, ie around Tours, the best known wines are Vouvray and Montlouis which range from sweet to very dry, as well as the ubiquitous Touraine which lends its name to a wide variety of red, rosé and white styles.

Finally in the upper reaches of the river, NE of Bourges, the world famous Sancerre and Pouilly-Fumé are made from the Sauvignon Blanc grape.

These are bone-dry, flinty green wines which can be deliciously refreshing; unfortunately popularity has brought steep prices, and imitators all over the world.

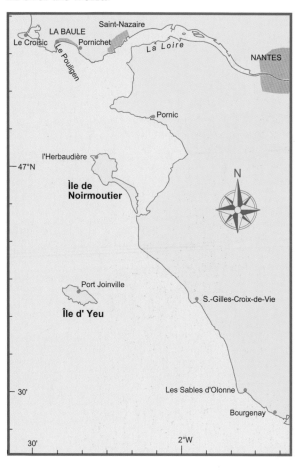

LE POULIGUEN

Le Pouliguen sits at the west end of the eponymous bay and should' properly be distinguished from La Baule its slightly ritzy neighbour, known to British soccer fans as the venue for team training (World Cup '98) – the lure of the beaches must have proved too much. Le Pouliguen is

in any case split from La Baule by the river (*Etier*) du Pouliguen in which you will berth. The split could hardly be more obvious: the east bank (La Baule) is lined by bland and anonymous apartment blocks (not typifying all of La Baule), whilst the Pouliguen side is a villagey mixture of architecture, restaurants, funfairs, trees, pubs, pavement cafés et cetera. To add to the idiosyncracies Le Pouliguen is twinned with Llantwit Major of all places, and the oddly-named town of Kisslegg in Germany!

Le Pouliguen has character and style and that can't be bad in this age of the Lowest Common Denominator. You'll like it.

TOURISM

Tourist Office Port-Sterwitz, 44510 Le Pouliguen. Tel 02.40.42.31.05. Fax 02.40.62.22.27. Open Jul/

Aug 0900-1230 & 1345-1900; out of season 0900-1200 & 1430-1800. The Affaires Maritime office is next door.

What to see/do Cycle down to Pointe de Penchâteau then westwards along the Côte Sauvage, very much less savage than some further north, but an attractive ride towards Batz-dur-Mer. The coast has low sandstone cliffs punctuated by many caves and tiny beaches, best seen at LW. See also the introduction to this chapter.

Beaches The pleasant Plage du Nau is immediately west of the river entrance. To the east, only 200m from the marina, the superb beaches of La Baule stretch for 7Km to Pornichet marina.

Bus Line 81 runs via La Baule (10 interesting mins) to St Nazaire (50 mins); and to Le Croisic.

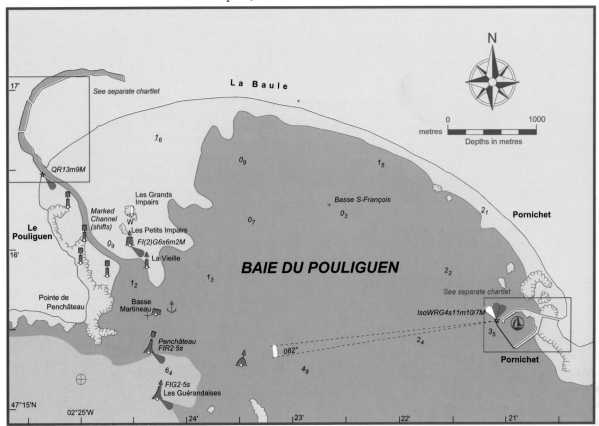

Labels on photograph: Church spire · 3rd PHM perch · PHM beacon, QR · River entrance

Approaching with about 7 cables to run

Railway Station (Tel 02.40.42.13.02) is 500m NW of the Tourist Office. Paris is 3h 5m by TGV, via St Nazaire and Nantes; timetable info Tel 08.36.35.35.35.

Taxi Tel 02.40.42.33.65; 02.40.42.33.66; 06.08.45.47.87; 06.07.53.41.67.

Ferry A passenger ferry (*navette du port*) crosses the river just south of the fuel berth HW ±3, 0900-2300, never on a Monday; short, cheap (3FF) and useful – saves walking on water.

Bike hire
- Cycles Peugeot, bd de l'Atlantique, Tel 02.40.42.32.72.
- Cyclocation, 27 rue du Gén Leclerc, Tel 02.40.62.32.94.

Car hire Ask at Tourist Office.

EATING ASHORE
Restaurants
- Le Duguay-Trouin, 26 quai Jules Sandeau. Tel 02.40.42.32.05. Menus 155FF; 215FF per head for a platter of sea food. American Express. Push the boat out in elegant surroundings.
- Marie-Claire, rue Jean Bart (opposite the PO). Tel 02.40.42.32.37. Menus 65-150FF. Slightly away from the quayside throng.

SHOPPING
Supermarkets Good old Spar, 8 Grande Rue, is north of the church, two blocks from the river. Intermarché, rue de Cornen (off bd de l'Atlantique) is a 1½km hike west of the marina.

Markets Daily in season at rue des Halles, close NNE of the church; out of season Tues, Fri and Sun 0800-1230. Stalls spill out into the surrounding streets.

Banks Several in the vicinity of Place Mauperthuis.

Launderette Boisseau Yves, 2 rue du Gare. Dry cleaning: Pressing de la Cote d'Amour, 13 rue du Bois. Tel 02.40.42.32.58.

NAVIGATIONAL MATTERS

Charts AC 2353 (1:75,000) and SHOM 7033 (1:50,000) cover Le Pouliguen and Quiberon Bay. AC 2986 and SHOM 7395 cover Le Pouliguen and the R Loire approaches at 1:50,000.

Approaches From the W/SW enter Pouliguen Bay via the waypoint 47°15´·20N 02°25´·00W, thence between Penchâteau and Les Guérandaises lateral light buoys, in the 3° white sector of Pornichet's directional light.

From the east, ie from anywhere within Pouliguen Bay, which is enclosed by a line of reefs stretching 5M ESE from Pointe de Penchâteau to Grand Charpentier light house, set course direct to Basse Martineau PHM buoy.

This line of reefs can safely be penetrated between Les Evens and Les Troves, marked by lateral buoys; less safely because unmarked, between Les Troves and Baguenaud; via Passage du Ronfle between Baguenaud and Pierre Percée NCM buoy; and

Chapter 5

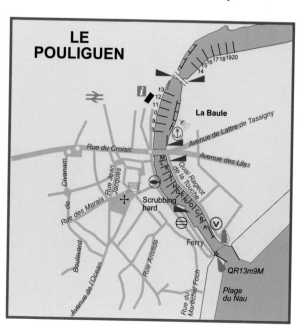

Le Pouliguen, looking NNW

finally by a variety of channels of your own devising between Pierre Percée, Le Grand Charpentier and the coast at Pte de Chémoulin. Note that Pouliguen Bay is quite shallow north of a line from Martineau buoy to Pornichet.

Pilotage The key starting position is close east of Martineau buoy at 47°15′·60N 02°24′·25W. From here survey the scene and identify all or most of the marks depicted on the chart(let). Set off on track 300° toward the southernmost of 3 decent-

sized PHM perches; this keeps you clear of the drying banks SW of La Vieille and Petits Impairs.

When close to said perch, alter approx 345° towards the 3rd of five green SHM perches which, with the other two PHM perches, will funnel you towards the entrance. Nearing the 3rd SHM perch and when the church spire bears 305°, turn slowly port as the harbour entrance (47°16′·44N 02°25′·30W) opens between two short training walls which cover.

Entrance and navigational marks near low water

Entrance looking seaward

From the above you will appreciate that the approach is a wide doglegged track, staying within the limits of an imprecise, sinuous and sometimes shifting channel. If entering at HW–3, expect to be searching around for sufficient water; better by far to wait until HW –1 when depths will be little problem even for a draught of 2m. A first-time approach at night is not advised.

Daymarks Petits Impairs is a stout SHM beacon tower which provides general orientation but does not directly contribute to pilotage. Together with La Vieille SHM beacon and Les Grands Impairs (now a small white beacon) they all mark nasties to the east of the approach channel. Pouliguen church spire is a distant mark which is hidden by buildings in mid-approach, only to re-appear when closer in. The PHM beacon, QR, at the river mouth is a slender, 13m high white 'winged' pylon, red top which you should pick up with binoculars asap – it is your eventual goal.

Tides HW Le Pouliguen at neaps is 20 mins after, and at springs 25 mins before HW Brest. LW Le Pouliguen at neaps is 25 mins, and at springs is 20 mins before LW Brest. MHWS is 5·4m, MLWS 0·7m; MHWN is 4·3m, MLWN 2·0m.

Tidal streams between Penchâteau and Les Guérandaises buoys reach 1½-2 knots at springs, setting NE/ SW. In the entrance and up-river the stream is said to reach 4 knots at half tide.

Access at HW±3 for 1·5m - 2·0m draught, best at HW –1; for 1·2m draught access is outside LW ±2½. There is a rocky sill 1·6m above CD at the harbour entrance; after crossing depths rapidly increase to at least 1·5m. In 1999 near 'A' pontoon 3·6m was sounded at HW –2½ neaps.

Hazards The drying banks and rocks either side of the approach channel, as discussed. The first bridge has only 3m air clearance.

Shelter in the marina is very good except in strong E-S winds. In the bay strong S-W winds raise a heavy sea but any swell breaks on the shallows.

Anchorage to await the tide is close east of Basse Martineau buoy in about 2m on sand.

Entrance marks, looking to seaward from 4th PHM

Chapter 5

'A' pontoon visitors   *Fuel berth*

MARINA

Bureau du Port is 500m beyond A pontoon, just past the road bridge on east side amongst trees. Square Général Masson, 44502 La Baule. Tel 02.40.11.97.97; Fax 02.40.11.97.98. VHF Ch 09. HM Pierre Le Clanche. Hours in season, daily 0800-2000; out of season 0900-1230 & 1400-1800, closed pm Sat & Sun. Weather forecasts are posted daily.

Showers are inside.

Visitors berth/raft on A pontoon, then check with the Bureau du Port.

Tariff Daily rates for LOA bands in Jul/Aug: 7-8·5m = 90-100FF; 8·5-10m = 105-118FF; 10-11·5m = 126-142FF; 11·5-13m = 150-170FF.

Fuel Diesel and petrol from pontoon on east side just before A pontoon.

NAUTICAL NEEDS

Chandlery & repairs

- SOS-Atlantique, chemin du Pré Malenpogne (700m west of the church). Tel 02.40.42.33.29.
- Ateliers Maritime Baulois (AMB), route du Guérande (near station). Tel 02.40.15.16.16.
- L'Atelier du Marin, Léniphen (1M north). Tel 02.40.15.16.74.
- Navy Plaisance, Léniphen (1M north). Tel 02.40.42.30.60.

First road bridge

'A' pontoon visitors

Foot ferry

Looking up harbour

PORNICHET

Pornichet, at the southeast end of the Baie du Pouliguen, is rather more enjoyable than you might expect from such a popular seaside resort area. The reason seems to be that away from the seething beach there are still traces of the grandeur and gentility of a century ago. Stroll up the Avenue du Général de Gaulle (how many streets, avenues and boulevards of that lofty name have I walked whilst researching this Companion?) and you cannot fail to be impressed by the Town Hall, set in immaculate flower gardens, and the village atmosphere nearer the station.

Around the Place du Marché, only a block or two from the beach, French provincial life goes on undisturbed by modern trends. A little further inland the racecourse has taken over from the former salt marshes. At Ste Sébastien to the east you may come across the *Poste des Gabelous* used as a lookout by customs officers in the days when salt was literally worth its weight in gold.

Yes, you could like Pornichet if the sheer functionality of the marina doesn't drive you away.

See also the introduction to this chapter.

TOURISM

Tourist Office 3 bd de la République (by market square), 44380 Pornichet. Tel 02.40.61.33.33. Fax 02.40.11.60.88. Open Jul/Aug 0900-1930, Sun 1000-1300 & 1500-1830; out of season 0915-1230 & 1400-1800, closed Sun.

Beaches From the marina, the superb beaches of La Baule stretch for 7km to Le Pouliguen. In the other direction cycle about 3km to Plage Ste Marguerite and two other beaches just short of Pointe de Chémoulin, less crowded and neatly tucked in between cliffy outcrops.

Bus Lines 82 & 83 run to St Nazaire (35 mins).

Railway Station (Tel 02.51.76.34.08) is 2km N of the marina, up ave du Gén de Gaulle. Paris is 2h 55m by TGV, via St Nazaire and Nantes; timetable info Tel 08.36.35.35.35.

Taxi Tel 02.40.15.21.36; 06.08.78.76.96; 06.07.06.35.46; 06.80.84.55.30.

Bike hire
• Air Bike, 52 bd des Océanides, Tel 02.40.61.58.17; from 50FF per day.

Fuel

Capitainerie

Pornichet, looking NNE

Capitainerie tower

- Balladou, 140 ave de Mazy, Tel 02.40.61.34.13.

Car hire
- Garage Hoquy, 5 ave du Général de Gaulle; Tel 02.40.61.03.12.
- Hertz, 16 bd de St Nazaire; Tel 02.40.61.08.16.
- Avis, 126 bd de la République; Tel 02.51.10.06.00.

EATING ASHORE

Restaurants At the marina there are about four eating places, crêperies etc. One such is:
- Le Brigantine. Tel 02.40.61.03.58. Eat inside or out, but not when Pornichet bridge club is there! Menus 88-98FF, cooking is over a wood fire.

Once truly ashore, bd des Océanides (the sea front) has a wide choice, mostly at resort prices, and with names like Le Sunset Beach, Parfums de Plage. Just off the Market square, try:
- Chez Pierette, 63 ave du Général de Gaulle. Tel 02.40.61.75.15. Sardines a speciality.

- La Chance, 4 ave Barthou. Tel 02.40.15.47.20. Traditional cuisine, plus moules/frites.
- Le Sud Bretagne, 42 bd de la République. Tel 02.40.11.65.00. A good hotel, restaurant/garden

SHOPPING

Supermarkets Spar, 16 bd de la République/ Place du Marché (8 mins walk from the marina); Mon-Sat 0800-1300 & 1500-2000, Sun 0830-1300.

Markets Wed and Sat mornings in the tree-lined Market Place. Stalls surround the conical-roofed covered market (Les Halles) in colourful and crowded chaos.

Banks Several in the vicinity of ave du Général de Gaulle.

Launderette La Pince à Linge, 4 ave Jeanne d'Arc (off ave Gén de Gaulle); Tel 02.40.61.49.99.

NAVIGATIONAL MATTERS

Charts AC 2353 (1:75,000) and SHOM 7033 (1:50,000) cover Le Pouliguen and Quiberon Bay. AC 2986 and SHOM 7395, both 1:50,000, cover Pornichet and the R Loire approaches. AC 2989 and SHOM 6797, both 1:15,000, cover Pornichet, the entrance to R Loire and St Nazaire.

Approaches are as for Le Pouliguen, modified slightly as follows:

From the W/SW enter Pouliguen Bay via the waypoint 47°15´·20N 02°25´·00W, thence between Penchâteau and Les Guérandaises lateral light buoys, to the marina staying in the 3° white sector of Pornichet's directional light. This is hard to make out against shore lights.

From the S and E, within Pouliguen Bay, which is enclosed by a line of reefs stretching 5M ESE from Pointe de Penchâteau to Le Grand Charpentier light house, set course direct to the marina.

The line of reefs can safely be penetrated between Les Evens and Les Troves, marked by lateral buoys; less safely because unmarked, between Les Troves and Baguenaud; via Passage du Ronfle between

Directional light IsoWG 4s

QR   QG

Marina entrance

Baguenaud and Pierre Percée NCM buoy; and finally by a variety of channels of your own devising between Pierre Percée, Le Grand Charpentier and the coast at Pte de Chémoulin. Notes: Pouliguen Bay is shallow north of a line from Martineau buoy to Pornichet. Pierre Percée islet is a Nature Reserve; no landing 1 Mar to 31 Aug.

Daymarks The marina can be hard to discern against the unbroken line of shore-side buildings, until within 1-2M, especially in poor visibility. There are no unique features other than masts.

Tides HW Pornichet at neaps is 20 mins after, and at springs 45 mins before HW Brest. LW Pornichet at neaps and at springs is 22 mins before LW Brest. MHWS is 5·5m, MLWS 0·8m; MHWN is 4·4m, MLWN 2·1m.

Tidal streams in the eastern end of Pouliguen Bay are not quoted.

Access at all tides and in all weathers. The entrance (47°15'·56N 02°21'·03W) faces north; a PHM & SHM pile inside mark the breakwater foundations.

Hazards None. The nearest reefs described above are 1M south of the marina.

Shelter in the marina is excellent. In the bay strong S-W winds raise a heavy sea and any swell breaks on the shallows.

Anchorage There are no recognised anchorages near the marina.

MARINA

Bureau du Port is on the 1st floor of a tower at the head of the marina. Port de Plaisance, BP 67, 44380 Pornichet. Tel 02.40.61.03.20; Fax 02.40.61.87.18. VHF Ch 09. HM Paul Marc Urvois. Hours in season, daily 0800-2100; out of season daily 0900-1215 & 1300-1800. Weather forecasts are posted daily. Showers at base of tower: 0815-1145 & 1730-2045; 10FF jetons.

Visitors <9m LOA berth on NE side of I pontoon; 9-12m LOA berth on the hammerheads of pontoons A, B, D, E, F, G, L, M and N; >12m LOA call VHF Ch 09 for instructions from the dory; max LOA is 25m. Depths in the marina vary from about 1·2m to 3·5m.

The marina is linked to the shore by a low road bridge, north of which is an unlit harbour almost full of local boats. This dries about 2m; access HW ±3. Nominally there are 21 ⚓s.

Tariff Daily rates for LOA bands in Jun-Sep: 7-8m = 96F; 8-9m = 113F; 9-10m = 125F; 10-11m = 140F; 11-12m = 155F; 12-14m = 190F.

Fuel Diesel and petrol at pontoon to port of the entrance, inside the head of the NW breakwater. In season 0800-2000; out of season 0900-1200 & 1400-1700.

NAUTICAL NEEDS

Chandlery & repairs

- Pornichet Marine, 166 bd des Océanides, BP 166, 44380 Pornichet. Tel 02.40.61.14.32. SHOM chart agent and chandlery.
- Electro Nautic, at marina. Tel 02.40.61.25.01. Electronic and electrical repairs.
- Inter Co-op Marine, at marina. Tel 02.40.61.09.37. Chandlery.
- Interventions Express, at marina. Tel 02.40.61.07.80. Engines and mechanical repairs.
- La Baule Nautic Chantier Naval, at marina. Tel 02.40.61.03.78. Boatyard. Repairs. Chandlery.
- Le Roy Plaisance, at marina. Tel 02.40.61.10.20. Chandlery.

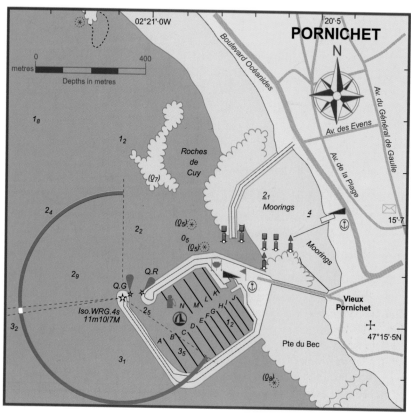

Looking NE up the Loire

ST NAZAIRE

Frank Cowper in his *Sailing Tours, Part III* had this to say in 1894:

'St Nazaire will not take long to explore. There are ninety acres of docks. There are 23,000 inhabitants. There is an old church in the old town and several hotels in the new town, and a Bureau du Santé. At the post office they do not seem to have much small change. Like many others I had to go away without the stamps I wanted because I had not got the exact amount of coin necessary. This seemed odd.'

Not his usual expansive style, but perhaps he was irked by the small change problem? Today the docks are much larger, shipbuilding appears to flourish and the population exceeds 65,000, or 200,000 if the suburbs are included. The town was bombed almost to extinction in WW2, but has been rebuilt (not to universal acclaim), along with a fine bridge across the Loire.

Two further historical notes: In WW2 the Joubert Dock was the only dry dock along the Atlantic coast big enough to berth the battleship *Tirpitz* for repairs, if damaged. Thus it was an obvious target if attacks by *Tirpitz* on Allied merchant ships were to be checked.

A British Commando raid in March 1942 destroyed the heavily defended dock gates by ramming them with the old American destroyer *Campbeltown* whose bows were packed with three tons of high explosive. Four VCs were won and many lives lost in that action which is recalled by a memorial on the seafront near the South Lock. *Tirpitz* remained in Norwegian waters, a threat to Russian convoys, until finally sunk in November 1944.

Her sister ship *Bismark*, completed at Kiel in early 1941, sailed on 18 May 1941 for the Atlantic. Ten days later, after being crippled by aircraft of the Fleet Air Arm, she was sunk.

TOURISM

Tourist Office place François Blancho, BP 178, 44613 St Nazaire (off rue Gén de Gaulle, 800m west of the Bassin de St Nazaire).
Web: www.capresse.com/saintnazaire
Tel: 02.40.22.40.65. Fax 02.40.22.19.80.

What to see/do Look round the town centre which is laid out in a grid pattern, alas with none of the charm of Rochefort, the product of an earlier age. The more pleasant residential area, with a vast green park and sports complex, is to the west and southwest. The centre is commercialised, with modern, slightly tawdry shops in the ave de la République. To the east are the docks, Atlantic Shipyards, Aérospatiale and all the hives of industry.

In the dock area, just south of the east lock, visit the Ecomuseum, in a bright yellow building, which tells the story of St Nazaire's maritime history (ocean liners and battleships). An adjunct is the French submarine *Espadon* berthed in rather sinister style in the covered lock used in WW2 by German submarines; open for visits.

Back in the fresh air enjoy the panoramic views from the concrete roof-top. Slightly further south wander round Le Petit Maroc, the former haunt of fishermen where you can pause in one or two nautical hostelries. On the west side of the Bassin de St Nazaire the former submarine base features a nautical exhibition "Escale Atlantique".

For a complete change of scene drive north out of town on the D50 to St Joachim, a village on the eastern side of the Brière Regional Natural Park. See also the introduction to this chapter.

Beaches Walk or cycle round to the Grand and Petit Traict, the first bay SW of the Avant Port. It is an attractive scene with yacht moorings, fishermen and safe bathing.

Bus Good local services.

Railway Station (Tel 02.51.76.34.62) is at the N end of bd Victor Hugo. Paris is 2h 55m by TGV, via Nantes; timetable info Tel 08.36.35.35.35.

Chapter 5

French submarine 'Espadon' in covered lock

Approaching East lock and covered submarine lock

Airport St Nazaire/Montoir, Tel 02.40.90.00.86, is just beyond the suspension bridge on the N bank. Nantes airport has daily flights to Gatwick by Britair (UK Tel 01293 502044).

Taxis Tel 02.51.76.04.04; 02.40.66.02.62.

Car hire Avis, 126 bd de la République; Tel 02.51.10.06.00. Other Tel numbers 02.40.22.25.25; 02.40.22.27.66; 02.40.22.21.22.

EATING ASHORE

Restaurants

- L'An II, 2 rue Villebois-Mareuil. Tel 02.40.00.95.33. Specialities: Seafood, La Godaille de St Nazaire. Menus 120-280FF.
- Le Moderne, 46 rue d'Anjou. Tel 02.40.22.55.88. The best of the day's catch. Menus 85-230FF.
- La Maricotte, 40 rue de la Paix. Tel 02.40.22.57.55. Seafood platter from only 49FF.
- La Pergola, 76 rue Jean Jaurès. Tel 02.40.66.79.73. Inexpensive Italian food and takeaway.

SHOPPING

Supermarkets Main shopping area, partly pedestrianised, in and around ave de la République.

Markets Tues, Fri and Sun mornings in the place du Commerce.

Banks Several in the vicinity of rue du Général de Gaulle.

Launderette Laverie Claire Nett, 101 ave de la République. Tel 02.40.66.41.87.

NAVIGATIONAL MATTERS

Charts AC 2986 and SHOM 7395 (both 1:50,000) cover the R Loire approaches. AC 2989 and SHOM 6797 (both 1:15,000) cover the entrance to R Loire and St Nazaire. AC 2985 and SHOM 7396 (1:20,000) cover the Loire up to Nantes.

Approaches The main 'Big Ship' Chenal du Sud starts at the SN-1 landfall buoy (47°00′·14N 02°39′·75W) and trends NE for 25M up a well-marked fairway to St Nazaire. From the WNW (Quiberon Bay) the broad unmarked Chenal du Nord runs ESE from Pte du Croisic and Plateau du Four; ESE of Le Grand Charpentier lighthouse it joins the Chenal du Sud. Yachts coming from due south past Île de Noirmoutier or from the southeast (Baie de Bourgneuf) should join the Chenal du Sud at any convenient point. Monitor VHF Ch 12 (16) St Nazaire Port Control throughout the approach.

A **waypoint** common to all approaches is 47°12′·11N 02°17′·24W (No 6 PHM buoy, Iso R 4s), 6M downstream of Saint Nazaire.

Pilotage From the waypoint buoy-hop just outside the line of PHM buoys, initially on a track of 025°. Between Nos 10 and 12 PHM buoys the channel veers onto 054°; 3·7 miles remain from abeam the conspicuous Pointe d'Aiguillon lighthouse to St Nazaire.

It is better to keep to the NW side of the channel, both in/out-bound, so as to:

a. retain easy access in emergency to the bays/ anchorages on the NW side;
b. keep clear of extensive drying shoals on the SE side (NB: Les Morées SHM beacon); and
c. avoid crossing the fairway near the sometimes busy port area.

The west and east jetties marking the entrance

East lock from the river

to the Avant Port and access to the South Lock (big ships) are easily seen. Before crossing this entrance, double-check that nothing is about to enter or leave – your rights of way are infinitesimal!

Skirt round the outside of the Avant Port to pass between the Vieux Môle (prominent lighthouse) and the SCM buoy marking Basse Nazaire. Continue to 47°16'·57N 02°11'·70W; from here the East Lock and its white control tower, the former submarine tunnel and the Joubert lock are all readily apparent, to the W and NW of you.

Daymarks The long elegant suspension bridge with two red/white towers (55m clearance) is just over 1M upstream of the East Lock, but in average visibility is easily seen from much further down-river. St Nazaire and the shipyard cranes are obvious but no feature is unique.

Harbour layout The Avant Port is almost enclosed by a pair of crab-like claws (the W and E jetties) which shelter the South Lock. Do not intrude here; it is not for yachts. Big ships transit the South Lock into Bassin de St Nazaire, the first of two colossal basins, 750m long.

At the north end of it a narrow passage, with swing bridge but no lock, leads into the Bassin de Penhoët which is an even more impressive 1150m long.

The East Lock (see under Pilotage) is the only item of real interest because through it yachts enter into the Bassin de St Nazaire, midway along the eastern side (for lock details see under Access); it is in effect a handy side-door, used by fishing vessels, yachts and other small fry.

The 350m long Joubert Dock (or *Forme-Écluse Louis Joubert*) lies at the SE corner of Bassin de Penhoët and is mainly used as a dry dock, rarely as a transit lock. At my last visit a new cruise ship *Mistral* had pride of place in it whilst being 'launched' by the French Prime Minister. It was the scene of a dramatic Commando raid in WW2 (see opening paragraph).

Tides HW St Nazaire at neaps is 30 mins after, and at springs 40 mins before HW Brest. LW St Nazaire at neaps and at springs is 10 mins before LW Brest.

MHWS is 5·8m, MLWS 0·8m; MHWN is 4·6m, MLWN 2·2m.

Tidal streams in the river are strong. Off the entrance to the Avant Port at mid-tide the spring ebb reaches 3·3 knots and the flood 3·0 knots.

Anchorage Yachts can stay afloat near 47°15'N 02°15'W, in the lee of Pte d'Aiguillon in about 4m on sand/mud, but keep clear of Roche Trébézy 0·9m. This anchorage is between the front and rear Portcé 025° leading lights and almost 3M downstream from St Nazaire. Or anchor closer to the town between the Avant Port's W jetty and Villès-Martin in 2-5m mud clear of the fairway.

BASSINS DE SAINT NAZAIRE AND PENHOËT

Capitainerie is at 3bis bd du Verdun, BP 422, 44616 St Nazaire. Tel 02.40.00.45.20; Fax 02.40.00.45.66. Open H24. VHF Ch 12. HM Gérard Patey.

Access at all tides and in all weathers. Time your approach so as to carry the flood tide up to St Nazaire, ideally arriving at about

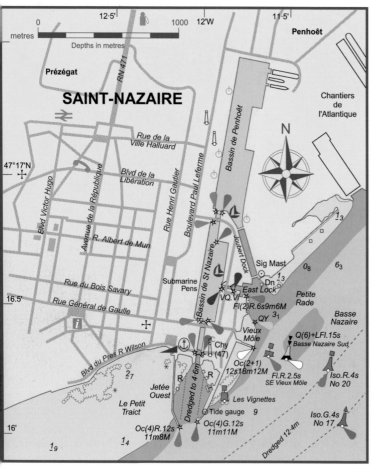

Locking out of East Lock; submarine pens behind.

slack water. Shelter in the Bassin de St Nazaire is excellent.

The **East Lock** (and associated swing bridge) opens for departures at even hours and for entrance at even hours + 10. Listen on VHF Ch 12 (24 hours).

Visitors are admitted temporarily without allocation of a berth. It is strongly advised to pre-book on Tel 02.40.00.45.20 (Capitainerie). On arrival the office in the lock control tower is a helpful source of information.

Berthing options in the Bassin de St Nazaire include: in the SW corner, south of the submarine pens; or on the E side, quai des Frégates, having turned 90° starboard out of the lock. Some live-aboard yachts and small fishing boats berth on quai Demange (turn 90° port out of the lock). In the Bassin de Penhoët immediately to starboard of the narrow inter-connecting passage, some yachts berth near the Joubert Dock. Call HM VHF Ch 12 for instructions if in doubt.

Alongside berths are those of a commercial port, ie against stone quays rather than pontoons. Both Bassins are dredged 8·7m. Fresh water is available; electricity on request. Security (against rogues) appears not to be a problem, despite appearances to the contrary, ie the usual run-down dockland ambience, with no security fencing nor lockable access gates.

Fuel None for yachts, nearest at Pornichet

NAUTICAL NEEDS

Chandlery & repairs (Pornichet is a far better place for all yachting needs).

Vieux môle
Oc(2+1) 12s   Oc(4)R 12s   Oc(4)G.12s

Avant Port and suspension bridge

- Le Comptoir de la Mer, quai Demange, 44600 St Nazaire. Tel 02.40.22.49.46. SHOM chart agent and chandlery. Also at 4 bd René Coty, Tel 02.40.22.21.71.
- L'Île aux Trésors, 2 quai des Frégates. Tel 02.40.22.46.16. Boatyard repairs, chandlery.

THE LOIRE TO NANTES

It is 28M from St Nazaire's East lock to the marina at Trentemoult, 47°11´·81N 01°34´·68W, on the W side of Nantes. The river is navigable by sea-going vessels. The first 9M are dredged from 6m to 13m; thereafter there is never less than 5m depth, usually more.

The river is well buoyed and lit, but also industrialised and uninspiring. Nearer to Nantes the scenery improves, but never attains the languid, almost majestic beauty which characterises the upper Loire of châteaux and vineyard fame.

Tides HW Nantes at neaps is 1h 35m, and at springs 55 mins after HW Brest. LW Nantes at neaps is 1h 25m and at springs 2h 15m after LW Brest.

MHWS is 6·3m, MLWS 0·9m; MHWN is 5·1m, MLWN 1·8m.

Tidal streams in the river are strong. Off St Nazaire at mid-tide the spring ebb reaches 3·3 knots and the flood 3·0 knots.

Pilotage Leave St Nazaire at HW Brest −4½, on the first of the flood; a 5 knot boat should allow about 4½ hours for the passage up-river, reaching Nantes about 1 to 1½ hours before local HW.

Trentemoult marina is on the S bank 1·4M up-river from the Pont de Cheviré (50m clearance)

and just before the Île de Ste Anne where the river divides. It is small and mostly dries, but is sheltered from all winds except NW gales. It is about 4km from the city centre.

Bureau du Port quai Surcouf, 44400 Rezé. Tel 02.40.84.09.14. HM M Legoeuil. In season open Mon-Sat 0830-1200 & 1400-1800; out of season, Tue-Sat same hours. No fuel except in cans from nearest garage.

Visitors berth alongside/raft up on the N side of pontoon A, the northernmost of threes. This dries at LW but fin keels sink into soft mud, no need for yacht legs. Max LOA 12m, max stay 8 days. No anchoring off the marina as it is a turning area for large vessels.

Nantes is a major city of half a million souls and capital of the Loire-Atlantique département, yet still retains its strong historical ties with Brittany. The old quarter, cathedral and Château des Ducs de Bretagne are among the many tourist attractions, as are the parks and flower gardens so much in evidence.

If you don't visit by boat, it is well worth a day trip by rail, bus or car from St Nazaire or Pornic. Rail and bus links are excellent; 2 hours by TGV to Paris. The airport is south of the city. The Tourist Office is off the place du Commerce; Tel 02.40.20.60.00. Web www.capresse.com/nantes

Canal connections De-masted vessels can enter the River Erdre via the St Felix lock (on the N side of the Île de Ste Anne) and a 900m tunnel below the city. The Erdre leads to Quiheix lock and into the Nantes-Brest canal which runs WNW to join the Vilaine River south of Redon.

Chapter 5

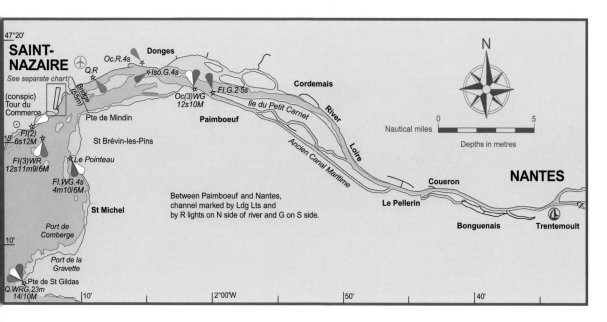

PORNIC

Pornic is the first significant harbour south of the River Loire. Brittany is astern, although historical ties remain strong. The Loire valley, famed for its châteaux and wines, is close to hand. Ahead lies the Vendée and beyond the Charente Maritime stretching south to the Gironde.

These two départements and their offshore islands encompass some of the finest cruising on the west coast. It's hot (or should be!), towns and villages are white-walled and red-tiled. The first hint of the Mediterranean is in the air ...

TOURISM

Tourist Office is at the railway station by the road bridge across the inner end of Le Vieux Port. Place de la Gare, BP 61, 44210 Pornic. Tel 02.40.82.04.40. Fax 02.40.82.90.12.

What to see/do Pornic goes hand in glove with Bluebeard's castle, at least in the tourist's mind. Gilles de Retz, he of the Blue Beard (*Barbe Bleu*), serial killer (6 wives) and chum of Jeanne d'Arc, built it back in the Middle ages; it has since been face-lifted, but still peers downriver from above the trees.

The setting is attractive and the riverside walk from the marina to the town is 15 minutes of pure delight. Fine summer residences shaded by parasol pines back the marina; sand and flowers everywhere vie with each other.

From the quays make the effort to clamber up the steep flights of steps to the upper town (*ville haute*) where you will be rewarded by the charming cobbled streets around the church and market place (markets are on Thursday and Sunday). Pause to sample the local vin du Pays Nantais made from the Gros Plant grape; it's light and tart, guaranteed to cleanse your palate!

Beaches Plage de La Noëveillard is an excellent beach immediately west of the marina. A series of good beaches extend further west past Ste Marie, and to the east if you across the river.

Bus Line 3/3E runs via Bourgneuf (20 mins) to Nantes (1h 10m). A Minibus goes to St Nazaire.

Railway Station (Tel 02.40.82.00.06) is at the end of Le Vieux Port. Change at Nantes (70 mins) for Paris 2h 10m by TGV; timetable info Tel 08.36.35.35.35.

Taxi Tel 02.40.82.17.13. Bike hire. Ask at the Tourist Office.

Car hire Tel 02.40.82.60.60.

Bluebeard's Castle and the drying harbour

EATING ASHORE

Restaurants A dozen or so restaurants, crêperies etc are at the west end of the marina. In town:
- Au Rendez-Vous des Pêcheurs, 10 quai Leray (north side of Vieux Port). Tel 02.40.82.02.51.
- Crêperie du Môle, 34 quai Leray. Tel 02.40.82.91.36.
- Chez Ange, quai du Cdt l'Herminier (south side of Vieux Port).
- Beau Rivage, plage de la Birochère (1·5km east of river). Tel 02.40.82.03.08. Menus 125-270FF.

SHOPPING

Supermarkets There are none close to the marina. The nearest is Super U, about 300m east of the rail station, on ave du Général de Gaulle. Or cycle about a mile west to Ste Marie where there is a Comod close to the high-spired church.

Markets Place du Marché (by the church) on Thursday and Sunday.

Banks Several in the upper town.

NAVIGATIONAL MATTERS

Charts AC 2981 and SHOM 7394, both 1:50,000, cover Pointe de St Gildas to Fromentine including Île de Noirmoutier and a 1:15,000 inset of Pornic. AC 2986 and SHOM 7395 cover the R Loire and western approaches to Pornic at 1:50,000.

Approaches From whichever direction you approach make for the waypoint 47°06′·10N 02°08′·70W.

You can only get at Pornic from the west or southwest, by entering the Baie de Bourgneuf between Pointe de St Gildas and the reefs off the northern end of Île de Noirmoutier. That assumes that you are not approaching via the Goulet de Fromentine at the south tip of Île de Noirmoutier. If you are, *bonne chance!*

Rounding Pointe St Gildas is non-stressful if you keep 5 cables off both it and Banc de Kerouars, a long dorsal shoal a mile or so south. Near its W end La Couronnée rock drying 2·2m is marked by

Nord-Couronnée NCM buoy; further west is a SHM buoy for the Loire's Chenal du Sud.

From the SW you will probably round Pte de l'Herbaudière via the Chenal de la Grise and Basse du Martroger NCM beacon tower, thence direct to Pornic. Chenal de la Grise is a fairly shallow, narrow passage and in heavy weather it might be wise to take the longer route to seaward of Île du Pilier and Grand Sécé NCM beacon.

Pilotage From the WPT set course 073°/1·5M direct to the marina 47°06′·53N 02°06′·59W. The small SWM buoy is a mere 50m from the marina entrance; leave it close to starboard and enter N of two PHM piles.

Daymarks At the waypoint Notre Dame isolated danger beacon is 7 cables SE of you – not so very isolated because it marks the west end of a string of drying rocks which lie 1·5M south and southeast of the marina; these and oyster beds extend all round the head of the Bay, eventually merging with those NE of Île de Noirmoutier.

Only La Noëveillard light house and the church spire are even remotely conspicuous, depending on the latest height of trees; they are in transit 055°. The former's white sector (in which the waypoint lies) leads between Banc de Kerouars and Notre Dame. A SPM buoy, Fl Y 2·5s and bearing 230° from the marina entrance 7 cables, marks the end of a sewer outfall.

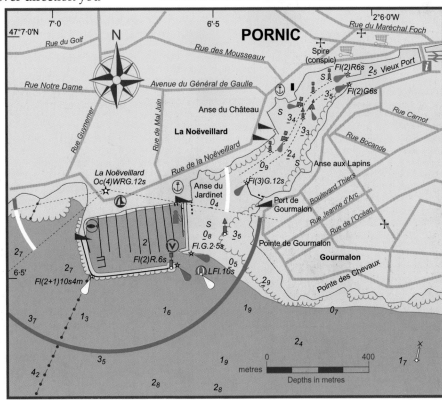

Unlit — Fl(2)R 6s — Fl.G 2·5s — LFl 10s

Marina entrance

Boat hoist — Drying, rocky ledge

Fuel berth

P3 pontoon — P2 pontoon visitors — P1 pontoon visitors — F Pontoon

Marina: pontoon identification

Tides HW Pornic at neaps is 50 mins before, and at springs 30 mins after HW Brest. LW Pornic at neaps and springs is 10 mins before LW Brest.

MHWS is 5·8m, MLWS 0·8m; MHWN is 4·6m, MLWN 2·2m.

Tidal streams one mile WSW of the marina set E at 1½kn and W at 2kn, max spring rates.

Access to the marina approx HW±5. At springs

(Coeff >75) there would be insufficient water to enter LW±1, due to silting. In >F7 southerlies the entrance would be dangerous.

Port de Gourmalon is a pleasant spot if you get bored with marinas. It is best approached above mid-flood on a first visit. The river channel is buoyed and perched; it dries 0·8m at the mouth. The moorings dry approx 2·4m, but shoal draft yachts on the outer trots probably stay afloat; the occasional foreign visitor moors there. It would be uncomfortable in strong S-W winds and is on the 'wrong' side of the river.

Le Vieux Port This is primarily for fishing boats, although few remain; it dries 2·5m. The quays are those of a working harbour. Although very central to the town, you would probably want to have strong reasons for shifting there from the marina and a land recce would be sensible.

Hazards Near LW the shoals at the mouth of the drying river are a trap for the unwary.

Shelter in the marina is good, but the **Ⓥ** berths on P1 and P2 are exposed to strong E/SE winds.

Anchorage A waiting anchorage is 5 cables west of the marina in 3m, on sand and mud.

MARINA

Capitainerie is at the NE corner of the marina. Port de Plaisance, La Noëveillard, BP 22, 44210 Pornic. Tel 02.40.82.05.40; Fax 02.40.82.55.37. www.port-pornic.com HM Gérard Bazin. VHF Ch 09. Office hours in season, daily 0900-1230 & 1400-1830. Weather forecasts posted daily.

Visitors Pontoon lettering is mildly confusing; say no more! All you need to remember is:

The 2nd & 3rd pontoons (P2 & P1) to starboard of the entrance have **Ⓥ** finger berths near their outer ends; P1 also has some alongside/rafting berths. Or berth on any vacant hammerheads of other pontoons. Very large yachts should pre-arrange to berth on pontoon PA (outer end of A) at the far end. Depths in the marina vary from about 2m to 2·5m, depending on silting.

Launderette/Showers (free and good; access H24) are next to the Capitainerie.

Tariff Daily rates for LOA bands in Jul/Aug; second figure is the rate for Jun & Sep. The Oct to May rates are half those for Jun & Sep:
LOA 7·5-8·5m = 100/84F; <9m = 108/93F; <10m = 118/100F; <11m = 136/115F; <12m = 152/127F; <13m = 174/147F; <14m = 197/160F.

Fuel Diesel and petrol pontoon is on the west side of the Boat Hoist, between P2 and P3. Daily 0900-1215 & 1400-1830 (1900 in season). Near LW manoeuvering space may be restricted by a drying ledge about 8m inshore of the rather small pontoon.

NAUTICAL NEEDS

Chandlery & repairs

- Pornic Nautic, at marina. Tel 02.40.82.11.82. Chandlery.
- Pro Océan, at marina. Tel 02.51.74.01.01. Chandlery, rigging, sails.
- Inter Co-op Marine, 2 rue du Maréchal Foch. Tel 02.40.82.01.95. Chandlery.
- Pornic Mécanique, ZI La Blavetiere (2km east on D751). Tel 02.40.82.00.55. Engine repairs.

The following companies are at ZA les Terres Jarries, about 500m NNW of the marina:

- Polypat. Tel 02.40.82.55.75. GRP hull repairs, engineering.
- Mecamer. Tel 02.40.82.28.04. Maintenance, engineering, Volvo, Tohatsu.
- Marine Service. Tel 02.40.82.28.04. Repairs, engineering, Volvo.

Looking up-river to the Vieux Port

Port de Gourmalon, looking seaward

Chapter 5

L'HERBAUDIÈRE

Red/white radio mast

LB shed

The town and harbour, looking WSW

L'Herbaudière sits in splendid isolation at the NW tip of Île de Noirmoutier, a 10·5M long thin strip of sand, soil and salt rarely more than 15 metres above, and in places below sea level. The principal town Noirmoutier-en-l'Île is on the NE side with a drying fishing harbour.

To the west a network of dykes protects the salt marshes and extensive saltpans; the polders (reclaimed land) have a distinctly Dutch look with several windmills. Further south long sandy beaches culminate in the potentially dangerous Goulet de Fromentine which the spring ebb scours at up to 8 knots – and the mainland bridge clears by 24m.

If you prefer the Gois causeway, drive your 4 wheels across only at LW–1½ to +1; for motorists who get their tidal sums wrong there are three refuges – smacks of a Peyton cartoon! Do not try to sail over it at any state of the tide; the causeway dries 3m and areas south of it dry 3·8m.

TOURISM

Tourist Office There is none in L'Herbaudière. In Noirmoutier-en-l'Île it is just downstream of the bridge at Route du Pont, BP 125. Tel 02.51.39.80.71. Fax 02.51.39.53.16.

What to see/do Cycle the 5km to Noirmoutier-en-l'Île to check out the harbour, pausing *en route* at Luzay to visit the goat cheese museum! In Noirmoutier-en-l'Île there are two museums: One is rather good on traditional boatbuilding, open in season 1000-1900 daily; the other, within the 15th century castle keep, houses an extraordinary selection of geological, ornithological, nautical,

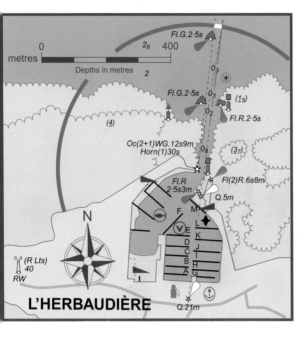

L'HERBAUDIÈRE

- Peugeot Garage de l'Île, 88 route de L'Herbaudière: Tel 02.51.39.16.45.

Ferries run from Bois de la Chaise to Pornic. Also from Pointe de la Fosse (island's south tip) to St Gilles-Croix-de-Vie.

EATING ASHORE

Restaurants The following restaurants are along the south side of the harbour:
- Le Jusant. Tel 02.51.39.71.44. Menus 82-185FF.
- La Courmaroune. Tel 02.51.39.06.02. Menus 78-148FF. Mme & M Le Boulh. Blue neon sign.
- La Marine (overlooking the fishing basin). Tel 02.51.39.23.09. Menus 80-250FF. Seafood specialities. I ate very well here on my last visit, good service and welcoming ambience. Book early.
- La Grande Voile (by the Fish market). Tel 02.51.39.09.30. Menus 60-161FF. Garish decor.

There is a far wider choice of restaurants in Noirmoutier-en-l'Île.

historical and other ...ical bits and pieces.

Across the bridge from Noirmoutier-en-l'Île you come to Océanile, an aquatic theme park which makes a 'definitely different' family day out. Open 1000-1900 daily. Tel 02.51.35.91.35.

On your return cycle along the attractive coastal route which includes the beautiful wooded Bois de la Chaise, where you can swim and recce the anchorage, qv. If you're in walking mode, a 2FF booklet suggests half a dozen good itineraries; take heart that there are no hills.

Beaches ESE of the harbour various beaches are interspersed amongst the rocky cliffs, leading to the Plage des Dames just northeast of Noirmoutier-en-l'Île. In contrast the west coast has huge almost endless stretches of fine sandy beach, backed by dunes.

Bus No 18 bus runs the length of the island: L'Herbaudière, via Noirmoutier, to Fromentine.

Taxis L'Herbaudière: Tel 02.51.39.12.69. Noirmoutier-en-l'Île: 02.51.39.07.07; 02.51.39.40.80.

Bike hire None in L'Herbaudière, but in Noirmoutier-en-l'Île contact:
- Charier Cycles, 23 ave Joseph-Pineau. Tel 02.51.39.01.25.
- La Boite à Pêche, rue du Boucaud. Tel 02.51.39.08.41.

Car Hire None in L'Herbaudière, but in Noirmoutier-en-l'Île contact:
- Europcar, 33 ave de la Victoire. Tel 02.51.39.98.14.

Capitainerie

Rear ldg mark

Fuel berth

Labels on image: Lifeboat shed · Fl(2)R 6s · Front 188° leading lights, both Q · Rear · Fl.R 2·5s · Dir.Oc(2+1)WG 12s · 2nd PHM perch

Closing the harbour entrance, slightly west of the leading line

SHOPPING

Supermarkets A convenient mini-market, Superette, is next to the Capitainerie; open 0800-1300 & 1500-2000. L'Herbaudière only has the usual butcher, baker, candle-stick etc...

Banks One in each of Noirmoutier-en-l'Île, Barbâtre and L'Épine.

NAVIGATIONAL MATTERS

Charts AC 2981 and SHOM 7394, both 1:50,000, cover Pointe de St Gildas to Fromentine including Île de Noirmoutier and with 1:15,000 insets of L'Herbaudière and Noirmoutier-en-l'Île. AC 2986 and SHOM 7395, both 1:50,000, cover the northern approaches to L'Herbaudière.

Approaches From NW to NE make for Basse du Martroger, a chunky NCM beacon light tower. The limits of this quadrant are marked by Grand Sécé NCM beacon to the NW and by Basse des Pères ECM spar buoy to the NE. In the middle of the quadrant (red sector of the Martroger light) Banc de la Blanche is about 2M N of the harbour with least depths of 1·1m; it is marked by a NCM spar buoy.

From the S or W, approach via Chenal de la Grise orientated 057° towards Martroger light and passing between the rocks off Pointe de L'Herbaudière and the rocky plateau surrounding Ile du Pilier to the NW. This narrowish channel is adequately marked and in Martroger's 055°-060° white sector; it is however quite shallow (2·6m) and the streams set along it at up to 3kn springs.

Pilotage The **waypoint** 47°02′·42N 02°17′·60W is at the intersection of L'Herbaudière's 187·5° leading line with the centre of Martroger's 055°-060° white sector. It is 7½ cables north of the harbour entrance.

By day the leading marks are hard to see (the rear mark looks like a yacht mast), so take bearings on the head of the west breakwater to ensure that you do not drift east of track towards very shallow patches (0·3m and 0·2m) and the Potée de Beurre rocks drying up to 2·9m; westerly drift is less serious. The final 400m is marked by two SHM light buoys, one PHM light buoy and two PHM perches; it is dredged 1·5m.

At night the narrow 2½° white sector (187·5°-190°) of the W breakwater ☆, Oc (2+1) WG 12s, overlaps the 187·5° leading lights, both Q, visible 098°-278°.

Daymarks Good general orientation is provided by: the twin light houses on Île du Pilier, 290°/2·7M from the harbour and by a 40m red/white radio mast and a water tower, respectively 500m west, and 1·4M ESE of the harbour – in addition to other marks mentioned in the text. The red-roofed,

NW jetty and daymarks

- Super U, rue du Nord (250m past the heliport): open Mon-Fri 0900-1230 & 1530-1930 (Fri-2015); Sat 0900-1930; Sun shut.

Markets Place du Marché every morning; ditto in St-Sauveur.

Banks Sufficient.

Launderette rue Neptune (400m south of Capitainerie); Tel 02.51.58.32.07; daily 0930-1930.

NAVIGATIONAL MATTERS

Charts AC 3640 covers Joinville at 1:10,000. However Île d'Yeu, and the shallow Pont d'Yeu with its anchoring and fishing prohibitions, are covered only by AC 2663 at very small scale (1:200,000). So too is the coast for 30M from Notre Dame de Monts, where AC 2981 (1:50,000) ends, to a point 1·5M SE of Bourgenay where AC 2641 (1:50,000) resumes.

French coverage, as might be expected, is very complete. SHOM 6613 (on which AC 3640 is partially based) also covers Joinville at 1:10,000. 6890 covers Île d'Yeu at 1:20,000; and 6853 covers Fromentine to St Gilles-Croix-de-Vie at 1:47,000. 6853 is substantially overlapped by the useful 6523 which covers Île d'Yeu to Les Sables d'Olonne at 1:47,200.

Approaches Île d'Yeu is about 5M long x 2M wide, orientated WNW/ESE, with the only major port, Joinville, on its N side. The 9.5M wide gap between the island and the mainland is reduced to half that width by the rocky shoals of Pont d'Yeu, marked at its seaward end by an unlit south cardinal buoy. Do not pass between this buoy and the mainland. A 2M wide band, where anchoring is prohibited due to cables and a water pipe, runs NE from the island to the mainland.

In effect the Joinville waypoint, 46°44'·80N 02°19'·50W, can be approached directly from either the W-N quadrant or from the E-SSE sector, or indirectly from around the ends of the island. Note that the island is generally foul for about 5 cables offshore.

Near the waypoint are Basse Mayence and La Sablaire shoals, marked respectively by north and south cardinal buoys, but deep enough for yachts to sail between these buoys. It is also safe to

Total tanks and marina

Avant port

navigate between the south cardinal and the island shore.

Pilotage The waypoint is 3 cables WNW of Basse Mayence NCM buoy, and on the 219° leading line, 1·3M from the harbour ent, 46°43'·82N 02°20'·68W. The leading marks are green-topped white towers, with the church tower almost in transit. The final approach is straightforward, utilising some or all of the numerous daymarks listed below.

On entering the outer harbour keep to port, closer to the distinctive concrete pillars and passerelle (warping piers) than to the drying NW side. At the ☆ Fl R 2·5s, turn 180° port into the marina, staying wide to allow outbound yachts to turn inside you; visibility is restricted here.

Daymarks A 50m high, white water tower (inverted cone shape) is the most conspicuous mark on Yeu. If the leading marks are not seen, an approach with it bearing 224° leads to the harbour entrance. The island lighthouse (Petite Foule, Fl 5s) may be seen beyond the water tower.

From a mile or two offshore the following are easily seen: Two conspicuous duck-egg blue Total oil tanks on the S side of the marina; and a brick chimney (which looks overdue for demolition) near the root of the NW Jetty and close SW of the helipad. The church tower with cupola leads 204° through the outer harbour.

Disregard a squat green-topped white light tower (now disused), 300m along the NW Jetty.

Tides At Joinville HW neaps is 40 mins before, and at springs 15 mins after HW Brest. LW at

neaps is 35 mins, and at springs 30 mins before LW Brest.

MHWS is 5·0m, MLWS 0·7m; MHWN is 4·0m, MLWN 1·9m.

Tidal streams 7 cables N of the harbour set roughly ESE/WNW at 0·8kn, max spring rates.

Access at all tides, day/night, and in all weathers.

Hazards When approaching along the coast from the east keep 5 cables offshore and at the entrance give La Galiote PHM buoy a wide berth to avoid 0·3m patches.

Shelter in the marina is very good, even when swell enters the harbour in northerly winds.

Anchorages Temporary, fair weather anchorage between the harbour entrance and La Sablaire SCM buoy to the east. A pleasant day ⚓ is 6 cables ESE in Anse de Ker Châlon on sand/mud in 3m, where there is a sandy beach for swimming or a picnic.

MARINA

Capitainerie is near C pontoon. Port de Plaisance, 85350 Île d'Yeu. Tel 02.51.58.38.11; Fax 02.51.26.03.49. VHF Ch 09. HM G Bezille. Office hours Jul/Aug 0700-2200; in season, daily 0800-1300 & 1400-2000; out of season 0800-1200 & 1400-1730. Weather forecasts posted daily.

Visitors may be directed to a berth by the HM's dory. If not, berth on *accueil* pontoon (beyond B pontoon). Do not berth on a hammerhead unless you have a large multihull. Depths in the marina vary from about 1·5m to 2·5m.

Fishing vessels, ferries and vedettes occupy the rest of the harbour. The Bassin à Flot, 3·7m deep, is used by a few trawlers and the occasional coaster. It may also be used by pleasure vessels too large for the marina or when the marina is full; it has no pontoons. Access HW±2 via a gate with traffic lights.

Showers are in the Capitainerie. Access 0700-1300 & 1400-2000; 5FF for 10 mins.

Tariff Daily rates for LOA bands in Jul/Aug: 7m = 98FF; 8m = 124FF; 10m = 153FF; 12m = 179FF.

Fuel Diesel & petrol pontoon is on the starboard side of the marina entrance. In season daily 0900-1200 & 1530-1900; out of season 0900-1030.

PORT DE LA MEULE

46°41'·70N 02°20'·60W, on the south coast is a delightful spot for a day trip (7M) or a possible overnight stay in very settled offshore conditions. It is better to anchor outside the tiny drying harbour which is totally exposed to the south; a prior recce by bike may help you decide. Distance is similar east or west about, so you might as well circum-navigate! SHOM chart 6890 is almost essential.

Port de la Meule has several good seafood restaurants., south side of marina.

NAUTICAL NEEDS

Chandlery & repairs

- Libraire Nautique, south side of marina. Sells a wide range of SHOM charts and publications. Open Mon-Sat 0930-1230 & 1430-1930; Sun 1030-1230 & 1600-1900.
- Compte Nautique, place du Champs de Foire (near Super U). Tel 02.51.58.73.40. Repairs.
- Inter Co-op Marine, quai Vernier. Tel 02.51.58.36.51. Chandlery.

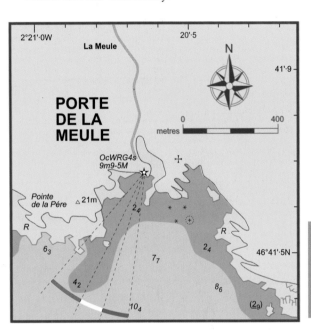

Chapter 5

Port de la Meule. Inner drying harbour

St Gilles, looking NW

Labels on image: Railway station · Grande Plage · Church spire · Fuel · Visitors' pontoons · New pontoons due to be installed

St Gilles-Croix-de-Vie

First this mouthful of a name: St Gilles-Croix-de-Vie is a commune made up of St Gilles to the east and Croix-de-Vie to the west of the dividing River Vie; usually abbreviated to St Gilles, as in the rest of this descriptive text. The marina is in Croix-de-Vie, although now spreading to the east bank. Port-la-Vie is a brand name, but more accurate than most marketing terminology! End of etymology lesson.

St Gilles is sometimes described disparagingly as a seaside resort, which it is – thanks to a vast amount of sand! But it is not in the same league as La Baule. Behind the beaches and the facade of hotels and apartment blocks, one can still find the old fishermen's cottages and two lively markets. The fish quays and market are very active and the marina has rather more character than some; it is also efficiently and pleasantly run.

TOURISM

Tourist Office bd de l'Egalité (near to the Capitainerie), BP 57, 85800 St Gilles-Croix-de-Vie. Tel 02.51.55.03.66. Fax 02.51.55.69.60. Mon-Sat 0930-1930; Sun 1000-1230 & 1500-1900.

What to see/do A stroll downriver, preferably at LW springs, is instructive. From the end of the Jetée de Boisvinet watch French yachts come barrelling in with typical abandon, only to stand on their stems abeam the first PHM buoy – having found least water the hard way! Take note of two good restaurants here (qv), but carry on out to Pointe de Grosse-Terre lighthouse.

Or from the marina walk upstream to the first bridge where you can cross to St Gilles proper, perhaps en route to the Super U, qv. Croix-de-Vie has the edge over St Gilles, despite its totally awful rue Général de Gaulle, a pedestrian street chock-a-block with tacky shops, candyfloss and grockles – the good Général's lofty nose would surely have wrinkled in disdain.

Finally a 9km bike ride (D38 north to Le Pissot, where fork right D69) takes you to the so-called Ecomusée du Bois Juquaud. This is a fascinating reconstruction of how people lived and worked in fairly primitive conditions a century ago on the marshlands (Marais Bretons).

Beaches No shortage of sand here! Plage de Boisvinet, just beyond the jetty of that name, is the nearest. Grande Plage, cross by dinghy or passeur (see under Ferries), stretches 13 miles to Les Sables d'Olonne; pick your patch. A mere 7 mile beach runs NW to St-Jean-de-Monts.

Bus Infrequent and slow service, Line 11, to Nantes (2h 10m); plus local services.

Railway Station is 300m NW of the marina, by the main fish basin. Paris is about 4 hours, change to TGV at Nantes (1h 25m). Local trains go to Fromentine (1h 15m) and Sables d'Olonne (45m).

Taxis Tel 02.51.55.04.26.

Bike hire
- Spad'Loc, bd de l'Egalité (behind the Capitainerie). Tel 06.12.49.98.54.
- Eurl Berthomé, 45/47 quai Gorin (west bank upstream from bridge). Tel 02.51.55.47.09.
- Ets Gérard Gateau, rue du Calvaire (next to Super U). Tel 02.51.55.48.56.

Car hire Agence Lambot Voyages (Avis, Hertz, Europcar), 2 rue Gén de Gaulle. 02.51.55.52.21.

Ferries to Port Joinville (55m) leave the embarkation jetty near Grand Môle at 0800, 1030, 1815 in Jul/Aug. Return from Yeu at 0915, 1700 and 1930. Tel 02.51.54.15.15.

A foot ferry (*passeur*) runs from the NW fish basin to Pointe de la Garenne. Brilliant short cut to the Grande Plage. Jul/Aug, every 15 mins from 1400-2000; 4FF single, 7FF return.

EATING ASHORE

Restaurants
Croix-de-Vie:
- Café Rochebonne, quai de la République (by front ldg lt). Popular, cheap seafood plat du jour.
- La Fauvette, 56 quai de la République. Tel 02.51.55.01.68. Menus 64-194FF. Traditional.
- Les Embruns, 16 bd de la Mer (by Jetée de Boisvinet). Tel 02.51.55.11.40. Elegant surroundings, glorious sea views and superb food. Patron Jean-Claude. Menus 85-380FF. Treat yourself!
- Le Boisvinet, 2 rue Louis Cristeau (next to Les Embruns). Tel 02.51.55.51.57. Menus 83-228FF.
- La Cotriade, 8-10 rue Louis Cristeau. Tel 02.51.55.31.37. Local fish and seafood.

St Gilles: Cross the bridge and turn right along the quayside for a variety, including
- La Godaille, 92 rue du Calvaire (*vers* Super U). Tel 02.51.55.46.43. Moules, oysters, fish soup.

SHOPPING

Supermarkets A convenient *boulangerie*, La Mie Câline, is across the street; open 0630-2000. Less convenient are the 2 nearest supermarkets:
- Intermarché, bd G Pompidou, is 20 mins walk northwest, following the railway. Jul/Aug, Mon-Sat 0830-2000; Sun 0830-1230. Sep-Jun, Mon-Sat 0900-1300 & 1500-1930; Sun 0900-1230.

Chapter 5

Entrance channel at low water, from Jetée de Boisvinet

- Super U, rue du Calvaire, is 15 mins walk; cross the bridge, fork right and look behind the big water tower. Mon-Sat 0830-2000; Sun 0830-1230.

Markets
Croix-de-Vie: Place Guy Kergoustin (in front of the church), Wed and Sat mornings.

St Gilles: Places du Vieux Port/du Marché aux Herbes (by church); Tues, Thur & Sun mornings.

Banks All the usual (open Tues-Sat), mostly along quai de la République, beyond the station.

Launderette place de la Fauvette (opposite first fish basin).

NAVIGATIONAL MATTERS

Charts AC 3640 has a blow-up of St Gilles at 1:15,000. Beyond that you will have to rely for coastal coverage on AC 2663 at very small scale (1:200,000).

French coverage is more complete: SHOM 6613 (on which AC 3640 is partially based) covers St Gilles at 1:10,000. 6853 (1:47,000) covers Fromentine to St Gilles, and is substantially overlapped by the useful 6523 (1:47,200) which covers Île d'Yeu to Les Sables d'Olonne.

Approaches Any approach from seaward to the waypoint lies within an arc 337° to 115° (138°),

ie from La Petite Barge SCM buoy off Les Sables d'Olonne to the Pont d'Yeu SCM buoy. There are no hazards within that arc and inshore dangers lie outside it – plain sailing in other words.

Daymarks Pointe de Grosse-Terre's sawn-off, white lighthouse is the most obvious feature with high-rise blocks close east of it. Four water towers are charted around the town; check that you have identified the right one – or else ignore them. In Croix-de-Vie the tall, gaunt church tower with 'minaret' top is just N of the marina; the smaller church spire of St Gilles is by the bridge.

Pilotage The waypoint is 46°41´·04N 01°58´·01W, Pill' Hours SCM light buoy, from where you can see 1·3M up the long entry channel to the 043·5° leading marks, both white towers with red tops. From a distance these blend uncannily with the white walls and red roofs which line the seafront behind, so initially binoculars may be needed, at least to pick out the front mark.

The buoyed channel is narrow and shallow, allegedly dredged 1·5m but silting is continuous; not so the dredging, so do not bank on more than about 0·8m.

St Gilles-Croix-de-Vie, looking NE

Above half-tide there is no problem, but near LW there is a fair chance of grounding. The buoys either side of the leading line (two PHM and one SHM) are placed at the very edge of the channel, so do not pass them too closely, even if you have to jink aside to avoid opposite direction vessels.

Abeam Pointe de la Garenne the 90° bend in the channel is marked by three SHM and one PHM buoys. Stay closer to the former as the tide (fierce at mid-flood) will tend to push you towards shoals on the outside of the bend.

Tides At St Gilles HW neaps is 30 mins before, and at springs 15 mins after HW Brest. LW at neaps and at springs is 32 mins before LW Brest.

MHWS is 5·1m, MLWS 0·7m; MHWN is 4·1m, MLWN 2·0m.

Tidal streams outside the harbour are weak, but in the buoyed channel reach 2kn on the flood and 3½kn, or even 6kn it is said, on the ebb. Care is needed when berthing at around mid-tide.

Access day/night, is best at HW −2 to HW to avoid the strongest streams. Due to a bar 0·5m at the entrance, do not enter LW ±2 if you draw >1·5m. In S to SW winds >F6 care is needed.

Hazards From the W or NW do not cut the corner between the Pill' Hours reefs (south of Pointe de Grosse-Terre) and the Pill' Hours SCM buoy.

Shelter within the marina is good in all weathers.

Anchorage To await the tide, ⚓ two cables S of Jetée de la Garenne in about 3m on sand/rock.

MARINA

Capitainerie faces No 4 pontoon. Port de Plaisance, BP 61, 85800 St Gilles-Croix-de-Vie. Tel 02.51.55.30.83; Fax 02.51.55.31.43. www.mairie-saintgillescroixdevie.fr VHF Ch 09. HM Mme Béatrice Bessonnet. Hours in season, daily 0600-2200; out of season 0800-1200 & 1400-1800. Weather forecasts posted daily. Depths in the marina are about 1·5m.

Visitors may be directed by the HM's dory to a berth, probably on Nos 4-6 pontoons. If not, berth

Waypoint and lighthouse, looking north

Pointe de Grosse-Terre lighthouse

Waypoint: Pill'Hours SCM buoy

Grand môle   043.5° ldg lights Dir Oc(3+1)R 12s   Jetée de la Garenne Q WG

beyond the fuel pontoon (No 7) alongside accueil pontoon No 8. Watch the tide!

Layout The first seven pontoons are numbered 0-6 from seaward. Nos 9 and 10 pontoons are on the south side of the fairway opposite the fuel pontoon. Note: Beyond these and connected to the east bank, three new pontoons (Nos 11, 12 & 14) with 200 berths were added in 2000.

Showers are behind the Capitainerie. Access H24; hot and free!

Chapter 5

Fishmarket

First fishing basin

PHM buoy

3 SHM buoys

The bend at low water, looking east

Tariff Daily rates for LOA bands, 1 Jun to 30 Sep; second figure is for 1 Oct to 31 May: 8-9·5m = 108/76FF; 9·5-11m = 131/91FF; 11-12m = 154/103FF; 12-13m = 169/115FF.

Fuel Diesel & petrol at No 7 pontoon. H24 by French card machine; otherwise in office hours.

Directions to visitors' pontoon

NAUTICAL NEEDS

Chandlery & repairs

- Inter Coop Marine, quai M Bernard. Tel 02.51.55.31.39. SHOM chart agent, chandlery.
- Massif Marine, route de la Roche. Tel 02.51.55.42.07. SHOM chart agent, chandlery.
- Alain Masson, at marina. Tel 02.51.54.26.97. Electronics.
- Méca Marine, ZI La Bégaudière, route de la Roche. Tel 02.51.55.42.93. Chandlery, repairs.
- Voilerie Simonin, at marina. Tel 02.51.39.41.87. Sail repairs.
- Ouest Électrique, 70 bd G Pompidou. Tel 02.51.55.47.20. Electrical repairs.

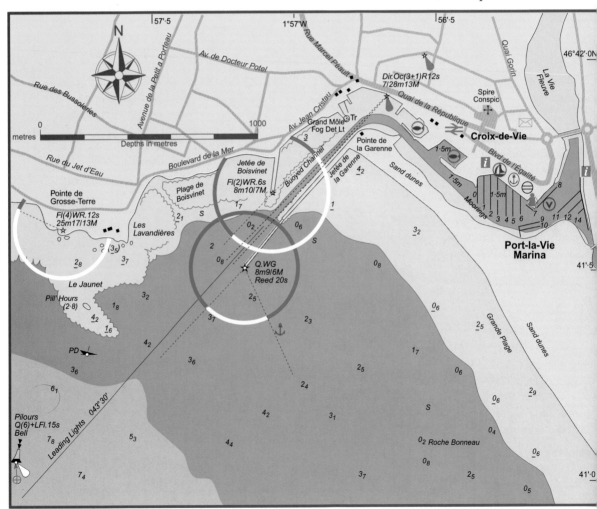

LES SABLES D'OLONNE

Les Sables is very proud of its association with the Vendée Globe. This, you may recall, is the single-handed, non-stop round the world race held every four years. It starts and finishes at Les Sables and the whole community and marina is completely taken over not only by the competitors but also by the total razzmatazz of the media. 2004 is the next year in which the race is due to be run. Vendée is of course the département within which Les Sables is situated.

The community is made up of Les Sables d'Olonne and La Chaume, divided by the waters of the River Vertonne which reaches the coast via a maze of salt pans. Les Sables is the large (40,000+ inhabitants) resort town on the east bank, La Chaume the much smaller and less sophisticated former fishing village on the west bank. Inland are the three suburbs of Château d'Olonne, Olonne-sur-Mer (it isn't on the sea) and l'Île d'Olonne.

The marina, Port Olona, lies roughly midway between Les Sables and La Chaume. The flavour is strongly Vendée, ie red tiled roofs and white walls; now there is a distinctly Mediterranean feel in the atmosphere.

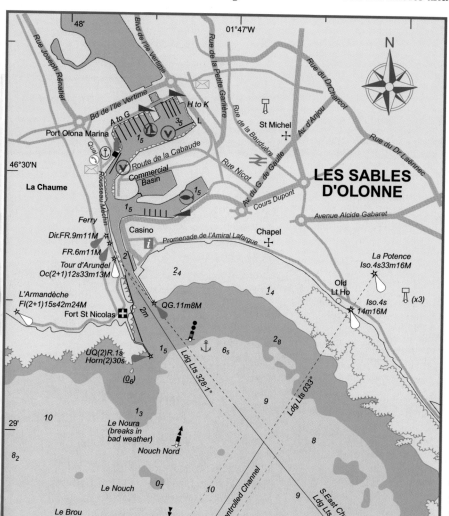

TOURISM

Tourist Office
1 promenade Joffré (near the east jetty), BP 146, 85104 Les Sables d'Olonne. Tel 02.51.96.85.85. Fax 02.51.96.85.71. Jul/Aug daily 0900-1900. Sep to Jun, Mon-Sat 0900-1215 & 1400-1830. Web www.ot-lessablesdolonne.fr E-mail: info@ot-lessablesdolonne.fr

What to see/do
Sunbathe and swim? Or if it's raining (unlikely) try the Musée de l'Abbaye Sainte Croix, rue de Verdun (800m east of the centre) home to a good collection of contemporary and modern art, plus exhibits of the marshland way of life. To renew your acquaintance with salt, visit Les Salines (semi-

Chapter 5

Les Sables d'Olonne, looking north

abandoned salt pans), either by bike or on a 2 hour boat trip from the marina (north of the sluices) – quite fun and certainly informative. Back in La Chaume wander round the old fishermen's houses behind the quays and stroll out to the elegant L'Armandèche lighthouse.

Beaches Grande Plage stretches 3km SE in a sun-baked curve from the harbour entrance; you could hire a bathing tent or cabin for the family! Behind it Le Remblai is a protective embankment on which everybody likes to promenade. From La Chaume the beaches extend 13M northwest to St Gilles and are less crowded, but interspersed with rocky outcrops and more difficult to reach.

Bus Good local services, timetable/map essential. Never as fast as trains in the wider area.

Railway Station is 1km SE of the marina, E of the fish basin. Paris is about 3h 40m, change to TGV at Nantes (1h 20m). Local trains go to Fromentine (2 hrs).

Taxis Tel 02.51.32.06.24; 02.51.95.40.80; 02.51.95.89.89.

Bike hire
- Le Cyclotron, 66 promenade Clemenceau (Grand Plage). Tel 02.51.32.64.15.
- Ets Le Roch, 65 rue Nationale (town centre). Tel 02.51.32.04.46.
- Cycles des Pays des Olonnes, 3 place du Poilu de France. Tel 02.51.32.03.48.

Car hire
- Pneus Sablais-ADA, 14 ave Jean-Jaurès. Tel 02.51.32.67.95.
- Havas Voyages (Avis), 5 place Collineau (town centre). Tel 02.51.95.08.86.

EATING ASHORE

Restaurants Along the marina quayside there are cafés, brasseries, restaurants; one such is:
- Sud Gascogne, 9 quai Prouteau. Tel 02.51.95.36.63. Popular, seafood; 0800-2200.Keep walking east across the bridge and the main road towards the Fire Station tower (conspic). Here you will find a superb fish restaurant , Le Charcot at 207 rue du Docteur Charcot; Tel 02.51.90.87.87, but closed Tue evening and all Wed.

- La Chaume and Les Sables are so spread out and with such a wide choice that it is better to indicate areas to explore rather than specifying individual retaurants.

La Chaume offers a wider selection of restaurants along quai George V, but get there early: The variously named Nos 10, 18, 20 and 24 are all worth a look.

If you don't like what you see, take the 'suicide' ferry (see Pilotage) across to Les Sables and go no further than quai Guiné (where you landed); every other place is a seafood restaurant, too numerous to list, but Le Clipper at No 19bis is recommended; Tel 02.51.32.03.61. Further east along the quai Garnier the choice becomes slightly, not a lot, more upmarket. Continue to Place du Poilu de France (town centre) and rue Nationale where Le Sablier at No 56 is recommended.

SHOPPING

Supermarkets

- A convenient Alimentation/Épicerie, amongst the apartment blocks opposite 'A' pontoon, sells most basic foods.
- The nearest supermarket is Super U, in La Chaume at the corner of rue de la Marne and rue de l'Aiguillon, about 10 mins walk (street map needed). Mon-Sat 0830-2000; Sun 0830-1230.
- Intermarché, rue de la Petite Garlière, is two blocks east of the marina. Jul/Aug, Mon-Sat 0830-2000; Sun 0830-1230. Sep-Jun, Mon-Sat 0900-1300 & 1500-1930; Sun 0900-1230.

Markets

La Chaume: Place Anselme Maraud, by the quayside just north of Tour de la Chaume; Tues, Thur & Sun 0800-1300.

Looking NNW from the waypoint

Les Sables: Halles Centrales, rue des Halles; 15 Jun-15 Sept daily, except Mon, 0800-1300. Fish market is at NE end of fish basin; Jul/Aug, Mon-Sat 0830-1230 & 1600-1930, Sun 0830-1230.

Banks All the usual in both La Chaume and Les Sables.

The near approach and Nouch Nord NCM buoy

St Nicholas Light tower
UQ(2)R 1s

Fort St Nicholas

Passerelle

Tour
d'Arundel

Light tower
QG

West side of entrance channel

NAVIGATIONAL MATTERS

Charts AC 3640 has a plan of Sables d'Olonne at 1:15,000. Beyond that you will have to rely for coastal coverage on AC 2663 at very small scale (1:200,000).

French coverage is more complete: SHOM 6551 (on which AC 3640 is partially based) covers Sables d'Olonne at 1:12,500. 6523 covers Île d'Yeu to Les Sables d'Olonne at 1:47,200, and is usefully overlapped by 6522 (1:47,400) which extends cover to the northern tip of Île de Ré.

Approaches From the NNW and W, La Petite Barge SCM buoy (46°28'·96N 01°50'·52W) must be rounded before turning E to the waypoint 46°28'·61N 01°47'·35W, Nouch Sud SCM buoy.

From the SW quadrant set course direct to the waypoint. From the SE steer for the harbour entrance (46°29'·33N 01°47'·30W), staying at least 3 cables offshore.

The two charted approaches, 033° and 320°, are primarily for large vessels, the former being for vessels carrying hydrocarbons (yachts to keep clear) and recommended in heavy weather.

Daymarks Les Barges, a dull grey lighthouse with helo platform, is conspicuous 1·5M west of L'Armandèche lighthouse. The latter is a slender,

white fluted tower, 5 cables west of the harbour entrance, with 3 high-rise blocks close east of it. The white buildings of Les Sables are massed along the coastline, too homogeneous to offer much guidance, if any is needed.

Pilotage From the waypoint, head northward towards the harbour entrance leaving Nouch Nord NCM spar buoy comfortably to port. The inner leading marks 328·1° are hard to see, and probably not needed by yachts.

Happily the red-topped white tower on St Nicolas' jetty is as plain as a pikestaff; north of it are a passerelle, fort, spending beaches and the bulky Tour d'Arundel (Tour de la Chaume on some charts), which is mostly hidden by a tall office block until it comes abeam. The best water lies well to starboard, so keep close to the eastern jetty initially. Outbound vessels, especially fishing boats, are vying for the same water and may pass a mere boathook's length from you – stand by to repel boarders!

Near the entrance to the commercial and fish basins, be alert for a suicidal pedestrian ferry which ploughs a triangular groove (as on AC 3640) between Les Sables and La Chaume. The driver may be blind; near-misses occur all around him.

Tides At Les Sables d'Olonne HW neaps is 30 mins before, and at springs 15 mins after HW Brest. LW at neaps and at springs is 3½ mins before LW Brest.

MHWS is 5·2m, MLWS 0·7m; MHWN is 4·1m, MLWN 2·0m.

Tidal streams outside the harbour are weak, and no more than 1 knot in the entrance channel. When the sluice gates at the N end of the marina are open for scouring, rates may be 1½ - 2kn.

Access day/night, at all tides. Sailing is prohibited in the entry channel which is dredged 2m. In southerlies >F5-6 care is needed as a heavy swell may also be present.

Front leading
mark, FR

Rear leading
mark, FR

328° leading marks, hard to see; not essential for yachts

Hazards Les Barges, drying rocky reefs, and other rocks extend 2M west and northwest of L'Armandèche lighthouse. Le Noura 1·3m and Le Nouch 0·7m are shoal patches south of the harbour entrance, the latter marked by north and south cardinal buoys.

Shelter within the marina is good in all weathers. Be aware of the sluice gates (see above).

Anchorage is 1 cable E of Jean Marthe isolated danger buoy in about 5m on sand, but this is totally exposed to the south and only safe in calm, settled weather.

MARINA

Capitainerie is among the trees near the fuel and accueil pontoon. Port Olona, BP 122, 85104 Les Sables d'Olonne. Tel 02.51.32.51.16; Fax 02.51.32.37.13. HM Jacques Archambaud. VHF Ch 09. Open daily 0700-2100. Weather forecasts posted daily. The marina staff are friendly, helpful and tolerant of *les fou anglais*.

Visitors should berth alongside the accueil pontoon (good chance to refuel) and check in at the office. Pontoons are lettered A-K from seaward in depths from 1·5m to 3·5m. Nominally the **V** pontoon is 'L' at the far end, but a smiling face may get you closer; depends in part whether you wish to be nearer to La Chaume or Les Sables and of course on how crowded the marina is.

Shower blocks are opposite E and G pontoons; open 0700-2000.

Launderette Laverie Océane, 3 quai Prouteau (opposite E pontoon). Tel 02.51.21.62.98.

Tariff Daily rates for LOA bands, July/August; second figure is for June and September:

8-9m = 116/82F; 9-10m = 133/93F; 10-11m = 149/105F; 11-12m = 166/117F; 12-13m = 195/136F.

Fuel Diesel & petrol at accueil pontoon. Open 0800-2000; all cards.

NAUTICAL NEEDS

Chandlery & repairs
- Sablaise Nautique, at marina. Tel 02.51.32.62.16. SHOM chart agent, chandlery.
- Littoral Maintenance, at marina. Tel 02.51.23.86.43. Engineering repairs. Volvo, Yanmar.
- Voilerie Tarot, at marina. Tel 02.51.21.22.87. Sail repairs.
- Eric Marine, at marina. Tel 02.51.21.29.79. Chandlery, engineering.
- A Masson, quai de la Cabaude. Tel 02.51.32.01.07. Electronics.
- Avenir Entente Cordiale, quai de la Cabaude. Tel 02.51.21.03.58. SHOM chart agent, chandlery.

Chapter 5

Port Olona marina, looking NE

BOURGENAY

This has all the makings of a sleepy hollow – and none the worse for that! Bourgenay is simply a small holiday village onto which a marina was grafted in 1989. It is not obvious why this artificial harbour was built when Les Sables d'Olonne is so close (6M) – unless to satisfy demand? Most southerly marina in the Vendée might be its best claim to fame.

Inland, Talmont St Hilaire is Big Brother, although it is little more than a small country town.

TOURISM

Tourist Office Place du Château, BP 18, 85440 Talmont St Hilaire. Tel 02.51.90.65.10. Fax 02.51.20.71.80. A useful annex by the crossroads in the centre of Bourgenay opens in season. Tel 02.51.22.23.18.

What to see/do Sunbathe and relax ... as Classic FM back in the sunless UK exhorts us to do! The beach to the east (see below) is rather more natural than the golden strands associated with Les Sables and St Gilles. Pine woods make pleasant walking. Local rainy-day attractions include:

A car museum on D949 west out of Talmont – is this why you came all the way to the Vendée?

The ruined 11/12th century castle in Talmont puts on the usual mediaeval spectacles of jousting, archery, harp-plucking and other Middle Ages activity. Richard the Lionheart was here! There are some interesting châteaux and gardens a little further afield (ask at the Tourist Office).

Beaches Plage du Veillon is a vast sandy expanse on a low spit at the mouth of the drying Payré river, 2km east; with lifeguards.

Bus A local bus, line 154, runs from the port and the central crossroads to Les Sables d'Olonne (30 mins) and to Talmont (15 mins). The timetable is obtainable from the Tourist Office.

Train Nearest station is at Les Sables d'Olonne, 11km WNW. Paris is about 3h 40m, change to TGV at Nantes (1h 20m).

Taxis Tel 02.51.90.60.82; 02.51.21.11.77.

Bike hire Carrosserie peinture, 503 ave des Sables, Talmont. Tel 02.51.90.20.35.

Roof-top statue of Notre Dame de l'Espérance

Car hire Ask at the Tourist Office or go to Les Sables d'Olonne.

EATING ASHORE

Restaurants Local specialities include oysters from the Payré river and brioche Vendéenne.
- Hôtel de Port Bourgenay*** is north of the marina, ave de la Mine. Tel 02.51.23.35.35.
- Hôtel Le St Hubert* is east of the marina, 760 ave de la Plage. Tel 02.51.22.24.04.

Amongst the cafés, bars, and crêperies in the NE corner of the marina are:
- Le Blé Noir, crêperie. La Bourlange, restaurant, crêperie. Le Triangolo, restaurant, pizzeria.

At Talmont try Auberge de la Boule d'Or, 3 rue du Château. Tel 02.51.90.60.23.

SHOPPING

Supermarkets A boulangerie just outside the marina is open daily 0715-1245 & 1630-2000 and sells the most mouth-watering pastries and tarts.
- A mini-supermarket, Superette de Bourgenay, is about 500m from the marina, daily 0800-1300 & 1530-2000.
- Super U, 86 ave des Sables, is 5km away in Talmont St Hilaire.

Banks Two or three in Talmont St Hilaire. Cash dispenser in Bourgenay village.

Launderette in the Village du Lac (sports and holiday centre inland from the marina).

NAVIGATIONAL MATTERS

Charts The small scale AC 2663 (1:200,000) is the only Admiralty chart to cover Bourgenay.

SHOM 6522 (1:47,400) covers Bourgenay, and from Les Sables d'Olonne to the northern tip of Île de Ré. 6522 is overlapped by 6523 (1:47,200) to the NW and by 6521 (1:47,500) to the SE, but both these charts exclude Bourgenay. There is no UK or French large scale harbour chart.

Approaches The coast 5M either side of Bourgenay is fringed with drying ledges, so it is best to keep at least 0·5M offshore. Make good the waypoint at 46°25′·34N 01°41′·86W, Bourgenay SWM buoy, which has a huge, faintly DIY topmark. From here the marina entrance bears 040°/1·35M, on the 040° leading line.

If you keep north of the SWM buoy, be aware of the Roches du Joanne (see below) which can be dangerous in bad weather. Even in calm weather it can be noticeably roly-poly in their vicinity.

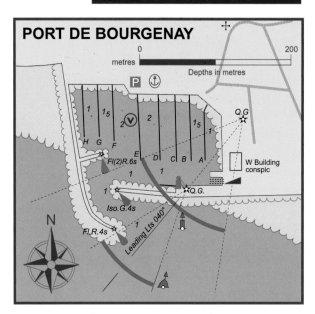

Daymarks The most conspicuous feature is a large white roofed/walled boatyard building at the east end of the marina. This is virtually on the 040° leading marks, which are both green □s with white border, QG; the green □s may blend all too easily with pine trees behind. A white patch on the head of the W breakwater is helpful, especially coming from the SE. The white statue

Safe water mark buoy with outsize topmark

Looking east across the marina

of Notre Dame de l'Espérance is visible, if you look for it, on the conical roof of a rest home whose residents probably derive more succour from it than you.

Pilotage From the waypoint, proceed to the marina entrance (46°26'·38N 01°40'·57W) noting that the Roches du Joanne are close to starboard 2·9m and to port 3·7m. At the entrance keep inside a SHM buoy and SHM perch which warn of rocky ledges to the east. The channel does a pronounced S-bend between the breakwater heads, first to port then to starboard. Horizontal red/white chevrons on the inside of the breakwater indicate the blind S-bend where the very sensible 3 knot speed limit should be heeded.

Tides Use the tidal data for Les Sables d'Olonne which is only 6M to the NW.

Tidal streams outside the harbour are weak.

Access day/night, at all tides, but care needed at LWS ±1. There is a 0·5m

patch off the end of the W breakwater. Elsewhere the channel is dredged 1m, but subject to silting. In SW winds >F5 care is needed. (The entrance is reminiscent of a very miniature Brighton marina).

Hazards Roches du Joanne either side of the 040° leading line. When there is a heavy swell, breakers form at the 40m wide entrance. There are rocky ledges east of the entrance.

Shelter within the marina is good in all weathers.

Marina entrance is to the left

Statue

Rear ldg mark

Capitainerie

Fuel

Conspic BY building

Visitors' pontoon E

Front ldg mark

SHM perch

Ldg line 040°

SHM buoy

Bourgenay, looking NNE

Anchorage is subject to the constraints of anchoring off any open coast with no natural shelter.

MARINA

Capitainerie is in a pseudo lighthouse on the N side of the marina. Port de Plaisance, 85440 Talmont St Hilaire. Tel 02.51.22.20.36; Fax 02.51.22.29.45. HM Pascal Loizeau and helpful staff. VHF Ch 09. Open daily in season 0800-2100;

Leading marks and conspicuous white-roofed building

out of season 0900-1200 & 1400-1800. Weather forecasts posted daily. The entrance and marina fairway are dredged 1m.

Visitors should berth in 2m at the *accueil* Pontoon E; fingers on the east side, alongside/rafting on the west side. Pontoons are lettered A-H from east to west in depths of 1m to 2m.

Showers (hot and free) are behind the Capitainerie; open 0700-2300/0900-1800 in/out of season.

Tariff Daily rates for LOA bands, July/August; second figure is for May, June and Sept: 8-9m = 97/73F; 9-10m = 112/85F; 10-11m = 131/97F; 11-12m = 148/110F; 12-13m = 172/122F.

Fuel Diesel & petrol at SE corner of the marina in 1m. Open 0830-1800; all cards.

NAUTICAL NEEDS

Chandlery & repairs
- Polypat, at marina (the conspic white-roofed building). Tel 02.51.23.73.94. Boatyard, chandlery, mechanical and electrical engineering, electronics.
- Atlantica, at marina. Tel 02.51.22.29.56. Chandlery, repairs.

Chapter 5

ÎLE DE RÉ TO POINTE DE LA COUBRE

CONTENTS

THE SEA AND THE LAND

South of Bourgenay the coastline becomes steadily more interesting, although still low-lying. We are now leaving the Vendée and cruising along the Charente-Maritime.

The first main feature is Pertuis Breton (the Breton strait) dividing Île de Ré from the mainland. On its mainland shore there are several minor drying harbours worth exploring on the tide: Jard-sur-Mer, La Tranche, L'Aiguillon with La Faute-sur-Mer and the canal up to Marans.

Le Douhet, fishing basin

Tour St Nicholas, La Rochelle

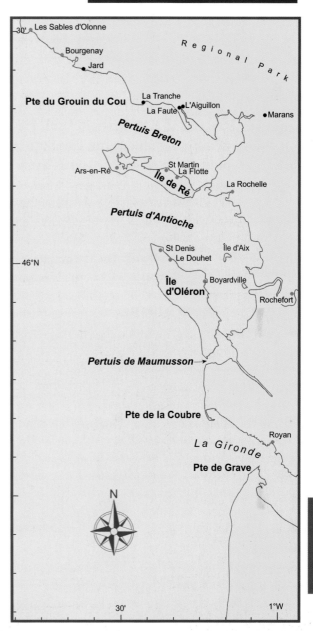

From La Tranche the Marais Poitevin (Poitou marshlands), now a Regional Natural Park, stretch eastwards for some 70km to Niort. The marshes are criss-crossed by waterways and dykes; the land between is green and fertile. The western part is known as the Dry Marsh, a pastureland for sheep and cattle and equally a rich arable land for cropping. The eastern or Wet Marsh is a fascinating area of poplars and swampy glades accessible only by flat-bottomed boats. Take your boat up to Marans and explore by bike or even dinghy.

Île de Ré is a charming island connected to the mainland by a long elegant bridge. A visit to St Martin is definitely a must, whilst Ars-en-Ré is a little more remote and challenging.

South again and the 6 mile wide Pertuis d'Antioche between Île de Ré and Île d'Oléron gives access to la Rochelle, although you will more likely have sailed under the bridge and past the commercial and fishing port of La Pallice.

La Rochelle is everything you could wish for: a well-preserved and interesting historic town, into which the sea penetrates to the very heart; a modern marina to satisfy your mundane needs; and good communications by road and rail.

Île d'Oléron is also attached to the mainland by a bridge, but manages to feel detached, perhaps because of its size. Most yachtsmen will know it only by St Denis, or possibly the lesser harbours of Le Douhet and Boyardville. Continue SE and up the Charente River to Rochefort, a C17 navy port which captivates all hearts by its rugged simplicity and the ordered layout of its streets and gardens.

For something different head 120km inland to Poitiers, a university town enhanced by Notre-Dame-la-Grande church and its commanding position. North of it is the Futuroscope, a 'Park of the Moving Image': an educational fun centre where architectural imagination has been allowed to run riot. The visual impact of the moving images will wow the family and flatten the Dome!

Chapter 6

ARS-EN-RÉ

I regret to tell you that Ars is pronounced exactly as if it had an 'e' on the end!
Having removed that nagging doubt, I should add that this is an intriguing place,
spiced with a little challenging pilotage on the way in.
The pace of life is slow and relaxed, even the crowds

seem less pressurised than in St Martin – when
they are not lost in the narrow back streets of the
town. Hollyhocks grow out of pavements and
along every wall; some of the buildings are
crumbling. It's that sort of place.

Most of the tourist information under St Martin
applies, so only differences are shown here.

TOURISM

Tourist Office Place Carnot (by the church), 17590
Ars en Ré. Open Mon-Sat 1000-1245 & 1500-1945;
Sun/Hols 1000-1300. Tel 05.46.29.46.09; Fax
05.46.29.68.30.

What to see/do This end of Ré feels remote and
detached. To enhance this feeling, take the minor
road from St Clément des Baleines to Les Portes

across salt pans, few of them actively worked,
and the coastal marshes which form the Lilleau-
des-Niges Nature Reserve, home to about 300
different bird species. The Fier d'Ars stretches in
front of you.

Clamber up Les Baleines lighthouse, a mere 53
metres high and 257 steps to the top for fabulous
views across Pertuis Breton and Pertuis
d'Antioche.

500m south of the lighthouse is L'Arche de Noé
(Noah's Ark), a floral amusement park, open 1030-
1930 Jun-Aug; Apr, May & Sep 1400-1800. Here
the family will find tropical birds, birds of Ré (not
prey), nautical history, animals from the North
Pole to the Amazon, shellfish and oceanographic
museums, not to mention butterflies and insects –
you name it ...

Beaches Leave the church on Route de la Grange to cross the D735 and on to the Plage Grignon on the SW coast, about a 1·2 km walk/bike ride. This is a perfectly adequate shingly beach with drying expanses of mud and seaweed in front of it – interesting exploration for the kids at LW. There are also good beaches eastward from Les Baleines lighthouse round to Pointe du Fier.

Bus The local Rébus operates 3 efficient routes: Line 1 links Ars to Les Portes (NW tip) and to La Rochelle via La Couarde, change for St Martin. Get the timetable from the Tourist Office.

Taxis Tel 05.46.29.25.65 (Mme Cotie).

Bike hire
- Cycland, at the Port. Tel 05.46.29.47.17. From 45FF per day.
- D Neveur, 2 place de la Chapelle. Tel 05.46.29.20.88.

EATING ASHORE

Restaurants
- Le Bistro de Bernard, 1 quai de la Criée, attractive flowery setting overlooking Bassin de la Prée. Tel 05.46.29.40.26. 130-175FF.
- Café du Commerce, 6 quai de la Prée, overlooking Bassin de la Prée. Tel 05.46.29.41.57. 98FF.

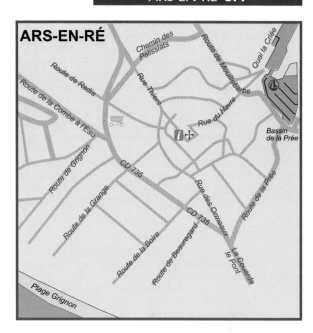

- Le Clocher, 14 place Carnot (shady spot by the church). Tel 05.46.29.41.20.
- L'Océane, 29 place Carnot/corner of rue du Hâvre. Tel 05.46.29.24.70. Restaurant/crêperie.
- Le Grenier à Sel, 20 rue de la Baie (east of church). Tel 05.46.29.08.62. Restaurant.

Chapter 6

Pointe du Fiers

Approx position of front ldg mark

Bûcheron SHM buoy

BUCHER

Bûcheron buoy and outer approach channel 265°

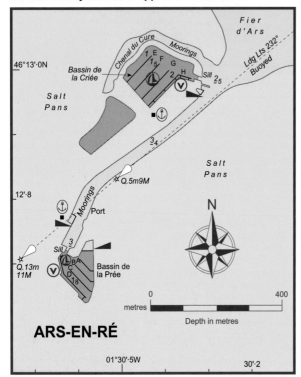

Fier d'Ars

Chenal du Cure

Moorings

Ldg Lts 232°
Buoyed

46°13'·0N

Bassin de la Criée

Salt Pans

7 E F G
1 5
2 H
Sill 2 5

3 4

Q.5m9M

Salt Pans

N

12'·8

Moorings
Port

Q.13m 11M

Sill
3
B A
C
D 18

Bassin de la Prée

0   400

metres

Depth in metres

ARS-EN-RÉ

01°30'·5W

30'·2

SHOPPING

Supermarkets Spar open 0830-2030 daily; from the church walk west on rue d'Angleterre until you meet the main D735, then look about you.

Markets Jul/Aug daily in and around the covered market, place du Marché, in front of the rear leading light. Other months in place Carnot (by the church), Tues and Friday.

Banks Crédit Agricole, 40 rue du Hâvre. Crédit Maritime, 7 rue Bardons.

Launderette Lav' en Ré, place du Marché.

NAVIGATIONAL MATTERS

Charts As per the St Martin entry. (next section)

Approaches Directions for the outer approaches are very much as per those for St Martin. From the ESE set a course direct to the waypoint, 46°14'·45N 01°23'·55W, which is in deep water four cables NNW of Les Ilates, a large NCM beacon tower.

From the NW the same waypoint will suffice, but if, en route to it, the Bûcheron SHM buoy is seen, then sensibly alter course for that buoy, noting the drying Banc du Bûcheron WNW of it. Despite two sets of leading lights, a first-time night approach is not recommended due to the number of unlit marks which have to be negotiated.

3 SHM buoys

L'Abbesse PHM beacon

6 PHM buoys

Looking NE across the Fiers d'Ars from the start of final approach channel

Daymarks The church spire at Ars is uniquely conspicuous throughout the approach, the top half being painted black and the lower half white; it is a ghostly but welcome pointer through the prevalent haze. The woods on Pte du Fiers stand out well above the surrounding flatlands, not to be confused with similar woods on Pte du Grouin,

The 232° leading marks

where a conspic white water tower is in Loix. Les Baleines lighthouse at the W end of Ré may be seen, north of the extended 265° leading line.

Pilotage The waypoint is on the 265° leading line, but the rear leading mark is notoriously hard to see until it is too close to be useful. So track 265° for the Bûcheron SHM buoy, 1·6M ahead, leaving it and the subsequent SHM buoy and beacon 50-100m to starboard for best water. Hop between these marks, noting that the outer bar dries 0·4m between the two buoys. A long pool with 2·2m lies between the 2nd buoy and the beacon and makes a possible anchorage.

As the first PHM beacon draws near, quit the 265° leading line and turn onto the 232° leading line, whose marks are also difficult to see! But the B/W spire is now firmly in your sights, 2° left of the line. After the turn, cross the inner bar drying 1·5m, and beyond enter a second pool; this is the main anchorage with 2m and a SHM beacon at its northeast end.

From here the leading marks, L'Abbesse PHM beacon and a line of 6 small PHM and 3 SHM buoys should be visible 1-1·5M ahead, leading across the wide expanse of Le Fier d'Ars. After the last lateral buoys you will see to starboard the entrance to Bassin de la Criée, whilst ahead a canalised section with gently sloping walls continues for about 800m to Bassin de la Prée.

Entrance to the Bassin de la Criée (1·3m over the sill)

Tides use the data for St Martin.

Tidal streams are strong near the Bûcheron SHM buoy, and at the entrance to Fier d'Ars they can reach $4\frac{1}{2}$ knots at springs.

Hazards All channel buoys and beacons are unlit. Banc du Bûcheron is gradually shifting south, so stay 50-100m off the SHM marks. The final canalised section has gently sloping walls; keep near mid-channel. Japanese seaweed was reported (1999) to be a problem here and elsewhere on this coast, although it was neither seen nor encountered over a 3 months period.

Shelter in both marinas is excellent in all weathers.

Anchorage is possible in the two pools described under Pilotage. Anchorage near the waypoint is exposed to wind and tidal streams.

Chapter 6

ACCESS

Windows into both marina basins, over sills drying 2·5m (with depth gauge), are summarised below for yachts of 1·2m and 1·6m draughts:

Coefficient	Windows for draughts of 1·2m and	1·6m	Min-max depths of water above sill at HW
40 (neaps)	HW$-1\frac{3}{4}$ to $+2\frac{1}{2}$.	HW-1 to $+1\frac{1}{2}$	1·5–1·9m
70 (average)	HW$-2\frac{1}{4}$ to $+3\frac{1}{2}$.	HW$-1\frac{3}{4}$ to $+2\frac{3}{4}$	2·2–2·8m
100 (springs)	HW$-2\frac{1}{2}$ to $+3\frac{3}{4}$.	HW$-2\frac{1}{4}$ to $+3\frac{1}{4}$	3·1–3·5m

Allow 1 hour or less for the 4M from the Bûcheron buoy to the marinas.

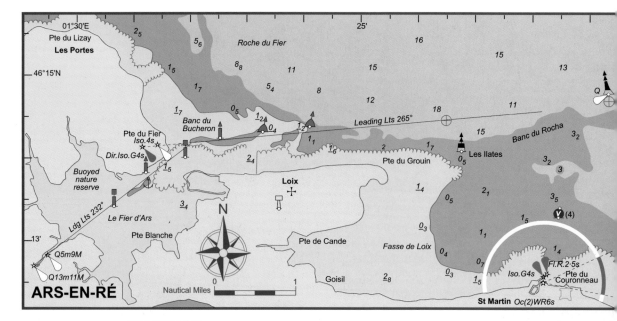

Map labels:
01°30'E — Pte du Lizay — **Les Portes** — Roche du Fier — 25' — 16 — 15 — 13
46°15'N — 2₅ — 5₆ — 8₈ — 11 — 15 — 15 — 1₅ — 1₇ — 5₄ — 8 — 12 — 18 — 11 — Q
Banc du Bucheron — 1₇ — 0₅ — 1₂ — 0₄ — 1₂ — Leading Lts 265° — 15 — Banc du Rocha — 3₂
Pte du Fier Iso.4s — 1₁ — 1₆ — 0₅ — Les Ilates — 3₂ — 3
Dir.Iso.G4s — 2₄ — 2 — 1₇ — Pte du Grouin — 3
Buoyed nature reserve — 1₅ — Loix — 1₄ — 2₁ — 3₅
Ldg Lts 232° — 3₄ — N — 0₅ — 1₅ — Y (4)
Le Fier d'Ars — Pte Blanche — Pte de Cande — Fasse de Loix — 0₃ — 1₁ — 1₄
13' — Q5m9M — Nautical Miles — 0₄ — 0₇ — 1₅ — Fl.R.2·5s
Q13m11M — Goisil — 2₈ — 0₃ — 1₅ — Iso.G4s — Pte du Couronneau
ARS-EN-RÉ — 0 — 1 — St Martin Oc(2)WR6s

MARINAS

Capitainerie is at quai de la Criée, 17590 Ars en Ré. Tel 05.46.29.25.10; Fax 05.46.29.66.91. HM Patrick Herail. VHF Ch 09. Open daily 1 Apr-30 Sep at HW±2 within hours of 0700-2200; Oct-Mar daily 0830-1230 & 1400-1800.

Bureau du Port, 23 quai de la Prée. Tel 05.46.29.08.52. Open daily 1 Apr-30 Sep: as above; closed out of season. Weather forecasts are posted daily at both offices.

Visitors have three options, from seaward:
a. Bassin de la Criée ('newer' marina about 500m NE of the Port area). H pontoon (depth 2m), berths 1-12 if LOA >10m; berths 13-30 if <10m.
b. Port, drying 3m to soft mud; access approx HW±2½. Berth on NE quay just before entrance to Bassin de la Prée, or pick up a buoy either side of the channel.
c. Bassin de la Prée. Berth alongside/raft up on D pontoon in 1·8m, 1st to starboard of entrance.

Shower blocks at both marinas; open office hours or H24 by code number.

Tariff Daily rates for LOA bands, Jul/Aug; 2nd figure is Apr-Jun & Sep:
7·5-8m = 102/77F; <9m = 117/88F; <10m = 136/102F; <11m = 155/116F; <12m = 169/126F; <13m = 186/139F; >13m, per extra metre add 10% of the 13m daily rate.

Fuel Diesel pump, mainly for fishing vessels, is on east side of the Port. Tel 05.46.29.40.43. Open Jul/Aug 0800-2000 at HW±2; other months by telephone.

NAUTICAL NEEDS

Chandlery & repairs Blondeau Marine, at the Port. Tel 05.46.29.04.89. Chandlery, workshops.

Drying moorings in the port

Looking north from Bassin de la Prée. 'D' pontoon for visitors is on the west side

St Martin-de-Ré, looking WSW (out of season)

Labels on image: Marina · Capitainerie · Waiting pontoon · IsoG 4s · Fish basin · Gate and bridge · Lt Ho Oc(2)WR 6s · Tourist office · Wooden breakwater · Fl.R 2·5s

St Martin-de-Ré

Monsieur Vauban was here, as you will guess when you first see the Citadelle sprawling east of the harbour although it is not as big as those in Lorient or Le Palais. St Martin is everybody's favourite – unfortunately. It is like a film set, a cameo of the France that we thought had disappeared

with WW2 but still keep stumbling upon to our surprise and delight. Golden stone walls, faded shutters, wrought iron balconies, peeling stucco, flagstones and cobbles – sip your wine and let images of the 17th century flood in upon you. St Martin is hot, vivid and intense ...

TOURISM

Tourist Office ave Victor Bouthillier, BP 41, 17410 St Martin-de-Ré. Tel 05.46.09.20.06. Fax 05.46.09.06.18. Open 1000-1200 & 1530-1730; closed Wed pm and Sun. The office is east of the fish basin in the fine Hôtel de Clerjotte (not a place of accommodation); the entrance is not very obvious. It also houses a museum (see below). On the opposite side of the road is the main bus stop (*gare routière*) for St Martin harbour.

What to see/do Sunbathe and relax. Wander the town. Climb the church tower up a narrow stairway past the bells; terrific views from the top. Take in the Ernest Cognacq museum, behind the Tourist Office; it is mostly devoted to the island's nautical past, and worth a visit not least to see the courtyard, galleries and tower, open 1000-1900.

If you want to get away from the slightly claustrophobic atmosphere of the marina, explore the island by bike via the many signposted cycle tracks which keep you off the roads. It is 20 km to Les Baleines from St Martin and 13km to Sablanceaux where the mainland bridge takes off for La Rochelle.

Chapter 6

Beaches Plage de la Cible, the nearest to the marina, is a small sandy beach close east of the Citadelle. Cycle east towards La Flotte for Plage de la Clavette and Plage de l'Arnérault; or cross the island to the southwest coast which is more or less continuous sand – take your pick.

Bus The local Rébus operates 3 efficient routes: Line 1, La Rochelle to Les Portes (NW tip); Line 2, La Rochelle to St Martin and Loix; Line 3, Sablanceaux via a devious route through St Martin to La Couarde. The timetable is obtainable from the Tourist Office.

Railway Nearest station is at La Rochelle, qv.

Taxis Tel 05.46.09.44.04; 05.46.09.43.44; 05.46.09.43.21.

Bike hire

- Cycland, Impasse de Sully. Tel 05.46.09.08.66. From 45FF per day.
- Cyclo-Surf, Clos Vauban (east of Tourist Office). Tel 05.46.09.08.28.
- Motive. Tel 05.46.09.92.98. Electric scooters with approx 30km range; recharge en route.

Car hire Ask at the Tourist Office. Bikes and buses are ideal on the island.

Fish basin and church

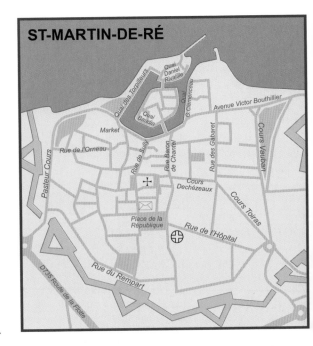

ST-MARTIN-DE-RÉ

EATING ASHORE

Restaurants Look no further than the quays around the marina and fish basin, but look carefully because menus are geared and priced for the ever present tourist.

- La Baleine Bleue, quai Launay Rozilly, overlooks the marina. Tel 05.46.09.03.30. 130-180FF.
- Les Remparts, 4 quai Daniel-Rivaille is just east of the swing bridge, somewhat away from the crowds. Tel 05.46.09.20.22.
- Le Bistrot du Port, 13 cours Pasteur (SW from marina). Tel 05.46.09.14.18. Menus 45-110FF.
- Le Bélem, on the quay, does a good self-service breakfast from 0700 – should you feel the need!

SHOPPING

Supermarkets Intermarché and Super U are on opposite sides of the road to La Flotte, about 1½km out of town.

Market Daily except Mon, rue Jean Jaurès near SW corner of the marina.

Banks Crédit Agricole and others on the south side of the fish basin.

NAVIGATIONAL MATTERS

Charts AC 2641 and AC 2746 (1:50,000) cover St Martin and Île de Ré from north and south.
   SHOM 6668 covers St Martin at large scale (1:15,000). 6521 (1:47,500) covers Pertuis Breton and Île de Ré. 6333 (1:47,510) covers Pertuis d'Antioche, Île de Ré and the north of d'Oléron.

Approaches From the WNW set a course direct to the waypoint 46°14´·78N 01°20´·68W (Rocha NCM buoy; see p194). On the north side of Pertuis Breton, Pointe du Grouin du Cou* should be cleared by 1 mile. On the south side Les Baleineaux light house should be rounded at least 1 mile off, 2 miles in heavy weather. Further east, be aware that the Banc du Rocha 1·2m extends ENE to within 1 mile of the waypoint; do not therefore cut inside Rocha buoy prematurely.

From the ESE set course from the Île de Ré bridge to the waypoint. If familiar with the north coast of Île de Ré, a more inshore track can be followed, noting shoal patches of about 0·8m.

*Not to be confused with Pointe du Grouin, 7·2M SSE on Île de Ré, between Ars-en-Ré entrance and St Martin-en-Ré.

Daymarks The 13m high white light tower with red top, Oc (2) WR 6s, sits conspicuously atop the ramparts on the east side of the entrance. The ruined church behind the harbour is clearly visible on the skyline; close west of it is the square church tower (which you can climb).

Pilotage From the waypoint the harbour bears 200°/2·4M. On a first visit the detached wooden breakwater across the harbour entrance appears to merge with the stone moles and ramparts; the entrances either side of it are not easily discerned until less than a mile away.

Of the two transits shown on the chartlet the 210° transit of the red topped light tower and church is by far the easier to see. Alternatively keep the church on a steady bearing of 200°. The stream sets across the approach and always seems stronger than it really is.

The NW entrance (46°12´·56N 01°21´·84W) to the Avant Port is normally used, but the SE entrance will do fine if you want to be different. Inside you are at once struck by the smallness of everything, accentuated by the encircling walls and ramparts. If you've just arrived from the wide open spaces of Les Minimes marina at La Rochelle, St Martin may feel positively claustrophobic at first. There really isn't much room to manoeuvre, lower sail, rig fenders, warps and all the other things which don't usually trouble the French yachtsman. If possible get ready before entering.

Squeeze through the narrows ahead – don't take the dead end gully in your one o'clock! Ignore the fishing basin which now stretches in front. Keep looking and steering to starboard and as you round the bend the entrance to the wet basin will open up, all of 12m wide. See under Access.

Tides At St Martin HW neaps is 15 mins after, and at springs 30 mins before HW Pointe de Grave. LW at neaps is 20 mins, and at springs 25 mins before LW Pointe de Grave.

MHWS is 6·0m, MLWS 0·9m; MHWN is 4·9m, MLWN 2·4m.

Tidal streams a mile or so offshore set roughly east/west at no more than 1 knot, but during the first and last hour or so of the in-going stream an eddy may set west or WNW.

Access day/night to the 1·5m drying outer harbour is possible in the top half of the tide depending on draught. However time your arrival for when the gate into the marina is open. This occurs when there is adequate water over the sill (dries 0·7m), and only within the 'administrative' windows of 0500-2300 Jul/Aug; 0630-2200 May, Jun & Sep; 0800-1800 winter. The following are representative neap and spring openings:

Based on a typical neap HW at 1400, the gate will only be open once in the day, ie approx 1100-1600, HW-3 to +2. At typical spring HWs of 0635 and 1850, the gate will be open approx 0500-0930 and 1600-2130, ie HW-3 to +3. For intermediate times interpolate between neaps and springs, or better still telephone the Capitainerie a day or two before your arrival! Timetables can be found at some harbours in the vicinity, eg La Rochelle.

Chapter 6

Oc(2)WR 6s   Detached breakwater   Fl.R 2·5s   -   Iso G 4s   Church tower

Entrance gate and swing bridge, looking out from marina

The pedestrian swing bridge opens in sympathy with the gate. There are Ⓡ Ⓦ Ⓖ (horizontal) entry lights to starboard just before the bridge: Ⓡ = no entry; Ⓦ Ⓖ = proceed with caution. They are hard to see and the HM is more likely to wave you in from the quayside! He will also direct you to your finger berth if one has already been assigned, or to alongside berthing/rafting.

Hazards Drying ledges either side of the harbour entrance extend about 5 cables offshore.

Shelter within the marina is excellent in all weathers.

Anchorage is possible near the white ⚓s (see below), but with no natural shelter.

MARINA

Capitainerie is on the N side of the entry gate. Port de Plaisance, quai Daniel-Rivaille, 17410 St Martin de Ré. Tel 05.46.09.26.69. HM Laurent Garnier. VHF Ch 09. Open daily in season 0700-1900; out of season 0800-1200 & 1400-1800. Weather forecasts posted daily. The marina depth is maintained at 3m.

Visitors have four options, from seaward:
a. Pick up one of 4 white ⚓s about 8 cables north of the harbour; no charge for 24 hours.
b. Berth alongside the waiting pontoon inboard of the NW mole, dredged 2·3m or less if silted. It is subject to uncomfortable undulations (Mexican Wave) in even quite moderate N'ly winds.
c. In the marina berth or raft up alongside the NW quay opposite the entry gate. Similar berths are at the southeast end of the marina.
d. Berth on a finger pontoon assigned by the HM. This is the best option, but a prior telephone call is essential as vacant finger berths are scarce. They are numbered 1-157 clockwise

from port of the entry gate; most likely berths are 5-50 and 122-157, all before the 90° bend.

Showers (free) and **Launderette** are in the Capitainerie; open 0600-1200 & 1400-2300.

Tariff
a. Alongside quay/rafted up. Daily rates for LOA bands, Jul/Aug; 2nd figure is May, Jun & Sep: 7·5-9m = 97/61FF; <10·5m = 121/76FF; <12m = 145/91FF; <13m = 158/99FF.
b. Finger pontoon. Daily rates for LOA bands, Jul/Aug; 2nd figure is May, Jun & Sep: 7·5-9m = 121/97FF; <10·5m = 152/121FF; <12m = 182/145FF; <13m = 197/158FF.

Fuel Diesel & petrol pumps are just before the swingbridge, N side; if not operating try the pumps on the west side of the fish basin.

NAUTICAL NEEDS

Chandlery & repairs
- Chantiers Navals (U Ship), quai Launay-Razilly. Tel 05.46.09.21.06. SHOM agent, chandlery.
- Océan Nautique, ZA St Martin. Tel 05.46.09.13.83. Chandlery, electronics, repairs.
- Ré Boat Service, 5 ZA La Couarde (5km west). Tel 05.46.29.49.62. Hull and engine repairs.
- Ré Plaisance, 8 Galerie de l'Îlot. Tel 05.46.09.02.44. Chandlery, engine repairs.

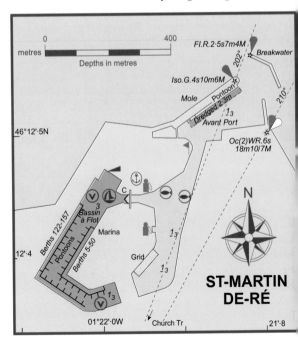

LA FLOTTE, ILE DE RÉ

La Flotte: Yachts to starboard will stay afloat; the inner harbour dries

The following notes about this rather pleasant little drying harbour may induce you to poke your bows in, especially if St Martin is full. They are barely 4M apart, allowing for intervening oyster beds; or 4km by bike if you plan to pre-recce. La Flotte does have some berths where you can stay afloat! Most of the tourist information under St Martin applies, so only differences are shown here. Do walk or cycle eastwards to L'Abbaye des Châteliers, a 12th century Cistercian abbey which was largely destroyed in 1623 by the Protestants. The golden ruins glow warmly in the early morning sun and there are good views of Pertuis Breton and the mainland bridge; it makes a brilliant site for Son et Lumière on a summer's evening. Its stones were used in building the nearby Fort de la Prée in 1625, to keep the Brits away from La Rochelle – *mais nous avons changé tout cela.*

Maison du Platin is a rainy day museum visit: local traditions and island history ...

TOURISM

Tourist Office quai Sénac, BP 5, 17630 La Flotte (inner harbour). Tel 05.46.09.60.38.

Beaches Plage de la Clavette is west of the harbour and Plage de l'Arnérault is to the east.

Bus The local Rébus operates three routes of which Line 2 links La Flotte to La Rochelle, St Martin and Loix; Line 3 also runs via La Flotte to Sablanceaux, St Martin and La Couarde. The timetable is obtainable from the Tourist Office.

Railway Nearest station is at La Rochelle, qv.

Taxis Tel 05.46.09.61.21; 05.46.09.60.26.

Bike hire Cycland, 17 rue du Marché. Tel 05.46.09.65.27. From 45FF per day.

EATING ASHORE

Restaurants Several restaurants line quai Sénac, the west side of the inner harbour, including:
- Le Français, at No 1. Tel 05.46.09.60.06. **Hôtel/ restaurant.
- L'Ecailler, at No 3. Tel 05.46.09.56.40. Fish restaurant, one of the best on Ré. About 200FF.
- Poissonerie du Port, at No 4. Tel 05.46.09.68.22. Taste before eating; also takeaway.
- Elsewhere try: Chez Ben, 1 rue Henri Lainé. Tel 05.46.09.50.01. Tunisian, for a change.
- Le Lavardin, rue Henri Lainé. Tel 05.46.09.68.32. Menus 95-340FF.
- Le Richelieu, 44 ave de la Plage. Tel 05.46.09.60.70. ***Hôtel/Restaurant. Menus 300FF+.

SHOPPING

Supermarkets A Superette (mini-supermarket) is in the town. Intermarché at ZA Michaud.

Market Daily in the Vieux Marché.

Banks Crédit Agricole and BNP in cours Félix Faure.

NAVIGATIONAL MATTERS

Charts As per St Martin entry.

Approaches From the NW in an arc to SE set a course direct to the waypoint, 46°11′·90N 01°18′·78W, noting the drying oyster beds between Couronneau NCM beacon off St Martin and La Flotte; some are marked by yellow SPM stakes. From the SE you can shape a course closer inshore, but the NCM beacon NE of La Flotte must be rounded. In the vicinity of the waypoint there are 5 white conical waiting buoys.

Daymarks A conspic water tower bearing 235°/ 1·3M from the harbour offers general guidance and the white Romanesque church tower with red roof is helpful, 3 cables west of the harbour. Closer in, the 10m high white light house with green top, Fl WG 4s, on the Grand Môle is easily seen. So too is a small black tower with white windows and a turreted top, almost in transit 212° with the light tower.

Pilotage From the waypoint the harbour (46°11′·35N 01°19′·25W) bears 212·5° at 6 cables. Maintain this track and pick up the Moiré indicator, below and to the left of the light tower. This is aligned on 212·5°; when on this bearing you see 2 vertical orange bars (electronic) against a black ■ background. If you deviate to port or starboard the vertical bars change to chevrons pointing horizontally in the direction to which you should turn to regain track. As you do so, they gradually revert to vertical bars. If you are not regaining track, more orange chevrons will appear!

The range of this indicator is about 500 metres, depending on day/night, visibility and whether the

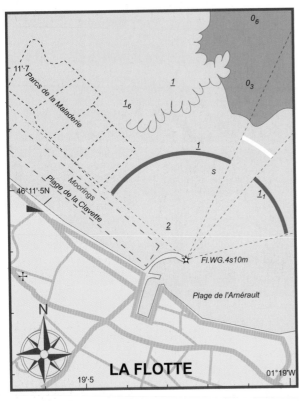

La Flotte at half-tide, looking west

Black tower and turret

Church tower

Inner harbour

Grand Môle

Mooring trots

E

F

Visitors

Fl.WG 4s

Moiré indicator

sun is in your eyes! Accurate, unambiguous and above all simple – Trinity House please note. In this instance it permits a precise track between oyster beds close on either side.

By night you will also be in middle of the 15° white sector (205°-220°) of the Fl WG 4s light.

Tides and **Tidal streams** use the data for St Martin.

Access HW±3. The outer harbour, where there are three pontoons, dries approx 2·4m. There is little chance of a berth in the crowded inner harbour, drying up to 2·8m.

Hazards Drying ledges either side of the harbour entrance extend about 6 cables offshore.

Shelter from NW'lies is good in the outer harbour, thanks to the curving Grand Môle, but it is exposed to fresh NE winds which may cause a scend in the harbour.

Anchorage is possible near the white waiting buoys (see above), but with no natural shelter.

HARBOUR

Capitainerie is on the W side of the inner harbour. Bureau du Port, 1 quai de Sénac, 17630 La Flotte. Tel 05.46.09.67.66. VHF Ch 09. HM Yves Gendron. Open daily in season 0800-1200 & 1400-1900; out of season HW±2. Weather forecasts posted daily.

Visitors should berth on the hammerheads of pontoons (F & E) immediately inside the Grand Môle; end of 'E' pontoon is dredged 2m, but availability in Jul/Aug is dire. Very small craft may berth in the inner harbour on the south side of the stub north jetty. Note: The 10 pontoons shown in a French almanac opposite pontoons E & F were not in place in August 1999; instead three long mooring trots were laid for small craft. There are plans for 250 extra berths by about 2004.

CNLF (Club Nautique de la Flotte), 1 quai de Sénac. Tel 05.46.09.97.34; mobile 06.07.28.67.20. VHF Ch 09. M Yves Ferrasson (in charge) is progressive and friendly, the local authority HM less so. CNLF reserves 8 berths on the ends of E/F pontoons for visitors. The hospitable Clubhouse has showers and bar.

Tariff Pontoons E/F: Daily rates for LOA bands, Jul/Aug; 2nd figure is Apr-Jun & Sep/Oct 7·5-8m = 124/82F; <9m = 144/96F; <10m = 163/108F; <11m = 181/122F; per extra m = 20/13F.

Fuel None; nearest is at St Martin.

NAUTICAL NEEDS

Chandlery & repairs Full facilities are at La Rochelle.
• Océan Nautique, 19 quai de Sénac. Tel 05.46.09.69.00. Chandlery, electronics, repairs.

Moiré   Fl.WG4s   Turreted
indicator   tower

Moiré indicator shows on course

Turn starboard...

Chapter 6

Turn much further starboard...
(at this stage the indicator is too close to use)

LA ROCHELLE

La Rochelle is a Mecca for yachtsmen on the west coast of France and with good reason. The town (it feels more like a city with over 72,000 Rochelais) is awash with history, although not quite in the Venetian sense. Thanks to far-sighted planning in the 1970s the blight of city traffic in 17th and 18th century streets has been at least minimised. Many streets are pedestrianised and a joy to stroll along between well-preserved historic buildings.

Many such buildings surround the Vieux Port where the magnificent twin towers of St Nicolas and La Chaine stand guardian. The drying basin bustles with vedettes, a few fishing craft and more yachts than the few pontoons can accommodate. Two non-tidal basins complete the nautical scene. La Rochelle has justly been described as the most attractive and unspoilt seaside town in France.

To seaward by 1½km is Les Minimes marina, by far the largest on the west and north coasts and possibly on the south coast as well. Yet despite some 3200 berths Les Minimes manages to preserve a friendly charm, epitomised by the *accueil* pontoon where the visitor is assured of a hospitable greeting from the girls who (paradoxically) man it.

La Lanterne

Chaine to La Lanterne. Return towards the Bassin d'échouage via rue St-Jean du Pérot, earmarking a restaurant for dinner. Pass through the Grosse Horloge gateway and up the arcaded rue du Palais towards Place du Verdun.

Pause for a glass of vino, then along rue Gargoulleau to the busy market place (every morning). Southward down rue des Merciers to the Hôtel de Ville, from which you can plunge into a maze of narrow streets (rue St Sauveur, rue du Port and Petite rue du Port). Cross the sunken canal into rue St Nicolas (bars/nightlife), over quai Valin to the south side of the Bassin des Yachts and a call at the Tourist Office.

If during this *tour de force* you have managed to squeeze in one or two of the many museums, it will now be lunchtime. Three hours later, you may decide to call it a day ... There's still plenty to see and another day or two will make no odds.

Oh, don't forget to 'do' the Aquarium when you get back to the marina.

TOURISM

Tourist Office Le Gabut (S side of Bassin des Yachts), 17025 La Rochelle. Tel 05.46.41.14.68. Fax 05.46.41.99.85. E-mail: tourisme.la.rochelle@ wanadoo.fr Website: www.ville-larochelle.fr Open Mon-Sat, Jul/Aug 0900-2000; Jun/Sep 0900-1900; Oct-May 0900-1230 & 1400-1800.

What to see/do La Rochelle is essentially a town for walking: From the water bus a circuit might take you along the ramparts past Tour de la

Beaches The nearest, in fact only, beach is close SW of the marina; hop across the breakwater.

Bus All buses originate from the south side of the vast Place de Verdun, from which 6 local and longer distance companies operate. No 10 bus runs from the marina to Place de Verdun. See also Water Bus under the Marina section.

Ferries/vedettes run from the Vieux Port to Île de Ré, Île d'Aix, Fort Boyard and Île d'Oléron.

Les Minimes marina, looking north

Railway The station is at bd Joffré (500m SE of Bassin des Yachts). Tel 08.36.35.35.35 for train info. Paris is 3 hrs by TGV. Coastal line runs to Nantes and via Saintes to Bordeaux and south.

Taxis Tel 05.46.41.55.55; 05.46.42.22.00; Autoplus municipal taxis 05.46.34.02.22.

Airport La Rochelle/Laleu is close NE of La Pallice. Tel 05.46.42.18.27. OK for your biz jet.

Bike hire
- Autoplus, 05.46.34.02.22 (municipal yellow bikes) on Cours des Dames, also at the bus station;
- Boobaloo, rue de la Monnaie (northwest of La Lanterne). Tel 05.46.41.02.24.

Car hire
- Budget, 1 ave de Gaulle; and others by the railway station.
- Electrique Autoplus, place du Verdun, hires mopeds and small cars by the half-day and day. Tel 05.46.34.02.22.

EATING ASHORE

Restaurants There are numerous convenient, if undistinguished, eateries around the S side of the marina, but in the town the choice is far greater and more intriguing. However the eating places around the Bassin d'Échouage and in the rue du Port and Petite rue du Port (tourist honey-pots) tend to be over-crowded & over-priced. Without wandering too far, try the following in/near rue St-Jean du Pérot which runs behind the Tour de la Chaine towards La Lanterne:
- André, at No 5. Tel 05.46.41.28.24. Seafood at affordable prices; eat outside.
- La Marmite, at No 14. Tel 05.46.41.17.03. Menus 200-400FF. Superb seafood and ambience.
- Bistrot de l'Entracte, at No 22. Tel 05.46.50.62.60. Menus from 150FF.
- L'Assiette Gourmande, at No 39. Tel 05.46.52.07.98. Menus 75-95FF. Good value fish and meat.
- Le Grillardin, at No 48. Tel 05.46.41.27.69. Relaxed atmosphere, brilliant steak *au poivre*. Sit at the bar and watch your food being cooked in front of you.
- Les Quatres Sergents, at No 49. Tel 05.46.41.35.80. Menus 89-132FF. More upmarket. Diners. Nearby: Le Verdière, rue de la Cloche. Tel 05.46.50.56.75. Menus 80-188FF. Closed Mon.

On the S side of the Bassin des Yachts (near Tourist Office) are several quieter restaurants. Try:

Chapter 6

- Bistrot du Ship, 7 quai du Gabut. Tel 05.46.41.22.93.

SHOPPING

Supermarkets There are convenient small food shops behind the Galerie Marchande, south of pontoons 10-12, but check with the Capitainerie for supermarkets within walking distance.

Markets Fri morning at rue Lucille, south of the marina. In La Rochelle: Daily in place du Marché. Fish market daily 1600-1800, except Sun, at Bassin d'Échouage.

Banks Crédit Mutuel, rue Lucille (south of pontoon 11). All banks in the town.

NAVIGATIONAL MATTERS

Charts AC 2743 and SHOM 7413 cover La Rochelle and La Pallice at 1:15,000. AC 2641 (1:50,000) and SHOM 6521 (1:47,500) cover Pertuis Breton and La Rochelle. AC 2746 (1:50,000) and SHOM 6333 (1:47,510) cover Pertuis d'Antioche and La Rochelle.

Approaches From the WNW (Pertuis Breton) transit the Ile de Ré bridge, skirt round La Pallice

Tour Richelieu

(no yachts, please) keeping a wary eye open for commercial/fishing vessels and set course direct to the waypoint 46°08´·23N 01°11´·88W.

From the west and south, steer as required to the waypoint, but note the following:

Le Lavardin drying reef and adjacent spoil ground area, about 2M west of the waypoint; Chauveau SCM and Roche du Sud WCM buoys near the leading line and 3M from the waypoint; and a waiting area for large ships at anchor is a mile or more south of the latter buoy.

Daymarks The 17m high, red octagonal Tour Richelieu near the marina entrance stands out well against the background of mainly white buildings. In amongst these buildings is a welter of forts, towers and churches of which just three will suffice for navigational orientation:

Tour St Nicolas, a massive 42m high tower is to starboard of the entrance to Le Vieux Port; from its top an equally massive French tricolour is invariably flown. On the port side the smaller Tour de la Chaine is rather less obvious. 200m to the west is La Lanterne, a round tower topped by a conspicuous spire. Ignore all the others until/ unless you are foot-slogging as a tourist!

The 059° leading marks are: front a red/white banded tower tucked amongst the trees close east of Tour St Nicolas; rear a tall, white, green-topped lighthouse on the far side of the inner basin.

Lights By day the leading lights are Fl 4s and in poor visibility seem none too bright. At night they are quick flashing. If coming from the WNW be aware that the 4° sector (061°-065°) of the rear leading light is obscured by the bulk of Tour St Nicolas, ie until you are within 2° of the 059° leading line.

Pilotage The waypoint is on the 059° leading line, 1·35M from the Tour Richelieu. Les Minimes WCM buoy is 3 cables SE of the waypoint, marking shoals further east.

The approach channel shoals to 0·7m with a few 0·1m patches and care is needed near MLWS. 200m after Tour Richelieu at a WCM buoy (46°08'·96N 01°10'·13W)turn starboard for Les Minimes marina; do not cut the corner. The short entry channel is marked by two small PHM buoys.

If bound for the Vieux Port, maintain the leading line, keeping as close to 4 PHM buoys as other vessels will allow. There is usually a steady stream of ferries and vedettes, the channel is 35m wide and depths are only 0·2m to 0·3m.

Tides At La Rochelle/La Pallice HW neaps is 15 mins after, and at springs 30 mins before HW

Looking seaward from inside the Vieux Port

Pointe de Grave. LW at neaps is 20 mins, and at springs 25 mins before LW Pointe de Grave.

MHWS is 6·0m, MLWS 0·9m; MHWN is 4·9m, MLWN 2·4m.

Tidal streams near the waypoint do not exceed ½ knot. 8 cables SW of Le Lavardin they set NE/SW at up to 1·9 knots.

Access day/night to Les Minimes marina, but do your tidal sums if approaching near LW springs.

For the Vieux Port HW–2½ is a sensible time to start an approach, ensuring adequate water in the Bassin d'Échouage and access to the inner wet basin.

Hazards Shallow approach channel, flanked by drying ledges.

Shelter in the marina and in the basins of the Vieux Port is excellent in all weathers.

Anchorage There is no recognised anchorage.

MARINA AND VIEUX PORT

Capitainerie is in a tower in the centre of the marina. Port des Minimes, 17026 La Rochelle. Tel 05.46.44.41.20; Fax 05.46.44.36.49. e-mail port.lratwanadoo.fr HM Jean Lorand. VHF Ch 09. Open H24. Weather forecasts are posted daily. Depths in the marina vary from 1m to 2m.

Bureau du Vieux Port by entrance to outer basin. Tel 05.46.41.32.05; Fax 05.46.44.36.49.

Visitors have three berthing options, from seaward:
a. In Les Minimes marina; vast, functional, friendly and efficient. Berth initially on the *accueil* pontoon, dead ahead of the entrance. After the paperwork you will be assigned an adjacent berth or one on pontoons 13-15 in the SW part of the marina.
b. In the Vieux Port, atmospheric (as they say), but also noisy and one is by no means certain to get a slot. In the Bassin d'Échouage the first pontoon is for fish vessels. Berth on Nos 1 or 2 pontoons, max depth 1·3m; fin keels will sink into soft mud. The edges of the Bassin dry about 1m.
c. In the inner basin (Bassin des Yachts; 3m depth), if a berth can be pre-arranged. Quieter but still very central. Enter via a gate close NE of Tour St Nicolas; access HW –2 to HW +5. Two pontoons with fingers extend from the N side. Around the outside, berth bows in/stern to buoy.
Note: Large yachts (max LOA 60m) may pre-arrange to berth in the outer basin (aka Bassin des Chalutiers; 5m depth), entered via a gate close south of Tour St Nicolas.

Showers 12FF in marina at Capitainerie or at a block west of 10 pontoon; 8FF in Vieux Port.

Tariff Applicable to Port des Minimes, Bassin d'Échouage and the inner and outer basins. Daily

Chapter 6

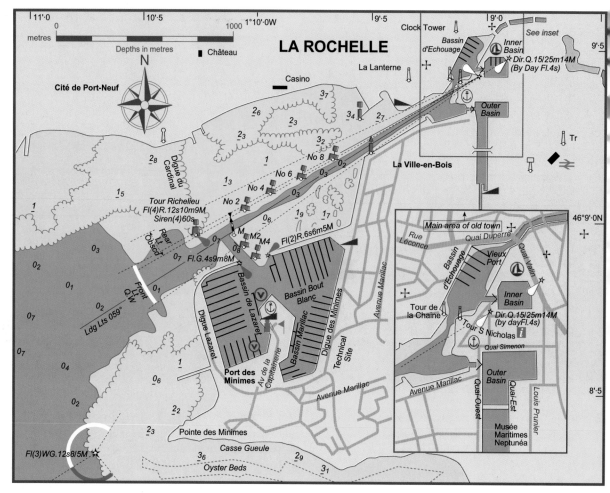

rates are for LOA bands in Jun-Sep; Apr/May 25% off; Oct-Mar 50% off. 3rd night free for cash payment (only once per week):
7·5-8·5m = 83FF; 8·5-9·5m = 95FF; 9·5-10·5m = 108FF; 10·5-11·5m = 123FF; 11·5-13m = 145FF; 13-15m = 184FF; 15-16m = 221FF; 16-18m = 256FF.

Fuel Diesel & petrol are next to the Capitainerie, 0800-2000 in season; H24 with French card.

Launderette 1 rue Lucille, south of the marina. Also ave Marillac, SE corner of the marina.

Water Bus This is the best way to get to/from town (Vieux Port). It leaves from the root of 10 pontoon as follows: Jul/Aug, 0900-2330 every 30mins, except 1300; Apr, May and Sep, 1030-1930 hourly except 1330; Jun 0930-1930 hourly except 1330; Oct-Mar, 1030-1830 hourly except 1330. Single 11FF, pay onboard.

NAUTICAL NEEDS

Chandlery & repairs
The following are SHOM chart agents, all located in or near Les Minimes marina. The ZA (Zone Artisanale) is along the east side of the marina:

- Navigatlantique, ZA. Tel 05.46.44.53.77.
- Comptoir Maritime Rochelais, ZA. Tel 05.46.44.34.97. Chandlery, mechanical & electrical work.
- Atlantic Loisirs, ave des Minimes. Tel 05.46.44.21.35.
- Accastillage Diffusion, ave Marillac. Tel 05.46.45.49.49. Chandlery, mechanical repairs.
- Marina Europe, ZA, BP 245. Tel 05.46.44.69.86.
- Librairie Nautique St Nicolas, 31 rue St Nicolas (one block NE of rear leading light). Specialist in charts and French and foreign Pilots etc. Tel 05.46.50.20.92. www.chez.com/stnicolas/

Around the marina there are some 80 companies capable of making general and specialist repairs, so that to include just a few companies in this book could only be highly selective. It would be more realistic to get well-informed advice from the Capitainerie on say two or three companies which can deal with your specific problem(s) – the decision is then yours!

LE DOUHET, ILE D'OLÉRON

See St Denis for general information about Île d'Oléron. Only differences concerning Le Douhet, both ashore and afloat, are covered below. Le Douhet is a small coastal village equidistant 2·5km from La Brée des Bains up the coast and St Georges inland beyond the salt marshes.

Campsites abound but are not usually intrusive. The marina is carved out of all pervasive sand and therein lies a problem: The entrance channel is very prone to silting and requires constant dredging ... but do not be offput; it's worth an away-from-it-all visit. You can always cycle down from St Denis for a prior recce.

Forget museums – the only local culture is sun-worshipping! Enjoy the beaches, swimming, *Le pique-nique* washed down with the distinctive tangy local wine; yes vines are grown near St Pierre and St Georges. Gorge yourself on local oysters and mussels ...

TOURISM

Tourist Office The two nearest are at 28 rue des Dames, 17190 St Georges d'Oléron. Tel 05.46.76.63.75. Fax 05.46.76.86.49. or at rue Ardillières, BP21, 17840 La Brée des Bains. Tel 05.46.47.96.73. Fax 05.46.75.96.73.

Beaches There's sand everywhere in this place and you have only to walk left or right out of the marina to be on a fine beach backed by pine trees and probably yet another campsite.

Bus The nearest bus stops are 2km away at La Brée des Bains or St Georges. See St Denis.

Taxi Tel 05.46.75.98.03.

EATING ASHORE

Restaurants
* La Coquille, at the port. Tel 05.46.76.74.74. Seafood menus; open daily in summer.

Le Douhet, near LW, looking WNW. White line indicates position of retaining wall/sill

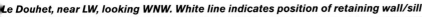

Capitainerie

Visitors' pontoon

Buoyed channel

Chapter 6

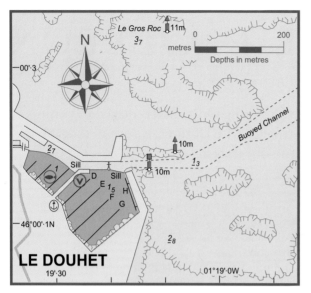

LE DOUHET

NAVIGATIONAL MATTERS

Approaches From the NW to N steer direct to the waypoint 46°00´·54N 01°17´·61W. From N to SE, skirt round La Longe and Le Boyard, a 4M long bank between Oléron and Île d'Aix. Either side of it are deepwater East and West channels. West of the latter, mussel racks between Le Douhet and Pointe des Saumonards are marked by an ECM and a NCM buoy, both lit. Further west a second lit NCM buoy is the approach waypoint.

Daymarks Fort Boyard, a massive artillery fortress with 27 metre high tower, is easily visible 4·5M east of Le Douhet. Le Douhet is distinguished by a gap in the trees and you may be able to make out the white tower and red roof of the Capitainerie behind 365 masts – or thereabouts.

Pilotage From the waypoint (NCM buoy, Q) a track of about 240°/7½ cables leads to the first of three pairs of small lateral buoys. These mark the entry channel which leads WSW to the marina entrance 46°00´·15N 01°19´·18W across inshore ledges drying about 1·3m.

Two short training banks at the harbour entrance are marked by a PHM/SHM perch. Enter the marina over a sill (drying 1·8m) between the east breakwater and a yellow post with tidal gauge. Beyond this a yellow SPM buoy marks the retaining wall joined to a central jetty. Small fishing boats berth to the NW in the Old Port.

A night approach is not advised due to lack of lights.

• Le Bord à Bord, at the port. Tel 05.46.76.62.61. Seafood.
• Le Brasero, at the port. Tel 05.46.76.64.24. Seafood.
• Pizzeria, at the port. Tel 05.46.76.72.79.

SHOPPING

Supermarkets None in Le Douhet. P'tit Marché at the port sells bread, vegetables, basic foods and wines; 0800-2000 in season. A Co-op is in rue des Dames, St Georges.

Markets St Georges, sous les Halles, daily 0800-1300. La Brée des Bains, place du Marché, daily in season; Wed, Fri & Sun out of season.

The Capitainerie

The marina entrance

Tides and **Tidal streams** are as for St Denis.

Access windows by day for coefficient 80 are as follows for draughts between 1m and 2m: 1·0m HW −4 to +3½; 1·2m HW −3¾ to +3¼; 1·5m HW −3½ to +3; 2·0m HW −2¾ to +2¼.

There are two waiting buoys outside the buoyed channel.

Anchorage is near the waiting buoys or at the west end of Anse de la Maleconche (E of marina).

Hazards La Longe and Le Boyard shoal, orientated NW/SE, is about 3M east of Le Douhet. At its SE end, near Fort Boyard, there are depths of 0·2m and a shoal drying 2·3m. The approach and entry channels to Le Douhet are shallow and cross drying ledges. Sand can block these channels almost overnight, given that the marina is virtually carved out of sandbanks.

Shelter from the prevailing westerlies is very good in the marina.

MARINA

Capitainerie is opposite D (Visitors) pontoon. Port de Plaisance du Douhet, 17190 St Georges d'Oléron. Tel 05.46.76.71.13; Fax 05.46.76.78.26. HM Pascal Proust. VHF Ch 09. Open at tide times 0730-2130 in season; out of season 0830-1200 & 1330-1800. Weather forecasts are posted daily. Depths in the marina are about 1·5m, <u>not</u> 2·5m as indicated in some publications and charts.

Visitors berth/raft up alongside the NW side of D pontoon or in finger berths on the SE side.

Showers and **Launderette** are in the Capitainerie.

Tariff applies also to Boyardville. Daily rates are for LOA bands Jul/Aug; 2nd figure is for 1 Sep-30 Jun. Third consecutive night is free:

8-9m = 82/46FF; <10m = 95/62FF; <11m = 108/62FF; <12m = 118/72FF; <13m = 128/72FF; <14m = 138/82FF; >14m = 154/82FF.

Fuel *Rien du tout.*

NAUTICAL NEEDS

Chandlery & repairs
• Société Oléronnaise Services-Plaisance, at the port. Tel 05.46.75.07.22. Chandlery, repairs.

Clearing the entrance; note first pair of lateral buoys

BOYARDVILLE,
ILE D'OLÉRON

See St Denis for general information about Île d'Oléron. Only differences affecting Boyardville, both ashore and afloat, are covered below.

Boyardville is a small village named after Fort Boyard whose workers were billeted there during its lengthy (1804-1859) construction. This fortress was intended as a gun platform to guard the approaches to Rochefort against the marauding British. By the time it was finished gunnery technology had moved on and the fort was redundant – haven't we heard that tale somewhere else? Today Boyardville is a pleasant little place with a small fishing fleet, superb beaches and shaded walking amongst the pines of Forêt des Saumonards.

Cycle 5km south to Le Marais aux Oiseaux, a bird sanctuary well worth visiting; so too is the ornithological Park at Maisonneuve close SW of St Pierre d'Oléron. Take a break at St Pierre, the island's attractive "capital", before completing your 16km circuit by heading up to Sauzelle and back across the marsh-lands.

TOURISM

Tourist Office ave de la Plage. Tel 05.46.47.04.76.

Beaches The nearest beach is just north of the marina, backed by pine trees.

Bus Three buses a day to Le Chateau d'Oléron, where change for Rochefort and Saintes.

Bike hire Roue Libre, 45 ave Albatros (opposite the market). Tel 05.46.47.38.71.

Vedettes Trips to Fort Boyard, Île d'Aix, La Rochelle and Île de Ré.

EATING ASHORE

Restaurants
- Les Bains, at the port. Tel 05.46.47.01.02. Hotel-restaurant. Menus 97-152FF; seafood.
- La Calypso, at the port. Tel 05.46.47.32.56.
- L'Escale, at the port; 64 rue Hippocampes. Tel 05.46.75.00.88.

SHOPPING

Supermarkets Boyardial, 135 rue 158ème. Tel 05.46.47.23.14.

Market A covered market is 50m from the **V** pontoon, open daily in Jul/Aug.

Banks Cashpoint by the market.

NAVIGATIONAL MATTERS

Approaches From the NW make for the waypoint 45°58´·37N 01°13´·20W (La Perrotine SHM buoy), via the West Passage or by the East Passage, respectively SW and NE of Le Boyard shoal. From the E the approach lies south of Île d'Aix, keeping between Les Palles NCM buoy and Le Boyard

Boyardville entrance

Near LW, looking east

SCM buoy; these marks also apply if coming out of the Charente river.

From the SE, when clear of Coureau d'Oléron set course direct to the waypoint, keeping clear of the extensive drying shoals off the east coast of Oléron.

Note: La Perrotine SHM buoy, and therefore the waypoint, is shifted *de temps en temps* in sympathy with the movement of the sandbanks.

Daymarks Fort Boyard, a massive artillery fortress with 27 metre high tower, is conspicuous 1·7M NNW of La Perrotine SHM buoy. The woods on Pointe des Saumonards are a clear feature.

Pilotage From the waypoint (SHM buoy) a track of 263°/4 cables leads to the end of the jetty, ☆ Fl (2) R 6s (45°58´·30N 01°13´·76W), which extends 2 cables ENE from Pointe de la Perrotine. For best water keep about 10m off this jetty until abeam the first slip to starboard; here take up a mid-channel course so as to clear a spit to port. After 100m turn starboard for the gate into the marina.

The 500m stretch of the canalised drying river between the marina and a low bridge is occupied by fishing boats.

Tides and **Tidal streams** are as for St Denis.

Access The gate into the marina opens automatically day/night when the water level is 4·3m above CD. The following windows are a guide, depending on the tidal coefficient (and to a much lesser extent on barometric pressure and wind):

Coeff <40 (neaps) HW ±1½; coeff 70 (average) HW ±2; coeff >90 (springs) HW ±2½.

Ⓡ lights warn when the gate is about to open/close.

Anchorage is 5 cables N of the jetty head near the yacht moorings in about 3m on sand; a good place to wait if early for the marina gate.

Hazards Between La Perrotine buoy and the jetty head maintain a straight track so as to avoid substantial sandbanks drying about 2·9m on either side.

Shelter is very good in the marina.

MARINA

Capitainerie is on the SE side of the marina. Port de Boyardville, 17190 St Georges d'Oléron. Tel 05.46.47.23.71; Fax 05.46.75.06.13. HM Pascal Proust. VHF Ch 09. Open 0800-2100 in season; out of season 0830-1200 & 1400-1730. Weather forecasts are posted daily.

Visitors berth/raft up alongside the Ⓥ pontoon to starboard of the entrance, or as directed. The 5 other pontoons are lettered A to E from the SW. Depths in the marina are about 2m. There is not a lot of room for manoeuvering.

Showers are next to the Ⓥ pontoon.

Tariff The Le Douhet tariff applies also to Boyardville.

Fuel is from a boatyard wharf on the opposite side of the river to the marina entrance. Tel 05.46.47.01.36. In season 0900-1215 & 1400-1800.

NAUTICAL NEEDS

Chandlery & repairs
• Chantiers Navals de la Perrotine, at the port. Tel 05.46.47.01.36. Chandlery, boatyard, repairs.

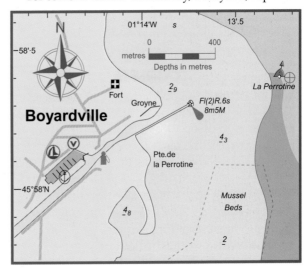

Chapter 6

ROCHEFORT

Rochefort is a great favourite with Brits and indeed all nations; I have never heard ill spoken of it. Warm golden stone, most elegant 17th century architecture, gardens, attractive squares and above all friendly people – no wonder foreign yachts winter here at affordable rates

and in surroundings of great character – in summer too it is a magnet, yet never presumes, is always gentle.

Jean-Baptiste Colbert, Navy minister in the reign of Louis XIV, deserves most of the credit. His task was to build a great naval base (almost like Chatham), ironically to keep the Brits out! The town is laid out with military precision in a grid of desirable streets; the riverside is redolent with history (see below) including reconstructions of how the Dockyard was over 300 years ago.

Pierre Loti is synonymous with Rochefort: retired naval officer, eccentric (aren't they all), author, sportsman and member of the Académie Française. Visit his bizarre house, crammed with exotic memorabilia, at 141 rue Pierre Loti.

Forgive the exuberant prose, but when you have visited Rochefort you will understand. Some people have described it as the highpoint of their French Atlantic cruise.

Belle Epoque railway station

building is occupied by the Chamber of Commerce and a library, but you will see exhibitions of rope and rigging in the International Centre of the Sea. Walk aboard the frigate Hermione being rebuilt in dry dock. Amongst a wealth of museums three stand out: the Navy Museum (Hôtel de Cheusses, just south of the former Dockyard); the museum of Naval aviation (guided tours Thurs 1430) and the museum Les Métiers de Mercure (12 rue Lesson), shops of another age – an absorbing time warp ... If you haven't already done so, pause for a drink in the attractive Place Colbert.

Bus The bus station (gare routière) is just off rue du Dr Peltier, about 200m south of the Tourist Office where timetables can be obtained.

Railway The station is at the N end of ave President Wilson (700m NW of Basin No 1). Paris is 3 hrs by TGV via La Rochelle. Coastal line runs to Nantes and via Saintes to Bordeaux and south.

Taxis Tel 05.46.99.07.64.

Airport Rochefort/St Agnant is 7km S of the town centre. Tel 05.46.83.05.20.

Ferries/vedettes run to Fort Boyard, La Rochelle and Île d'Aix.

Bike hire Espace-Nature, 35 rue Audrey de Puyravault. Tel 05.46.83.91.68. 6FF for half day, 12FF for whole day; 250FF returnable deposit required.

Car hire Ask at the Tourist Office.

TOURISM

Tourist Office ave Sadi-Carnot, 17300 Rochefort. Tel 05.46.99.08.60. Fax 05.46.99.52.64. Open daily, mid-Jun to mid-Sep 0900-1900 (2000 Jul/Aug); mid-Sep to mid-Jun 0900-1230 & 1400-1830, closed Sun. Website www.tourisme.fr/rochefort

A secondary office is by the Musée de la Marine; opening hours are more restricted.

What to see/do Visit La Corderie Royale (rope factory) and surrounding gardens; you won't see a 374m long warp stretched out full length because much of this elegant classical-style

EATING ASHORE

Restaurants In the vicinity of the marina are:
- Hotel***/Restaurant de la Corderie Royale, south of Basin 1. Tel 05.46.99.35.35. Superb setting, elegant C17th building, excellent food at almost affordable prices; menus 150-320FF.
- La Flore, 1 quai Bellot, south of Basin 1. Tel 05.46.87.21.06. Eat inside or out looking across the basin; popular, some character and readily affordable prices; menus 100-170FF.
- Le Gabier, east side of Basin 2. Restaurant/ brasserie; convivial place for a drink, a snack or meal.
- L'Escale de Bougainville, northeast corner of Basin 2. Tel 05.46.99.54.99. Modern building, very good food; menus 98-230FF. (Launderette next door!).

Up in the town, try:
- Le Tourne Broche, 56 ave de Gaulle. Tel 05.46.99.20.19. Menus 110-210FF; one of the best.
- Bruno Berton, 76 rue Grimaux. Tel 05.46.83.95.12. Small, pre-book. Menus 125-190FF.

SHOPPING

Supermarkets seem almost intrusive in Rochefort.
- The nearest is Lidl, about 250m ENE of the lifting bridge between Basins 2 and 3. Continue 1½km ENE along ave de la Libération to Stoc.
- The much larger LeClerc is about 2km due south of the marina in Martrou shopping centre, on the way to the transporter bridge; or
- Intermarché is 2km NW in the Quatranes shopping centre.

You can also shop very entertainingly at a host of enticing food shops and in one of the most active street markets you could wish to roam.

Markets Off Place Colbert and at Les Halles by Porte de l'Arsenal a.m on Tues, Thur and Sat.

Banks All banks in the town.

Launderette On NE side of Basin 2, next door to the restaurant L'Escale de Bougainville.

For Bookworms The Librairie at the corner of rue Thiers and rue Audrey de Puyravault is full of old books, especially about the WW2 liberation of Rochefort.

NAVIGATIONAL MATTERS

Charts AC 2746 (1:50,000) and SHOM 6333 (1:47,510) cover Pertuis d'Antioche as far as Île d'Aix. SHOM 6334 (1:47,600) considerably overlaps 6333 and covers Pertuis d'Antioche, the Charente and Rochefort. AC 2748 (1:20,000) and

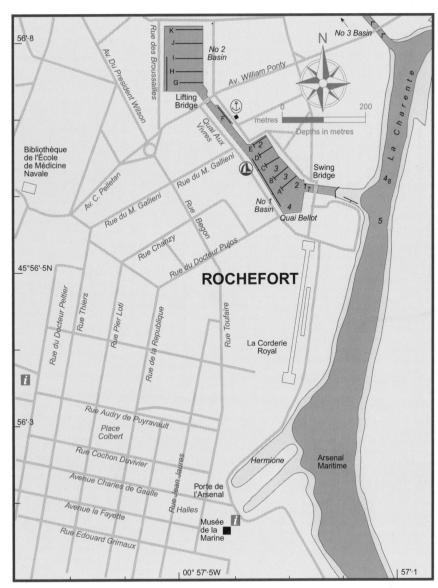

Chapter 6

Short stay pontoon downstream of the entrance

SHOM 4333 (1:15,000) cover the Charente and Rochefort in greater detail.

Approaches From the NW (Pertuis d'Antioche) take the east passage between Île d'Aix and La Longe & Le Boyard bank, on track to the waypoint 45°59′·58N 01°09′·53W, Les Palles NCM buoy (not to be confused with Les Palles NCM beacon 9M WNW, near St Denis d'Oléron).

From the S and W make for the waypoint keeping clear of drying shoals.

Leave the waypoint on the flood at about HW Rochefort −2½ to arrive at the entry gate into No 1 Basin at HW assuming a ground speed of 6kn, probably more, but it is better to arrive early.

Daymarks In a low-lying area Fort Boyard, as described under Île d'Oléron, is conspicuous 2·3M west of the waypoint. So too are the twin white towers, red tops, of Île d'Aix lighthouse.

Leading lights & mark Initially the river is lit by two sets of leading lights (115° and 134·5°), but night navigation by pleasure craft is prohibited. Upstream a succession of unlit leading lines guide large commercial ships. These charted lines/ beacons are lettered TT to AA going up-river and are of only passing interest to yachts.

Pilotage From the waypoint yachts should buoy-hop past 3 unlit SHM buoys and a SPM light buoy off Port des Barques, 4·5M upriver. Note that a bar 0·6m lies between the first and second SHM buoys. Thereafter the fairway gradually narrows, but the remaining 10·5 miles are simple, keeping in mid-river or nearer the outside of bends. Depths are about 2m, except for a few 0·8m patches, up to Soubise after which 4m - 8m is the norm. The river makes a wide 180° bend and several lesser turns, so you need to keep yourself orientated.

At Martrou the D733 road bridge (32m clearance) and an old aerial transporter bridge 400m upstream warn that Rochefort is 2M ahead; between these two "bridges" a former lifting bridge is no more, apart from its abutments. The transporter bridge is used in summer and raises intriguing questions about rights of way! It is in essence an airborne raft suspended a few feet above the water by wires from a trolley moving on rails aloft. Its "pilot" monitors VHF Ch 12/16.

Tides At Rochefort HW neaps is 35 mins after, and at springs 10 mins before HW Pointe de Grave. LW at neaps is 1h 25m, and at springs 30 mins after LW Pointe de Grave.

MHWS is 6·5m, MLWS 0·8m; MHWN is 5·3m, MLWN 2·2m.

Tidal streams near the second SHM buoy reach 2kn on the spring flood and 3 kn on the ebb. Up-river in the narrows beyond the bridges the rate reaches 4 knots.

Access to Bassin No 1 is possible 0600-2200 May-Sep, 1 hour's notice required; and 0700-2000 Oct-Apr, with 24 hours notice. Within these windows the single pair of gates opens at HW La Rochelle, ie 20 mins before HW Rochefort, for no more than 30 mins to permit departures and arrivals. The pedestrian swing bridge opens in unison, as does the lifting bridge between Basins.

There is a drying waiting pontoon on the port side just short of the entry gate (45°56´·60N 00°57´·20W). A second waiting pontoon, for short stay with electricity and water, is 1 cable south of the entrance on the west bank, almost opposite the Corderie Royale; yachts can remain afloat here.

Hazards Shallow approach channel from the waypoint to about the 3rd SHM buoy.

Shelter in the marina is excellent in all weathers.

Anchorages Off Île d'Aix there are fair weather anchorages outside the following white ⚓s, all in 2m: 3 ⚓s (PL 40-42) off Pte de Coudepont; 4 ⚓s (PL 43-46) 3 cables NW of the lighthouse; and 5 ⚓s (PL 47-51) 3 cables ESE of the island's southern tip. The only anchorages in the river are clear of the fairway at Soubise and Martrou; there are also 4 white ⚓s off the latter.

MARINA

Capitainerie is between Basins 1 and 2, starboard side. Port de Plaisance, quai Lemoyne de Sérigny, 17300 Rochefort. Tel 05.46.83.99.96; Fax 05.46.99.80.56. HM Ghislaine Caquineau. VHF Ch 09. Open in season, Mon-Sat 0830-1200 & 1330-1730, Sun 1000-1200 and gate opening times.

Weather forecasts are posted daily. Depths in the marina vary from 2m to 3m.

Visitors berth where directed. Basin No 1 (pontoons A-E and the west quayside) has an historic atmosphere with shady chestnut trees near the entrance and fine buildings on the SW and S sides. Pontoons C & D have finger berths; alongside berthing/rafting on all other pontoons/quays. Basin No 2 (pontoons G-K) is more functional; it is reached via a short canal (pontoon F) and a lifting bridge which stays open whilst the entry gate is open. All pontoons have finger berths. Basin No 3 upstream is for commercial vessels only.

Showers 10FF are below the Capitainerie.

Tariff Daily rates are for LOA bands in season (not defined):
7-8m = 52FF; <9m = 55FF; <10m = 68FF; <11m = 72FF; <12m = 81FF; <13m = 88FF; <14m = 107FF; <15m = 116FF.

Fuel The diesel & petrol pumps to port just before the entry gate are regrettably out of commission. They have been vandalised (no hoses) and should be regarded as dead for the foreseeable future.

However any of several garages within 1km of the marina will fill cans and deliver to your boat.

NAUTICAL NEEDS

Chandlery & repairs
- Chantier nautique du Port, No 1 Basin, east side. Tel 05.46.82.07.97. Chandlery, engineering.
- Charente Océan, No 2 Basin. Tel 05.46.82.07.97. Chandlery, engineering repairs.

Inoperative fuel pumps

Entry gate

Waiting pontoon

Entrance to No 1 Basin

POINTE DE GRAVE TO THE SPANISH BORDER

CONTENTS

From a hill on the south bank of the Adour, the twin spires of Bayonne cathedral dominate the town's narrow lanes

THE SEA AND THE LAND

France is full of surprises and contrasts and the final 140 miles of your voyage are no exception. From Pointe de Grave at the mouth of the Gironde the coast runs almost ruler-straight for 60M to Cap Ferret and the entrance to the Bassin d'Arcachon.

Thus far the only possible surprise may have been the entrance to Arcachon, if the weather has been unkind – but in high summer it is usually benevolent and settled for several days at a time. You are after all only looking for a cast-iron 12 hour window.

Assuming that the Gods have smiled upon you, the passage will have been bum-numbingly dull. The coast is an endless ribbon of sand, the Côte d'Argent, and let's face it, one grain of sand looks much like another. Pause in Arcachon for a few days to "ease springs". Then plunge on for the same distance south to Capbreton.

One solution is to knock off these two passages at night, the big advantage of this ploy being that there is no worry about violating the Landes missile range as it is never active at night. This must be one of the few coastlines in Europe where you can be only 3M offshore in total blackness and not a shore light to be seen – for hour after hour.

Arcachon is an intriguing place to visit, a contrast between the 19th century and, I suppose, the 21st in which we now find ourselves. It is over-crowded in summer, mostly by the Bordelais escaping from Bordeaux. Since your coastal voyage is probably at variance with a passage up the Gironde and on through the canals to the Mediterranean (chapters 8 and 9), this might be a good time to jump on the train to Bordeaux (40 mins) which you cannot fail to enjoy.

It is from Capbreton onwards that the surprising contrasts start to crowd in upon you – I refer to the looming foothills of the Pyrenees and the almost Alpine charm of the Basque country. After the never-ending, austere flatlands of pine forest it is pure joy to see the land rise into "bumpy country", dotted with oak and split by green valleys. Add to that the traditional white-fronted, red-beamed Basque houses and the quiet charm of the French Basques who celebrate high days and feast days with traditional song and dance – and suddenly Aquitaine has come alive again! Capbreton, Bayonne (but not Anglet), St Jean-de-Luz and Hendaye are all delightful places.

Which is why yachtsmen should try not to bypass this corner on their way westward to Spain. In fact they should make every effort to include it in their plans. Once there trek inland, take to the hills – enjoy a revitalising break from the two-dimensional view out of the cockpit of your boat.

LANDES FIRING RANGE

Limits: The Centre d'Essais des Landes (CEL) firing range lies between Pte de la Negade and Capbreton and extends 45M offshore. Its N boundary bears 065° from 45°12'N 02°00'W; the S boundary bears 115° from 44°N 02°25'W. The W boundary joins these two lat/long positions. The inshore limit parallels the coast 3M off, except in 3 places where it joins the coast:

a. at Sector 31H, off Hourtin, between 45°14'N and 45°09'N;

b. at Sector 31K, between 44°31'N and 44°28'N; and

c. at Sector 31A, between 44°28'N and 44°13'N, which itself extends 12M offshore. (This is the most often used sector).

Sector designations: The range is split into blocks 31N and 31S, to the N and S of a clear corridor (31B) 8M wide bearing 270° from Arcachon. 31N and 31S are sub-divided into N/S sectors delineated by distance off the coast. Thus, 31S 27.45 means the S block, in a sector 27-45M offshore.

Range activity: Various sectors are active from 0830-1800 LT Mon-Fri; but never on Sun, rarely on a Sat. The range is not active in August. Navigation through active sectors is prohib from the coast to the 12M territorial limit; beyond 12M it is strongly discouraged.

Information: Landes broadcasts range activity on VHF Ch 06, after warning on Ch 06 and 16, at 0815 & 1615LT Mon-Thurs, and at 0815 & 1030LT Fri. For more info on request (Mon-Thurs 0800-1700LT; Fri 0800-1100) call Landes VHF Ch 06 or e 05.58.78.18.00 (same hrs); also recorded data H24 on e 05.58.82.22.42/43. Other sources of info include: Hr Mr's, Aff Maritimes, CROSS Soulac and Sémaphores at La Coubre, Cap Ferret and Socoa; all on request Ch 16, which should be monitored on passage.

Transit options include: sailing by night or at weekends or in August; or routeing outside the 45M limit.

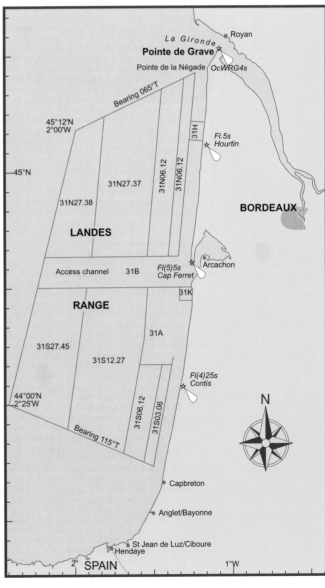

ARCACHON

Dune du Pyla from Cap Ferret

Arcachon is, or perhaps was, one of those superb watering places to which the wealthy retreated to while away the summer months around the turn of the century- and even up to the Thirties. They still do, but so does everybody else! Indeed every weekend, and not just in summer, the people of Bordeaux (*Bordelais*) rush like lemmings to the silver beaches and sheltered waters of the Bassin d'Arcachon, barely an hour's drive away.

The fine houses and villas of a century ago slumber amongst the pines, mimosas and broad avenues which make up the *Ville d'hiver* (winter town), set behind and above the coastal strip which is known as the *Ville d'été* (summer town). There are even spring and autumn towns, but with not quite the same clear identity as the other two seasons!

The *Ville d'été* is where the action is with marina, good shops, a casino, bars, cafés and excellent restaurants spread along the promenades and adjacent streets. Needless to say in July and August it gets grossly overcrowded, driving is a nightmare and even walking is not much fun.

Escape, if you will, to the Bassin d'Arcachon, a vast roughly equilateral (10M sides) expanse of drying waters stretching from Cap Ferret, past Arcachon to Le Teich in the east and up to Arès in the north. Much of it is accessible only on the tide via a network of minor channels.

Oyster farming communities (*ostréiculture*) straggle along its sides. Oyster beds (*parcs d'huitres*) and yet more oyster beds form Arcachon's great glory. Île aux Oiseaux is encircled by them. If you are already an oyster buff, you will know the ropes. To the uninitiated a cruise round the Bassin, taking in an oyster farm with tasting, might be a good start. The port of Gujan-Mestras is a good place to see any of six picturesque oyster farms where you can learn more about the inmates. Read, sleep and above all eat oysters! The best are said to come from Cap Ferret and Banc d'Arguin. Compare them with those of the Belon River and Cancale or even Whitstable on your return to the UK.

TOURISM

Tourist Office is on Place Roosevelt, near to the rail and bus stations. Address: BP 137, 33311

Arcachon. Tel 05.56.83.01.69. Fax 05.57.52.22.10. Hours in season Mon-Sat 0900-1900; Sun 0900-1230; Hols 0900-1900. E-mail tourisme@arcachon.com Website: www.arcachon.com

What to see/do Sailing within the Bassin is more suited to shoal draft boats and those which can take the ground (not on an oyster bed, please). About the only places where a deep-draught fin keeler can safely stay afloat are along the Cap Ferret peninsula at anchorages off La Vigne, L'Herbe, Le Canon and Grand and Petit Piquet, all sheltered from westerlies.

Another more unusual, but popular cruise is a day trip to the Banc d'Arguin. Head out towards Cap Ferret, but at No 11 SHM buoy leave the main channel where a NCM buoy marks the division. Follow the secondary channel, marked by four ECM buoys, south to Banc d'Arguin. This part-drying bank includes a bird sanctuary, oyster farm and a 'museum' of terns. Anchor in a sheltered lagoon almost at the foot of the towering (103m) Dune du Pyla (also spelled Pilat). Great for swimming and a picnic!

Back on terra firma you will not regret making a bus trip (every 30 mins from Arcachon) to the Dune du Pyla. Walk through the pines and clamber up a man-made stairway to the 103m high summit. The view south along the dorsal spine of this extraordinary sand-dune is breathtaking. So too is

Breakers off Cap Ferret with spar buoy in Passe Nord just visible in the centre background

the view to seaward, tracing the buoyed channel which you so skilfully negotiated!

Finally for something slightly different, visit Le Teich ornithological park, NE of Gujan-Mestras, by bus or train. The park roughly equates to the Slimbridge Wildfowl Trust in Gloucestershire (do any birds migrate from one to t'other?) and is set amongst the salt marshes, dykes and pools of this remote and peaceful corner of the Bassin. Take your choice of three walks: short (aviaries 400m, $\frac{1}{2}$ hour); medium (storks, 2km, $1\frac{1}{2}$ hrs); long (geese, 5km, 3 hrs). Short cuts are possible. There are observation points and hides in which to settle down and observe les oiseaux. Bring your binoculars and watch up to 260 species. Open to 2200, entry 36FF. Tel 05.56.22.80.93. You can also walk a 10km path around the outside of the park, free of charge but it may be muddy.

Dune du Pyla, looking south

Cap Ferret lighthouse

Bus Buses run from near the railway station to all local communities and to the Dune du Pyla.

Railway Station, Tel 05.56.83.88.88, is at bd du Général Leclerc 20 mins walk west from the marina. All trains connect to Bordeaux, 40 mins, whence Paris is about $3\frac{1}{4}$ hours by TGV.

Airport Bordeaux/Merignac (70km). Tel 05.56.34.50.00. Flights to most major cities.

Taxis Tel 05.56.83.30.03; 05.56.83.80.80; 05.56.83.11.11.

Ferries/vedettes From the three jetties along the waterfront to Andernos and Cap Ferret. Trips around Île aux Oiseaux ($1\frac{1}{2}$ hrs) and to Banc d'Arguin ($2\frac{1}{2}$ hrs). Try shark-fishing on the ocean.

Bike hire
- Locabeach, 326 bd de la Plage; Tel 05.56.83.39.64.
- Locarêve, 210 bd de la Côte d'Argent; Tel 05.56.83.62.83.

Car hire
- Europcar, 35 bd du Général Leclerc (opposite the station); Tel 05.46.83.48.00.
- Ada, 1 rue Sully Mélendès; Tel 05.46.22.54.45.

Beaches Immediately west of the marina is Plage d'Eyrac, followed by Plage d'Arcachon and more or less continuous sand right round to Dune de Pyla. There is also a beach outside the north wall of the marina.

EATING ASHORE

Bear in mind that the marina is approx 2km from the town centre.

Restaurants Within reach of the marina, mostly on bd Mestrezat and invariably fishy, are:
- La Bouée, bar/brasserie. Cheerful eatery with *terrasse*. Menus 60-90FF.
- Le Chipion, corner of rue des Pêcheries. Tapas, steak, fish, oysters. Menus 70-90FF.
- Le Patio, 10 bd de la Plage, opposite rue du Port. Gastronomy from 160FF. Tel 05.56.83.02.72.
- La Taverne du Pêcheur, bd de la Plage. Popular and recommended.

Nearer to town:
- L'Ombrière, 79 cours Héricart de Thury. Menus from 135FF. Tel 05.56.83.86.20.

Marina entrance, approaching from the NW

- Chez Yvette, opposite Tourist Office. People come from Bordeaux just to eat fish dishes here.

In the heart of the Summer Town, rue du Maréchal de Lattre de Tassigny is a pedestrian street, full of eating places of every kind and price range. Try, for example:

- La Marée, at No 21, popular with inexpensive seafood fresh from the market. Tel 05.56.83.24.05.
- Les Baguettes d'Or, at No 45bis. Vietnamese specialities. Menus 60-85FF. Tel 05.56.83.84.79.

SHOPPING

Supermarkets Petit Casino, by tourist stand at corner of bd Mestrezat and rue des Pêcheries. Further south: LIDL, ave du Gen Leclerc, towards La Teste.

Markets Daily in season, near the Mairie, place Lucien de Gracia.

Banks All the usual in town. Nearest cashpoint is at Credit Maritime, quai du Capitaine Allègre.

Marina entrance from inside, looking north. Fuel berth is on the right

NAVIGATIONAL MATTERS

Charts AC 2750 and SHOM 6766 (1:48,800) covers the approaches and the Bassin d'Arcachon. AC 2664 (1:200,000) covers from Pertuis de Maumusson southwards almost to Capbreton.

Hazards in a nutshell are depth of water, swell and wind; see also tidal streams. Least charted depth is 3·9m on the bar between 4N and 5N buoys, but over a period of time depths vary and the channel shifts. You should therefore get up-to-date information before leaving your previous port. On arrival call the Semaphore on Ch 16 or mobile phone Service de la Marine Gironde 05 56 82 32 97 for present conditions, if in doubt.

Town and marina, looking west

Cap Ferret peninsula

Fuel

Capitainerie

Nautical centre

Technical site

Swell can reduce under-keel clearance significantly and perhaps unacceptably; hence the need to be at the waypoint near HW when depth of water should be about 8.2m springs and 7·3m neaps. Swell higher than 1 metre may make the bar dangerous.

Strong onshore winds from SW to N will raise quite a sea, exacerbated by swell, and may make pilotage harder, especially if lightly crewed. Whilst experienced and prudent yachtsmen should not be put off by all this, bear in mind that boats are lost every year in the Passe usually because they were ill-equipped or crew exceeded their abilities. In poor conditions local fishing boats will divert to La Rochelle. In good conditions the approach is rewarding and not too demanding.

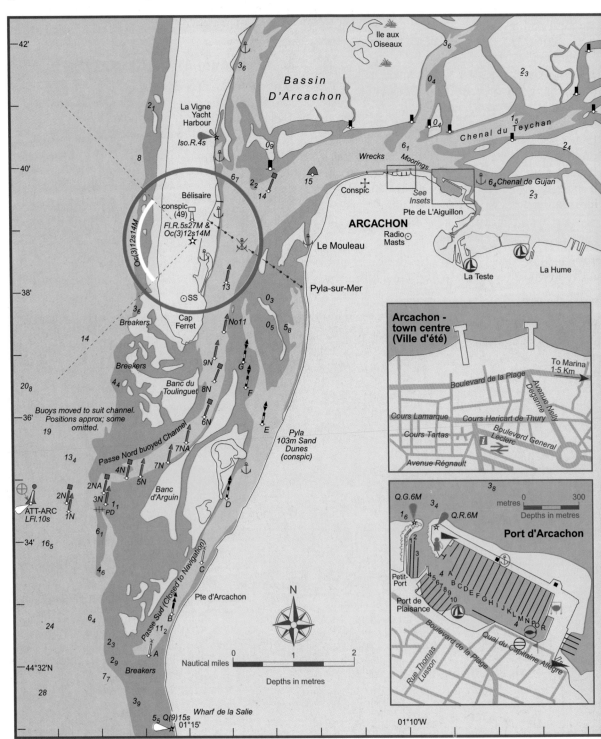

Access Leave the waypoint at HW –2 to –1 to carry the last of the flood for 10M to the marina. If later than HW+1, the strength of the ebb (up to 6kn at springs) may preclude arrival. At LW slack there may be insufficient water, so wait until HW –2. A night arrival is out of the question as channel buoys are unlit. The South Channel (Passe Sud) was closed to navigation in late 1996 and should not be attempted; many of the buoys have been withdrawn.

Best time to depart from Arcachon is around HW –1 so as to cross the bar near slack water.

Approach The waypoint is 44°34´·78N 01°18´·60W, the ATT-ARC buoy, <u>Att</u>errisage (landfall) <u>Arc</u>achon. From here the first lateral buoys will be visible 8 cables to the east; all are large, well-painted spar buoys. The sea breaks on the drying Banc du Toulinguet to port and Banc d'Arguin to starboard. The sight is impressive but in moderate conditions need not intimidate. The channel between these banks

Passe Nord: typical breakers and spar buoy

unfolds as you hop from buoy to buoy. Buoy numbers are suffixed 'N' for Passe Nord; see Table for positions, which are referenced to ED50 and may change frequently.

Daymarks Cap Ferret is low-lying; a signal station and prominent oil exploration rig (1999) are on its southern tip. 1M north the lighthouse and a large water tower are conspicuous. Dune de Pyla, 103m high, is an enormous sand dune about 2M SSE of Cap Ferret; on a hazy day it may be hard to discern until quite close.

Cap Ferret, signal station

POSITION OF BUOYS 19 JULY 2000		
Buoy	**Type**	**Position**
ATT/ARC .... SWM .... 44°34´·66N .... 01°18´·66W		
Passe Nord buoys:		
1N .... SHM .... 44°34´·49N .... 01°17´·74W		
2N .... PHM .... 44°34´·65N .... 01°17´·74W		
2Na .... PHM .... 44°34´·81N .... 01°17´·01W		
3N .... SHM .... 44°34´·66N .... 01°16´·89W		
4N .... PHM .... 44°35´·01N .... 01°16´·50W		
5N .... SHM .... 44°35´·03N .... 01°16´·04W		
6N .... PHM .... 44°36´·04N .... 01°14´·59W		
7N .... SHM .... 44°35´·31N .... 01°15´·46W		
7Na .... SHM .... 44°35´·60N .... 01°14´·91W		
8N .... PHM .... 44°36´·53N .... 01°14´·39W		
9N .... SHM .... 44°36´·96N .... 01°14´·34W		
Main fairway inwards to marina:		
11 .... SHM .... 44°37´·35N ..... 01°14´·10W		
13 .... SHM .... 44°38´·16N .... 01°14´·04W		
14 .... PHM .... 44°39´·60N .... 01°13´·06W		
15 .... SHM .... 44°39´·85N .... 01°12´·04W		
Buoys from North to South, marking approach to		
Banc d'Arguin and former Passe Sud (closed):		
G .... ECM .... 44°37´·10N .... 01°13´·52W		
F .... ECM .... 44°36´·49N .... 01°13´·37W		
E .... ECM .... 44°35´·85N .... 01°13´·24W		
D .... ECM .... 44°34´·60N .... 01°14´·08W		
C .... SPM .... 44°33´·66N .... 01°14´·73W		
B .... NCM .... 44°32´·87N ..... 01°15´·40W		
A .... SPM .... 44°32´·14N .... 01°15´·98W		
To seaward of Wharf de la Salie, WCM beacon,		
Q(9)15s19m10M .... 44°30´·95N .... 01°15´·59W:		
La Salie Fl(2)6s . IDM .... 44°30´·50N .... 01°17´·67W		

Banc d'Arguin anchorage and the Dune du Pyla

Tides HW Arcachon at neaps is 10 mins, and at springs 25 mins after HW Pointe de Grave. LW at neaps is 20 mins after, and at springs the same as, LW Pointe de Grave. HW Cap Ferret at neaps is 15 mins before, and at springs 5 mins after HW Pointe de Grave.

MHWS is 4·3m, MLWS 0·4m; MHWN is 3·4m, MLWN 1·3m.

Tidal streams near ATT-ARC buoy do not exceed 0·7 knots, but at the bar and entrance to the Bassin the flood sets E at up to 2 knots; the ebb sets NW at 4 knots (6kn at coefficients >115). Inside the Bassin, north of the town, the spring stream reaches $3\frac{1}{2}$ knots, setting ENE/WSW. There is no UK or SHOM Tidal stream atlas; figures must be read from the chart.

Marina (Ent 44°39'·83N 01°09'·04W)
Capitainerie is on the N side of the marina, abeam G pontoon. Address: quai de Goslar, 33313 Arcachon. Tel 05.56.22.36.75; Fax 05.56.83.26.19. VHF Ch 09. HM Didier Carpentey. Hours, daily 0730-2030. Weather forecasts are posted daily. www.port-arcachon.com

Visitors There is no *accueil* pontoon and ❶ berths are no longer advertised. Request a berth on VHF Ch 09 or berth on the hammerhead of any pontoon and check in at the Capitainerie. The problem is that there is a 20 (twenty) year waiting list for berths! Visitors do not therefore feature anywhere on the list of priorities. The fairway is ostensibly dredged 4m but silting persists.

Shelter in the marina is good, but some swell enters in strong NW-N winds.

Anchorage No anchoring in the marina, but outside good holding can be found to the N or NE in the Chenal du Gujan, clear of the fairway and oyster beds in about 3·5m.

Tariff Daily rates for LOA bands, Apr-Sep; second night is free:
7-8·5m = 112-136FF; 8·5-10m = 150-173FF; 10-11·5m = 187-208FF; 11·5-14m = 213-294FF.

Fuel is immediately to port on entry; depth 1·6m. Open 0730-2000 in season. Tel 05.56.22.36.76.

Showers are in the Capitainerie, 0730-2030.

Launderette in the Capitainerie.

NAUTICAL NEEDS

Chandlery & repairs The following is only a small selection:
- Co-op Maritime, Quai Goslar. Tel 05.46.83.46.60 Chandlery. SHOM chart agent.
- Co-op Maritime d'Avitaillement, 2 quai Silhouette. Tel 05.46.83.42.12. Chandlery. SHOM agent.
- Servimer, 52 bd de la Plage. Tel 05.56.83.70.25. Electronics.
- Aiguillon Service, 6 bd Chanzy. Tel 05.56.83.56.07. Rigging, sails, chandlery.
- Nautic Service, 2 rue d'Aiguillon. Tel 05.56.54.98.99. Engines (Volvo, Suzuki, Mercury)
- Centre Marin, 37 ave de l'Atlantique, Cap Ferret. Tel 05.56.60.63.56. Engines (Volvo). Chandler.

Cap Ferret peninsula from the east, with Cap Ferret lighthouse and conspic water tower

CAPBRETON

Capbreton is a seaside resort and not a bad one at that. It also has an undisputed claim to be the only port in the département of Landes, which partly explains why the French military have overlaid the featureless Gironde and Landes coastline with a vast weaponry range.

This is described in some detail on p221. It runs 12M south from Pointe de Négade off the mouth of the Gironde to Capbreton and extends about 15M offshore. It can be crossed when it is closed, ie usually at night and on Sundays, most Saturdays, and throughout August.

The harbour entrance, 55M south of Pointe d'Arcachon, momentarily interrupts the unbroken strand of beach (Côte d'Argent) which then continues a further 8M south to Anglet/Bayonne, backed as always by interminable pine forests.

Capbreton lies south of the harbour and Hossegor to the north and NE, both holiday communities nestling rather attractively amongst sand and pines.

TOURISM

Tourist Office is on ave Georges Pompidou, 40130 Capbreton. Tel 05.58.72.12.11; Fax 05.58.41.00.29.

What to see/do Swimming and sunbathing are top of the priorities however long you plan to stay. If however the weather is unsuitable you might consider hiring a car and heading into the Pyrennees or Basque country, particularly if you do not intend calling in at any of the remaining French harbours before the Spanish border (St Jean-de-Luz is definitely worth a visit by sea).

If you are still around in the second week of August you will be able to watch the world professional surfing championships at Hossegor.

Bus Buses run to Bayonne, Biarritz and all local communities.

Railway Nearest station is at Bayonne (20km), Tel 08.36.35.35.35 for timetable information. All trains route via Dax to Bordeaux, whence Paris is about $3\frac{1}{4}$ hours by TGV.

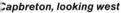
Capbreton, looking west

Chapter 7

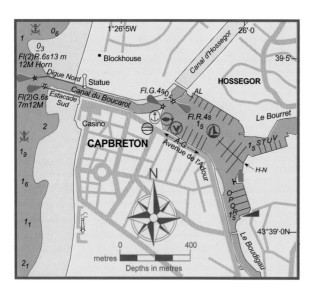

Entrance two hours after low water

Airport Biarritz (27km). Tel 05.59.43.43.83. Flights to most major French cities.

Taxis Tel 05.58.72.05.11; 05.58.72.48.81.

Bike hire Locavélo, pont Bonamour/rue du Cdt l'Herminier; Tel 05.58.72.48.68.

Car hire
- Shell station, ave Maréchal Leclerc, Tel 05.58.72.12.86.
- Bayonne railway station, Tel 05.59.55.06.56.
- Biarritz airport, Tel 05.59.43.80.20.

Beaches are immediately south and north of the harbour entrance, stretching for miles. So your patch of sand should not be under too much threat.

EATING ASHORE

Restaurants Pavé du Port, in La Pêcherie which is the area at the SE end of the marina.
- Le Régalty, at the marina (La Pêcherie). Tel 05.58.72.22.80. Excellent menus from 150FF.
- La Sardinière, 87 ave Pompidou, Tel 05.58.72.10.49.
- Le Bellevue, ave Pompidou, Tel 05.58.72.10.30. Very good menus 135-180FF.

SHOPPING

Supermarkets Intermarché, bd des Cigales, Tel 05.58.72.40.21.

Market Daily in season; Tues, Thurs & Sat out of season.

Banks Most of the usual, including cashpoints, are in the town centre.

NAVIGATIONAL MATTERS

Charts SHOM 6586 (1:10,000) and 6557 (1:49,600) cover Capbreton and its approaches. AC 1102 (1:200,000) and SHOM 6786 (1:130,000) cover Capbreton and the coast at smaller scale.

Tides HW Capbreton at neaps is 30 mins, and at springs 35 mins before HW Pointe de Grave. LW at neaps is 20 mins, and at springs 25 mins before LW Pointe de Grave.

MHWS is 4·2m, MLWS 0·7m; MHWN is 3·3m, MLWN 1·7m.

Tidal streams off the entrance do not exceed 0·5 knots. A current sets north at about 0·5 knots, unless counteracted by northerly winds.

Hazards Strong W to N winds make the entrance impassable. Silting occurs around the south pier head and in the narrow Canal du Boucarot.

Approach The waypoint is a fairly arbitrary 43°39´·38N 01°27´·25W from which the N Jetty

South Estacade

North jetty and statue of the Virgin Mary

near low water with an onshore force 3–4

...ight bears 082°/3 cables. This position is in deep water and enables you to see into the entrance to assess conditions. There are no leading lines.

Daymarks are few and far between; essentially the red roofs, mainly S of the entrance, punctuate the white and green of sand and tree. There is a water tower, one of three; also a long, red-roofed Sanatorium respectively 4 cables SE and S of the entrance – and that's it. When close to the entrance (43°39´·42N 01°26´·82W), note that there are two light towers at the end of the south *estacade*; the outer one, a white post with green top, is operational, the inner taller one is defunct.

Access The entrance is only 40 metres wide and totally exposed to the Atlantic. Do not attempt to enter if seas are breaking across it; nor at LW ±2½ because of insufficient water and the likelihood of a confused lumpy sea even in a modest F3 onshore wind, exacerbated by any swell. HW –3 to +1 is probably the optimum window with an underkeel clearance of at least 1m.

Enter close to the N jetty for best water, paralleling it until abeam the inner end of the wooden south jetty (*estacade*). Here, to avoid shoals, move into mid-channel or even towards the southern half and maintain this until the marina entrance opens to starboard, beyond the Capitainerie.

MARINA

Capitainerie is on the S side of the marina entrance. Address: BP 49, quai Georges Pompidou, 40130 Capbreton. Tel 05.58.72.21.23; Fax 05.58.72.40.35. VHF Ch 09. HM Mme Claude Jaunin. Hours, Jul/Aug daily 0700-2000; out of season Mon-Sat 0800-1200 & 1330-1800. Weather forecasts are posted daily. e-mail: port-capbreton@wanadoo.fr Web: www.port-capbreton.com

The drying rocks provide a good reason to stay on the north side of the entrance channel

Chapter 7

Marina entrance from inside, looking NW

Visitors The *accueil* pontoon is B, second to starboard from marina entrance; check in at the Capitainerie, *svp*, if you would like a berth elsewhere. The marina is dredged 1·5m.

Shelter in the marina is good, but the harbour entrance may be impassable; see Access.

Anchorage No anchoring in the marina. See notes above about the Gouf de Capbreton.

Tariff Daily rates for LOA bands in high season; second night is free:
7-8·5m = 95-109FF; 8·5-10m = 119-131FF; 10-11·5m = 143-160FF; 11·5-14m = 165-182FF.

Fuel (diesel and petrol) is at quai de la Pêcherie, between M and O pontoons. Open 0830-1200 & 1400-1800 in season; out of season 1500-1800; and on request to Tel 05.58.72.15.66.

Showers are in the Capitainerie, also across the road from B pontoon and near O and AL pontoons; open 0730-2030.

Launderette is across the road from B pontoon and in the old Capitainerie.

Pedestrian ferry A small electric ferry (*passeur*) 'Le Boucarot' plies a triangular course from 'A' pontoon to AL pontoon on the north side and then eastwards to La Pêcherie between N and S pontoons. Apr- Sept; 5FF per trip or 10 trips for 40FF.

NAUTICAL NEEDS

Chandlery & repairs Most repair facilities are in La Pêcherie or the technical zone ENE of it.
- Okeanos, quai de la Pêcherie. Tel 05.58.72.29.89. Chandlery, boatyard, engine, electronics.
- S'té Deschamps, quai de la Pêcherie. Tel 05.58.49.30.64. Engines.
- Nautical Service Landes (NSL). Tel 05.58.72.29.52. Chandlery, engines, electronics.

GOUF DE CAPBRETON

Gouf de Capbreton is a gigantic underwater canyon which extends seaward almost from the harbour entrance for more than 25M across the continental shelf. Its origin is unknown. Normally along this coast depths increase progressively with distance from the shore. Off Capbreton the 3m contour is 1 cable west of the jetty heads, but within the next cable the depth has increased abruptly to 30m; and to 100m six cables further offshore. Depths continue to increase to 1300m and more, whilst the adjacent depths on the shelf are only about 120m.

In bad onshore weather the sea does not break in the Gouf, except to either side where depths are less than 50m. In these conditions ships have been able to anchor safely in the Gouf in about 60m depth, but Yachts should stay at sea or possibly take refuge in the bay of St Jean-de-Luz (18M SSW).

ANGLET & BAYONNE

At last the Pyrenees, or at least their foothills, are in sight, hull down on the southern horizon .... The area east and south of Bayonne and Biarritz is particularly attractive wooded country with small hills – so different from the flat pine forests of the Landes. This is the Pays Basque. The River Adour,

fed by the lesser R Nive, flows seaward past the fine old town of Bayonne and the much less attractive industrial areas around Bouceau. Anglet is sandwiched between the almost contiguous towns of Bayonne and Biarritz. The marina is on Anglet's northern fringe, on the river's south bank, 7 cables from excellent beaches and with the pine woods of Chiberta to the south.

The marina's inescapable downside, it must be said, is the industrial complex on the opposite bank. This includes a major cement works which is lethal when the wind is in the NNW; and possibly one of the largest scrap metal works in Europe, which would have been the envy of Steptoe & Son!

Scrap metal loading...

TOURISM

Tourist Office is in Place des Basques, BP 819, 64100 Bayonne. Tel 05.59.46.01.46; Fax 05.59.59.37.55. Hours Jul/Aug, Mon-Sat 0900-1900; Sun 1000-1300; other months, Mon-Fri 0900-1830; Sat 1000-1800. There is a lesser office at the delightfully named No 1 ave de la Chambre d'Amour, close N of Pte St Martin lighthouse; Tel 05.59.03.77.01.

What to see/do Swimming and sunbathing are a high priority (see beaches). Anglet itself has little to offer. Bayonne and Biarritz are well worth visiting.

Bayonne is divided by the River Nive into Grand (W) and Petit (E) Bayonne, both within the ramparts designed by (guess who?) Monsieur Vauban. The twin spires of the Gothic cathedral dominate the town's narrow streets and half-timbered houses with reddish-brown balconies and shutters (see p220). The atmosphere is part Basque, part Spanish. Picturesque quays line the Nive and in Petit Bayonne the Musée Basque is due to re-open in 2001.

Biarritz is long past its nineteenth century glory and has a slightly faded air, but the beaches are as superb as ever. You will get the general flavour if you walk south from Pte St Martin along the

Chapter 7

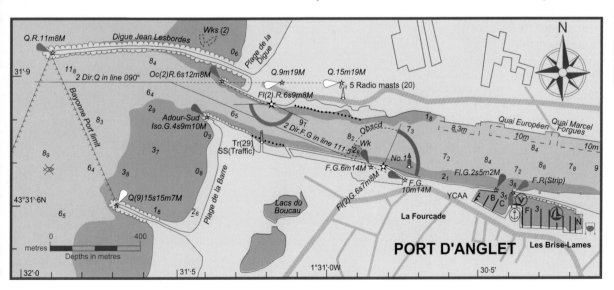

PORT D'ANGLET

...and a cement works

Grande Plage to the Vieux Port; take a look at the Rocher de la Vierge, a symbol of Biarritz. Then stroll inshore to the place Clemenceau, the main square, and return past the restored Casino.

When tired of town life, take the train from Bayonne up into the mountains following the valley of the River Nive, past Cambio-les-Bains to St Jean-Pied-de-Port, about an hour's trip through the peaceful green foothills. St Jean-P-de-P is the old capital of Basse Navarre and many latter day pilgrims leave here on the long walk to Santiago de Compostela in the footsteps of St James. A good centre for walking into Spain – and a total break from nautical life!

Bus STAB covers the whole Bayonne/Biarritz complex. No 4 bus to Bayonne (20 mins) stops at the marina. For Biarritz (40 mins) take the No 4 in the opposite direction to La Barre (by the ice rink) then change to No 9 bus.

Railway Bayonne station is on the N bank; Tel 08.36.35.35.35 for timetable information. All trains route via Dax to Bordeaux, whence Paris is about $3\frac{1}{4}$ hours by TGV.

Airport Biarritz (7km as the crow flies; difficult and slow by bus, taxi advised). Flights to most major French cities and some to the UK. Tel 05.59.43.83.83.

Taxi Tel 05.59.63.17.17.

Bike hire V-Tonic, route des Pontôts. Tel 05.59.52.36.48.

Car hire
- Budget, 32 ave de Bayonne, Tel 05.59.63.11.77.
- Bayonne rail station, Tel 05.59.55.06.56
- Biarritz airport, Tel 05.59.43.80.20.

Beaches The nearest is Plage de la Barre, sheltered by the south outer breakwater. Further south a series of good beaches, quaintly named, stretches down past St Martin to Biarritz and beyond.

Mouth of R Adour and Anglet marina, looking west

Biarritz — Pte St Martin lighthouse

IPTS

Marina entrance

Capitainerie

Deep water quays

Industrial zone

Signal tower and IPTS, looking up-river

EATING ASHORE

Restaurants Across the road from the marina you can eat at Les Terrasses du Port which is friendly and quite adequate. Almost next door a Vietnamese/Chinese restaurant is also a takeaway. For more serious eating in Bayonne try:
- Le Chistera, 42 rue Port Neuf, Tel 05.59.59.25.93. Delicious Basque specialities from 95FF.
- Auberge du Cheval Blanc, 69 rue Bourgneuf. Tel 05.59.59.01.33. Excellent menus from 120FF.

Good eateries can be found along the R Nive quaysides and in the back streets of Petit Bayonne.

SHOPPING

Supermarkets Across the road from the marina there are a few basic shops. For supermarkets go to the centre of Anglet or to Bayonne.

Market In Anglet proper the market on Thurs at place Quintaou is difficult to reach. In Bayonne there is a major market daily, except Sun, in Les Halles by the R Nive quayside.

Banks All you need in Bayonne and Biarritz.

NAVIGATIONAL MATTERS

Charts SHOM 6536 and AC 1343 (both 1:10,000) cover the R Adour. SHOM 6557 and 6558 (1:49,600) cover the approaches. AC 1102 (1:200,000) and SHOM 6786 (1:130,000) cover the coast at smaller scale.

Tides HW Bouceau (close to the marina) at neaps is 30 mins, and at springs 35 mins before HW Pointe de Grave. LW at neaps is 40 mins, and

at springs 25 mins before LW Pointe de Grave.

MHWS is 4·2m, MLWS 0·7m; MHWN is 3·3m, MLWN 1·7m.

Tidal streams In the entrance the spring flood reaches 2-4 knots and the ebb 3-5 knots; off the marina 1·5kn and 2·4kn respectively. Slack water periods last only about 15 minutes. Coastal streams are weak; a north-going current of $\frac{1}{2}$ knot is usual, unless counteracted by N winds.

Hazards Strong onshore winds may make the entrance impassable due to backwash.

Daymarks and lights Pointe St Martin lighthouse, white with black top, and the building blocks of Biarritz are 2·4M SSW. The industrial works on the north side of the river are too easily seen. The north breakwater is prominent and at the entrance a white signal tower with vertical black stripe is conspicuous on the south bank.

At night the powerful (19M range) 090° leading lights help locate the entrance, but by day their metal framework towers are less obvious. Inner leading lights lead 111·5° through the entrance and toward the south bank. The marina entrance is lit, the eastern light being a red neon strip.

Approach The waypoint is 43°32′·66N 01°32′·68W, 'BA' landfall buoy from which the harbour entrance (43°31′·88N 01°31′·92W) bears 144°/0·97M. From the buoy, however, it is advisable to steer more southerly until the entrance opens up.

From the SW keep a safe distance offshore and proceed direct to the harbour entrance.

Access At all tides, but note the tidal streams. In onshore winds above force 5 backwash off the

Harbour entrance and two incongruous policemen

inner piers may make the entrance difficult or even hazardous, especially on the ebb.

The 0·5M long north breakwater (Digue Jean Lesbordes; aka Digue du Large) provides considerable protection from NW and N winds. To a lesser extent the Digue du Sud (WCM light beacon) protects the entrance from S/SW winds.

The inner entrance between two short piers is approx 160 metres wide. Charted depths are about 10m in the entrance, reducing to about 7m near the marina.

International Port Traffic signals, only 3 Ⓡ or 3 Ⓖ, are shown from the signal tower and must be obeyed; if not shown, entry/exit is permitted. Ships up to 20,000 tons use the port; monitor VHF Ch 12/16 *Pilotage de l'Adour* or call 05.59.63.16.18 for advance warning of their movements.

Pilotage There is little or no pilotage as such. Six cables east of the signal tower the usual forest of masts will be seen beyond the trees; there are large white sheds at the eastern end of the marina.

The river is navigable by masted craft for 2·5M beyond the marina to a 5·2m bridge at Bayonne, but holds little appeal for yachts.

MARINA

Capitainerie is in the centre of the marina. Address: Port de Plaisance du Brise-Lames, 118 ave de l'Adour, 64600 Anglet. Tel 05.59.63.05.45; Fax 05.59.52.17.66. VHF Ch 09. HM Georges Damestoy, and his friendly, enthusiastic staff.

Hours, Jun-Sep daily 0730-2000; other months Mon-Sat 0730-1830. Weather forecasts are posted daily. Max LOA 18m, draught 2·5m.

Visitors The *accueil* pontoon is E, in front of the entrance. The marina has W and E basins dredged 3m near to the Capitainerie, but 1·1m at the far ends. Pontoons are lettered A-D in the W basin and F-N in the east; piles are red with black tops, *à la Cunard* or Clyde Puffer.

Shelter in the marina is good, but strong NW winds may affect boats on the accueil pontoon.

Anchorage None; anchor in the river only in emergency.

Tariff Daily rates for LOA bands 1 Jun-30 Sep (reduced by approx 50% for the rest of the year): 7·5-9m = 84-96FF; 9-10·5m = 100-117FF; 10·5-12m = 125-141FF; 12-14m = 150-167FF.

Fuel (diesel and petrol) is at the *accueil* pontoon. Open 0730-2000 in season; out of season 0800-1800; and on request to Tel 05.59.63.05.45.

Showers are in the Capitainerie; open office hours.

Launderette Enquire at the Capitainerie.

NAUTICAL NEEDS

Chandlery & repairs
- Librairie Jakin, 8 ave Maréchal Foch, Bayonne. Tel 05.59.46.13.15. SHOM chart agent.
- Cote Basque-Adour Nautique, at the E end of the marina. Tel 05.59.63.56.53. Chandlery and repairs to hull and engines.

Marina entrance, accueil and fuel pontoon, looking down-river

Bay of St Jean-de-Luz, looking west

ST JEAN-DE-LUZ AND CIBOURE

St Jean-de-Luz and adjacent Ciboure are arguably the most attractive of the four Basque coastal towns in this Companion. St Jean is by far the larger and boasts an extensive beach; Ciboure has great charm with Basque houses smiling down across the marina and with a perfectly adequate beach to match. Socoa with a massive circular fort and drying harbour lies at the NW corner of the bay. The Pyrenees, on a clear day, provide a magnificent backdrop.

The Bay of St Jean is semi-circular, one mile across and protected by east, central and west breakwaters. The River Nivelle flows in from the south dividing St Jean from Ciboure, although they share a common harbour entrance, quite narrow – be warned! Here the yachtsman will stand straight on for Ciboure marina whilst fishing vessels apply full port helm followed by full starboard to slalom into St Jean's fishing basin with some panache.

Donibane-Lohizune and Ziburu are the Basque names for St Jean-de-Luz and Ciboure.

TOURISM

Tourist Office is at 4 Place du Fronton, 64500 Ciboure (a stone's throw SW of the marina).

Tel 05.59.47.49.40; Fax 05.59.47.85.77.

In St Jean the Tourist Office is near the railway station. Tel 05.59.26.03.16; Fax 05.59.26.21.47. Hours Jul/Aug, Mon-Sat 0900-2000; Sun 1030-1300 & 1500-1900; other months, Mon-Sat 0900-1230 & 1400-1900.

What to see/do Both Ciboure and St Jean are interesting and attractive towns, bedecked with flowers wherever possible; it is a real pleasure to stroll through their narrow streets.

The composer Maurice Ravel is Ciboure's most famous son, born of a Basque mother and a Swiss father. The family house, with a distinctive Dutch 17th century pediment, overlooks the marina.

If or when you tire of the beaches, take the local bus up past Ascain, a typical Basque village, to Col de St Ignace where you can jump on the rack-and-pinion railway to the top of La Rhune (see under Daymarks); or of course you can foot-slog up in about 2½ hours. Then on to Sare (½ hour) via a twisting mountain road. This little jaunt may

La Rhune, the local mountain

whet your appetite for sorties into the higher sierras. See also under Anglet/Bayonne for the train trip to St Jean Pied-de-Port which is much further south in the Pyrenees.

Bus The bus station is next to St Jean rail station; timetables are available at the Tourist Office.

Railway St Jean station is 400m east of the marina; Tel 08.36.35.35.35 for timetable information. TGV via Dax and Bordeaux to Paris is about 5¼ hours.

Airport Biarritz (15km as the crow flies; difficult and slow by bus, taxi advised). Flights to most major French cities and some to the UK. Tel 05.59.43.83.83.

Taxi Tel 05.59.26.07.37.

Bike and Car hire At the railway station.

Beaches The nearest is tucked in behind the west training wall at the harbour entrance. Beyond that is the Plage de Socoa. The beaches at St Jean-de-Luz embrace most of the E side of the bay.

EATING ASHORE

Restaurants Next to the marina on quai Maurice Ravel, you will not be disappointed by:
- Chez Dominique, at No 15. Tel 05.59.47.29.16. Menus from 140FF. Described by a local as "Absolutely Fabulous"!
- La Taverne du Pêcheur, at No 19. Tel 05.59.47.21.29. Menus 125-180FF.
- Chez Mattin, 63 rue E Baignol (beyond the Mairie). Tel 05.59.47.19.52. Traditional fish menus.

Or walk round to Socoa's little harbour, where in the bd du Cdt Passicot you will find:
- Chez Margot, Tel 05.59.47.18.30. Fresh grilled *langoustines* with *estragon* sauce.
- Chez Pantxua, Tel 05.59.47.13.73. Menus from 150FF. Terrific food and views across the bay.

SHOPPING

Supermarkets are further out of town on the N10; ask at the Tourist Office. Local food shops in Ciboure are adequate for daily needs.

Market Regional produce every morning in the place Camille Jullian, opposite the town hall.

Banks are "open Saturday and closed Monday" – quote from local guide! You will find all you need in St Jean, if not in Ciboure.

Launderette Laverie du Port, 23 quai Ravel (near Ravel's house). Tel 06.80.06.48.36. Daily 0700-2200.

Entrance channel, looking NNW across bay

NAVIGATIONAL MATTERS

Charts AC 1343 (1:10,000) and SHOM 6526 (1:7,500) cover St Jean-de-Luz. SHOM 6558 (1:49,800) covers the approaches. AC 1102 (1:200,000) and SHOM 6786 (1:130,000) cover the coast at much smaller scale.

Tides HW Socoa at neaps is 40 mins, and at springs 45 mins before HW Pointe de Grave. LW at neaps is 45 mins, and at springs 30 mins before LW Pointe de Grave.

MHWS is 4·3m, MLWS 0·6m; MHWN is 3·3m, MLWN 1·5m.

Tidal streams In the bay there is a continuous clockwise circulation, with the flood stream entering more strongly through the east entrance and the ebb flowing out through the west entrance. In the NW yacht anchorages the flood sets N at $\frac{1}{2}$ knot and the ebb at 1 knot. Coastal streams are weak; a north-going current of $\frac{1}{2}$ knot is usual, unless counteracted by N winds.

Hazards Offshore shoals can be dangerous in heavy weather; see under Approach. Les Briquets, a dangerous drying reef, is about 3M west of Socoa.

Fishing vessels enter/leave at speed through the relatively narrow harbour entrance.

Daymarks 5·5M SE of the harbour, La Rhune is a distinctive 898m high mountain with buildings

Chapter 7

Ciboure marina, looking seaward. The front leading mark is the white tower in the centre

and a red/white TV mast on its conical top (see picture). Visibility permitting, a bearing on it of 160° leads to the west entrance.

Approach The Plateau de St Jean-de-Luz (a coastal shelf with depths of around 23m) lies about 4M offshore between Biarritz and Cabo Higuer. In heavy weather the sea breaks on it and on the shallower inshore shoals in depths of 15-20m.

In moderate weather and good visibility yachts can follow the coast at least 1·5M offshore until St Jean-de-Luz is identified. From the W be aware of Les Briquets, a dangerous drying reef about 2M east of Cabo Higuer and 3M west of Socoa.

In heavy weather yachts should consider following the 3 charted sets of leading lines, viz:

i. Outer, 138°, is the only safe approach in bad weather or at night. It leads between Illarguita and Belhara Perdun banks to a position 43°24'·30N 01°41'·76W, 7 cables NW of the front leading light, where the second leading line 101° is intercepted. The front leading mark (Socoa) is a white, □ tower with a black stripe; not to be confused with a white signal station tower 100m SSW of it. The rear mark (Bordagain) is difficult to see; 200m SSW of it, the stone Bordagain tower is more distinctive on a hill top. Both lights are Dir Q, the front light also has a R sector (264°-282°).

ii. Middle, 101°, leads 8 cables E to the

waypoint, 43°24'·16N 01°40'·71W, where the inner leading line 150·7° is intercepted. By day the Ste Barbe leading marks are: Front, a white △ on a white building; rear a black ▲ on a white square tower. Both lights are Dir Oc (4) R 12s.

iii. Inner, 150·7°. This leads through the west entrance towards the harbour/marina at

Entrance channel with fishing vessel leaving at speed

Ciboure; see under Pilotage. The leading marks are conspicuous tall white towers, front with a red vertical stripe, rear with a green vertical stripe; both QG.

Access Best at HW±3, due to patches of about 1m near the harbour entrance. Stormy weather from the west causes a bar to form at the entrance; the resultant eddies make departure, and especially entry, dangerous except near HW. Note: The Passe de l'Est entrance, between Digue d'Artha and Digue de Ste Barbe, is not advised in bad weather.

Pilotage From the waypoint the Passe de l'Ouest entrance (between the west mole, Digue des Criquas, and the detached central mole, Digue d'Artha) bears 150·7° at 2·7 cables and the marina is a further 8 cables ahead on the same bearing, which is of course the inner leading line.

Within the outer harbour the fairway is marked by 9 small SHM and 2 PHM buoys.

The inner harbour entrance lies between two training walls. It is about 3m deep and 40m wide with sloping sides; near LW keep a mid-course. Sailing vessels must motor into/out of the harbour; speed limit 5 knots. Keep a sharp lookout for opposite direction fishing vessels.

Anchorages Within the bay two areas west of the 150·7° leading line and one area NE of the harbour entrance are designated as yacht anchorages; the latter is less exposed to swell. Other areas are for fishing vessels and water sports. The beaches are protected by anti-pollution booms.

Marina (43°23´·23N 01°39´·94W)

Capitainerie is at the S end of the marina. Address: Port de Larraldenia, 64500 Ciboure. Tel 05.59.47.26.81; Fax 05.59.47.86.11. VHF Ch 09. HM Jean Aguirre. Hours, Jun-Sep daily 0630-1300 & 1330-2000; other months, daily 0730-1230 & 1330-1830. Weather forecasts posted daily.

Showers in the Capitainerie, 10FF.

Visitors Berth on the hammerheads of the first 2 pontoons to starboard, which also have fingers; check in with the Capitainerie. 6 **V** berths are advertised. Depths are 1·5m to 2·5m. No anchoring. Beware slipways in SE corner of the marina, marked by 2 PHM perches. There are 20 ⚓s out in the bay.

Shelter in the marina is good.

Tariff Daily rates for LOA bands Jul/Aug: 7m = 82FF; 8m = 95FF; 10m = 120FF; 12m = 188FF.

Fuel is only available by bowser, Tel 05.59.26.06.98.

NAUTICAL NEEDS

Chandlery & repairs
• Comptoir de la Mer, at the marina. Tel 05.59.47.13.54. Chandlery.

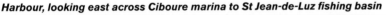

Harbour, looking east across Ciboure marina to St Jean-de-Luz fishing basin

HENDAYE

Looking south: France to port, Spain to starboard

France and Spain meet in the Bay of Fuentarrabía which faces NE in a broad sweep between Pte Ste Anne in the east and Cap Higuer in the west. The Bidassoa river flows into the SW corner of the bay, dividing Hendaye on the French side from Spanish Fuenterrabía, Hondarribia in Basque.

All is strikingly handsome: green fields and (palm) trees predominate; the rocks off each headland merge into golden beaches; La Rhune and the Pyrenees are the backdrop.

Hendaye is really two towns: Hendaye-Ville and Hendaye-Plage, about 2 km apart. The former has a pleasant enough centre on rising ground and the rail station is below it by the bridge over the Bidassoa. Hendaye-Plage is a modern seaside resort looking out across a vast well-manicured beach towards Cap Higuer. Hendaye as a whole is rather incongruously twinned with Peebles in the Scottish lowlands, on the banks of the Tweed and some way from the nearest salt water.

TOURISM

Tourist Office is at 12 rue des Aubépines, 64700 Hendaye (900m east of the marina). Tel 05.59.20.00.34; Fax 05.59.20.79.17. E-mail: tourisme.hendaye@wanadoo.fr Hours Jul/Aug, Mon-Sat 0900-2000; Sun 1000-1300; other months, Mon-Fri 0900-1230 & 1400-1830(1800 Sat).

What to see/do Swimming and sunbathing remain as attractive as ever. In the evening a visit to the Casino will either make you or break you. But, if you feel like total respite from the boat, the Basque country and the Pyrenees are surely the primary attractions:

For a brief, interesting and rewarding appetizer (especially if your booze locker is depleted), hire a car and drive up to Col d'Ibardin, 4km west of La Rhune (Michelin road map 78). Go east from Hendaye on N10 towards St Jean-de-Luz. After 12km turn off south at Urrugne onto the tiny D4 to the village of Herboure (5km); thence onto D404 a twisty mountain road which leads to Col d'Ibardin (4km) on a remote part of the Franco-Spanish border. Not only are the views fabulous, but more importantly spirits, beer and wines can be had at duty-free prices from a series of large Basque buildings. A litre of genuine Scotch for 65FF can't be bad! To complete the circuit, carry on into Spain to Bera/Vera, then return down the Bidassoa valley by N121A to Hendaye.

Port of Refuge which is tucked in below the slopes of Cap Higuer.

Anchorage or a vacant mooring are also possible near the moorings SE of the marina entrance, ie in the Baie de Chingoudy in depths of around 2·5m.

MARINA

Bureau du Port is at the NW corner of the marina. Address: Port de Plaisance, BP 534, 64705 Hendaye. Tel 05.59.48.06.10; Fax 05.59.48.06.13. VHF Ch 09. HM Michel Garcia. Hours H24. Weather forecasts posted daily.

Showers There are 3 shower blocks along the N edge of the marina.

Visitors Berth on ❶ pontoon 'A', at the NW corner of the marina in front of the Bureau du Port. Depths are 3m in the west of the marina and 2·5m in the east. No anchoring.

Shelter in the marina is very good.

NOTE: On the Spanish side a marina is being completed as we go to press. The entrance is at about 43°22'·65N 01°47'·45W, ie halfway along the western training wall and the marina is situated south of the beach.

Tariff Daily rates for LOA bands, Jul-Aug; /second figure is Apr-Jun & Sep; 3rd night free:

6-8m = 95/71FF;
8-10m = 135/101FF;
10-12m = 190/143FF;
12-14m = 240/180FF;
14-16m = 295/221FF.

Fuel (diesel and petrol) berth is at the SE corner of the marina. H24 with French bank card; otherwise office hours.

NAUTICAL NEEDS

Chandlery & repairs The Technical area stretches from the roundabout at the E end of the marina to the Fish quays:

- Comptoir Maritime Basque, quai de la Floride, at the fishing area. Tel 05.59.20.22.14. SHOM chart agent, chandlery.
- Scaph-Atlantique, 4 rue des Orangers. Tel 05.59.20.56.04. Chandlery. Boat repairs.
- Mareva, rue des Orangers. Tel 05.59.48.01.48. Chandlery. Boat repairs.
- Delta Voiles, rue des Orangers. Tel 05.59.20.55.72; mobile 06.80.32.97.04. Sailmakers, riggers.

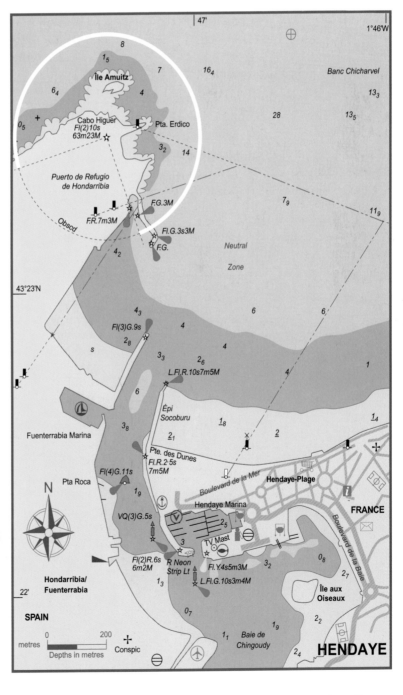

Chapter 7

THE GIRONDE, ROYAN TO BORDEAUX

CONTENTS

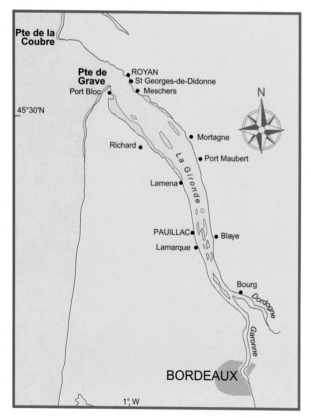

THE SEA AND THE LAND

Quote from a recent letter received from an apparently experienced yachtsman:

'This summer (1999) sections of pontoon were missing in the area to starboard of the reception pontoon due to storm damage. I would not recommend Royan to anyone'.

Yet friends of mine who have kept their boat at Royan for many years, arrived there a day or two after the ferociously destructive storms of Christmas 1999, expecting to deal with a major insurance claim, only to find their boat completely unscathed, albeit covered in glass and debris from the surrounding quays. The neighbouring (downwind) boat had her stanchions bent in contact with the pontoon, so hard over was she heeled by the wind.

The moral of this little yarn is not so much about the security of Royan (which is pretty good), as about the strongly-held and often contentious views that many yachtsmen express on almost any topic under the sun! Is that how the pinch of salt originated?

The Gironde may not rank with the Mississippi in terms of power, but it is still a mighty river. Do not be afloat on it after heavy rains and gales because your boat is likely to be encumbered by whole trees and a raft of flotsam. Do the same at Springs and you are inviting trouble!

Turning now to kinder weather and gentler thoughts there is the little matter of Bordeaux wines to be discussed. Let us hope you are safely ensconced in Pauillac, Bourg or Bordeaux as you read these jottings. If you are a wine-buff you will doubtless already have made your plans for visiting the vineyards and re-stocking your cellar.

If, like me, you are a lesser mortal, it would certainly be wise to do a little sightseeing either by car (best from Bordeaux) or by bike from Pauillac, surrounded as you are by all those Premières Crus. No harm in asking the advice of the local Tourist Office, particularly if you need to book a visit to a particular château (see under Pauillac). Spur of the moment visits are unlikely to be a success and may result in little more than a taste of the château's second wine.

Here is a brief resumé of the Vignoble de Bordeaux, without preaching about the wine itself:

The Médoc extends from Bordeaux's northern fringe along the west bank of the Gironde almost to Port Bloc. It is low-lying very gently undulating country, as if affected by the Atlantic swell. The soil is thin and pebbly, home to the Cabernet Sauvignon grape and others. The small stones have the dual role of storing heat on the surface (to ripen the grape), whilst preventing rapid evaporation of moisture from under them; hence stable temperature and humidity. The gravelly soil makes for good drainage.

Wine makers say that the character of a wine comes from the grape and the soul from the soil. In the Médoc they say that if you can see the river and feel the gravel under your feet, you can make good wine! In addition to Cabernet Sauvignon, the four main grapes grown for the red wines are Merlot, Cabernet Franc, and, in lesser amounts, Malbec and Petit Verdot.

The famous names are there in abundance and even if you cannot afford to buy the wine, you can at least derive a vicarious pleasure from seeing the great châteaux themselves – many of them gracious manor houses.

Going anti-clockwise, the Graves (gravelly) region skirts around Bordeaux and continues SE for 50km up the west bank of the Garonne. Some vineyards are no more than clearings amid the pine forests of the Landes. The drier whites are predominantly made from the Sauvignon Blanc grape. At the southern end (not far from the first lock into the Canal latérale à la Garonne at Castets-en-Dorthe) are the sweet white wines of Barsac and Sauternes, made from the Semillon grape. The grapes are left on the vine to encourage the noble rot (*pourriture noble*) which, with a delicate blend of damp, misty mornings and warm, sunny afternoons, raises the sugar content to produce top quality sweet white wine. If you stay away from the expensive big-name wines, you may find in Graves some interesting, affordable and appetizing wines, both white and red.

Crossing the Garonne at Langon, the Premières Côtes de Bordeaux area flanks the east bank as far downstream as Lormont, at the Pont d'Aquitaine in Bordeaux. Here the vines grow cheek by jowl

**St Estèphe: Château Calon-Ségur.
Note the dry pebbly soil**

Pauillac: Château Pichon Longueville-Baron

Finally the circuit is completed as we move downstream to Côtes de Bourg and de Blaye, where the Dordogne flows into the Gironde. Côtes de Bourg is far smaller than Côtes de Blaye which extends some 25km N and E of Blaye itself. The wines in both regions are not in the big league, but are nevertheless good, easy-to-drink reds and whites which fill the lower and more affordable end of the price bracket. Back in the C15/16 these wines, especially the Bourg, were considered the best in all of Bordeaux; merchants would only sell if the buyer was prepared to take some of the 'plonk' from the Médoc as well!

with other crops (wheat, maize, tobacco, fruit and vegetables) and the roads are shaded by tall poplars. Sweet whites and fruity reds are produced, the latter being more attractive. Cadillac by the way has nothing to do with American cars; it is better known for its strong, sweet whites.

The rest of the great wedge of land between the Garonne and the Dordogne is the Entre-deux-Mers region where good dry whites are produced in large quantities, representing value for money. Big estates and mechanical harvesting are the norm in this pleasing area.

North of the Dordogne, near Libourne, are two important regions: St Émilion and Pomerol.

St Émilion, centred around the eponymous and attractive mediaeval town, is small and compact. The wine, made from the Merlot grape, is rich red, noted for its solid tastiness in contrast to the greater delicacy of the Médoc. NE of St Émilion, and bearing that name, are five satellites where much cheaper, but still good, wines are made: Montagne, Lussac, Parsac, Puisseguin and St Georges.

Pomerol is on the NE side of Libourne, adjoining St Émilion but even smaller (4 x 3km). There is nothing much to see, but the wines are soft, warm and gentle clarets of very high quality; do not expect to stumble upon bargain prices. Fronsac and Lalande are satellites to the W and N.

After tasting as many wines as possible, you may have found one or more which delight both your taste buds and your purse. The question then arises Where best to buy? If the wine appears to be available only at some small château, then you would probably have no choice but to buy a case or two on the spot.

Supermarkets however generally dominate wine buying and selling as much in France as in the UK. Possibly in France the market is more discriminating and therefore prices lower. At any rate this would be a good starting point, especially if you have taken the trouble to price some well-known wines in the UK in order to compare them with French prices. You may be pleasantly surprised at what is on offer for as little as 20-30FF per bottle.

Another option is to buy from a wine wholesaler/export retailer where stocks are large and prices competitive. One such in Bordeaux is:

Cash Alcools, 41 Place des Capucins, 33000 Bordeaux. Tel 05.56.92.62.96; Fax 05.56.94.54.98. This is a friendly and helpful place next to the Marché des Capucins.

One of the lesser marinas on the Gironde, frequented by Mole, Ratty, Badger and Toad

THE GIRONDE:
ESTUARY AND RIVER

The Gironde is one of France's most fascinating rivers although at first sight it may appear broad, bland and flanked by flatlands. But what flatlands, at least on the western side! The great vineyards and châteaux of the Médoc are visible from the river and surely merit a land recce by bike from Pauillac or hire car from Bordeaux. No Gironde cruise would be complete without berthing in Bordeaux for

INTRODUCTION

These notes offer navigational guidance for entering the estuary – not always a straightforward process – and for passage up-river.

   They also include information on Port Bloc and five other lesser ports. There are separate entries for Royan, Pauillac and Bordeaux. Chapter 9 covers the canal route to the Mediterranean.

a few days – not only to explore this interesting city but also to radiate out into the famous wine regions to the south and east of the city: Graves, Sauternes, Barsac, Entre-deux-Mers and Premières Côtes de Bordeaux. You can also take a pleasure cruiser ("Alienor") down river to Blaye where the sole pontoon is not very suitable for yachts.

   Bourg on the River Dordogne has yacht pontoons to enable you to visit their less famous, but more affordable vineyards. Further up the Dordogne (covered by SHOM 7029, but not AC 2916) Libourne is a rocky and difficult option, so it

Chapter 8

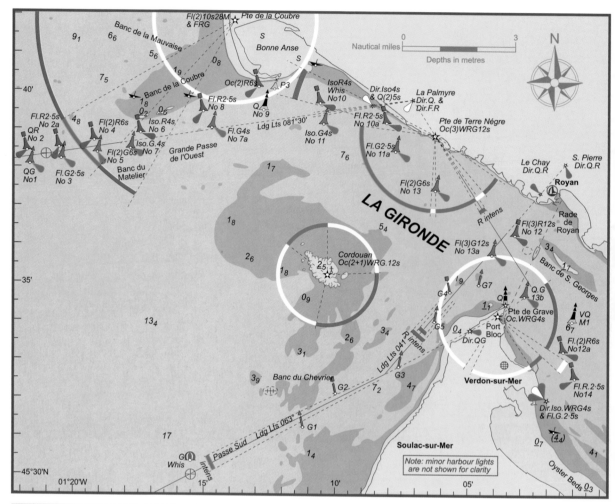

Bec d'Ambès, looking SSW. Vineyard of Château Eyquem is in the foreground

would be better to sample the delights of Pomerol and St Emilion by car. (The Rivers Dordogne and Garonne, as not all the world knows, unite at Bec d'Ambès, 12M downstream from Bordeaux, to flow seaward under the 'new' name of La Gironde).

Finally on a historical note spare a thought for the "Cockleshell Heroes" who in five dark nights of December 1942 paddled their five two-man canoes up-river from 10M southwest of Pointe de Grave. Only two crews made it to Bordeaux, where their limpet mines blew up five large cargo ships. After beaching their canoes near Blaye, only two men survived to reach Blighty via Spain.

NAVIGATIONAL MATTERS

Charts The approaches to the Gironde and Royan are covered by AC 2910 (1:50,000). AC 2916 (1:50,000) continues to Bordeaux, with detailed insets at 1:25,000. SHOM 7028 and 7029 (both 1:45,000) are the equivalents. SHOM 7030 (1:20,000) is a detailed chart of Bordeaux.

The mouth of the Gironde estuary is about 12M wide between Pointe de la Coubre in the north and Pointe de la Négade, 7M SSW of Pointe de Grave. However extensive shoals,

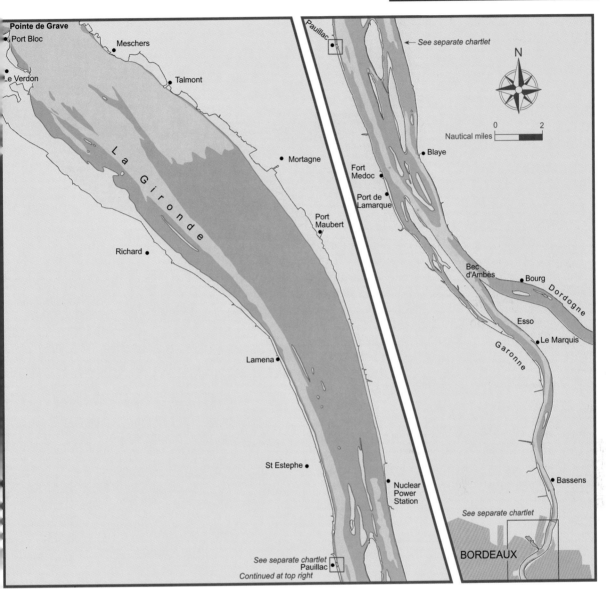

centred on the drying Cordouan plateau and its unusual light-house, block off the middle of this vast arena.

Approaches The two approaches, for which directions are given below, are:

The Grande Passe de l'Ouest (main deep water channel, dredged 13·5m), which passes close to Pointe de la Coubre and is used by large commercial vessels and others; and the shallower Passe Sud which sneaks in past Pointe de Grave, mainly for the benefit of yachts and fishing vessels.

Problems, affecting both channels in varying degree, arise from a combination of Atlantic swell, opposing winds greater than about Force 5 and strong tidal streams. The yachtsman should stay at sea or in harbour when the first two ingredients are present.

To make best use of the streams, timing of the approach must be calculated with some care.

Timing as always, is of the essence. Allowing 2 hours on a fair tide from the waypoint to Royan, (8.2), your most likely first port of call, there are two options for the Passe de l'Ouest:

a. Leave the waypoint at about HW–2, so as to make Royan not later than HW; or

b. Leave the waypoint at about LW+1 on the first of the flood, so as to carry a fair tide to Royan or even to Pauillac some 27M further up-river, halfway to Bordeaux.

Option (a) is more usually adopted because of the stronger tidal stream, but has the disadvantage that a seriously delayed departure (for whatever reason) from the waypoint might mean bucking the ebb before reaching Royan. The likelihood of being affected by swell and breakers is greater.

Chapter 8

Option (b) means a weak stream initially and less swell, but it can come unstuck if the start of the flood is much delayed; hence the addition of an extra hour after LW. River current, especially at neaps, can significantly delay the flood.

It is not always easy to forecast such tidal quirks with any certainty. However useful information can be gleaned (if your French is sufficiently fluent) by monitoring VHF Ch 17 broadcasts of tidal heights at various points on the river. These are given every 5 minutes and, as water levels first begin to rise, for example, a picture emerges of when the flood is starting to make. Reports are broadcast, by a computerised voice, from Bordeaux in sequence to seaward: Bordeaux, Bassens, Le Marquis, Bec d'Ambès, Fort Médoc, Pauillac, Lamena, Richard and Le Verdon.

Well, the best laid plans of mice and men ...

Despite having done your homework, do not assume that you will be guaranteed a smooth ride! Anticipate a brief encounter with short steep seas in the main channel, usually between Nos 5 & 7 buoys. In bad conditions the seas may break, allegedly reaching heights of up to 5 metres – in which conditions you should not be attempting the entry.

West approach (Grande Passe de l'Ouest). By day/night make good the waypoint (45°38′·30N 01°21′·10W), between Nos 2 and 2a lateral buoys and on the 081·5° leading line. Yachts do not need to route via Nos 1 and 2 buoys, still less via the BXA landfall buoy over 5M to seaward of the

Meschers, outer harbour

waypoint. Do not however try a short cut east of the waypoint or you may cross shoals to the S or N of the channel: Banc du Matelier, the aptly named Banc de la Mauvaise and the equally dangerous drying Banc de la Coubre on which seas break even in calm conditions.

The 081·5° leading line is purely intended to get Big Ships (keep a good lookout astern) as far as No 7 SHM buoy, only 2·3M east of the waypoint, after which its line slowly diverges from the buoyed channel.

For yachts buoy hopping is the norm, ticking them off as you progress and keeping to the edge of the channel. So from the waypoint track 078° for 6M, direct to the bend at No 9 NCM buoy (45°39′·49N 01°12′·72W). Here take up a track of 109° for 8M, just outside the buoyed channel, to close the coast at Pointe du Chay if bound for Royan (qv). If bound up-river a track of 126°/8.5M will take you to No 13b SHM buoy off Pointe de Grave where you enter the river proper.

South approach (Passe Sud, or Passe de Grave; used only by the Cockleshell Heroes, yachts and fishing vessels). From the south, this channel saves many miles and is perfectly safe in moderate conditions. In bad weather it can be every bit as rough as the Grande Passe de l'Ouest. It passes between fairly adjacent shoals, but is adequately buoyed. In haze (quite common) the leading marks are hard to see, so buoy-hopping is again the order of the day.

The waypoint is 45°30′·00N 01°15′·47W, 4 cables south of

Meschers: Troglodytes and Hermit

the SWM buoy 'G', and on the 063° leading line. Pass G1 and G2 lateral buoys and just short of G3 buoy, take up the next leading line 041°, skirting Pointe de Grave on course to No 13a SHM buoy. Platin de Grave, between G4 and G7 buoys, is shoal (1·9m – 2·6m) and almost on the leading line.

From No 13a Royan is 2·2M ahead on the far side of the estuary; anticipate a large drift angle to offset the main tidal stream (3·6 kn max spring flood).

If proceeding up-river, route via G4 and G7 to No 13b SHM buoy, then to No 12a and onward ....

On a clear, moonlit night (or with radar) Passe Sud may be used, but not for a first approach. Keep both sets of leading lights (063° St Nicolas, QG, and Pte de Grave, Oc WRG 4s; and 041° Le Chay and St Pierre, both QR) exactly in transit. Bear in mind that G1 to G7 buoys are unlit.

Daymarks Pte de la Coubre light house is white, with the top one third a handsome blood-red. Three cables ENE of it is a big, red and white coastguard station tower, not shown on AC 2910. The light houses at La Palmyre, Pointe de Terre-Nègre and Cordouan will all be seen, rather than utilised for navigation. Admire the last named from a safe distance – if not too busy even to notice it! Pointe de Grave is low lying with sandy beaches and continuous pine woods.

Tides Pointe de Grave is the Standard Port. Differences are published in the MRNA for Royan (qv), Richard, Lamena, Pauillac (qv), Le Marquis, Bordeaux (qv) and Libourne (R Dordogne).

MHWS is 5·4m, MLWS 1·0m; MHWN is 4·4m, MLWN 2·1m.

Tidal streams In the Grande Passe de l'Ouest the spring ebb reaches 4·2 knots near No 9 buoy, and in Passe Sud 2·2 knots; flood rates are 2·5 and 1·8 knots respectively. The stream sets parallel to both channels. SHOM Tidal stream atlas (559-UJA: St Nazaire to Royan) refers.

Anchorages There are few recognised yacht anchorages in the mouth of the estuary. A possible safe anchorage out of the tide is in the bight between the drying Bonne Anse and the front

Mortagne, inner basin

Port Maubert, 'the muddy trench'

081·5° leading light. A small marina (Port de Bonne Anse, 1·5m depth) is tucked into the NE side of the Bonne Anse.

In emergency or sudden fog (sometimes very thick), it is obviously important to clear the shipping channels, even by no more than a cable. Up-river this will usually be possible, except where the channel is narrow and closely flanked by shoals or drying banks. In some circumstances, for example if the boat is making water, a deliberate beaching might be sensible.

MINOR HARBOURS BETWEEN POINTE DE GRAVE AND PAUILLAC

8.1.1 PORT BLOC, 45°34'·18N 01°03'·64W

(harbour entrance). Tucked away at the tip of the Médoc peninsula, a stone's throw from Pointe de Grave, Port Bloc is hardly a yachtsman's mecca, especially when the facilities and delights of Royan are only 3½M away across the river. PB is in fact rather a bleak place, still surrounded by WW2 gun emplacements and bunkers. The town is

Chapter 8

Port Maubert. Berth bows-in

Capitainerie is open around HW, Tel 05.46.02.56.89; HM Jean-Luc Rat. Pre-booking advised or anchor off and recce by dinghy. Talmont church is visible 2M to the SE. Meschers is a pleasant little town. Visit the caves where troglodytes lived in the C14 whilst on pilgrimage to see the local hermit.

8.1.3 MORTAGNE, 45°28´·28N 00°48´·65W

(entry waypoint), is a rather larger harbour 7·5M SE of Meschers. Make good the waypoint where a ruined beacon was replaced (1999) by a large red buoy, with two lateral perches. The entry channel leads 064° for almost a mile to the long, drying, outer harbour, beyond which is a fair-sized wet basin entered via a lock gate (opens HW –1 to HW in season). Here the pontoons, instead of being prosaically labelled A-F, are charmingly named Açores, Bermudes, Canaries, Delos, Elbe and, along the SE wall, Fidji. 80FF first night, 2nd night free. Capitainerie, 9 rue de l'Europe, 17120 Mortagne, is abeam the lock gate; Tel 05.46.90.63.15; HM M. Gouzien. Use tidal differences for Richard.

To the north on low cliffy hills, the ancient town, once fortified and occupied by the English, overlooks the port.

neither large nor vibrant. It is a ferry port – and how! Ferries from Royan are frequent and large, filling the entrance with their beam and the inside of the harbour with their wash. Local boats lead a tough life and certainly there is no provision for visiting yachts.

One and a half miles to the south, the cranes and oil tanks at Le Verdon stand stark and unappealing. Plans for a marina midway between Port Bloc and Le Verdon are well documented but as yet unrealised.

On the east bank there are three small harbours, not often visited by cruising yachts. In the first two yachts will stay afloat, the third is faintly reminiscent of the creeks of the Thames estuary.

8.1.2 MESCHERS, 45°33´·15N 00°56´·55W

is a very small harbour on the east bank, 5·5M upstream from Royan. The outer part dries about 1·5m, best access HW–3 to HW. An inner wet basin, 2m depth, is entered HW ±2½ via a lock gate. Approach on north between two PHM beacons. After 150m the 8m wide channel turns port 328° into the dinky-toy outer harbour. A nominal *accueil* pontoon is to port or berth on pontoons A-C to starboard; max LOA 9m. The lock gate into the wet basin, pontoons D-F, is ahead with 3 small waiting pontoons to starboard.

Bourg pontoons, looking up R. Dordogne

For good Charentaise food try the Auberge de la Garenne, 2 Impasse ancienne gare; run by Catherine and Daniel Denis. Tel 05.46.90.63.69. If you haven't already tried it, a glass of the local Pineau is a must; actually it is grape juice whose fermentation has been stopped by the addition of cognac, making it into a pleasantly warming liqueur.

8.1.4 PORT-MAUBERT, 45°25′·00N 00°45′·80W

(entry waypoint on the drying contour). Welcome to ditch-crawling up a delightful muddy trench! Pyramide de Beaumont (66m) beacon is conspic to the N of the port. Approach near HW on 024·5° although the leading marks are hidden by trees. The perched channel squirms through densely-rushed banks, before reaching the home straight. Berth bows-in on fingers; keels sink into soft mud. Picnic on the grassy banks, away from it all. Or eat sturgeon and other good fishy things at L'Écluse on the N bank at the east end.

Secondary Channel From Port Maubert, or indeed from Royan, yachts can safely navigate up-river to Bec d'Ambès, keeping a mile or less off the east bank in least depths of about 3m. But it is not easy to cross back to the main channel due to shallow and drying ridges in mid-river.

At the 60km post S1 is the first of 5 SHM buoys marking the mid-river side of the secondary channel which at S9 buoy narrows to about 1 cable. Blaye is about 2M south of S9.

Across to the Médoc bank and almost midway between Royan and Bordeaux is the useful port of Pauillac – see separate entry, 8.3.

Upstream from Pauillac but still on the east bank take a look at:

8.1.5 BLAYE, 45°07′·55N 00°39′·93W (pronounced

Bligh). The pontoon for yachts is short and very exposed. Tidal streams are strong. Blaye cannot therefore be 100% recommended for visiting yachts. The small drying gully just south of the Citadelle, marked by a PHM beacon, Q(3) R 5s, is for local boats only. Capitainerie Tel 05.57.41.13.63. VHF Ch 12. HM M. Penot.

But, if you are driving around the region, the village has much leafy charm and is a good base for exploring the Premières Côtes de Blaye vineyards. The Tourist Office, Tel 05.57.42.12.09, on the river front will help organise visits and tastings. There is a traditional market in the main square on Wed and Sat mornings. Vauban's C17 Citadelle is worth a visit: a village within a village, still inhabited and with good views over the river. It was built to keep the dastardly Brits away from Bordeaux. A convenient car ferry crosses the river almost hourly from Lamarque to Blaye.

8.1.6 BOURG, 45°02′·33N 00°33′·52W

Although listed as Bourg-sur-Gironde, the town is firmly on the N bank of the Dordogne, 2M up-river from Bec d'Ambès. Visit the attractive, hilly Côtes de Bourg vineyards where some good, reasonably priced red wines may be found; they were once more highly rated than Médoc. Long gallery caves below the town are now used as wine cellars. Visit caves of another kind, prehistoric, at Pair-non-Pair, 6km east of Bourg.

The long pontoon is accessible at all tides, but is exposed to fresh west winds which against the ebb raise a nasty chop; rafting up is prohibited. There is a drying wreck off the west end of the pontoons. Bilge keelers can dry out in a small inlet. Capitainerie, Tel 05.57.68.40.06.

Bourg market

Chapter 8

ROYAN

Royan is GOOD NEWS – for a variety of reasons which will emerge as you read on. It is a friendly relaxed sort of place, far enough south not to get frostbite should you elect to swim in the river; it feels more like the seaside anyway.
It is twinned with Gosport although anything but identical.

Between the wars Royan was an elegant, fashionable resort and traces of its heyday are still visible out at Pontaillac. The town was virtually flattened towards the end of WW2 and has been rebuilt with broad, open avenues and boulevards. The feeling of space is enhanced by the wide sweeping bay and the ever-present vista across to Pointe de Grave.

Royan is safely and strategically located just inside the mouth of the mighty Gironde estuary. It is therefore a good starting point: to cruise up the Gironde, visiting famous-name ports like Pauillac, Bourg and Bordeaux; or try a venture up the Dordogne as far as Libourne. Berth in Bordeaux for a few days – to explore this interesting city and/or hire a car and continue a land recce of vineyards and châteaux, great and not so great! (See separate entries for the Gironde, Pauillac and Bordeaux).

Or from Bordeaux your plans may include passage through the canals to the Mediterranean.

Finally Royan is the last jumping-off point for Spain's north coast, if you intend to keep seaward of the Landes missile range – as opposed to coast-crawling down via the Basque Country.

TOURISM

Tourist Office is at Place de la Poste, near the NE end of Front de Mer; address BP 138, 17207 Royan. Tel 05.46.05.04.71; Fax 05.46.06.67.76. Hours in season Mon-Sat 0900-1930; Sun/Hols 1000-1300 & 1500-1800. Out of season Mon-Sat 0900-1230 & 1400-1800.

What to see/do Sunbathe, swim, sleep, drink, eat. In between these epicurean pursuits visit La Tremblade, La Marennes and the oyster beds of the River Seudre. Reconnoitre the nautical scene at Pertuis de Maumusson and Pointe de la Coubre. There's even a zoo at La Palmyre!

Cycle 16km on the D25 via St Georges and Meschers to Talmont. This is an enchanting village and tiny port built on a small promontory which juts out into the Gironde. The squat 12th century church of Sainte-Radegonde stands foursquare on a low cliff with commanding river views. It is an architectural showpiece in the Romanesque style which you must relish for yourself, since no words of mine can do it justice.

Don't risk your own boat – jump on a cruise *bateau*, weather permitting, to visit the oldest light house in France. Cordouan it is, remote and often inaccessible on its rocky plateau. The tower is a bewitching mixture of flamboyant Renaissance

Mother duck on an uninvited scrounge

Royan, looking NW

Labels on image: Cathedral tower, Market, Capitainerie, 'D' pontoon visitors, Accueil pontoon, Ferry terminal

architecture, topped by the more severe lines of the Classical school. 301 steps will get you to the top, dead or alive ...

Finally try to be in Royan for the Feast of the Assumption, 15 August. You will witness from the deck of your boat a brilliantly executed Son et Lumière, followed by a most spectacular firework display. Local yachts vacate the marina en masse, fearful that pyrotechnic cinders and half-spent rockets will land on their decks. Rig a hosepipe, fill a couple of buckets with water and you're unlikely to come to any harm!

Bus Line 1 to Talmont, 40 mins; Line 2 to La Coubre light house, 62 mins; Line 3 to Rance-les-Bains (mouth of R Seudre), 90 mins. Bus to Saintes, 65 mins (very slow).

Railway Station, Tel 05.46.05.20.10, is at Place du Gare 20 mins walk NE from the marina. A local train to Saintes connects with the Brest-Bordeaux line. Paris is about 4 hrs by TGV.

Taxis Tel 05.46.05.02.79; 05.46.39.88.88.

Ferry Car/passenger ferries shuttle all year round to/from Port Bloc (30 mins), continuously in Jul/Aug and very frequently in other summer months. Tel 05.46.38.35.15.

Bike hire Cycles, Tel 05.46.05.16.42. Neway, esplanade du Bac, Tel 05.46.39.87.26.

Car hire
- Avis, 75 ave de Pontaillac. Tel 05.46.38.48.88.
- Hertz, Tel 05.46.05.24.34.
- Europcar, 13 place du Dr Garnier, Tel 05.46.05.20.88.

Roscoff is about 6 hours drive via Saintes, Fontenay le Comte, Nantes, Rennes and St Brieuc. St Malo is 5 – 5½ hours drive.

Beaches are known locally as *Conche* (cove, inlet). Those to the west of the marina are sheltered by rocky cliffs; they include E to W: Foncillon, Chay/Le Pigeonnier and Pontaillac (the best). East of the marina La Grande Conche stretches for ever (2km), beneath a thick layer of sizzling human flesh. Walk a bare 100m from the marina and you're on it. The beaches are delightful, but inevitably crowded in summer. Slightly further SE at St Georges the beach is backed by pines, less crowded and more relaxed. There is a villagey atmosphere and a good market. It is safe to swim in the Gironde, which looks like *café au lait* with too much *lait*.

EATING ASHORE

Restaurants Le Lido, bld Frédéric Garnier. Looks like a shack, but excellent, cheap seafood and good service.

roasts, oriental spices, slightly wild chef! Also take-away.

- La Tortue II, 11 rue des Bains. Tel 05.46.05.89.75. Run by Martine Klein and chef Jean-Luc. A warm welcome, super food and service and not too expensive. Beat that!

SHOPPING

Supermarkets
- Near the Central market there is a small Co-Op and a small Casino.
- At Pontaillac the Intermarché is favoured by locals.
- Leclerc hypermarket, rue Lavoisier (Tel 05.46.05.11.89), is about 4km NE, just off the N150 to Saujon and Saintes, near the little airfield.

Markets Daily in the Central Market, covered by a parachute-shaped roof, and surrounded by stalls; all the magic of the market-place at the far end of the wide, tree-lined bld Aristide Briand.

Banks All the usual. Cashpoints on the marina quayside.

- Les Filets Bleus, 14 rue Notre Dame (near the cathedral). Tel 05.46.05.74.00. Alain, the owner catches the fish. Open kitchen. Good value set menus, but the à la carte can be dear.
- Restaurant l'Anjou, 17 rue Font de Cherves. Tel 05.46.05.09.49. Menus 62-192FF. Good fish and a friendly welcome from Françoise and Jean-Pierre Anjou.
- Cortez Maltése, place Charles de Gaulle; near the central market. Cheap and friendly; spit

NAVIGATIONAL MATTERS

Charts Royan and the approaches to the Gironde are covered by AC 2910 (1:50,000). AC 2916 continues to Bordeaux at 1:50,000, with detailed insets at 1:25,000. SHOM 7028 and 7029, both at 1:45,000, are the French equivalents. SHOM 7030 (1:20,000) is a detailed chart of Bordeaux.

For entry to the Gironde estuary see 8.1. Both approaches into Royan share a common final waypoint 45°36´·89N 01°02´·00W. From here the marina entrance (45°37´·20N 01°01´·38W) is 4 cables NE, and R1 SHM buoy is 3 cables SSE.

West approach As you pass Pointe du Chay from

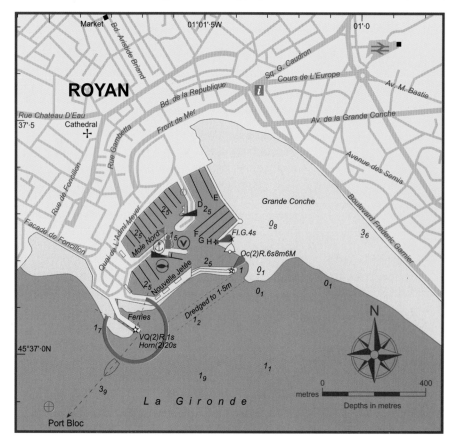

Passing Pointe du Chay. The 041° Passe Sud leading marks are just off the left edge of this photograph

the NW, Royan cathedral is abeam to port and the harbour comes into view around the headland. Do not be bamboozled by the conspicuous disused light house, 1·5M to the SE; it has nothing to do with Royan!

South approach From 13a buoy Royan is 2·2M ahead on the far side of the estuary. Counter the main tidal stream (3·6 knots, spring flood) so as to avoid being set onto Banc de St Georges.

Daymarks Royan's modern cathedral (or church) is unique in appearance, so unique in fact that you might not guess it to be cathedral or church. Its tower is a jagged spike and the roof line has pronounced sheer; its appearance changes sharply, depending on your viewpoint – say no more!

Tides HW Royan at neaps is the same as, and at springs 5 mins before, HW Pointe de Grave. LW, at neaps and springs, is 5 mins before LW Pointe de Grave.

MHWS is 5·1m, MLWS 1·0m; MHWN is 4·2m, MLWN 2·1m.

Tidal streams within the inner part of the Rade de Royan set continuously NW due to an eddy which forms during the in-going flood stream. Further offshore the stream aligns with the river. SHOM Tidal stream atlas (559-UJA: St Nazaire to Royan) refers.

Access is at all tides and in all weathers, but near LW keep carefully to the final channel between the ferry terminal and Nouvelle Jetée, said to be dredged 1·5m – but it is silted to 1m around the head of Nouvelle Jetée where a small yellow SPM buoy marks the outer edge of the channel. There ain't much water; the extensive beach is encroaching!

The marina is supposedly dredged 2·5m in both the main basin and the newer NE basin, but there is probably only 1·5m.

Approaching the Accueil pontoon stern-first

Hazards The Banc de St Georges, drying 1·7m, may be a trap for the unwary – or the lost – but it is over a mile south of the harbour and marked by a SCM light buoy on its SE side. R1 SHM light buoy marks 2 wrecks, but loosely warns of Banc de St Georges. Keep clear of the ferries. Be alert for fast fishing boats and yachts appearing round Nouvelle Jetée, as you enter/leave.

Shelter in the marina is very good in all weathers.

Anchorage No anchoring in the marina.

MARINA

Capitainerie conspicuous in centre of harbour. Tel 05.46.38.72.22; Fax 05.46.39.42.47. VHF Ch 09. HM Yves Guirriec. Hours in season, daily 0800-2000; out of season 0900-1800. Weather forecasts are posted daily. Inner basins: Pontoons 1-12.

Visitors check in at *accueil* pontoon, dead ahead as you enter. Probable ❶ berths are on D pontoon in the NE basin, where a flotilla of ducks are quite likely to board your boat!

Tariff Daily rates for LOA bands, all year round. 7-8·5m = 73-87FF; 8·5-10m = 93-106FF; 10-11·5m = 111-126FF; 11·5-14m = 135-157FF.

Talmont church, 8 miles upriver

Fuel berth is just beyond the Accueil pontoon. H24 by French bank card, or 0900-1230 & 1430-1900 if paying by non-French cards/cash.

Showers are in the Base Nautique (0800-2130, except Fri 0800-2030; 12FF). Or further along the quay, underneath the arches, f.o.c. in a rather claustrophobic block; hours "*très variable*".

Launderette Laverie de Pontaillac, 9 bd de la Côte de Beauté. Tel 05.46.38.66.91.

NAUTICAL NEEDS

De-masting There is a 1·5 ton crane on the inner East jetty, near the boat-hoist.

Chandlery & repairs

- Chantier Navale de Cordouan, 30 bld Thiers, at marina. Tel 05.46.38.11.72. Boatyard.
- Pierre Michel (at marina). Tel 05.46.39.43.75. Engineering repairs.
- Cap Océan, by the ferry ramp. Tel 05.46.39.20.20. Chandlery.
- Depan' Elec' Marine, at fish harbour. Tel 05.46.38.35.34. Electronics.
- Royan Marine, 14-16 Voutes du Port. Tel 05.46.38.54.00. Chandlery, SHOM chart agent.
- La Voilerie, Voutes du Port. Tel 05.46.38.36.95. Chandlery, SHOM chart agent.

PAUILLAC

Pauillac looking ENE at low water

Famed for the illustrious quality of its wine, this Commune contains three out of the five Médoc Premières Crus (Châteaux Lafite-Rothschild, Latour and Mouton-Rothschild). Many other well-known châteaux are within 4km of the town, easy cycling distance for a picnic or to visit the vineyards.

The huge Shell oil depot, 3km north of the marina, does nothing for the landscape.

TOURISM

Tourist Office (Maison du Tourisme et du Vin) is on the front just south of the marina; address La Verrerie, 33250 Pauillac. E-mail: tourismeetvin depauillac@wanadoo.fr Tel 05.56.59.03.08; Fax 05.56.59.23.38. Hours in season Mon-Sat 0900-1930; Sun/Hols 1000-1300 & 1500-1800. Out of season Mon-Sat 0900-1230 & 1400-1800.

What to see/do Wine, wine and yet more wine! Visit the châteaux, walk the vineyards, see how the finest wines (arguably) in the world are made and above all swirl, nose, taste, assess, describe and even drink the stuff! Have an on-board wine tasting and get each member of the crew to describe the same wine, in writing – a fascinating and difficult exercise.

' ... Many claret lovers would tell you that the wines of Pauillac have the quintessential flavour they look for in Bordeaux – a combination of fresh soft-fruit, oak, dryness, subtlety combined with substance, a touch of cigar-box, a suggestion of sweetness. Even the lesser growths of Pauillac approach their ideal claret'.

Hugh Johnston, *The World Atlas of Wine.*

The Tourist office organises visits to certain châteaux or you can make your own arrangements. The following Châteaux accept visits, usually with English-speaking tours:

- Mouton Rothschild, where there is also a wine museum and art collection (Tel 05.56.73.21.29);

- Lafite-Rothschild (Tel 05.56.73.18.18);

- Latour (Tel 05.56.73.19.80);

Chapter 8

Looking NW into marina at low water springs

- Croizet-Bages, Mon-Fri (Tel 05.56.59.66.69);
- Pichon Longueville Comtesse de Lalande (Tel 05.56.59.19.40);
- Batailley (Tel 05.56.59.01.13), Mon-Fri 0800-1200 & 1400-1600, including tasting.
- The Cave Co-opérative La Rose Pauillac (Tel 05.56.59.26.00) on rue du Maréchal Joffre, is

worth a visit to learn a little more about the region and to acquire affordable and yet drinkable Pauillac wine.

Buses run to Bordeaux, about 1½ hours, 6 times daily and to Le Verdon. Stop is just N of marina.

Railway Station, Tel 05.56.59.00.66, is at Place de Verdun 10 mins walk NW from the marina. Trains

Enter close to the outer (east) breakwater

to Port Bloc and Bordeaux.

Taxis Tel 05.56.59.14.67; 05.56.59.06.38; 05.56.59.05.32.

Ferry Passenger/bike/car ferries cross almost hourly from Lamarque (12km upriver) to Blaye.

Bike hire Ask at the Tourist Office which also provides routes; 50FF half day, 70FF whole day.

Car hire Hertz, quai Albert de Pichon, opposite the marina. Tel 05.56.59.04.53.

EATING ASHORE

Restaurants There are the usual eateries *touristique* along the front, but good restaurants in the village are hard to find. Cycle along the shoreside D2/E4 road 8km north to Ste Estephe where you can enjoy the menu du jour (65FF) including "out of this world" vegetable soup, washed down with the *vin du maison* at Le Peyrat, 19 rue du Littoral (by the river). Tel 05.56.59.71.43.

De-masting crane, near high water

SHOPPING

Supermarkets Intermarché in rue de la République.

Markets Tues and Sat mornings, covered and open air markets on rue de la République. 10FF for a bag of delicious *crevettes grises*, fresh from the river; eat with an apéritif.

Banks Credit Lyonnais; BNP, 10 rue Albert; and others, plus cashpoints.

NAVIGATIONAL MATTERS

Charts AC 2916 (1:50,000) covers the river, with detailed insets at 1:25,000. SHOM 7028 and 7029, both at 1:45,000, are the French equivalents.

Daymarks The Shell tanker jetties and oil tanks at Trompeloup, 1-2 miles downstream of the marina are conspicuous. Pauillac church tower is a very good landmark, visible from afar.

The waypoint, arriving from down-river, is 45°12´.51N 00°44´.25W, No 43 SHM buoy, 65 cables NNE of the marina. The west jetty at the marina entrance sports a uniquely welcoming, giant-sized claret bottle marked PAUILLAC.

Tides HW Pauillac at neaps and at springs is 1 hour after HW Pointe de Grave. LW, at neaps is 1 hour 35 mins, and at springs 2 hours 5 mins, after LW Pointe de Grave.

MHWS is 5·5m, MLWS 0·5m; MHWN is 4·4m, MLWN 1·1m.

Tidal streams In the channel the ebb sets north for 7 hours (HW Pointe de Grave +2 to –4), and reaches 4·5/2·4 knots at springs/ neaps. The flood does not exceed 3·0/1·4 knots at springs/neaps. The weakest streams, 0·6/0·3 knots springs/neaps, occur at HW Pointe de Grave –3 and +2.

Access in all weathers. Keep close to the starboard breakwater and well off the Bottle, as you slalom through the entrance. If possible berth when the tidal stream is weakest (see below).

Hazards The strong tidal stream runs through the marina, via outlets in the north mole. For a first visit consider anchoring off to await slackish waters at HW Pointe de Grave –3 and +2.

Chapter 8

Shelter in the marina is good in all weathers.

Anchorage No anchoring in the marina. Outside, anchor in about 5m, aligned with the outer breakwater, but no nearer than 500 metres south of the marina due to charted underwater cables.

MARINA

Capitainerie is on north breakwater. Port de Plaisance, 33250 Pauillac. Tel 05.56.59.12.16; Fax 05.56.59.23.38. VHF Ch 09. HM Alain Crouzal. Hours 0800-1200 & 1400-1800 daily. Weather forecasts are posted daily.

Visitors berth on A and B pontoons, first two to starboard on entering, least depth 2m. Pontoons are springy and rickety (see the page following the Introduction). There are 150 berths of which 20 are for visitors.

Caution: strong tidal stream can make berthing difficult. The weakest streams, 0·6/0·3 knots springs/neaps, occur at HW Pointe de Grave –3 and +2; just to make this important point for the third time!

Tariff Daily rates for LOA bands:
7-8·5m = 62-81FF; 8·5-10m = 85-99FF; 10-11m = 115FF; 11-12m = 141FF; 12-16m = 167FF.

Fuel berth (diesel and petrol) is at the entrance, beside The Bottle. 0700-2000. Tel 05.56.59.04.53.

Showers etc are in a block at the south end of the marina.

Launderette Salon Lavoir, 7 rue Bossuet (west of main square). Daily 0700-2100.

NAUTICAL NEEDS

De-masting There is a 1 ton electric crane on a jetty, just south of the Capitainerie, but not accessible LW±3. Free bottle of Pauillac if the job is done by the professionals! A 15 ton mobile crane is available for boat lifts.

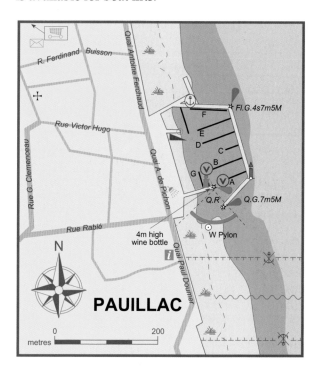

Leaving at high water

Nuclear power station on far bank

'A' pontoon

BORDEAUX

Bordeaux – city of wine! For 300 years capital of Aquitaine under the English, who were finally ejected in 1453. And even today Bordeaux, eighth largest city of France, does not feel itself to be particularly French and there is no love lost with Paris as you will glean from even a brief perusal of the history books. In the C18 the mediaeval walls and houses were knocked down and rebuilt in the fine stone which we see today. Take a long hard look at the Grand Théâtre a superbly executed example of neo-Classical architecture, not to mention similar elegant buildings all around. Walk the old city with guide book in hand, since these notes cannot possibly do justice to such a well-endowed and friendly city. You will rarely find people who think ill of Bordeaux.

TOURISM

Tourist Office (main) is near Esplanade des Quinconces, at 12 cours du 30 Juillet, 33080 Bordeaux. Tel 05.56.00.66.00; Fax 05.56.00.66.01. E-mail: otb@bordeaux-tourisme.com

Internet: www.bordeaux-tourisme.com Hours in season Mon-Sat 0900-2000; Sun/Hols 0900-1900. Out of season Mon-Sat 0900-1900; Sun/Hols 0945-1630. Wine tours can be booked here. There is also a tiny office at Gare St Jean.

What to see/do Depending on your interests this may be good news or bad: Bordeaux boasts rather a lot of museums! If you're in Basin No 2, you've probably realised that the grandly-titled Conservatoire International de Plaisance is right on your nautical doorstep in the submarine pens. For 20FF you can enter these forbidding pens, or admire the view from the roof, but the museum pieces are a random array of boats supposedly tracing the history of yachting ... maybe.

Meanwhile back in downtown Bordeaux, continue the museum trail by sampling the Musée: of Aquitaine; of contemporary Art; of Fine Arts; of decorative Arts; of Customs and Excise (!); of Natural History; of wine (Chartrons); of photographic prints (Goupil); of the Resistance (Centre Jean Moulin); of printing; of wine (Vinorama); of science (Cap Sciences); and of architecture. Don't say you haven't been warned. Get the leaflets from the Tourist Office and go to it!

Alternatively fan out into the world's greatest wine-growing region. Surely not a difficult decision to make?

Bus Line 9 from city centre to Basin No 2 (direction Pl René Maran), get off at Place Latule.

Pont d'Aquitaine

Pont du Jour (private marina)

Lormont YC pontoon

Lock entrance to Bassin No2

View downstream towards Pont d'Aquitaine at low water

Chapter 8

Railway Gare St Jean, Info tel 08.36.35.35.35, is at rue Charles Domecq, 3km SE of city centre. Trains to La Rochelle, Nantes, Arcachon, Toulouse. Paris is about 3 hrs by TGV.

Airport Bordeaux-Mérignac, 12km west of city centre by regular bus shuttle. Tel 05.56.34.50.50

Taxi ranks Centre Grand Théâtre 05.56.81.99.15; Pl Gambetta 05.56.81.99.05.

Car hire Gare St Jean (arrivals):
• Budget, 05.56.91.41.70.
• Hertz, 05.56.91.01.71.
• Europcar, 05.56.31.20.30.

Useful tip: The city's ring road is called La Rocade and is sign-posted as such.

EATING ASHORE

Restaurants There is no justice in this world, - how can one city be endowed with so many super eating places? Here are just a few, all to be found in the very heart of the city and its people:
• Le Plat dans l'Assiette, 8 rue Ausone. Tel 05.56.01.05.01. Excellent food, friendly hosts in characterful surroundings. Across the street is a very good, inexpensive Italian restaurant.
• Chez Ducon, allées de Tourny. Tel 05.56.81.61.61. Up-market, wood panelling, good service, jazz accompaniment.

La Garonne, 1M south of Bec d'Ambès, 10M from Bordeaux

• Les Noailles, also in allées de Tourny; good lunch, but get there early!
• Brasserie des Quinconces, place des Quinconces. Tel 05.56.81.48.87. Lunch 65FF, dinner 95FF.

Place du Parlement, in the Quartier St Pierre, is a delightful cobbled square, encircled by Louis XV buildings, a magical place to dine under the stars in any of half a dozen restaurants.
• Try the mid-price L'Ombrière, twinned with Le Café de la Place. Tel 05.56.44.82.69. Menus 80-119FF.

The pedestrianised rue des Faussets and rue des Bahutiers are not far away, with all types/prices of open-air restaurants.
• Didier Gélineau, 26 rue du Pas-St-Georges. Tel 05.56.52.84.25. Gourmet cuisine, elegant decor. Menus 215-340FF.

And from the sublime to life's basics: there is a McDonald's at Basin 2, better than UK versions!

SHOPPING

The main shopping street is the pedestrianised rue Ste Catherine, running N/S through the centre. More good shops and elegant buildings are at its north end in a triangle defined by the Places Gambetta, de Tourny and de la Comédie. About 400m west of the Cathédrale St André is the Mériadeck shopping Centre, an ultra-modern, hideous concrete sprawl in stark contrast to the gracious, eighteenth century architecture of the Vieux Quartier.

Supermarkets Mostly away from the city centre. Ask at the Capitainerie if in Bassin 2.

Markets There are many, one of the best known being the newly enlarged Marché des Capucins in Place Capucin, near the Place de la Victoire; here you can buy fresh produce from 0500 daily, especially good on Saturdays. Also Grands Hommes where there is a daily market. Grand Marché in cours Victor Hugo; Chartrons in place Chartrons. Not to mention flea markets.

Banks All banks and many cashpoints.

NAVIGATIONAL MATTERS

Charts The approaches to the Gironde are covered by AC 2910 (1:50,000). AC 2916 continues to Bordeaux at 1:50,000, with detailed insets at 1:25,000. SHOM 7028 and 7029 are the French equivalents, both at 1:45,000. SHOM 7030 (1:20,000) is a detailed chart of Bordeaux.

For entry to the Gironde estuary and passage up-river see 8.1. The final approaches into Bordeaux are straightforward. At Bec d'Ambés the Dordogne flows into the Gironde; leave No 62 WCM buoy to port and enter the River Garonne, 12M downstream of Basin No 2. The east bank of this river is industrialised most of the way to Bordeaux.

Waypoints seem superfluous. You will readily find Lormont, almost beneath the Pont d'Aquitaine. The entrance to Bassin No 2, 44°51'·73N 00°32'·93W, is 1·3M further up-river.

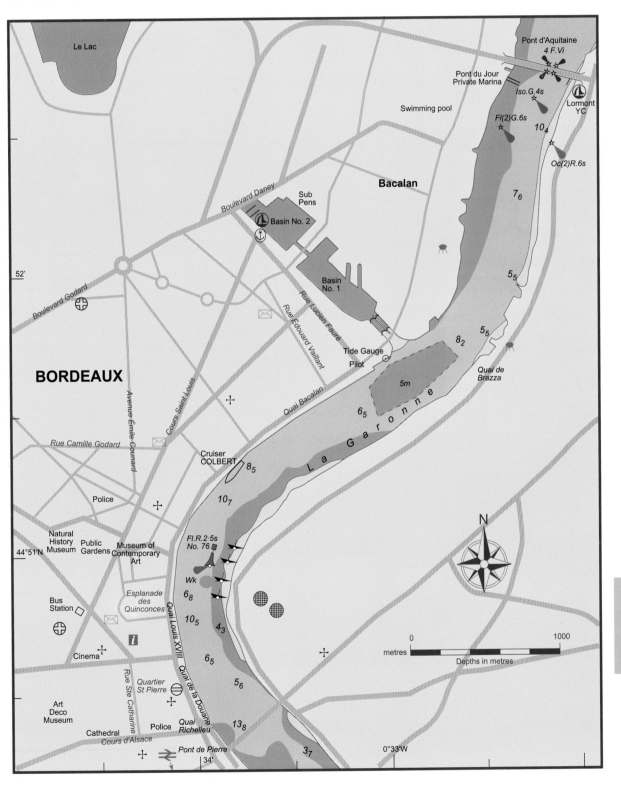

Chapter 8

Lormont, de-masting crane and Pont d'Aquitaine Pont du Jour private marina on opposite bank

Daymarks The large suspension bridge, Pont d'Aquitaine, dominates the skyline; it has an air clearance of 51m.

Tides HW Bordeaux at neaps is 2 hrs, and at springs 2 hrs 25 mins, after HW Pointe de Grave. LW, at neaps is 3 hrs 30 mins, and at springs 4 hrs 5 mins, after LW Pointe de Grave.

MHWS is 5·3m, MLWS 0·0m; MHWN is 4·2m, MLWN 0·4m.

Tidal streams at Bordeaux: At HW Bordeaux $-2\frac{1}{2}$ hrs, the flood reaches $2\frac{3}{4}$ kn at springs and $2\frac{1}{4}$ kn at neaps. At HW Bordeaux $+1\frac{3}{4}$ hrs, the ebb reaches 4 kn at springs and $2\frac{3}{4}$ kn at neaps. The approximate times of slack water are HW Bordeaux +15 mins, and +7 hrs (springs) or $+8\frac{1}{4}$ hrs (neaps). Slack water lasts very briefly, only 5-10 mins at the start of the flood.

Access to Lormont YC pontoon is at all tides and in all weathers; Basin 2 at HW Bordeaux $-1\frac{1}{2}$.

Hazards Large ships, strong tides, floating debris.

Shelter at Lormont is degraded by wash and may be only moderate in strong

north or south winds. Basin 2 is very sheltered in all weathers.

Anchorage Anchoring in the river is really only feasible in emergency, when a deliberate grounding on the muddy banks might be a better course of action, depending on the problem.

BERTHING

There are 3 options for yachts, from seaward:

i. Lormont YC. This is a private club pontoon on the east bank virtually underneath the Pont d'Aquitaine suspension bridge. The YC is friendly, but visitors should appreciate that berths are entirely subject to space being available and at the Club's discretion; check with the YC boatman that an overnight stay is acceptable (longer stays may not be). Yachts can lie afloat at all tides on either side of the southerly pontoon (the northerly pontoon is for small workboats and fishing craft); berths are affected by wash. On the pontoon a little electric crane is adequate for small-medium size masts. Showers in the YC: Halte Nautique de Lormont, quai Chaigneau-Bichon, 33310 Lormont. Tel 05.56.31.50.10.

Note: The former Pont du Jour marina on the opposite bank is now strictly private and visitors are not accepted, allegedly due to an insurance problem. A large Alsatian and his equally discouraging owner keep watch!

ii. Basin No 2 is on the west bank 1·3M upstream of the suspension bridge; entered via a lock and across Basin No 1. It is run for the Bordeaux Port Authority by the local Capitainerie on its SW side, Tel 05.56.90.59.57, Fax 05.56.90.59.96; HM Alain Bechard mobile 06.13.79.10.75. Two days or so before arrival get authorisation to berth in the Basin on Tel 05.56.90.59.57. It is 3km from the city centre and although the surrounding

Bassin No2, lock entrance from the river, near low water

warehouses, submarine pens and scarcity of grass would not win it any beauty prizes, it is acceptable and appears to be reasonably secure. Facilities tend to be basic.

For entry arrive at HW Bordeaux $-1\frac{1}{2}$, departures at HW $+\frac{1}{2}$. Call VHF Ch 12 *"Capitainerie Port de Bordeaux"* for clearance to lock in; or telephone 05.56.31.58.64. Expect to use the wider, southerly of two locks (swing bridges open in unison with lock gates); there are no traffic lights. In the vast Basin No 2 yachts berth along the SW side (sternline to buoy) or on pontoons at the NW end; the concrete WW2 submarine pens frown across from the NE side.

Note: The aerial photograph below was taken in light snow, low cloud and poor visibility!

iii. A Halte Nautique, for de-masted yachts only, is on the NE bank just upstream of the 4·2m high Pont de Pierre beyond which masted yachts cannot safely go! Electricity is provided, but no water. This is 20 mins walk to the city centre but is intended as a short-stay berth. Café/bar and chandlery are close by. See photograph on page 277.

Tariff Bassin No 2 is keen to encourage visitors who may well receive free berthing for a few days. Longer periods by negotiation over a bottle of wine. Tariff requested, but not received; charges would be minimal in keeping with the facilities. The same applies at Lormont.

Fuel is not available by hose to yachts in Bordeaux.

Pontoons at NW end of Bassin No 2

NAUTICAL NEEDS

De-masting There is a small crane on the Lormont YC pontoon and a mobile crane in Basin 2.

Chandlery & repairs
- Le Compas, Basin No 2. Tel 05.56.50.60.02. Good chandlery. SHOM chart agent.
- Corderie et Voilerie de l'Atlantique, 271 bld Alfred Daney (business park behind Basin 2). Tel 05.56.43.19.61. Rigging, sails. SHOM chart agent.
- Accastillage Diffusion, 11 place Stalingrad (E end of Pont de Pierre). Tel 05.56.86.70.81. Wide range of chandlery.
- Le Froid à Bord, Warehouse 27, rue Lucien Faure (SW side of basin). Tel 05.56.50.60.60. Refrigeration, heating, desalination.

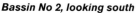
Bassin No 2, looking south

BORDEAUX TO THE MEDITERRANEAN VIA THE CANALS

CONTENTS

This chapter does not pretend to be anything more than a thumbnail sketch of the route from Bordeaux to the Mediterranean. But as such it may help to crystallise your thoughts by presenting the Big Picture from which you will be able to refine your planning in more detail. The route is covered from Bordeaux to the Med purely because this continues the north-to-south direction of the book.

Geography From Bordeaux to Sète on the Med coast is approx 506km/274M, with 118 locks. (To put this in perspective, the distance is about the same as that from Carlisle to Beachy Head by rhumbline). The route is made up of 3 main sections:

i. River Garonne, Bordeaux to Castets-en-Dorthe: 55km/30M. No locks.

ii. Canal latéral à la Garonne, Castets-en-Dorthe to Toulouse, 193km/104M. 53 locks.

iii. Canal du Midi, Toulouse to Sète (including Étang de Thau), 258km/140M. 65 locks.

Note: The Canal may also be exited/entered further west at Grau d'Agde and, via the Canal de la Robine, at Port La Nouvelle.

Distance and Time Whether 'tis better to take the 'outside' offshore route via Portugal and Gibraltar or the Canal route? – may seem an obvious question, but the answers are interesting.

It is mainly a time and distance equation, but your boat's draught could be the deciding factor (see below). Crew strength, prevailing winds and other factors also need to be considered.

Approximate distances and possible passage times, with an unknown number of stops, are:

The 'outside' route could total 1630M and take at least 16 days:

- Brest (or anywhere between there and Lorient) to La Coruña, 330M in 3 days;

- La Coruña to Lisbon, 330M in 3 days;

- Lisbon to Gibraltar, 300M in 3 days; and

- Gibraltar to Sète, 670M in 7 days.

The Canal route could total 560M and also take 16 days. To compare like with like, it includes

- Brest to Royan, 230M in 3 days;
- Royan to Bordeaux, 55M in 1 day; and
- Bordeaux to Sète, 274M in 12 days.

Information The two available Guides to the Canals may be summarised as follows:

Voies Navigables du Midi, No 11 in the Navicarte series on river/canal guides. By Claude Vergnot, published by Éditions Grafocarte; 4th edition 1996; 120pp, small A4 size. Price £17.50. This is written in English, French and German (the 3 languages are awkwardly laid out on the pages). The route is covered from Royan to the Med in the first 87pp; the rest of the book covers the lower reaches of the Rhône and the Baïse river.

The text is perfectly adequate, good on most practicalities and quite strong on historical aspects. Translations can be quaint (Do you have a Certificate of Aptitude?). The colour photographs are small. The yellow/blue strip maps at 1:50,000 scale are properly detailed with margin notes; as far as possible they face the accompanying text. Due to the many bends in the canals, these maps are not orientated with north at the top of the page, which can be confusing.

Canaux du Midi, No 7 in the Guide Vagnon series of river/canal guides. By Jean Merlot, published by Vagnon Dec 1998, 240pp A4 size. Price 109FF. The route is covered in the reverse direction (ie Med to Royan) with substantial sections on the lower reaches of the Rhône, the Lot and Baïse rivers. Thus the two Canals of interest are covered in 140 pages (54-193).

This is a larger book with all pages in landscape style making map-reading easier whichever way you are heading – you do not need to hold the book upside down! The text is clear and bold, but economical in content. It is also in English, French and German, but the 3 languages are kept separate. There are many colour photographs and the maps are big, clear and colourful, strongly schematic by intent rather than cartographically exact; orientation is the same as the other Guide.

You will definitely need one of these guides, but only you can decide which one ...

The CEVNI buoyage, signs and rules of the road used on the canals, together with notes on locking and moorings, are published in two books, one of which should be on board:

a. Vagnon Carte de Plaisance, in French, English and German, approx £12; and

b. RYA book of Euro-regs for Inland waterways (1998) by Marian Martin, approx £5.00.

Land-orientated guides (Cadogan, Michelin, Rough etc) are too numerous to be listed here, but all offer interesting information. Michelin maps (1:200,000) Nos 79, 82, 83 and 86 will help to keep you aware of the countryside through which you are crawling. For more detail, use the French O.S. maps (Cartes IGN; 1:100,000).

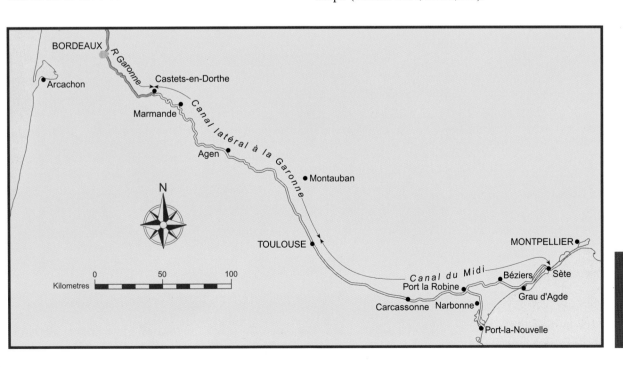

Draught (*Tirant d'eau*). If you draw more than about 1·6m/5ft3in, you may not get through. It is almost as simple as that. Almost, because the least depths in the Canals vary from year to year and greatly depend on rainfall or drought and on how much winter dredging and clearance may have been achieved.

The quoted least depths are: River Garonne 1·8m (but the river is tidal up to and beyond the first lock at Castets-en-Dorthe); Canal latéral à la Garonne 1·8m; Canal du Midi 1·5m-1·6m.

Maximum depths will usually be found in the middle of the canal, the bed of which may have a gradual upward slope to either side. The bottom is often soft mud, so if you do touch you may be able to keep going with a little more power. Be wary of some reported depths which you may hear along the way, both pessimistic and optimistic; some people speak of ploughing a groove with their keel(s) for considerable distances, probably with a draught of 1·7m or even 1·8m. Lock-keepers however are a good source of accurate and up-to-date information.

Voies Navigables de France (VNF), the canal managers, are reluctant to specify actual depths until the last moment. So, if depths look like being marginal for your draught, obtain the latest information from the relevant VNF station before you de-mast (in Royan, Pauillac or Bordeaux; or at the Med port of entry).

There are 80 local offices, managed by 17 regional branches. The regional branches relevant to the Canal Latéral à la Garonne are:

- Service Maritime et de Navigation Gironde, BP 61, 33028 Bordeaux. Tel 05.56.90.58.00.

- DDE Lot & Garonne, Service de Navigation, 1722 ave Colmar, 47916 Agen. Tel 05.53.69.33.33.
- Direction Régionale de VNF, 2 Port St-Etienne, BP 7204, 31073 Toulouse. Tel 05.61.36.24.24.

Canal du Midi regional branches include Toulouse (above) and four local offices:

- Service Navigation, 115 rue Amidonniers, 31000 Toulouse. Tel 05.62.15.11.91.
- Service Navigation, Écluse Frequel, 11000 Carcassonne. Tel 04.68.25.01.50.
- Service Navigation, 9 quai d'Alsace, 11100 Narbonne. Tel 04.68.32.02.35.
- Service Navigation, ave du Prado, 34500 Béziers. Tel 04.67.11.81.30.

Tolls are due on waterways managed by Voies Navigable de France (VNF). A detailed brochure in English can be obtained from: French National Tourist Office, 178 Piccadilly, London W1V 0AL; Tel 020 7629 2869, Fax 020 7493 6594; Info 0891 244123.

Licences are available for periods of 1 year, 30 days (not necessarily consecutive; known as *Loisirs*), 16 consecutive days (known as *Vacances*) or 1 day. The 2000 rates, based on 5 sizes of boat area, ie LOA x Beam (m) = m^2, were as follows (in French francs):

VNF LICENCE FEES					
	$<12m^2$	$12\text{-}25m^2$	$25\text{-}40m^2$	$40\text{-}60m^2$	$>60m^2$
1 Year	469	678	1356	2191	2713
30 days	271	485	855	1330	1649
16 days	104	209	313	417	521
1 day	51	102	153	204	256

Pole to be rotated   Approach signals   Explanatory board

Approaching an automatic lock

POTTED HISTORY

The need for an efficient trade route between the Atlantic and Mediterranean was recognised long ago by the Emperors Augustus and Charlemagne amongst others. For centuries goods could only be transported by barges up the River Garonne as far as Toulouse, whence they had to be carried overland to the Mediterranean ports.

The major problem in designing and building the Canal du Midi (Toulouse to the Med) was how to provide enough water to keep the canal filled. Bear in mind the very hot, dry summers of the Midi and more particularly the fact that the canal, as designed, would start from Toulouse at 127m/418ft above sea level, climb to a peak altitude of 190m/623ft at the Col de Narouze (53km SE of Toulouse) before making the 187km long descent to sea level, at the Med.

The man who solved the problems was Pierre Paul Riquet, a wealthy tax-collector, who with the backing of the finance minister, Colbert, obtained royal patronage from Louis XIV. Riquet and the State funded the project jointly and work started in 1667. Water was tapped from the Black Mountains through minor rivers and feeder canals to a massive holding basin at St Ferréol (15km NE of Castelnaudary). From here water was supplied to the Canal. The work of digging the canal by hand, building bridges and surmounting obstacles was immense and costly. A budget of £15 million, a work-force of 12,000 men and engineering skills and ingenuity of the highest order were required.

The task was completed in 1681, six months after Riquet died. His memorial, a rather severe obelisk, stands at the summit of Naurouze. In 1996 the Canal du Midi was fittingly designated a World Heritage site by UNESCO. It is a great architectural monument to one man's vision and determination. *Si monumentum requiris, circumspice.*

At the Mediterranean end, there were frequent delays due to silting up of the ports of Narbonne and Sète. This is no longer the case at Sète which was later linked by canal eastwards to Aigues-Mortes. In 1808 the Canal du Rhône à Sète extended the link to Beaucaire on the Rhône, so that the dangerous Rhône delta could be short-circuited.

Finally, given the uncertainties and problems of navigating the Garonne river between Bordeaux and Toulouse, both in turbulent winter floods and the drying shallows of high summer, the next project was to construct a canal parallel (latéral) to the river. This had already been suggested by Monsieur Vauban, and the Canal latéral à la Garonne was eventually opened in 1856.

Licence stickers (*vignettes*) must be visibly displayed starboard side forward. You can buy them by post from VNF Head Office, 175 rue Ludovic Boutleux, BP 820, 62400 Béthune, France. Tel 03.21.63.24.24; Fax 03.21.63.24.42. Web site: www.vnf.fr Also from Librairie VNF, 18 Quai d'Austerlitz, 75013 Paris; Tel 01.45.84.85.69; and from other main offices.

Enclose a Eurocheque* made out in FF and quote: Owner's name/address; boat's name, LOA, beam, draught; registration number; type of licence required, with validity dates for 1 day and 16 day periods; SAE; photocopy of your Certificate of Competence, boat's registration certificate and proof of engine power output. *Eurocheques will be withdrawn from use on 31 Dec 2001.

Or you can buy them in person from VNF offices on the canals at:
- Castets-en-Dorthe, Écluse 53. Tel 05.56.62.83.07.
- Toulouse, 2 Port St-Etienne. Tel 05.61.36.24.24.
- Narbonne, 9bis quai d'Alsace, Écluse du Gua. Tel 04.68.42.23.27.
- Agde, Écluse Ronde. Tel 04.67.94.23.09.
- Sète, 1 quai Philippe-Régy. Tel 04.67.46.34.67.

Automatic lock signals

Chapter 9

Air clearance/headroom (*Tirant d'air*). The least quoted clearance is 3·3m, on the Canal du Midi. This occurs at the centre of a bridge span; when 5·5m away from the centre, clearance may be as little as 2m. Radomes and spreaders may need some thought.

But clearance is not usually a limiting factor; the average mast can be laid quite close to the deck, from pulpit to sheer legs aft. Ensure sufficient headroom in the cockpit and a reasonable view forward. A red plastic bucket at the forward end of the mast gives some protection and visual warning; at the other end, invert your VHF aerial and fly some flag or bunting to warn others.

SOME PRACTICALITIES

Times of lock operations Apr-Sep 0800-1930; Oct/Nov 0800-1800; Dec-Feb 0800-1730; Mar 0800-1800. Locks are closed on public holidays. Lock-keepers usually have a lunch break from 1230-1330. All these times are subject to annual re-negotiations. Navigation by leisure craft is only permitted in daytime. On the Canal latéral à la Garonne where leisure traffic is less than on the Midi, lock-keepers may ask where you will be night-stopping so as to forewarn the next locks ahead; they may also ask you to group with other boats. Canal sections are closed for maintenance, as far as possible in the winter, but check for any such closures (*chomages*) which may affect your dates, especially in late spring and early autumn.

LOCK OPERATION

Manually operated locks, some electrically powered, are described in the canal Guides. Bow and stern lines rigged on both sides ensure flexibility if the situation changes rapidly.

Closed (Panama) fairleads, which stop a warp jumping out if an upward pull is applied, as when the boat is at the bottom of a deep lock, are best but, for just one canal passage, (snatch) blocks will serve equally well.

Large fenders, or tires (with inflated inner tubes) in canvas bags and attached by two lanyards, are essential. A scaffold plank rigged outboard of your fenders gives added protection against lock and quay walls; it also serves as a gangplank.

Automatic locks account for 28 out of the 53 locks on the Canal Latéral à la Garonne, none of the 65 locks on the Canal du Midi, and 9 out of the 13 on the Canals de Jonction/de la Robine.

How to activate an automatic lock, noting that minor variations will be met.

The photographs are of a fairly typical lock, at Narbonne on the Canal de la Robine:
i.   Note the light signals before and/or at the lock: ⓇⓇ (vert) = lock out of service; Ⓡ or ⓇⓇ (horiz) = do not enter (lock shut or already in use); ⓇⒼ = standby to move, lock being readied; Ⓖ or ⒼⒼ (vert or horiz) = proceed.
ii. Advance to a pole suspended from a cable across the canal; rotate the pole a $\frac{1}{4}$ turn, (this action means that you wish to enter the lock, which will be readied).

Pole to be rotated ——

i. When readied, ⓇⒼ or Ⓖ is shown; enter the lock only when you have a Ⓖ.

v. Land a crewman, as usual, who presses the green button, when lit, on the control panel [to continue the sequence of filling/emptying and closing/opening gates.

. Leave the lock without delay, re-embark crewman and proceed on your merry way.

Speed limits are 8km/hr (4·3 knots) on the canals and 16km/hr (8.6 knots) on the river Garonne, reducing to 10km/hr (5.4 knots) when passing incoming boats and moored vessels.

River banks are named Left or Right as you face downriver towards the sea. On the canals the flow direction is less obvious, so this terminology may prove confusing. Therefore, because sea-going yachtsmen are well used to compasses, this book refers to the N, S, E or W bank as the case may be. Note: Water flow is from the summit of the Canal du Midi (53km east of Toulouse) towards Bordeaux and in the opposite direction towards the Med.

The frequent **Haltes Nautiques** are municipally run and are usually free, at least for one or two nights. Commercially run places, especially those which are bases for charter companies, will charge per night. Kilometre posts, most of which are clearly marked, are a useful reference.

Fuel Diesel by hose is available on the Canal latéral à la Garonne at: Mas d'Agenais (Crown Line), Agen (Locaboat), Moissac (Port de plaisance) and at Toulouse (Port Sud); on the Canal du Midi at: Castelnaudary (Crown Line), Port la Robine, Colombiers, Cassafieres, Grau d'Agde and at Sète (Vieux Port); and on the Canal de la Robine at Port-la-Nouvelle. Petrol by hose is rare.

Weeds and grass cuttings can block engine cooling water intakes. Make frequent checks in the initial stages to establish the extent of any problem. Clean filters at least once a day.

A GLOSSARY OF 'CANAL' WORDS

accostage = mooring;
amarrer = to moor/berth;
amont, montant = upstream;
aval, avalant = downstream; *bac* = ferry;
barrage = weir;
bief = pound (as in water impounded between two locks);
chomage = maintenance closure;
écluse = lock;
épi = groyne;
essence = petrol;
gazole = diesel;
mascaret = tidal bore;
pont-canal = aqueduct;
rive gauche/droite = left/right bank.

Low bridge with houses above

Weir

Control box

The automatic lock at Narbonne and low Pont des Marchands beyond

Chapter 9

THE RIVER GARONNE
(*Garonne fluviale*)

Be prepared. This part of the voyage starts almost certainly in Bordeaux 8.4 where tidal timing is not too difficult. The mast is down and securely lashed on deck. The engine has been double-checked, especially engine and gearbox oil levels. The cooling water filter is clean and will be re-checked many times over the next 300M. Fuel tanks and spare jerry cans are brimfull.

inside for the night. Alternatively secure to the three red/white waiting piles just before the lock entrance.

TIMING

The aim is to leave Bordeaux, Pont de Pierre (km 70), in daylight so as to reach the lock in Castets-en-Dorthe at about local HW which is approximately 2h 10m after HW Bordeaux. The distance is some 54km/30M, so with 6 hours of flood tide all the way, allow 5-6 hours passage time; leave Bordeaux 4 or 5 hours before local HW, ie near LW.

If you are leaving from Bassin No 2, it will be necessary to lock out at the previous HW +30 and then position the boat either on the Lormont YC pontoons or at the Halte Nautique immediately upstream of Pont de Pierre on the east bank – so as to leave on the first of the daytime flood.

It is a good idea to forewarn the lock-keeper at Castets-en-Dorthe (Tel 05.56.62.83.07) of your ETA. If you arrive slightly after 1930 (closing time Jun-Aug) he may open the lock for you or at least leave the gates open so that you can berth

TIDES

HW Bordeaux at neaps is 2 hrs, and at springs 2 hrs 25 mins, after HW Pointe de Grave. MHWS is 5·3m; MHWN is 4·2m. The approximate times of slack water are HW Bordeaux +15 mins; and, near LW, at HW Bordeaux +7 hrs (springs) or +8¼ hrs (neaps). Slack water lasts very briefly, only 5-10 mins at the start of the flood.

The following table is published by the Bordeaux Port Authority for neap, average and spring tides. It shows the times, relative to HW or LW Bordeaux at which HW and LW occur at four places up-river. It also shows the heights of HW and LW at these places, relative to chart datum at Castets, but these vary widely with the seasons (see below).

Seasonal variations in water levels. April to July: Depth of water at Castets varies 0·2 to 0·7m from about 2m. River currents are weak; the flood stream is noticeable and must be utilised.

TIDAL TIMES AND HEIGHTS UP-RIVER										
Coefficient	**Bordeaux**		**Portets** (km50)		**Cadillac** (km36)		**Langon** (km25)		**Castets** (km17)	
	Time	Ht (m)	Time	Ht (m)	Time	Ht (m)	Time	Ht (m)	Time	Ht (m)
45 (neaps)	HW	3·95	+0h30m	3·9	+0h50m	3·2	+1h10m	1·3	No tidal effect	
	LW	0·1	+2h00m	−0·1	+2h40m	−0·2	+3h40m	0·0	No tidal effect	
70 (average)	HW	4·7	+0h40m	4·4	+1h00m	3·4	+1h30m	1·0	+2h10m	0·7
	LW	0·15	+1h20m	0·1	+2h20m	0·1	+3h40m	0·0	+5h10m	0·0
100 (springs)	HW	5·2	+0h50m	5·0	+1h20m	4·0	+1h50m	2·3	+2h10m	1·3
	LW	0·0	+1h30m	−0·1	+2h30m	−0·2	+3h40m	0·0	+5h10m	0·0

August to September: In the dry season water levels are low and shoals and pilings are barely covered at LW. Boats often run aground in the upper reaches between Langon and Castets; a spring tide will help to avoid this.

CHARTS

There are no official charts of the river, but both Guides publish clear chartlets which show the best line, main features and any hazards; these are summarised below.

PASSAGE NOTES

The passage should be done in one day. In Bordeaux pass under one of the three white-painted arches of the Pont de Pierre, which is followed by road and rail bridges and the ring-road (*rocade*) bridge at Bègles.

Keep W of Île d'Arcins (km65) and E of Île de la Lande (km59). At Langoiran bridge (km49) take the centre span. Between km44 and 42 beware pilings on both banks. At Cadillac (km36) use the two eastern spans and be aware of current. Between Cadillac and Langon there are pilings on both banks.

At Langon (km25) use the southern bridge spans and be aware of the piles of a former bridge upstream of the rail bridge; the current is often strong here. Nearing Castets keep to the south bank and use the S bridge span. The lock-keeper is keeping a look-out for you; see 9.2.

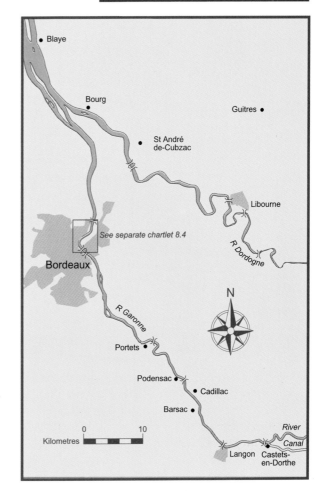

Bordeaux, looking SE up the R Garonne

Chapter 9

CANAL LATÉRAL À LA GARONNE

As you approach Castet's functional metal road bridge, the Garonne diverges away to the east. A château sits high above you to starboard. Lock 53 is dead ahead if you have kept to the S bank and gone through the S span of the bridge. There are 3 red/white waiting piles if the lock is not open.

On a green light enter the larger south lock; the north lock is disused. The lock is deep and the lock-keeper will lower a long boathook onto which you loop your longest warps so that he can secure them for you. No need to go ashore here; VNF licences can be bought at lock 51.

Once over the initial novelty of this tidal lock, negotiate the equally novel automatic lock 52 to berth at the pleasantly shaded Halte Nautique beyond – a sensible first night-stop, with showers 10FF and the usual facilities. The small town of Castets straggles up the hillside.

A minor excursion – you are now in land-lubber mode – would be to visit a C13 château, Benedictine abbey and museum at La Réole, about 10km east by bike or taxi; take the backroads not the busy N113. Les Fontaines is a good restaurant in this charming mediaeval town.

Outline The canal, between Castets-en-Dorthe and Toulouse, is 193km long with 53 locks many of which are automatically operated. It cuts across the départements of Gironde, Lot-et-Garonne, Tarn-et-Garonne and Haute-Garonne. The main towns on or close to the canal are Marmande, Damazan/Aiguillon, Agen, Valence d'Agen, Moissac, Castelsarrasin, Montech/Montauban and Grisolles.

These notes do not attempt to detail every lock, every hazard and every stopping place, for which your guide book should suffice. They merely set the scene, comment on the country through which you are passing and indicate some of the towns and villages where a pause might be a good idea – or not, as the case may be! Navigation is hardly a problem; you always know that around the next bend is another bend, followed by a lock … seemingly ad infinitum.

Next day, as you press on, note that the kilometre posts have re-started at 193km and count down to

Navigation is hardly a problem

First lock, at Castets-en-Dorthe, looking E from the bridge

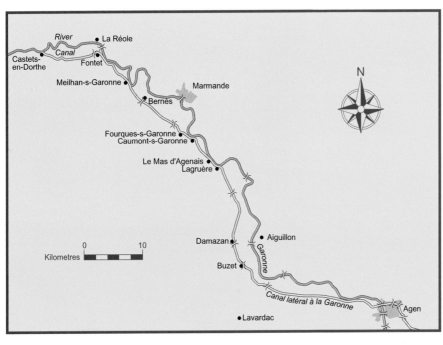

the N bank, from which you can cycle 5-10km into the town of Marmande on the N113.

Mas d'Agenais (km155) has a Crown Blue Line base on the N bank, where diesel is available, and a *halte* Publique opposite on the village bank. Lagruère (km153) is a peaceful Halte just beyond the bridge, with a campsite and crêperie amongst the trees, and across the canal the very good restaurant 'Les Terrasses de Garonne'. A good stop for the first night?

zero at Toulouse. Your progress is very much an individual matter: some will need to keep to a schedule and set themselves a daily target; others will take pot luck and stop when they feel like it. For convenience the canal is covered in 5 sections, each of approximately 40km.

Castets (km193) to Lagruère (km153)
Fontets (km182) has a natural basin with the usual facilities and good play areas for the kids, but not a sliver of shade. If night-stopping, berth on the concrete jetty rather than the floating pontoon which is locked. The village boasts a museum of 'monuments' made of matchsticks – strike a light!

Meilhan (km176) is a good *halte* on the north bank, opposite the village where La Tertre is an upmarket restaurant with panoramic views from the ramparts; pre-booking essential.

Bernès (km171), Fourques (km163) and Caumont (km161) are small stopping places on

Lock and bridge at Castets-en-Dorthe, looking down-river

Lagruère (km153) to Agen (km108)
Villeton (km149) and La Falotte (km146) are small *haltes* before reaching Damazan (km140), an attractive Bastide town 5km by road from the larger town of Aiguillon. Buzet (km136) gives its

Buzet vines

Chapter 9

name to the Appellation Controlée wine-making region; visit the excellent wine Cooperative, between Buzet and Damazan. A horse and cart will collect you free of charge from the moorings.

Buzet is also where you can lock onto the Baïse river (pronounced Bay-eez) if you are feeling bored; but it does get shallow (1m) beyond Lavardac and further progress, except by dinghy, might be unwise. The Baïse is crossed by the Canal latéral (aqueduct) and by the autoroute.

After Buzet the canal runs east for an unremarkable and fairly straight 25 km to the outskirts of Agen. Here there is a flight of 4 automatic locks before the canal crosses the Garonne river on an impressive aqueduct (km109), then skirts round the N and E sides of this large provincial town (40,000+ inhabitants).

Agen is at the centre of a fruit and vegetable-growing area and is perhaps best known for its famous prunes (*pruneaux*). In the Tourist Office (107 bd Carnot; Tel 05.53.47.36.09) they have a bowl of prunes always on the counter and very good they are! The town is spaciously set out with an interesting *vieux quartier*, full of good quality restaurants.

Night-stop options include: the public pontoons after the aqueduct and behind the railway station (therefore noisy); or the Locaboat hire base in the next basin eastwards, more civilised, quieter but not free; diesel is available. Both are handy for the town centre. At Boé on the SE outskirts (km102) there is a *halte nautique* (Montalembert) in parkland, but the pontoons are very short. Close by is Château St Marcel, now a small hotel with a very good restaurant.

Agen (km108) to Moissac (km64)
The two cooling towers of a large nuclear power station will have been visible in the east from soon after leaving Agen. Almost opposite the power station the little villages of Lamagistère and

Buzet Halte Nautique

Damazan, is an attractive Bastide town

Halte Nautique at Valence d'Agen

Damazan Halte Nautique

Agen, the aqueduct looking east

Golfech are brilliant with flowers, as is the town of Valence d'Agen (km82) just beyond. There is a *halte nautique* here which sadly has been vandalised recently, although Valence itself is an interesting C13 Bastide town.

Keep going for another 17km to reach Moissac (km 65), a super town which might tempt you to take a day off working locks. The waterways get a little complex just before you reach Moissac:

The Garonne which has been paralleling the Canal little more than a boathook's length away now swings away to the south and as it does so is joined by the river Tarn flowing through Moissac from the east.

The Canal goes into Moissac and just past the excellent Port de Plaisance (good quays, facilities, fuel) turns 90° to the south in the outskirts and crosses the Tarn via a handsome pink aqueduct.

But Moissac's crowning glory is the C12 Abbey-church of St Pierre set back a little from the town centre. The south entrance porch (narthex) is justifiably famous and beyond my words – stand and wonder at it. Then step aside to enter the adjoining cloister through the Tourist Office; sounds odd but the way in which the cloister surrounds a

Pont Napoléon across the R. Tarn at Moissac

Chapter 9

Moissac, Port de Plaisance project

garden courtyard built around a huge cedar tree is elegant, simple and contemplative.

Moissac (km64) to Grisolles (km27)

6km south of Moissac at Castelsarrasin (km57) the new port should have been finished in 2000. Quays are on the townside where you can berth alongside or stern in, bow to buoys. There is a very good market on Thursday mornings.

Montauban is 21km east by road or a 10 minutes train ride, or can be reached by the 11km long side canal which branches off at Montech (pronounced Montesh); but first check that this side canal has now re-opened. Montauban was

possibly the original Bastide town and the tightly-knit pink houses cluster together in the centre. Have a drink or a meal in the Place Nationale and admire the splendid architecture all around you.

Montech (km43) has a flight of 5 locks and running in parallel is the water slope *(Pente d'eau)* which is not available for leisure boats and is only rarely used by the occasional tourist cruiser. It bypasses the locks by pushing a moving basin of water, in which a vessel is enclosed, up a 3% slope, rising 13·3m in a distance of 443m – now a bit of a white elephant.

Once clear of Montech you will be thinking ahead about your next night-stop. Grisolles (km27) is not far ahead but is an unprepossessing former commercial port. Indeed the canal becomes increasingly industrialised as you approach Toulouse; the railway hugs the east bank.

Grisolles (km27) to Toulouse (km 0) and to Port Sud (km12 on the Canal du Midi)

Entering Toulouse keep a close check on where you are! The last lock (No 1 on the Canal Latéral) is at the 4km post. At the zero mark you go through the last bridge and enter the vast expanse of the Port de l'Embouchure. This is the end of the Canal latéral à la Garonne and the start of the Canal du Midi (9.4). See under Toulouse (9.3) for berthing and tourist information.

Lagruere Halte Nautique

TOULOUSE

The town hall in Place du Capitole

There are four night-stop possibilities on what is now the Canal du Midi (km posts counting up from zero) which curves clockwise around the N and E sides of the inner city: Port de l'Embouchure, hardly enticing by virtue of its impersonal size

and because of the Brand's Hatch-style motorway traffic which roars around it at all hours; buses to the city centre (3km). When leaving via the Canal du Midi, be sure to take the middle of three bridges!

- The disused Canal du Brienne is accessed via the right hand of the 3 bridges. From here to the first lock it is possible to secure alongside the bank using your own stakes.
- Port St Sauveur (km5·5), a collection of pontoons with FW and electricity adjacent to some run-down buildings (to be renovated), but an easy walk to the city centre. Tel 05.62.15.11.91.
- Port Sud (km12·5), a large purpose-built marina on the southern outskirts, is encircled by smart

high-rise blocks but is pleasant enough and the only safe place in Toulouse to leave a boat for any length of time; there are quite a few liveaboards. All facilities including diesel, showers 10FF, launderette and an excellent *alimentation*, restaurant and Intermarché. Tel 05.61.75.07.64. Tariff. Daily rates for LOA bands, all year: 6-8m = 36FF; <10m = 42FF; <12m = 50FF; <14m = 59FF; <16m = 68FF. No 68 bus into the city (9km) requires a change; a taxi is easier.

Note: 1km before you reach Port Sud, on the east bank there is a large boatyard for leisure craft which appears to have extensive engineering facilities; Tel 05.61.73.86.11.

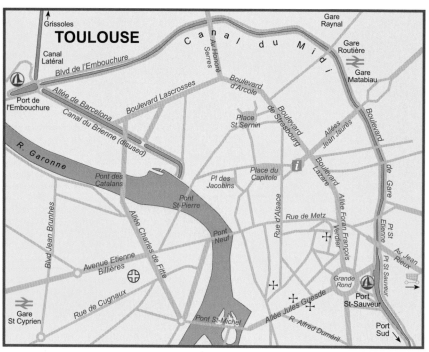

TOURISM

Tourist Office Donjon du Capitolium, Place Charles de Gaulle, BP0801, 31080 Toulouse. Tel 05.61.11.02.22; Fax 05.61.22.03.63. E-mail: ottoulouse@mipnet.fr

Port St Sauveur, pontoons to starboard

What to see/do Toulouse, the pink city (*Ville Rose*), is France's fourth largest at over a million souls. It is vibrant, beautiful and thoroughly enjoyable! It is also an obvious crew-change point midway between Bordeaux and the Mediterranean, with excellent road, rail and air links.

Here are just a very few of the many things to see or visit:

Place du Capitole, the vast main square surrounded by beautiful arcaded buildings and the hugely impressive Capitolium itself (the town hall). Behind it is the Tourist Office in the Place Charles de Gaulle amid trees and shaded gardens.

Radiate out on foot from this centre point into the old city, delineated by the River Garonne from Pont Neuf along rue de Metz; then north up the rue d'Alsace Lorraine, the main shopping street

behind the Place du Capitole; and back to the river at Pont St-Pierre via the church of St Sernin and the University.

The basilica of St Sernin is the largest Romanesque church in France and 'a must' for its amazing architecture and carvings. Les Jacobins is a large rectangular church whose octagonal bell-tower overlooks the peace of a cloistered courtyard.

Place St Georges is a popular café area which you are sure to stumble upon if

Port de l'Embouchure

you are walking from a berth at Port St Sauveur. Further north in Place Victor Hugo there is a superb food market above which are clustered excellent and atmospheric eating places, lunch only. In the evening after a drink in the Place du Capitole, head NE to the rue Bayard to eat at No 14, Le Colombier, where cassoulet (a stew of pork, lamb and sometimes duck with haricot beans) will keep hunger at bay until next day.

Outside the city visit the City of Space (*Cité de l'Espace*) which, with its planetarium, model of the Ariane rocket and a full scale replica of the Mir space station, symbolises the involvement of

Toulouse in space exploration. Closer to earth and near the airport, Aérospatiale admits the public to its assembly halls where the Caravelle and Concorde and now the Airbus is built.

Taxis Tel 05.34.25.02.50; 05.61.42.38.38; 05.61.52.22.22; 05.61.21.55.46.

Airport (Toulouse-Blagnac). Tel 05.61.42.44.00; Info 05.61.42.44.64; Forecast 08.36.68.12.34.

Railway Gare Matabiau, alongside the Canal at km4. Tel 05.61.10.10.00.

Buses SEMVAT runs a comprehensive network; plan & timetable desirable. Tel 05.61.61.67.67.

Port Sud marina

CANAL DU MIDI TO PORT LA ROBINE

Toulouse is approximately halfway between Bordeaux and the Med – a cause for celebration? The Canal du Midi is more enjoyable than the Latéral Canal. It snakes and winds it way along the contour lines so that at times the bends are quite sharp and a great relief from never-ending straight stretches. The terrain is more interesting, the towns and villages more dramatic and charming and even the oval-shaped locks have greater elegance. The curved walls were built that way so as to withstand the inward pressure of the surrounding earth better. After more than three centuries they have stood the test well.

There are more leisure boats on the Midi than on the Latéral, especially in high summer. A few are only marginally in control of their vessels and you need to be wary of their movements. In a flight of locks, the prime example being Fonserannes near Béziers, try to go through as a singleton rather than sharing each chamber with the 'bumper cars'. Some of the bridges are low and/or narrow and these are mentioned in the text below. The locks are still manually operated (a few of the flights are electrically powered), but none are automatic. After the first 50km to the summit you have the satisfaction of knowing that it is downhill all the way, which makes locking so much more relaxing!

On the Canal du Midi you will traverse the départements of Haute-Garonne, Aude, and Hérault. Aquitaine has slipped astern and the region of Languedoc-Roussillon lies ahead. The Black Mountains and Haut Languedoc Regional Park flank the Canal to the north and offer the chance of an invigorating diversion for a day or two away from the routine of lock-bashing. Further to the south the foothills of the Pyrenees can be glimpsed; even Andorra is only some 80km south of Carcassonne.

The major towns, cities and features along the way include the summit stretch at Naurouze,

Le Segala, delightful with wide quays

Castelnaudary, Carcassonne; and Narbonne if you have taken the Canal de la Robine, branching south to enter the Med at Port La Nouvelle. After Béziers the Canal du Midi ends at Les Onglous, just beyond Agde where the second entrance/exit for the Med lies. Finally cross the Étang du Thau to reach Sète and the Med again. Here this voyage ends, and another starts.

The Canal between Toulouse and the junction with Canal de la Robine (for Port la Nouvelle) divides for convenience into three sections each of about 50kms.

Port Sud (km12) to Castelnaudary (km64)
Once out of Toulouse the canal winds charmingly through pleasant farmland. There are minor stops at Negra (km33), Gardouche (km38), Villefranche (km41) and Renneville (km43).

Memorial to Pierre-Paul Riquet

At Port Lauragais (km50) the stop is larger and unusually combined with an autoroute service station (which does not intrude; fill up a jerry can with diesel here if you look like getting low). The highlight of Lauragais is a fascinating exhibition on the design and building of the Canal, illustrated with many old maps and drawings; Pierre-Paul Riquet features large, as well he might. There is also a rugby museum since the Midi is the heartland of the French game.

The autoroute crosses the canal here (discreetly) and around the corner is the last of the uphill locks, No 17 aka L'Océan – which might inspire those heading downhill all the way to Biscay. You are now on the level, at the summit of the Canal. Look carefully to your left at km52·5 and you should see above the trees the obelisk which is the memorial to Pierre-Paul Riquet.

Castelnaudary: flight of four locks at St Roch (No23)

Castelnaudary: Le Grand Bassin

At km54 the little village of Le Segala hoves into view and may I suggest that this could be a good night-stop, if it fits your schedule. The village is delightful in its own right with its wide quays, a fair amount of berthing space and a good, informal restaurant (Relais de Riquet; menus 65-130FF; get in early) on the quayside. It is an excellent base from which to leap on your bikes and ride back 1½km to the Col de Narouze and the memorial to get the feel of this spot. Notice also the feeder canal (*rigole*) from the St Ferreol Basin 24km away up in the Black Mountains.

25km east of Le Segala is the first of the downhill locks, No 18 (aka the Mediterranean – *pour encourager les autres*) followed quickly by a double and a treble flight plus two singles. The 2nd lock of the 2 singles (No 22, Laplanque) has a low, narrow bridge dating back to the C16, so try not to scrape it (height 3·4m at centre, 2.25m at the edges; 5·8m wide).

Castelnaudary (km64) is a fair sized provincial town serving the rolling farmlands of Lauragais, often brilliant with fields of sunflowers. Berth on the north side public quay between the Pont Neuf and Pont Vieux for easy access to the picturesque areas. Or enter the Grand Bassin which is a much photographed expanse of water (part of Riquet's supply system). On its S side a Crown Blue Line base has good facilities including showers and diesel; Tel 04.68.94.52.72. The railway station is a 450m walk. If you haven't already tried it, pitch into some Cassoulet ... *dormez bien!*

Castelnaudary (km64) to Trèbes (km117)

In the next 14km you negotiate the quadruple No 23 lock (electrical), double No 24, triple No 25 and nine singles, descending 46m in 16km; fortunately most of it is pleasantly shaded. At Bram take a breather and decide whether to stop short of Carcassonne at the delightful haltes of Villesequelande (km91), Caux and Sauzens (km94); or press on another 10km into Carcassonne (km104) where there is a big, chaotic and rather noisy canal basin

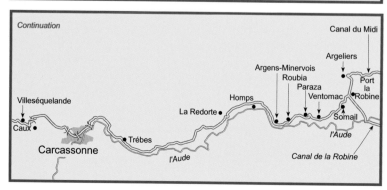

Carcassonne: La Cité floating on high

Carcassonne: the office

or quieter tree-lined banks to the east beyond lock No 40.

Carcassonne's lower town (*Ville basse*) is large, bustling and laid out in a grid of streets within the ramparts. The basin is on the N side next to the station. The hub is Place Carnot where there are cafés, restaurants and a market on Tuesdays, Thursdays and Saturdays.

Of course La Cité, the famous mediaeval fortress-city on the SE outskirts is what everybody has come to see. I first saw it from the autoroute and was immediately entranced by its almost too-perfect fairy-tale image, apparently floating on high. At night it is imaginatively floodlit and even more magically breathtaking; the Pont Vieux is a favourite viewpoint. From the Canal it is quite a long, and usually hot, walk; or take the No 2 bus from the railway station.

The River Aude, flowing down from the Pyrenees, turns east at Carcassonne and more or less parallels the Canal for the next 60km. On leaving Carcassonne take care at the bridge over the lock; at 3·3m high and 6m wide it is regularly swiped by hire cruisers. Once clear, salute the Emperor Charlemagne's great fortress off to starboard and then get down to the next 6 locks before Trèbes; the Fresquel flight of No 42 (double) and 43 is electrically operated.

Trèbes (km117) is a small town with most facilities and shops. The *halte nautique* is on the N bank just before the town bridge, beyond which there is a bassin where Connoisseur Cruisers have a base, but no fuel for sale. Berth on the S bank where best you may. Immediately east an avenue of tall plane trees casts glorious deep shade, at the end of which No 46 triple locks lead out of town.

Trèbes (km117) to Port la Robine (km168)

In the next 28 km stretch to Homps (km145) there are only 11 locks to contend with and few worthwhile stopping places, so make good speed through the valley of the Aude. At Laredorte (km139) there are some tight bends which require care; also an enticing looking waterside restaurant, Le Rivassel, which has a good reputation.

At Homps there is a base, Port Minervois, for two charter companies: Luc Lines and Camargue Plaisance. Tariff daily rates for LOA bands, 1 April to 30 September:

Trèbes: a charter company base

Trèbes: an avenue of plane trees casts glorious deep shade

<7m = 28FF; <9m = 36FF; <11m = 44FF; <13m = 54FF; <15m = 59FF; per metre >15m = 4FF.

But there are also long public quays and a relaxed bar-restaurant, Les Tonneliers, where food and ambience are pleasing even if the service is a little quaint. There is an excellent Tourist Office. The lock bridge is low.

5km further along the Canal is Argens-en-Minervois (km151), another purpose-built Locaboat base (Port Occitanie), with a rather charming hilltop village right behind. Prices are said to be high; 15FF for a shower. Just beyond at km152·5 is the last lock, No 56, on the Canal for 54km (the longest pound in France).

So press on for the next lock-free 15km, past haltes at Roubia, Paraza (where slow down for a very sharp bend and small aqueduct) and Ventenac, until you reach Le Somail (km166).

This is a picturesque old canal port and village with a much photographed bridge – indeed the whole thing is getting too touristy for its own good. There are no shops, not even a *boulangerie*! Berth against the stone quays and eat at either of the two good restaurants, Le Poivre Vert and the Auberge le Somaillou.

Or keep on for 2km to Port la Robine (km168), which is run by the ever-helpful Marion and Ted Bateman (BP 6, 11120 Mirepeisset; Tel 04.68.46.11.46) and is in a small strategically placed creek. It offers limited short-stay berths,

boatyard facilities, diesel and showers (be wary of an adjacent cement works if the wind is in the NE), but there is no village or restaurant.

Tariff daily rates for LOA bands, June to September:
6-8m = 33FF; <10m = 38FF; <12m = 52FF; <14m = 57FF; <16m = 61FF.

There is a 1km long one-way stretch either side of Port la Robine between the aqueduct over the River Cesse and the small railway bridge to the east. Within this stretch there is a T-junction where:
a. the Canal de Jonction branches off SE to Sallèles d'Aude and into the Canal de la Robine through Narbonne towards Port La Nouvelle on the Mediterranean Sea (Section 9.5); whilst
b. the Canal du Midi continues N then E towards Béziers (Section 9.6).

Homps, quays looking east

CANAL DE LA ROBINE TO PORT LA NOUVELLE AND THE MED

This, your first chance to get into the Med, may save quite a lot of time if you are going to/coming from Spain. For example by sea Port-la-Nouvelle is 37M SW of Sète and 24M SW of Grau d'Agde. From the Canal du Midi to Port-la-Nouvelle by canal is only 37km and 13 locks.

But it does require a shallow draft boat, bilge keeler or a lifting keel. The HM at Port-la-Nouvelle told me that in the final 2km between the last lock, Ste Lucie (km28·5), and the bridges at the head of his port there were depths of only 1·2 to 1·4m. He stated that the canal bed was clean, contrary to another report that old iron railings had been thrown in!

The passage divides naturally into three short sections:

a. Canal de Jonction, 5km and 8 locks from the Canal du Midi to Moussoulens;

b. Canal de la Robine, 10km and 3 locks from Moussoulens to Narbonne; and

c. Canal de la Robine, 22km and 2 locks from Narbonne to Port-la-Nouvelle.

The Canal de Jonction lined by shapely umbrella pines, runs dead straight for 3km to Sallèles d'Aude via 5 locks, all automatic. It was built in 1776 to connect Narbonne with the Canal du Midi. Sallèles is quite a large village where the Halte is well-shaded by plane trees; it has a restaurant, supermarket and other shops.

After Sallèles the canal crosses the River Aude 'on the level' and if the current is strong this may be tricky. But first negotiate the double Gailhousty electric locks, on which you will see posted the likely depth of water on the Aude crossing. After leaving the locks, keep well to starboard and turn upstream into the Aude; when 25m past an overhead marker line do a U-turn back and across to the far bank and on course down the Aude for about 700m to the Moussoulens lock, which normally remains open. Note: the object of the turn upstream and hairpin back downriver is simply to avoid a shoal in mid-channel which greatly reduces the navigable width.

The Canal de la Robine with a couple of manual locks, leads straightforwardly into the very heart of Narbonne –

truly a historic city - of flowers, fine buildings, good shops and markets. Try to spend a day or two here even if you have no intention of going on to Port-la-Nouvelle. It was capital of the first Roman province in France, Gallia Narbonensis, and Roman remains survive, the most obvious being the Horreum (grain store), a direct relation of the *horreos* along Spain's north coast. The tall tower of the massive Cathedral St Just is visible from miles away and, along with the Archbishop's Palace, dominates the city centre.

There are two stopping places: first a Connoisseur Cruiser base just after the Gua lock (km8·5). The river then turns 90° to port and dives under a series of bridges ending in the automatic Narbonne lock and famous 3·3m low bridge (*Pont des Marchands*), seemingly weighed down by the houses which sit on top of it! (See photographs on pages 272-275).

The second stopping place follows in short order on the S bank in a shaded cutting, a mixture of municipal *halte* and hire cruiser base. Both stops are almost equidistant from the city centre.

In the final 22km to Port-la-Nouvelle the **Canal de la Robine** runs like water upon water, the narrow ribbon of canal passing between the very extensive Étang de Bages et de Sigean (look out for flamingos) on the west side and the only slightly smaller Étang de l'Ayrolle on the east. Also to the east you will see the 214m high Montagne de la Clape, where a sea-tangy local wine is made. Étang translates loosely as a lagoon, lake, wetland, salt marsh or pond.

At **Port-la-Nouvelle** the Canal turns 90° port into the harbour which runs for 1M to the beaches and môles beyond. The N side is a dusty industrialised sprawl (cement, petroleum, chemicals) where quite large ships berth; the town opposite is an unremarkable seaside resort. There

Looking seaward from Port-la-Nouvelle

is a small marina after the 2 bridges at the top end of the harbour and masting can be done at D'Gees Nautique, Tel 04.68.48.04.18, which also sells diesel; beware wash and the *tramontane* NE wind.

OFFSHORE

Charts AC 1506 (1:75,000 & 1:15,000) and SHOM 7002 cover the approaches and the port itself. The harbour entrance is at 43°00′·84N 03°04′·30E; the fairway is dredged 7·8m.

To seaward there is a circular Regulated Area about 1M diameter and a traffic separation scheme extending 7·5M offshore and aligned with the leading lights on 294·4°; these measures are for use by ships carrying hydrocarbons and dangerous cargo.

Sailing ships and small craft <20m LOA may only enter the Regulated Area in order to access the port and anchorages. They must give way to warships and power-driven vessels >50m LOA.

Tides HW Port-la-Nouvelle at neaps and at springs is $4\frac{1}{2}$ hours before HW Gibraltar. LW at neaps and springs is 4 hours before LW Gibraltar (see the MRNA for Gibraltar tidal predictions).

MHWS is 0·4m, MLWS 0·2m; MHWN is 0·3m, MLWN 0·3m. These values are based on Port Vendres, approximately 30M to the south.

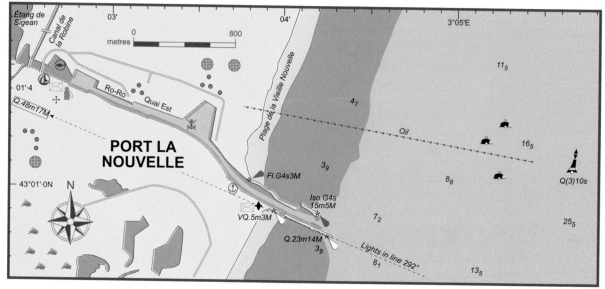

Poilhes quayside and restaurant

CANAL DU MIDI, PORT LA ROBINE TO AGDE

This Section continues the Canal du Midi from Section 9.4. The intervening Section 9.5 deals with the Canal de la Robine, Narbonne and Port-la-Nouvelle.

Port la Robine (km168) to
Fonserranes locks (at Béziers, km206)

This stretch is 38km long with no locks at all, but the 6 lock flight at Fonserranes will shortly redress this imbalance! Planning-wise allow at least half a day to negotiate this flight, probably a whole day in high season and at weekends when the hire boats are queuing bumper-to-bumper to get through; best to keep away from these peak periods altogether.

There is a straight stretch to the minor halte at Argeliers (km172) with berths in front of a waterside restaurant 'Au Chat qui Pêche'. Thereafter the Canal characteristically snakes its way along the contours on the north side of the Aude valley; there are glorious views south to the Pyrenees. (The Aude itself has disappeared, after crossing the Canal de la Robine north of Narbonne, to empty into the sea south of Béziers).

Capestang (km188) is an attractive small town with massive church on the S bank. Slow down for the bridge which is 6m narrow and 3·6m low. The Halte's official address is Place Danton Cabrol, 34310 Capestang; Tel 04.67.49.85.95, Fax 04.67.93.38.62. Excellent food in the Relais Bleu, S side of town on the D11 Béziers-Carcassonne road.

More superb views and delightful contouring brings us suddenly round a corner into the pretty little village of Poilhes (km194). Berth on the stone quays and enjoy some local walking and/or a meal at La Tour Sarrasine, upmarket and priced accordingly (set menus from 130-295FF), Tel 04.67.93.41.31.

En route to the next stopping place you will pass through the Malpas tunnel (km198), 160m long x 8m wide x 8m high, generous for a canal tunnel which incredibly is said to have been built in 6 days! Amazingly a railway line (1855) passes

Chapter 9

Malpas tunnel, looking SW

Looking north from Oppidum d'Enserune at Montady irrigation system

2m below the Canal and below that is a drainage basin for the Montady irrigation scheme. Sound your horn and look before entering as there is only room for single file traffic.

1 km further on you arrive in **Colombiers (km200)**, having negotiated the 3·5m low bridge with its adjacent *lavoir*. Berthing here is almost sure to be in the unashamedly modern, semicircular basin carved out of the S bank and used by two charter boat companies. All mod cons including diesel, supermarket, chemist, cafés etc –

FONSERANNES LOCKS

You will see the number of locks misleadingly quoted as 7, 8 or 9. Confusion arises because there were originally 8 locks in the flight, plus the Orb lock (No 58) separate at km208. The bottom two locks, slightly separate from the main flight, were used when the Canal actually joined the River Orb, which flows past the W side of Béziers. When a handsome aqueduct was built (1856) to carry the Canal <u>over</u> the Orb these last two locks became redundant, but can still be seen in a stagnant backwater (Port Vieux).

---

undeniably convenient for stocking up before moving on to night-stop elsewhere. The village fortunately seems to have escaped and is unspoilt. A fine timbered roof on the wine store (Cave de Colombiers) is worth a second look. It is also worth jumping on your (mountain) bike and sweating up to the top of the nearby hill to see the Oppidum d'Enserune, ruins of, and museum – a pre-Roman settlement dating back to C6 BC. The views from the top also justify the sweat, in particular of the disused Montady radial irrigation scheme below your feet.

After Colombiers there is a narrow stretch (km202-204) where single file is the rule; if you meet oncoming vessels there are "lay-bys" (*refuges*) to pull into.

And so to **Fonserannes (km206)** on the SW outskirts of Béziers where the six lock flight ends the previously mentioned 54km long pound of lock-free navigation.

At km206 there is a waiting pontoon on the N bank. Allow at least half a day to lock through.

The locking schedule is as follows:

Going down (NE, towards Béziers) 0800-0930 and 1330-1530.

Going up (SW, towards Toulouse) 1030-1145 and 1630-1845.

Tourist cruise vessels are pre-booked and have priority. Get in the queue and if you have a long overhanging mast, try to arrange to go through as a singleton so as to avoid the very real risk of

Fonserannes locks: the water slope engines; lock in the foreground

damage by hire cruisers. All the locks are electrically operated and manned by the Canal staff. The only bridge over the flight is 3·4m low and 6·1m narrow.

The locking procedure is a major spectator sport and half the population of Béziers turns out at weekends to watch the fun! There is also a Son et Lumière show held in season.

The water slope (*Pente d'eau*) runs alongside the flight of locks, but is now rarely used having suffered various failures since it was built in 1983, and there are few commercial or tourist barges.

Béziers Having completed the transit, cross the aqueduct over the River Orb and berth in the Port Neuf between locks 58 and 59. The large basin is next to the railway station and busy roads; it is also a 20 minutes walk up into the town centre. Cross under the railway and from the station climb up to the wooded Plateau de Poètes which leads into the tree-lined Allées Paul Riquet, where salute the statue of the great man who was born here. Béziers is a large and attractive city with mediaeval streets around the cathedral. Languedoc wine, rugby and bullfighting (in no particular order) are the local pursuits which suggest this is a macho place – blood was shed in the 1970s when rioting took place over the cost of wine! The Tourist Office is at Palais de Congrès, 29 ave St. Saëns, 34500 Béziers; Tel 04.67.76.47.00; Fax 04.67.76.50.80.

If you seek a quieter place to stop the night, continue south through lock Nos 60 & 61 for 5km to Villeneuve-Les-Béziers (km214). On the N bank there is a peaceful, well-shaded *halte nautique* (Les Berges du Canal, Tel 04.67.39.36.09), allied to a campsite, with all facilities, restaurant/shop and closer to a supermarket (Co-op) than in the city basin. The town is charming.

Béziers (km209) to Agde (km232)

Even from the Port Neuf in Béziers this 23km stretch with 3 locks should not take more than half a day. 7km after Villeneuve-Les-Béziers there is a Crown Blue line base at Port Cassafieres on the S bank. It has diesel and the beach is only 2km south – have a swim in the Med!

3km further on the little Libron stream crosses the Canal at 90° 'on the level'. To facilitate this

Fonserannes locks: looking up the flight of six locks

Chapter 9

River Hérault:
exit to Grau d'Agde

Canal du Midi
exit to Étang de Thau

Canal du Midi:
enter from Béziers

Yacht berthed
in 'lay-by'

Agde, Round Lock

there is a barrage arrangement of sluices and mini-lock gates under an overhead structure. The whole thing is normally open and free of obstructions, but you should transit with due caution (4 kph/2½ knots speed limit); only in times of flooding are there likely to be any restrictions.

... and now for Agde. Take the centre span of the triple-arched bridge at km230 into the lengthy port area. Berth on either side, the south being

Agde, cathedral tower

nearer the town; for the Round Lock wait here as close as possible to the E bridge.

When cleared by a green light, go under the bridge and into the Round Lock. Lock hours are 0800-1230 & 1330-1930. *Nota Bene*: The Lady lock-keeper reigns supreme and nothing moves without her prior permission. Secure properly once inside to combat some strange up-wellings.

The lock is not truly round; it has a 'lay-by' section to your left (9 o'clock) where de-masted yachts are more easily berthed whilst waiting for other lock gates to open. Ahead of you (12 o'clock) is the gate into the Canal du Midi for the final 8 km to Les Onglous, thence on to Sète (see 9.7). To your right (3 o'clock) the other gate opens at sea level to the River Hérault and out to the Med at Le Grau d'Agde (see next page).

The ancient port of Agde is rather pleasant, despite black basalt being the building material. Visit the C12 cathedral and the market on Thursdays.

Agde to Grau d'Agde and the Mediterranean

On leaving the Round Lock go under a metal railway bridge, then down a shortish tree-lined cut and into the R Hérault. Turn immediately some 45° to starboard to pass under the wide centre span of the stone road bridge and head down-stream in mid-channel; the almost black cathedral tower is conspicuous on the far bank.

Masting/de-masting can be done at the very helpful Chantier Michel (where diesel is available) on the east bank between the new road bridge (clearance 12m) and the fishing port of Le Grau d'Agde. Berthing may be difficult in the strong current and space may have to be made below the mobile crane.

Depths are adequate in the river except close to the banks. The river mouth is shallower and some turbulence is likely. Masting/de-masting can also be done in the marina at Cap d'Agde.

If arriving from sea via the R Hérault, you must pre-book a Round Lock entry slot with the lock-keeper (Tel 04.67.94.23.09). A VNF licence can be bought at the small basin on the N side of the port, after locking out of the Round Lock.

Offshore AC 1705 (1:300,000) and SHOM 7054 (1:50,000) provide offshore and inshore cover respectively. The lat/long of the harbour entrance is 43°16′·80N 03°26′·70E. About 3M to the east is the marina at Cap d'Agde where, from the west, a SCM buoy and Île Brescou must be rounded before entering.

Tides The times and heights interpolated for Sète (see 9.7) apply with sufficient accuracy to Grau d'Agde, some 12M to the SW.

Agde, Canal du Midi looking west from the Round Lock

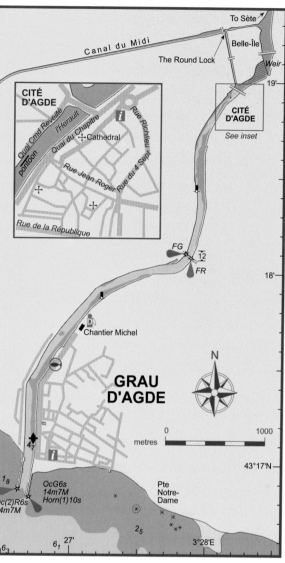

Chapter 9

AGDE TO SÈTE AND THE MED

This passage is made initially on the final 8km of the Canal du Midi, from the Round Lock at Agde to the training walls at Pointe des Onglous. The remainder of the route is across the Étang de Thau, a shallow inland sea.

Canal du Midi Out of the Round Lock at Agde turn port onto a short stretch of the R Hérault and transit No 64 (Prades) lock which is only closed in flood conditions. At km235 Bagnas lock, No 65, is the final one (Hurray!) and officially marks the start of sea-going waters. As if to make the point there is a lighthouse, the first since Bordeaux, at Les Onglous (km240). There is also a Glénans sailing base, but the nearest yacht harbour is at Marseillan, 8 cables to the north.

Re/de-masting can be done at Marseillan and Sète. The former is rather a pleasant old place with a marina built outside the original harbour; it is also home to Noilly Prat (guided tours) and the Château du Port restaurant with tables on the quayside. A 2·5 ton crane is next to the Capitainerie (Tel 04.67.77.34.93) and on balance conditions here are likely to be more favourable than at Sète where the YC crane is in a more exposed position.

Weather The Étang de Thau can be decidedly choppy if a strong NW'ly *Mistral* or the NE'ly *Tramontane* is blowing. Select your Navtex to La Garde (W) for the weather messages at 1140 and 2340 UT. The CROSS MRSC at Agde broadcasts weather info on VHF Ch 79 in French at 0715, 1245 and 1915 local times.

Navigation across the Étang de Thau is simple enough if you steer a middle course between the continuous oyster beds (stakes) which cover the NW side and the drying SE side. Head east out of Marseillan for about 1M to clear the oyster beds and then make good 048°/7M to the Rocher de Roquerols IDM beacon at the NE end. On your starboard bow should be Mont St Clair, the conspicuous rounded hill 175m high, which marks Sète. From Rocher de Roquerols steer 135°/1M past Pte de Barrou and into the buoyed channel which gives access to the port areas.

Canal de Sète: a poor man's Venetian Grand Canal (not navigable due to very low bridges)